An Examination of the Testimony of the Four Evangelists, by the Rules of Evidence Administered in Courts of Justice. With an Account of the Trial of Jesus

AN

EXAMINATION OF THE TESTIMONY

OF THE

FOUR EVANGELISTS.

AN

EXAMINATION OF THE TESTIMONY

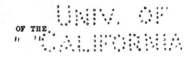

OF THE

FOUR EVANGELISTS,

BY

THE RULES OF EVIDENCE ADMINISTERED

IN

COURTS OF JUSTICE.

WITH AN ACCOUNT OF THE TRIAL OF JESUS.

BY SIMON GREENLEAF, LL. D.

ROYALL PROFESSOR OF LAW IN HARVARD UNIVERSITY.

BOSTON:

CHARLES C. LITTLE AND JAMES BROWN.

1846.

Entered according to Act of Congress, in the year 1846, by
SIMON GREENLEAF,
in the Clerk's Office of the District Court of the District of Massachusetts.

5400

BOSTON:
PRINTED BY FREEMAN AND BOLLES,
DEVONSHIRE STREET.

TO THE

MEMBERS OF THE LEGAL PROFESSION.

GENTLEMEN,

The subject of the following work I hope will not be deemed so foreign to our professional pursuits, as to render it improper for me to dedicate it, as I now respectfully do, to you. If a close examination of the evidences of Christianity may be expected of one class of men more than another, it would seem incumbent on us, who make the law of evidence one of our peculiar studies. Our profession leads us to explore the mazes of falsehood, to detect its artifices, to pierce its thickest veils, to follow and expose its sophistries, to compare the statements of different witnesses with severity, to discover truth and separate it from error. Our fellow-men are well aware of this; and probably they act upon this knowledge more generally, and with a more profound repose, than we are in the habit of considering. The influence, too, of the legal profession upon the community is unquestionably great; conversant, as it daily is, with all classes and grades of men, in their domestic and social relations, and in all the affairs of life, from the cradle to the grave. This influence we are constantly exerting for good or ill; and hence, to refuse to acquaint ourselves with the evidences of the Christian religion, or to act as though, having fully examined, we lightly esteemed them, is to assume an appalling amount of responsibility.

The things related by the Evangelists are certainly of the most momentous character, affecting the principles of our conduct here, and our happiness forever. The religion of Jesus Christ aims at nothing less than the utter overthrow of all other systems of religion in the world; denouncing them as inadequate to the wants of man, false in their foundations, and dangerous in their tendency. It not only solicits the grave attention of all, to whom its doctrines are presented, but it demands their cordial belief, as a matter of vital concernment. These are no ordinary claims; and it seems hardly possible for a rational being to regard them with even a subdued interest; much less to treat them with mere indifference and contempt. If not true, they are little else than the pretensions of a bold imposture, which, not satisfied with having already enslaved millions of the human race, seeks to continue its encroachments upon human liberty, until all nations shall be subjugated under its iron rule. But if they are well founded and just, they can be no less than the high requirements of heaven, addressed by the voice of God to the reason and understanding of man, concerning things deeply affecting his relations to his sovereign, and essential to the formation of his character and of course to his destiny, both for this life and for the life to come. Such was the estimate taken of religion, even the religion of pagan Rome, by one of the greatest lawyers of antiquity, when he argued that it was either nothing at all, or was everything. *Aut undique religionem tolle, aut usquequaque conserva.*[1]

With this view of the importance of the subject, and in the hope that the present work may in some degree aid or at least incite others to a more successful pursuit of this interesting study, it is submitted to your kind regard, by

Your obedient servant,

SIMON GREENLEAF.

HARVARD UNIVERSITY, }
DANE HALL, MAY 1, 1846. }

[1] Cicero, Phillip. II. § 43

CONTENTS

AND

SYNOPSIS OF THE HARMONY.

CONTENTS.	MATT.	MARK.	LUKE.	JOHN.
Sect.				
PART I.				
EVENTS CONNECTED WITH THE BIRTH AND CHILDHOOD OF OUR LORD.				
TIME: *About thirteen and a half years.*				
1. Preface to Luke's Gospel.			1, 1-4	
2. An Angel appears to Zacharias. *Jerusalem.*			1, 5-25	
3. An Angel appears to Mary. *Nazareth.*			1, 26-38	
4. Mary visits Elizabeth. *Jutta.*			1, 39-56	
5. Birth of John the Baptist. *Jutta.*			1, 57-80	
6. An Angel appears to Joseph. *Nazareth.*	1, 18-25			
7. The Birth of Jesus. *Bethlehem.*			2, 1-7	
8. An Angel appears to the Shepherds. *Near Bethlehem.*			2, 8-20	
9. The circumcision of Jesus, and his presentation in the Temple. *Bethlehem. Jerusalem.*			2, 21-38	
10. The Magi. *Jerusalem. Bethlehem.*	2, 1-12			
11. The flight into Egypt. Herod's cruelty. The return. *Bethlehem. Nazareth.*	2, 13-23		2, 39-40	
12. At twelve years of age Jesus goes to the Passover. *Jerusalem.*			2, 41-52	
13. The Genealogies.	1, 1-17		3, 23-38	
PART II.				
ANNOUNCEMENT AND INTRODUCTION OF OUR LORD'S PUBLIC MINISTRY.				
TIME: *About one year.*				
14. The Ministry of John the Baptist. *The Desert. The Jordan.*	3, 1-12	1, 1-8	3, 1-18	
15. The Baptism of Jesus. *The Jordan.*	3, 13-17	1, 9-11	3, 21-23	
16. The Temptation. *Desert of Judea.*	4, 1-11	1, 12, 13	4, 1-13	

2

CONTENTS.	MATT.	MARK.	LUKE.	JOHN.
Sect.				
108. James and John prefer their ambitious request. *Perea.*	20, 20-28	10, 35-45		
109. The healing of two blind men near Jericho.	20, 29-34	10, 46-52	18, 35-43	
110. The visit to Zaccheus. Parable of the ten Minae. *Jericho.*			19, 1 19, 2 28	
111. Jesus arrives at Bethany six days before the Passover. *Bethany.*				11, 55-57 12,1.9-11

PART VII.

OUR LORD'S PUBLIC ENTRY INTO JERUSALEM, AND THE SUBSEQUENT TRANSACTIONS BEFORE THE FOURTH PASSOVER.

TIME: *Five days.*

CONTENTS.	MATT.	MARK.	LUKE.	JOHN.
112. Our Lord's public Entry into Jerusalem. *Bethany, Jerusalem.*	21, 1-11. 14-17	11, 1-11	19, 29-44	12, 12-19
113. The barren Fig-tree. The cleansing of the Temple. *Bethany, Jerusalem.*	21,12.13. 18. 19	11, 12-19	19, 45-48 21, 37.38	
114. The barren Fig-tree withers away. *Between Bethany and Jerusalem.*	21, 20-22	11, 20.26		
115. Christ's authority questioned. Parable of the Two Sons. *Jerusalem.*	21, 23-32	11, 27-33	20, 1-8	
116. Parable of the wicked husbandmen. *Jerusalem.*	21, 33-46	12, 1-12	20, 9-19	
117. Parable of the Marriage of the King's Son. *Jerusalem.*	22, 1-14			
118. Insidious question of the Pharisees: Tribute to Cesar. *Jerusalem.*	22, 15-22	12, 13-17	20, 20-26	
119. Insidious question of the Sadducees: The Resurrection. *Jerusalem.*	22, 23-33	12, 18-27	20, 27-40	
120. A lawyer questions Jesus. The two great Commandments. *Jerusalem.*	22, 34-40	12, 28-34		
121. How is Christ the son of David? *Jerusalem.*	22, 41-46	12, 35-37	20, 41-44	
122. Warnings against the evil example of the Scribes and Pharisees. *Jerusalem.*	23, 1-12	12, 38.39	20, 45.46	
123. Woes against the Scribes and Pharisees. Lamentation over Jerusalem. *Jerusalem.*	23, 13-39	12, 40	20, 47	
124. The Widow's mite. *Jerusalem.*		12, 41-44	21, 1-4	
125. Certain Greeks desire to see Jesus. *Jerusalem.*				12, 20-36
126. Reflections upon the unbelief of the Jews. *Jerusalem.*				12, 37-50
127. Jesus, on taking leave of the Temple, foretells its destruction and the persecution of his Disciples. *Jerusalem. Mount of Olives.*	24, 1-14	13, 1-13	21, 5-19	
128. The signs of Christ's coming to destroy Jerusalem, and put an end to the Jewish State and Dispensation. *Mount of Olives.*	24, 15-42	13, 14-37	21, 20-36	
129. Transition to Christ's final coming at the Day of Judgment. Exhortation to watchfulness. Parables: The ten Virgins. The five Talents. *Mount of Olives.*	24, 43-51 25, 1-30			

TABLE

<small></small>

FOR

FINDING ANY PASSAGE IN THE HARMONY.

————

MATTHEW.

Chap.	Verse.	Sect.	Chap.	Verse.	Sect.	Chap.	Verse.	Sect.
i.	1-17	13	xiii.	1-23	54	xxii.	41-46	121
	18-25	6		24-53	55	xxiii.	1-12	122
ii.	1-12	10		54-58	61		13-39	123
	13-23	11	xiv.	1, 2	63	xxiv.	1-14	127
iii.	1-12	14		3-5	24		15-42	128
	13-17	15		6-12	63		43-51	129
iv.	1-11	16		13-21	64	xxv.	1-30	129
	12	24		22-36	65		31-46	130
	13-16	28	xv.	1-20	67	xxvi.	1-16	131
	17	26		21-28	68		17-19	132
	18-22	29		29-38	69		20	133
	23-25	32		39	70		21-25	135
v.	1-48	41	xvi.	1-4	70		26-29	137
vi.	1-34	41		4-12	71		30	142
vii.	1-29	41		13-20	73		31-35	136
viii.	1	41		21-28	74		36-46	142
	2-4	33	xvii.	1-13	75		47-56	143
	5-13	42		14-21	76		57, 58	144
	14-17	31		22, 23	77		59-68	145
	18-27	56		24-27	78		69-75	144
	28-34	57	xviii.	1-35	79	xxvii.	1, 2	146
ix.	1	57	xix.	1, 2	94		3-10	151
	2-8	34		3-12	104		11-14	146
	9	35		13-15	105		15-26	148
	10-17	58		16-30	106		26-30	149
	18-26	59	xx.	1-16	106		31-34	152
	27-34	60		17-19	107		35-38	153
	35-38	62		20-28	108		39-44	154
x.	1	62		29-34	109		45-50	155
	2-4	40	xxi.	1-11	112		51-56	156
	5-42	62		12, 13	113		57-61	157
xi.	1	62		14-17	112		62-66	158
	2-19	44		18, 19	113	xxviii.	1	160
	20-30	45		20-22	114		2-4	159
xii.	1-8	37		23-32	115		5-7	161
	9-14	38		33-46	116		8-10	162
	15-21	39	xxii.	1-14	117		11-15	165
	22-37	48		15-22	118		16	169
	38-45	49		23-33	119		16-20	170
	46-50	50		34-40	120			

2½

MARK.

Chap.	Verse.	Sect.	Chap.	Verse.	Sect.	Chap.	Verse.	Sect.
i.	1-8	14	vii.	24-30	68	xii.	41-44	124
	9-11	15		31-37	69	xiii.	1-13	127
	12, 13	16	viii.	1-9	69		14-37	128
	14	24		10-12	70	xiv.	1-11	131
	14, 15	26		13-21	71		12-16	132
	16-20	29		22-26	72		17	133
	21-28	30		27-30	73		18-21	135
	29-34	31		31-38	74		22-25	137
	35-39	32	ix.	1	74		26	142
	40-45	33		2-13	75		27-31	136
ii.	1-12	34		14-29	76		32-42	142
	13, 14	35		30-32	77		43-52	143
	15-22	58		33	78		53, 54	144
	23-28	37		33-50	79		55-65	145
iii.	1-6	38	x.	1	94		66-72	144
	7-12	39		2-12	104	xv.	1-5	146
	13-19	40		13-16	105		6-15	148
	19-30	48		17-31	106		15-19	149
	31-35	50		32-34	107		20-23	152
iv.	1-25	54		35-45	108		24-28	153
	26-34	55		46-52	109		29-32	154
	35-41	56	xi.	1 -11	112		33-37	155
v.	1-21	57		12-19	113		38-41	156
	22-43	59		20-26	114		42-47	157
vi.	1-6	61		27-33	115	xvi.	1	159
	6-13	62	xii.	1-12	116		2-4	160
	14-16	63		13-17	118		5-7	161
	17-20	24		18-27	119		8	162
	21-29	63		28-34	120		9-11	164
	30-44	64		35-37	121		12, 13	166
	45-56	65		38, 39	122		14-18	167
vii.	1-23	67		40	123		19, 20	172

LUKE.

Chap.	Verse.	Sect.	Chap.	Verse.	Sect.	Chap.	Verse.	Sect.
i.	1-4	1	v.	29-39	58	ix.	37-43	76
	5-25	2	vi.	1-5	37		43-45	77
	26-38	3		6-11	38		46-50	79
	39-56	4		12-19	40		51-56	81
	57-80	5		20-26	41		57-62	56
ii.	1-7	7		27-30	41	x.	1-16	80
	8-20	8		31	41		17-24	89
	21-38	9		32-36	41		25-37	86
	39, 40	11		37-49	41		38-42	87
	41-52	12	vii.	1-10	42	xi.	1-13	88
iii.	1-18	14		11-17	43		14, 15	48
	19, 20	24		18-35	44		16	49
	21-23	15		36-50	46		17-23	48
	23-38	13	viii.	1-3	47		24-28	49
iv.	1-13	16		4-18	54		29-36	49
	14	24		19-21	50		37-54	51
	14, 15	26		22-25	56	xii.	1-59	52
	16-31	28		26-40	57	xiii.	1-9	53
	31-37	30		41-56	59		10-21	94
	38-41	31	ix.	1-6	62		22-35	95
	42-44	32		7-9	63	xiv.	1-24	96
v.	1-11	29		10-17	64		25-35	97
	12-16	33		18-21	73	xv.	1-32	98
	17-26	34		22-27	74	xvi.	1-13	99
	27, 28	35		28-36	75		14-31	100

LUKE CONTINUED.

Chap.	Verse.	Sect.	Chap.	Verse.	Sect.	Chap.	Verse.	Sect.
xvii.	1-10	101	xx.	47	123	xxiii.	13-25	148
	11-19	82	xxi.	1-4	124		26-33	152
	20-37	102		5-19	127		33-34	153
xviii.	1-14	103		20-36	128		35-37	154
	15-17	105		37, 38	113		38	153
	18-30	106	xxii.	1-6	131		39-43	154
	31-34	107		7-13	132		44-46	155
	35-43	109		14-18	133		45	156
xix.	1	109		19, 20	137		47-49	156
	2-28	110		21-23	135		50-56	157
	29-44	112		24-30	133	xxiv.	1-3	160
	45-48	113		31-38	136		4-8	161
xx.	1-8	115		39-46	142		9-11	162
	9-19	116		47-53	143		12	163
	20-26	118		54-62	144		13-35	166
	27-40	119		63-71	145		36-49	167
	41-44	121	xxiii.	1-5	146		50-53	172
	45, 46	122		6-12	147			

JOHN.

Chap.	Verse.	Sect.	Chap.	Verse.	Sect.	Chap.	Verse.	Sect.
i.	1-18	17	ix.	1-41	90	xviii.	13-18	144
	19-34	18	x.	1-21	90		19-24	145
	35-52	19		22-42	91		25-27	144
ii.	1-12	20	xi.	1-46	92		28-38	146
	13-25	21		47-54	93		39, 40	148
iii.	1-21	22		55-57	111	xix.	1-3	149
	22-36	23	xii.	1	111		4-16	150
iv.	1-3	24		2-8	131		16, 17	152
	4-42	25		9-11	111		18-24	153
	43-45	26		12-19	112		25-27	154
	46-54	27		20-36	125		28-30	155
v.	1-47	36		37-50	126		31-42	157
vi.	1-14	64	xiii.	1-20	134	xx.	1, 2	160
	15-21	65		21-35	135		3-10	163
	22-71	66		36-38	136		11-18	164
vii.	1	66	xiv.	1-31	138		19-23	167
	2-10	81	xv.	1-27	139		24-29	168
	11-53	83	xvi.	1-33	140		30, 31	173
viii.	1	83	xvii.	1-26	141	xxi.	1-24	169
	2-11	84	xviii.	1	142		25	173
	12-59	85		2-12	143			

ADVERTISEMENT.

THE notes to the Gospels, credited to Archbishop Newcome, without other reference, are selected from the notes to his Greek Harmony.

In following Dr. Robinson's arrangement of the Gospels, I have in several places omitted his transposition of the verses of the text, occurring within the limits of a section; it being more convenient to insert them in the order in which they were written by the Evangelists.

The text, except in a few places where the article *a* was accidentally printed instead of *an*, in the words *an house, an hungered*, &c., is conformable to the common octavo edition of the American Bible Society.

PRELIMINARY OBSERVATIONS.

§ 1. IN examining the evidences of the Christian religion, it is essential to the discovery of truth that we bring to the investigation a mind freed, as far as possible, from existing prejudice and open to conviction. There should be a readiness, on our part, to investigate with candor, to follow the truth wherever it may lead us, and to submit, without reserve or objection, to all the teachings of this religion, if it be found to be of divine origin. "There is no other entrance," says Lord Bacon, "to the kingdom of man, which is founded in the sciences, than to the kingdom of heaven, into which no one can enter but in the character of a little child." [1] The docility which true philosophy requires of her disciples is not a spirit of servility, or the surrender of the reason and judgment to whatsoever the teacher may inculcate; but it is a mind free from all pride of opinion, not hostile to the truth sought for, willing to pursue the inquiry and impartially to weigh the arguments and evidence, and to acquiesce in the judgment of right reason. The investigation, moreover, should be pursued with the serious earnestness which becomes the greatness of the subject — a subject fraught with such momentous consequences to man. It should be pursued as in the presence of God, and under the solemn sanctions

[1] Nov. Org. 1. 68 His words are "Ut non alius fere sit aditus ad regnum hominis, quod fundatur in scientiis, quam ad regnum cœlorum, in quod, nisi sub persona infantis, intrare non datur."

3

created by a lively sense of his omniscience, and of our accountability to him for the right use of the faculties which he has bestowed.

§ 2. In requiring this candor and simplicity of mind in those who would investigate the truth of our religion, Christianity demands nothing more than is readily conceded to every branch of human science. All these have their data, and their axioms; and Christianity, too, has her first principles, the admission of which is essential to any real progress in knowledge. "Christianity," says Bishop Wilson, "inscribes on the portal of her dominions, 'Whosoever shall not receive the kingdom of God as a little child, shall in no wise enter therein.' Christianity does not profess to convince the perverse and headstrong, to bring irresistible evidence to the daring and profane, to vanquish the proud scorner, and afford evidences from which the careless and perverse cannot possibly escape. This might go to destroy man's responsibility. All that Christianity professes, is to propose such evidences as may satisfy the meek, the tractable, the candid, the serious inquirer." [1]

§ 3. The present design, however, is not to enter upon any general examination of the evidences of Christianity, but to confine the inquiry to the testimony of the Four Evangelists, bringing their narratives to the tests to which other evidence is subjected in human tribunals. Of course several things, sometimes controverted, will here be assumed as true.

§ 4. (1) It will, in the first place, be assumed that God has, at some times, revealed himself to man, by special and express communications. The reality of such a revelation has been argued from its necessity. That man is a religious being, is universally conceded, for it has been seen to be universally true. He is everywhere a worshipper. In every age and country, and in every stage, from the highest intellectual culture to the darkest stupidity, he bows with homage to a superior being. Be it the rude carved idol of his own fabrication, or the unseen divinity that stirs within him, it

[1] Bishop Wilson's Evidences, p. 38.

is still the object of his adoration. This trait in the character of man is so uniform, that it may safely be assumed, either as one of the original attributes of his nature, or as necessarily resulting from the action of one or more of those attributes.

, § 5. The object of man's worship, whatever it be, will naturally be his standard of perfection. He clothes it with every attribute, belonging, in his view, to a perfect character; and this character he himself endeavors to attain. He may not, directly and consciously, aim to acquire every virtue of his deity, and to avoid the opposite vices; but still this will be the inevitable consequence of sincere and constant worship. As in human society men become assimilated, both in manners and in moral principles, to their chosen associates, so in the worship of whatever deity men adore, they "form to his the relish of their souls."

· § 6. How it came to pass that man, originally taught, as we doubt not he was, to know and to worship the true Jehovah, is found, at so early a period of his history, a worshipper of baser objects, it is foreign to our present purpose to inquire. But the fact is lamentably true, that he soon became an idolater, a worshipper of moral abominations. The Scythians and Northmen adored the impersonations of heroic valor and of bloodthirsty and cruel revenge. The mythology of Greece and of Rome, though it exhibited a few examples of virtue and goodness, abounded in others of gross licentiousness and vice. The gods of Egypt were reptiles and beasts and birds. The religion of Central and Eastern Asia was polluted with lust and cruelty, and smeared with blood, "rioting, in deadly triumph, over all the tender affections of the human heart and all the convictions of the human understanding." Western and Southern Africa and Polynesia are, to this day, the abodes of frightful idolatry, cannibalism, and cruelty; and the aborigines of both the Americas are examples of the depths of superstition to which the human mind may be debased. In every quarter of the world, however, there is a striking uniformity seen, in all the features of paganism. The ruling principle of her religion is terror, and her deity is lewd and cruel. Whatever of purity the earlier forms of paganism may have possessed, it is evident from history that it was of brief duration. Every form, which history has preserved, grew rapidly and steadily worse and more corrupt, until the entire heathen world, before the coming of Christ, was infected with that loathsome leprosy of pollution, described with revolting vividness by St. Paul, in the beginning of his Epistle to the Romans.

§ 7. So general and decided was this proclivity to the worship of strange gods, that, at the time of the deluge, only one family remained faithful to Jehovah; and this was a family which had been favored with his special revelation. Indeed it is evident that nothing but a revelation from God could raise men from the degradation of pagan idolatry, because nothing else has ever had that effect. If man could achieve his own freedom from this bondage, he would long since have been free. But instead of this, the increase of light and civilization and refinement in the pagan world has but multiplied the objects of his worship, added voluptuous refinements to its ritual, and thus increased the number and weight of his chains. In this respect there is no difference in their moral condition, between the barbarous Scythian and the learned Egyptian or Roman of ancient times, nor between the ignorant African and the polished Hindu of our own day. The only method, which has been successfully employed to deliver man from idolatrous worship is that of presenting to the eye of his soul an object of worship perfectly holy and pure, directly opposite in moral character, to the gods he had formerly adored. He could not transfer to his deities a better character than he himself possessed. He must forever remain enslaved to his idols, unless a new and pure object of worship were revealed to him, with a display of superior power sufficient to overcome his former faith and his present fears, to detach his affections from grosser objects, and to fix them upon that which alone is worthy. This is precisely what God, as stated in the Holy Scriptures, has done. He rescued one family from idolatry in the old world, by the revelation of himself to Noah; he called a distinct branch of this family to the knowledge of himself, in the person of Abraham and his sons; He extended this favor to a whole nation, through the ministry of Moses; but it was through that of Jesus Christ alone that it was communicated to the whole world. In Egypt, by the destruction of all the objects of the popular worship, God taught the Israelites that he alone was the self-existent Almighty. At the Red Sea, he emphatically showed them that he was the Protector and Savior of his people. At Sinai, he revealed himself as the righteous Governor who required implicit obedience from men, and taught them, by the strongly marked distinctions of the ceremonial law, that he was a holy Being, of purer eyes than to behold evil, and that could not look upon iniquity. The demerit of sin was inculcated by the solemn infliction of death upon every animal, offered as a propitiatory sacrifice. And when, by this system of instruction, he had prepared a people to receive the perfect revelation of the character of God, of the nature of his worship and of the way of restoration to his image and favor, this also was expressly revealed by the mission of his Son.[1]

§ 8. (2.) It will, in the next place, be assumed, that the books of the Old Testament, as we now have them, are genuine; and that they existed in the time of our Savior, and were commonly received and referred to, among the Jews, as the sacred books of their religion. We shall also assume that the text of the Four Evangelists has been handed down to us in the state in which it was originally written, that is, without having been materially corrupted or falsified, either by heretics or Christians.

§ 9. The genuineness of these writings really admits of as little doubt, and is susceptible of as ready proof, as that of any ancient writings whatever. The rule of municipal law

---

[1] The argument here briefly sketched, is stated more at large, and with great clearness and force, in an essay entitled " The Philosophy of the Plan of Salvation," p. 13 – 107. See also Bishop Wilson's Evidences of Christianity, vol. i. p 45 – 61, Horne's Introduction to the Study of the Holy Scriptures, vol. i. p. 1 – 39 Mr. Horne has so freely cited the authors who have written upon the Evidences of Christianity, that it is now superfluous to do more than to refer to his own work.

on this subject is familiar, and applies with equal force to all ancient writings, whether documentary or otherwise. The first inquiry, when an ancient document is offered in evidence in our courts, is whether it comes from the proper repository; that is, whether it is found in the place where, and under the care of persons with whom, such writings might naturally and reasonably be expected to be found; for it is this custody which gives authenticity to documents found within it.[1] If they come from such a place, and bear no evident marks of forgery, the law presumes that they are genuine, and they are admitted to be read in evidence, unless the opposing party is able successfully to impeach them.[2] The burden of showing them to be false and unworthy of credit, is devolved on the party who makes that objection. The presumption of law is the judgment of charity. It presumes that every man is innocent until he is proved to be guilty; that everything has been done fairly and legally, until it is proved to have been otherwise; and that every document, found in its proper repository, and not bearing marks of forgery, is genuine. Now this is precisely the case with the Sacred Writings. They have been used in the church from time immemorial, and thus are found in the place where alone they ought to be

[1] Per Tindall, Ch. Just. in the case of the Bishop of Meath v. the Marquis of Winchester, 3 Bing. N. C. 183, 200, 201. " It is when documents are found in other than their proper places of deposit," observed the Chief Justice, " that the investigation commences, whether it was reasonable and natural, under the circumstances of the particular case, to expect that they should have been in the place where they are actually found ; for it is obvious, that, while there can be only one place of deposit strictly and absolutely proper, there may be many and various, that are reasonable and probable, though differing in degree, some being more so, some less ; and in these cases the proposition to be determined is, whether the actual custody is so reasonably and probably accounted for, that it impresses the mind with the conviction that the instrument found in such custody must be genuine." See the cases cited in 1 Greenleaf on Evidence, § 142. It is this defect, namely, that they do not come from the proper or natural repository, which shows the fabulous character of many pretended revelations, from the Gospel of the Infancy to the Book of Mormon.

[2] 1 Greenleaf on Evid. § 34, 142, 570

looked for. They come to us, and challenge our reception of
them as genuine writings, precisely as Domesday Book, the
Ancient Statutes of Wales, or any other of the ancient documents which have recently been published under the British
Record Commission, are received. They are found in familiar
use in all the churches of Christendom, as the sacred books
to which all denominations of Christians refer, as the standard
of their faith. There is no pretence that they were engraven
on plates of gold and discovered in a cave, nor that they were
brought from heaven by angels; but they are received as the
plain narratives and writings of the men whose names they
respectively bear, made public at the times when they were
written; and though there are some slight discrepancies
among the copies subsequently made, there is no pretence that
the originals were anywhere corrupted. If it be objected that
the originals are lost, and that copies alone are now produced,
the principles of the municipal law here also afford a satisfactory answer. The multiplication of copies was a public fact,
in the faithfulness of which all the Christian community had an
interest. In matters of public and general interest, all persons
must be presumed to be conversant, on the principle that
individuals are presumed to be conversant with their own
affairs; and therefore, in such matters, the prevailing current
of assertion is resorted to as evidence, for it is to this that
every member of the community is supposed to be privy.[1]
The persons, moreover, who multiplied these copies, may be
regarded, in some manner, as the agents of the Christian public, for whose use and benefit the copies were made; and on
the ground of the credit due to such agents, and of the public
nature of the facts themselves, the copies thus made are entitled to an extraordinary degree of confidence, and, as in the
case of official registers and other public books, it is not
necessary that they should be confirmed and sanctioned by the
ordinary tests of truth.[2] If any ancient document concerning

---

[1] Moorewood v. Wood, 14 East, 329, n. Per Lord Kenyon. Weeks v
Sparke, 1 M & S 686, The Berkley Peerage Case, 4 Campb 416. Per
Mansfield, Ch J See 1 Greenleaf on Evidence, § 128.

[2] 1 Starkie on Evidence, p 195, 1 Greenleaf on Evidence, § 483.

our public rights were lost, copies which had been as universally received and acted upon as the Four Gospels have been,
would have been received in evidence in any of our courts of
justice, without the slightest hesitation. The entire text of
the Corpus Juris Civilis is received as authority in all the
courts of continental Europe, upon much weaker evidence of
its genuineness; for the integrity of the Sacred Text has
been preserved by the jealousy of opposing sects, beyond any
moral possibility of corruption; while that of the Roman
Civil Law has been preserved only by tacit consent, without
the interest of any opposing school, to watch over and preserve
it from alteration.

§ 10. These copies of the Holy Scriptures having thus been
in familiar use in the churches, from the time when the text
was committed to writing; having been watched with vigilance
by so many sects, opposed to each other in doctrine, yet all
appealing to these Scriptures for the correctness of their faith;
and having in all ages, down to this day, been respected as
the authoritative source of all ecclesiastical power and government, and submitted to, and acted under in regard to so many
claims of right, on the one hand, and so many obligations of
duty, on the other; it is quite erroneous to suppose that the
Christian is bound to offer any further proof of their genuineness or authenticity. It is for the objector to show them spuri-
ous; for on him, by the plainest rules of law, lies the burden
of proof.[1]   If it were the case of a claim to a franchise, and a

---

[1] The arguments for the genuineness and authenticity of the books of the
Holy Scriptures are briefly, yet very fully stated, and almost all the writers
of authority are referred to, by Mr Horne, in his Introduction to the Study of
the Holy Scriptures, vol. 1, *passim*   The same subject is discussed in a more
popular manner in the lectures of Bp. Wilson and of Bp. Sumner of Chester,
on the Evidences of Christianity.   In America the same question, as it
relates to the Gospels, has been argued by Bp. McIlvaine, in his Lectures,
and by Mr. Norton, in his Evidences of the Genuineness of the Gospels.   "The direct historical evidence for the genuineness of the Gospels," the latter observes, "consists in the indisputable fact, that throughout
a community of millions of individuals, scattered over Europe, Asia and
Africa, the Gospels were regarded with the highest reverence, as the works
of those to whom they are ascribed, at so early a period, that there could be

copy of an ancient deed or charter were produced in support of the title, under parallel circumstances on which to presume its genuineness, no lawyer, it is believed, would venture to deny its admissibility in evidence, nor the satisfactory character of the proof.[1]

§ 11. Supposing the reader, therefore, to admit that it is not irrational, nor inconsistent with sound philosophy, to believe that God has made a special and express revelation of his character and will to man, and that the sacred books of our religion are genuine, as we now have them, our present object is, to compare the testimony of the Four Evangelists, as witnesses to the life, doctrine, and miracles of Jesus Christ, in order to determine the degree of credit to which, by the rules of evidence applied in human tribunals, they are justly entitled. The proper inquiry will be, not whether it is possible that the testimony may be false, for this is not the manner in which evidence is examined in courts of justice; but, whether there is sufficient probability that it is true. The subject of inquiry is matter of fact, and not matter of abstract mathematical truth. The latter alone is susceptible of that high degree of evidence which we call demonstration, which excludes the possibility of error, and which therefore may reasonably be required in support of every mathematical deduction. But the proof of matters of fact rests upon moral evidence alone; by which is

no difficulty in determining whether they were genuine or not, and when every intelligent Christian must have been deeply interested to ascertain the truth. And this fact does not merely involve the testimony of the great body of Christians to the genuineness of the Gospels; it is in itself a phenomenon admitting of no explanation, except that the four gospels had all been handed down as genuine from the Apostolic age, and had everywhere accompanied our religion as it spread through the world." See Norton's Evidences, &c. vol. 1. Additional Notes, p. ccxc.

[1] In a recent case in the House of Lords, an old manuscript copy, purporting to have been extracted from ancient Journals of the House, which were lost, and to have been made by an officer, whose duty it was to prepare lists of the peers present and absent, was held admissible evidence, upon a claim of peerage. See the case of the Slane Peerage, 5 Clark and Finelly's Reports, p. 24. See also the case of the Fitzwalter Peerage, 10 Clark and Finelly's Reports, p. 948.

meant not only that species of evidence which is employed in cases respecting moral conduct, but all the evidence which we do not obtain either from our own senses, from intuition, or from demonstration. In the ordinary affairs of life we do not require nor expect demonstrative evidence, because it is inconsistent with the nature of matters of fact, and to insist on its production would be unreasonable and absurd. And it makes no difference, whether the facts to be proved relate to this life or to the next, the nature of the evidence required being in both cases the same. The error of the skeptic consists in pretending or supposing that there is a difference in the evidence, where there is no difference in the nature of the things to be proved, and in demanding demonstrative evidence concerning things which are not susceptible of any other than moral evidence alone, and of which the utmost that can be said, is, that there is no reasonable doubt of their truth.[1]

§ 12. In proceeding to weigh the evidence of any proposition, the previous question to be determined is, *when* may it be said to be proved? The answer plainly is, when its truth is established by competent and satisfactory evidence. By competent evidence, is meant such as the nature of the thing to be proved requires; and by satisfactory evidence, is meant that amount of proof, which ordinarily satisfies an unprejudiced mind, beyond any reasonable doubt. The circumstances which will amount to this degree of proof can never be previously defined ; the only legal test to which they can be subjected is, their sufficiency to satisfy the mind and conscience of a man of common prudence and discretion, and so to convince him, that he would venture to act upon that conviction in matters of the highest concern and importance to his own interest.[2] If, therefore, the subject is a problem in mathematics, its truth is to be shown by the certainty of demonstrative evidence. But if it is a question of fact in human affairs, nothing more than moral evidence can be required, for this is the best evidence which,

[1] See Gambier's Guide to the Study of Moral Evidence, p. 121.
[2] 1 Stark Evid. 514 ; 1 Greenl. on Evid. 4.

from the nature of the case, is attainable. Now as the facts, stated in Scripture History, are not of the former kind, but are cognizable by the senses, they may be said to be proved when they are established by that kind and degree of evidence which, as we have just observed, would, in the affairs of human life, satisfy the mind and conscience of a common man. When we have this degree of evidence, it is unreasonable to require more. A juror would violate his oath, if he should refuse to acquit or condemn a person charged with an offence, where this measure of proof was adduced.

§ 13. Proceeding further, to inquire whether the facts related by the Four Evangelists are proved by competent and satisfactory evidence, we are led, first, to consider on which side lies the burden of establishing the credibility of the witnesses. The very statement of such a question startles us, because, in the affairs of ordinary life, the uniform course is to presume every witness to be credible until the contrary is shown; the burden of proof lying on the objector. But this only serves to show the injustice with which the writers of the Gospels have ever been treated by infidels; an injustice silently acquiesced in even by Christians ; in requiring the Christian affirmatively, and by positive evidence, *aliunde*, to establish the credibility of his witnesses above all others, before their testimony is entitled to be considered, and in permitting the testimony of a single profane writer, alone and uncorroborated, to outweigh that of any single Christian. This is not the course in courts of chancery, where the testimony of a single witness is never permitted to outweigh the oath even of the defendant himself, interested as he is in the cause; but, on the contrary, if the plaintiff, after having required the oath of his adversary, cannot overthrow it by something more than the oath of one witness, however credible, it must stand as evidence against him. But the Christian writer seems, by the usual course of the argument, to have been deprived of the common presumption of charity in his favor; and, reversing the ordinary rule of administering justice in human tribunals, his testimony is unjustly presumed to be false, until it is proved to be true. This treatment

moreover, has been applied to them all in a body ; and, without due regard to the fact, that, being independent historians,
writing at different periods, they are entitled to the support of
each other, they have been treated, in the argument, almost
as if the New Testament were the entire production, at once,
of a body of men, conspiring, by a joint fabrication, to im-
pose a false religion upon the world. It is time that this injustice should cease ; that the testimony of the Evangelists
should be admitted to be true, until it can be disproved by
those who would impugn it ; that the silence of one sacred
writer, on any point, should no more detract from his own
veracity or that of the other historians, than the like circumstance is permitted to do among profane writers ; and that the
Four Evangelists should be admitted in corroboration of each
other, as readily as Josephus and Tacitus, or Polybius and Livy.[1]

[1] This subject has been treated by Dr. Chalmers, in his Evidences
of the Christian Revelation, chapter III.   The following extract from
his observations will not be unacceptable to the reader.   " In other
cases, when we compare the narratives of cotemporary historians, it is
not expected that all the circumstances alluded to by one will be taken
notice of by the rest , and it often happens that an event or a custom
is admitted upon the faith of a single historian , and the silence of all
other writers is not suffered to attach suspicion or discredit to his testimony.   It is an allowed principle, that a scrupulous resemblance betwixt two
histories is very far from necessary to their being held consistent with one
another   And, what is more, it sometimes happens that, with cotemporary
historians, there may be an apparent contradiction, and the credit of both
parties remain as entire and unsuspicious as before. Posterity is, in these
cases, disposed to make the most liberal allowances   Instead of calling it a
contradiction, they often call it a difficulty   They are sensible that, in many
instances, a seeming variety of statement has, upon a more extensive knowledge of ancient history, admitted of a perfect reconciliation.   Instead, then,
of referring the difficulty in question to the inaccuracy or bad faith of any of
the parties, they, with more justness and more modesty, refer it to their own
ignorance, and to that obscurity which necessarily hangs over the history of
every remote age   These principles are suffered to have great influence in
every secular investigation ; but so soon as, instead of a secular, it becomes
a sacred investigation, every ordinary principle is abandoned, and the suspicion annexed to the teachers of religion is carried to the dereliction of all
that candor and liberality with which every other document of antiquity is
judged of and appreciated.   How does it happen that the authority of Jose-

§ 14. But if it were conceded, that the burden of establishing the credibility of the Evangelists, as witnesses, rested upon those who affirm the truth of their narratives, it is still capable of a ready moral demonstration, if we consider the nature of their testimony, and the essential marks of difference between narratives of facts, as they actually occurred, and the creations of falsehood. It is universally admitted that much of the credit to be given to witnesses, depends on their ability to discern and comprehend the nature of what they saw and heard, their opportunities for observation, and the degree of accuracy with which they are accustomed to mark passing events. But much also depends on their integrity; for without this requisite, very little reliance can be placed on any other, aside from corroborating and foreign testimony. After a witness is dead, and his moral character is forgotten, we can ascertain it only by a close inspection of his narrative, comparing its details with each other, and with contemporary accounts and collateral facts. This test is much more accurate than may at first be supposed. Every event which actually transpires, has its appropriate relation

phus should be acquiesced in as a first principle, while every step, in the narrative of the evangelists, must have foreign testimony to confirm and support it? How comes it, that the silence of Josephus should be construed into an impeachment of the testimony of the evangelists, while it is never admitted, for a single moment, that the silence of the evangelists can impart the slightest blemish to the testimony of Josephus? How comes it, that the supposition of two Philips in one family should throw a damp of skepticism over the gospel narrative, while the only circumstance which renders that supposition necessary is the single testimony of Josephus; in which very testimony it is necessarily implied that there are two Herods in that same family? How comes it, that the evangelists, with as much internal, and a vast deal more of external evidence in their favor, should be made to stand before Josephus, like so many prisoners at the bar of justice? In any other case, we are convinced that this would be looked upon as *rough handling*. But we are not sorry for it. It has given more triumph and confidence to the argument And it is no small addition to our faith, that its first teachers have survived an examination, which, in point of rigor and severity, we believe to be quite unexampled in the annals of criticism." See Chalmers's Evidences, pp 72 – 74, Amer ed 1817.

and place in the vast complication of circumstances, of which
the affairs of men consist; it owes its origin to the events
which have preceded it; it is intimately connected with all
others which occur at the same time and place, and often
with those of remote regions, and in its turn it gives birth
to numberless others which succeed. In all this almost in-
conceivable contexture, and seeming discord, there is perfect
harmony; and while the fact, which really happened, tallies
exactly with every other contemporaneous incident related to
it in the remotest degree, it is not possible for the wit of man to
invent a story, which, if closely compared with the actual occurrences of the same time and place, may not be shown to
be false.[1] Hence it is that a false witness will not willingly
detail any circumstances in which his testimony will be open
to contradiction; nor multiply them, where there is danger of
his being detected, by a comparison of them with other accounts, equally circumstantial. He will rather deal in general
statements and broad assertions; and if he finds it necessary
for his purpose to employ names and particular circumstances
in his story, he will endeavor to invent such as shall be out
of the reach of all opposing proof; and will be most forward
and minute in his details, where he knows that any danger of
contradiction is least to be apprehended.[2] Therefore it is that
variety and minuteness of detail are usually regarded as certain
tests of sincerity, if the story, in the circumstances related,
is of a nature capable of easy refutation if it were false.

 . § 15. There is this remarkable difference between artful or
false witnesses, and those who testify the truth, in their detail of circumstances. The former are often copious and even
profuse in their statements, as far as these have been previously fabricated, and in relation to the principal matter; but
beyond this, all will be reserved and meagre, from the fear
of detection. Every lawyer knows how lightly the evidence
of a *non-mi-recordo* witness is esteemed. The testimony of
false witnesses will not be uniform in its texture, but will be
unequal, unnatural and inconsistent. On the contrary, in

---

[1] 1 Stark. Evid. 496.   [2] 1 Stark. Evid. 523.

the testimony of true witnesses there is a visible and striking naturalness of manner, and an unaffected readiness and copiousness in the detail of circumstances, as well in one part of the narrative as another, and evidently without the least regard either to the facility or difficulty of verification or detection.[1] It is easier, therefore, to make out the proof of any fact, if proof it may be called, by suborning one or more false witnesses to testify directly to the matter in question, than to procure an equal number to testify falsely to such collateral and separate circumstances as will, without greater danger of detection, lead to the same false result. The increased number of witnesses to circumstances, and the increased number of the circumstances themselves, all tend to increase the probability of detection if the witnesses are false, because thereby the points are multiplied in which their statements may be compared with each other, as well as with the truth itself, and in the same proportion is increased the danger of variance and inconsistency.[2] Thus the force of circumstantial evidence is found to depend on the number of particulars involved in the narrative; the difficulty of fabricating them all, if false, and the great facility of detection, the nature of the circumstances to be compared, and from which the dates and other facts are to be collected; the intricacy of the comparison; the number of the intermediate steps in the process of deduction; and the circuity of the investigation. The more largely the narrative partakes of these characters, the further it will be found removed from all suspicion of contrivance or design, and the more profoundly the mind will repose on the conviction of its truth.

§ 16. The narratives of the sacred writers, both Jewish and Christian, abound in examples of this kind of evidence, the value of which is hardly capable of being properly estimated. It does not, as has been already remarked, amount to mathematical demonstration; nor is this degree of proof justly de-

---

[1] 1 Stark Evid. 487 The Gospels abound in instances of this. See, for example, Mark, xv. 21. John, xviii. 10. Luke, xxiii. 6. Matt. xxvii. 58–60. John xi. 1. [2] 1 Stark. Evid. 522.

mandable in any question of moral conduct. In all human transactions, the highest degree of assurance to which we can arrive, short of the evidence of our own senses, is that of probability. The most that can be asserted is, that the narrative is more likely to be true than false; and it may be in the highest degree more likely, but still be short of being absolutely certain. Yet this very probability may be so great as to satisfy the mind of the most cautious, and enforce the assent of the most reluctant and unbelieving. If it is such as usually satisfies reasonable men, in matters of ordinary transaction, it is all which the greatest skeptic has a right to require; for it is by such evidence alone that our rights are determined, in the civil tribunals; and on no other evidence do they proceed, even in capital cases. Thus, where a house had been feloniously broken open with a knife, the blade of which was broken and left in the window, and the mutilated knife itself, the parts perfectly agreeing, was found in the pocket of the accused, who gave no satisfactory explanation of the fact, no reasonable doubt remained of his participation in the crime. And where a murder had been committed by shooting with a pistol, and the prisoner was connected with the transaction by proof that the wadding of the pistol was part of a letter addressed to him, the remainder of which was found upon his person, no juror's conscience could have reproached him for assenting to the verdict of condemnation.[1] Yet the evidence, in both cases, is but the evidence of circumstances; amounting, it is true, to the highest degree of probability, but yet not utterly inconsistent with the innocence of the accused. The evidence which we have of the great facts of the Bible history belongs to this class; that is, it is moral evidence; sufficient to satisfy any rational mind, though falling short of mathematical demonstration. If such evidence will justify the taking away of human life or liberty, in the one case, surely it ought to be deemed sufficient to determine our faith, in the other.

§ 17. All that Christianity asks of men, on this subject, is, that they would be consistent with themselves; that they

---

[1] See 1 Stark. Evid. 498. Wills on Circumstantial Evidence, pp. 128, 129.

would treat its evidences as they treat the evidence of other things; and that they would try and judge its actors and witnesses, as they deal with their fellow-men, when testifying of human actions and affairs, in human tribunals. Let the witnesses be compared with themselves, with each other, with their contemporaries, and with surrounding facts and circumstances; and let their testimony be sifted, as if it were given in a court of justice, on the side of the adverse party, the witnesses being subjected to a rigorous cross-examination. The result, it is confidently believed, will be an undoubting conviction of their integrity, ability and truth. In the course of such an examination, the undesigned coincidences will multiply upon us at every step in our progress; and the probability of the veracity of the witnesses and of the reality of the occurrences which they relate, will increase, till it acquires, for all practical purposes, the force of demonstration.

§ 18. The discrepancies between the narratives of the several evangelists, when carefully examined, will not be found sufficient to invalidate their testimony. Many seeming contradictions will prove, upon closer scrutiny, to be in perfect agreement; and it may be confidently asserted that there are none that will not yield, under fair and just criticism. If these different accounts of the same transactions were in strict verbal conformity with each other, the argument against their credibility would be much stronger; since the character of human testimony, as Dr. Paley has justly observed, is that of substantial truth under circumstantial variety. All that is asked for these witnesses is, that their testimony may be regarded as we regard the testimony of men in the ordinary affairs of life. This they are justly entitled to; and this no honorable adversary can refuse. We might, indeed, take higher ground than this, and confidently claim for them the severest scrutiny; but our present purpose is merely to try their veracity by the ordinary tests of truth, admitted in human tribunals

§ 19. If the evidence of the evangelists is to be rejected because of a few discrepancies among them, we shall be obliged to discard that of many of the contemporaneous histories on which we are accustomed to rely. Dr. Paley has

4

noticed the contradiction between Lord Clarendon and Burnett and others in regard to Lord Stafford's execution; the former stating that he was condemned to be hanged, which was done on the same day; and the latter all relating that on a Saturday he was sentenced to the block, and was beheaded on the following Monday. Another striking instance of discrepancy has since occurred, in the narratives of the different members of the royal family of France, of their flight from Paris to Varennes, in 1792. These narratives, ten in number, and by eye-witnesses and personal actors in the transactions they relate, contradict each other, some on trivial and some on more essential points, but in every case in a wonderful and inexplicable manner.[1] Yet these contradictions do not, in the general public estimation, detract from the integrity of the narrators, nor from the credibility of their relations. In the points in which they agree, and which constitute the great body of their narratives, their testimony is of course not doubted; where they differ, we reconcile them as well as we may; and where this cannot be done at all, we follow that light which seems to us the clearest. Upon the principles of the skeptic, we should be bound utterly to disbelieve them all. On the contrary, we apply to such cases the rules which, in daily experience, our judges instruct juries to apply, in weighing and reconciling the testimony of different witnesses; and

---

[1] See the Quarterly Review, vol. xxviii. p. 465. These narrators were, the Duchess D'Angoulême herself, the two Messrs. De Bouillè, the Duc De Choiseul, his servant, James Brissac, Messrs. De Damas and Deslons, two of the officers commanding detachments on the road, Messrs. De Moustier and Valori, the garde du corps who accompanied the king, and finally M. de Fontanges, archbishop of Toulouse, who, though not himself a party to the transaction, is supposed to have written from the information of the queen. An earlier instance of similar discrepancy is mentioned by Sully. After the battle of Aumale, in which Henry IV. was wounded, when the officers were around the king's bed, conversing upon the events of the day, there were not two who agreed in the recital of the most particular circumstances of the action. D'Aubigné, a contemporary writer, does not even mention the king's wound, though it was the only one he ever received in his life. See Memoirs of Sully, vol. i. p. 245. If we treated these narratives as skeptics would have us treat those of the sacred writers, what evidence should we have of any battle at Aumale, or of any flight to Varennes?

which the courts themselves observe, in comparing and reconciling different and sometimes discordant reports of the same
decisions. This remark applies especially to some alleged
discrepancies in the reports which the several evangelists have
given of the same discourses of our Lord.[1]

[1] Far greater discrepancies can be found in the different reports of the
same case, given by the reporters of legal judgments, than are shown among
the evangelists , and yet we do not consider them as detracting from the
credit of the reporters, to whom we still resort with confidence, as to good
authority. Some of these discrepancies seem utterly irreconcilable. Thus,
in a case, 45 Edw. III. 19, where the question was upon a gift of lands to
J de C. with Joan, the sister of the donor, and to their heirs, Fitzherbert
(tit. *Tail*, 14) says it was adjudged fee simple, and not frankmarriage ; Stat-
ham (tit *Tail*) says it was adjudged a gift in frankmarriage ; while Brook
(tit. *Frankmarriage*) says it was not decided. (Vid 10 Co. 118.) Others
are irreconcilable, until the aid of a third reporter is invoked. Thus, in the
case of Cooper *v* Franklin, Croke says it was not decided, but adjourned ;
(Cro. Jac 100) , Godbolt says it was decided in a certain way, which he
mentions ; (Godb. 269) ; Moor also reports it as decided, but gives a different account of the question raised ; (Moor, 848) , while Bulstrode gives
a still different report of the judgment of the court, which he says was
delivered by Croke himself But by his account it further appears, that the
case was previously twice argued , and thus it at length results that the
other reporters relate only what fell from the court on each of the previous
occasions Other similar examples may be found in 1 Dougl. 6, n. compared
with 5 East, 475, n. in the case of Galbraith *v*. Neville , and in that of
Stoughton *v*. Reynolds, reported by Fortescue, Strange, and in Cases temp.
Hardwicke (See 3 Barnw. & Ald. 247, 248.) Indeed, the books abound in
such instances. Other discrepancies are found in the names of the same
litigating parties, as differently given by reporters , such as, Putt *v*. Roster,
(2 Mod. 318) ; Foot *v*. Rastall, (Skin. 49), and Putt *v*. Royston, (2 Show.
211,) also, Hosdell *v*. Harris, (2 Keb. 462) ; Hodson *v*. Harwich, (Ib. 533),
and Hodsden *v*. Harridge, (2 Saund. 64), and a multitude of others, which
are universally admitted to mean the same cases, even when they are not
precisely within the rule of *idem sonans* These diversities, it is well known,
have never detracted in the slightest degree from the estimation in which the
reporters are all deservedly held, as authors of merit, enjoying, to this day,
the confidence of the profession. Admitting now, for the sake of argument,
(what is not conceded in fact,) that diversities equally great exist among
the sacred writers , how can we consistently, and as lawyers, raise any
serious objection against them on that account, or treat them in any manner
different from that which we observe towards our own reporters ?

§ 20. It may be further observed of the sacred writers in general, that very little of the literature of their times and country has come down to us; and that the collateral sources and means of corroborating and explaining them are proportionally limited. The contemporary writings and works of art which have reached us, have invariably been found to confirm their accounts, and to reconcile what was apparently contradictory, and supply what seemed defective or imperfect. We ought therefore to conclude that if we had more of the same light, all other similar difficulties and imperfections would vanish.[1] Indeed, they have been gradually vanishing, and rapidly too, before the light of modern research, conducted by men of science in our own times. And it is worthy of remark, that of all the investigations and discoveries of travellers and men of letters, since the overthrow of the Roman empire, not a vestige of antiquity has been found, impeaching, in the slightest degree, the credibility of the sacred writers; but, on the contrary, every result has tended to confirm it.

§ 21. Having thus briefly adverted to the nature of the evidence which is to be required and expected, in regard to the facts of our Savior's ministry, we may now turn our attention to the witnesses themselves; to ascertain who they were, what were their opportunities for observation, their accuracy as observers, and their disposition to write and speak the truth. We take them in their order as evangelists; stating the prominent traits only in their lives and characters, as they are given to us by the concurring accounts of all credible writers

§ 22. MATTHEW, called also LEVI, was a Jew of Galilee, but of what city is uncertain. He held the place of publican, or tax-gatherer, under the Roman government; and his office

---

[1] "To understand the meaning of any writer, we must first be apprized of the persons and circumstances that are the subjects of his allusions or statements; and if these are not fully disclosed in his work, we must look for illustration to the history of the times in which he wrote, and to the works of contemporaneous authors." Per Lord Abinger, in Hiscocks v. Hiscocks, 5 Mees. & W. 368

seems to have consisted in collecting the taxes within his district, as well as the duties and customs levied on goods and persons, passing in and out of his district or province, across the lake of Genesareth. While engaged in this business, at the office or usual place of collection, he was required by Jesus to follow him, as one of his disciples; a command which he immediately obeyed. Soon afterwards, he appears to have given a great entertainment to his fellow publicans and friends, at which Jesus was present; intending probably both to celebrate his own change of profession, and to give them an opportunity to profit by the teaching of his new master.[1] He was constituted one of the twelve apostles, and constantly attended the person of Jesus as a faithful follower, until the crucifixion; and after the ascension of his Master he preached the gospel for some time, with the other apostles, in Judea, and afterwards in Ethiopia, where he died.

He is generally allowed to have written first, of all the evangelists; but whether in the Hebrew or the Greek language, or in both, the learned are not agreed, nor is it material to our purpose to inquire; the genuineness of our present Greek gospel being sustained by satisfactory evidence.[2] The precise time when he wrote is also uncertain, the several dates given to it among learned men varying, from A. D. 37 to A. D 64 The earlier date, however, is argued with greater force, from the improbability that the Christians would be left for several years without a genuine and authentic history of our Savior's ministry; from the evident allusions which it contains, to a state of persecution in the church at the time it was written; from the titles of sanctity ascribed to Jerusalem, and a higher veneration testified for the temple than is found in the other and later evangelists; from the comparative gentleness with which Herod's character and conduct are dealt with, that bad prince probably being still in power; and from the frequent mention of Pilate, as still governor of Judea.[3]

---

[1] Matt. ix. 10; Mark, ii. 14, 15; Luke v. 29.

[2] The authorities on this subject are collected in Horne's Introduction, vol. iv. p. 231–238, part 2, chap. ii. sec. 2.

[3] See Horne's Introduction, vol. iv. p. 229–232.

§ 23. That Matthew was himself a native Jew, familiar with the opinions, ceremonies, and customs of his countrymen; that he was conversant with the Sacred Writings, and habituated to their idiom; a man of plain sense, but of little learning, except what he derived from the Scriptures of the Old Testament; that he wrote seriously and from conviction, and had, on most occasions, been present, and attended closely to the transactions which he relates, and relates, too, without any view of applause to himself; are facts which Dr. Campbell considers established by internal evidence, as strong as the nature of the case will admit. He deems it equally well proved, both by internal evidence and the aid of history, that he wrote for the use of his countrymen the Jews. Every circumstance is noticed which might conciliate their belief, and every unnecessary expression is avoided which might obstruct it. They looked for the Messiah, of the lineage of David, and born in Bethlehem, in the circumstances of whose life the prophecies should find fulfilment, a matter, in their estimation, of peculiar value; and to all these this evangelist has directed their especial attention.[1]

§ 24. Allusion has been already made to his employment as a collector of taxes and customs; but the subject is too important to be passed over without further notice. The tribute imposed by the Romans upon countries conquered by their arms was enormous. In the time of Pompey, the sums annually exacted from their Asiatic provinces, of which Judea was one, amounted to about four millions and a half, sterling, or about twenty-two millions of dollars. These exactions were made in the usual forms of direct and indirect taxation; the rate of the customs on merchandise varying from an eighth to a fortieth part of the value of the commodity; and the tariff including all the principal articles of the commerce of the East, much of which, as is well known, still found its way to Italy through Palestine, as well as by the way of Damascus and of Egypt. The direct taxes consisted of a capi-

[1] See Campbell on the Four Gospels, vol. iii. pp 35, 36 ; Preface to St. Matthew's Gospel, § 22, 23.

tation-tax and a land-tax, assessed upon a valuation or census, periodically taken, under the oath of the individual, with heavy penal sanctions.[1] It is natural to suppose that these taxes were not voluntarily paid, especially since they were imposed by the conqueror, upon a conquered people, and by a heathen too, upon the people of the house of Israel. The increase of taxes has generally been found to multiply discontents, evasions and frauds on the one hand, and, on the other, to increase vigilance, suspicion, close scrutiny, and severity of exaction. The penal code, as revised by Theodosius, will give us some notion of the difficulties in the way of the revenue officers, in the earlier times of which we are speaking. These difficulties must have been increased by the fact that, at this period, a considerable portion of the commerce of that part of the world was carried on by the Greeks, whose ingenuity and want of faith were proverbial. It was to such an employment and under such circumstances, that Matthew was educated; an employment which must have made him acquainted with the Greek language, and extensively conversant with the public affairs and the men of business of his time; thus entitling him to our confidence, as an experienced and intelligent observer of events passing before him And if the men of that day were, as in truth they appear to have been, as much disposed as those of the present time, to evade the payment of public taxes and duties, and to elude, by all possible means, the vigilance of the revenue officers, Matthew must have been familiar with a great variety of the forms of fraud, imposture, cunning, and deception, and must have become habitually distrustful, scrutinizing, and cautious; and, of course, much less likely to have been deceived in regard to many of the facts in our Lord's ministry, extraordinary as they were, which fell under his observation.

---

[1] See Gibbon's Rome, vol. 1, ch vi. and vol 3, chap xvii and authorities there cited   Cod. Theod. Lib. xi. tit. 1–28, with the notes of Gothofred.   Gibbon treats particularly of the revenues of a later period than our Savior's time , but the general course of proceeding, in the levy and collection of taxes, is not known to have been changed since the beginning of the empire.

This circumstance shows both the sincerity and the wisdom of Jesus, in selecting him for an eye-witness of his conduct, and adds great weight to the value of the testimony of this evangelist.

§ 25. MARK was the son of a pious sister of Barnabas, named Mary, who dwelt at Jerusalem, and at whose house the early Christians often assembled. His Hebrew name was John; the surname of Mark having been adopted, as is supposed, when he left Judea to preach the gospel in foreign countries; a practice not unusual among the Jews of that age, who frequently, upon such occasions, assumed a name more familiar than their own to the people whom they visited. He is supposed to have been converted to the Christian faith by the ministry of Peter. He travelled from Jerusalem to Antioch with Paul and Barnabas, and afterwards accompanied them elsewhere. When they landed at Perga in Pamphylia, he left them and returned to Jerusalem; for which reason, when he afterwards would have gone with them, Paul refused to take him. Upon this, a difference of opinion arose between the two apostles, and they separated, Barnabas taking Mark with him to Cyprus. Subsequently he accompanied Timothy to Rome, at the express desire of Paul. From this city he probably went into Asia, where he found Peter, with whom he returned to Rome, in which city he is supposed to have written and published his Gospel. Such is the outline of his history, as it is furnished by the New Testament.[1] The early historians add, that after this he went into Egypt, and planted a church in Alexandria, where he died.[2]

§ 26. It is agreed that Mark wrote his Gospel for the use of Gentile converts; an opinion deriving great force from the explanations introduced into it, which would have been useless to a Jew;[3] and that it was composed for those at Rome, is believed, not only from the numerous Latinisms it contains,

[1] Acts xii. 12, 25; xiii. 5, 13; and xv. 36–41; 2 Tim iv. 11; Phil. 24; Col. iv 10; 1 Pet. v 13
[2] Horne's Introduction, vol. iv pp 252, 253.
[3] Mark vii. 2, 11; and ix. 43, and elsewhere.

but from the unanimous testimony of ancient writers, and from the internal evidence afforded by the Gospel itself.

§ 27. Some have entertained the opinion that Mark compiled his account from that of Matthew, of which they suppose it an abridgment. But this notion has been refuted by Koppe, and others,[1] and is now generally regarded as untenable. For Mark frequently deviates from Matthew in the order of time, in his arrangement of facts; and he adds many things not related by the other evangelists; neither of which a mere epitomizer would probably have done. He also omits several things related by Matthew, and impefectly describes others, especially the transactions of Christ with the apostles after the resurrection; giving no account whatever of his appearance in Galilee; omissions irreconcilable with any previous knowledge of the Gospel according to Matthew. To these proofs we may add, that in several places there are discrepancies between the accounts of Matthew and Mark, not, indeed, irreconcilable, but sufficient to destroy the probability that the latter copied from the former.[2] The striking coincidences between them, in style, words, and things, in other places, may be accounted for by considering that Peter, who is supposed to have dictated this Gospel to Mark, was quite as intimately acquainted as Matthew with the miracles and discourses of our Lord; which, therefore, he would naturally recite in his preaching; and that the same things might very naturally be related in the same manner, by men who sought not after excellency of speech. Peter's agency in the narrative of Mark is asserted by all ancient writers, and is confirmed by the fact, that his humility is conspicuous in every part of it, where anything is or might be related of him; his weaknesses and fall being fully exposed, while things which might redound to his honor, are either omitted or but slightly mentioned; that scarcely any transaction of Jesus is related,

---

[1] Mr. Norton has conclusively disposed of this objection, in his Evidences of the Genuineness of the Gospels, vol. 1 Additional Notes, sec. 2, p. cxv–cxxxii.

[2] Compare Mark x. 46, and xiv. 69, and iv. 35, and i. 35, and ix. 28, with Matthew's narrative of the same events.

at which Peter was not present, and that all are related with that circumstantial minuteness which belongs to the testimony of an eye-witness.[1] We may, therefore, regard the Gospel of Mark as an original composition, written at the dictation of Peter, and consequently as another original narrative of the life, miracles, and doctrines of our Lord.

§ 28. LUKE, according to Eusebius, was a native of Antioch, by profession a physician, and for a considerable period a companion of the apostle Paul. From the casual notices of him in the Scriptures, and from the early Christian writers, it has been collected, that his parents were Gentiles, but that he in his youth embraced Judaism, from which he was converted to Christianity. The first mention of him is that he was with Paul at Troas.;[2] whence he appears to have attended him to Jerusalem; continued with him in all his troubles in Judea; and sailed with him when he was sent a prisoner from Cæsarea to Rome, where he remained with him during his two years' confinement. As none of the ancient fathers have mentioned his having suffered martyrdom, it is generally supposed that he died a natural death.

§ 29. That he wrote his Gospel for the benefit of Gentile converts is affirmed by the unanimous voice of Christian antiquity; and it may also be inferred from its dedication to a Gentile. He is particularly careful to specify various circumstances conducive to the information of strangers, but not so to the Jews; he gives the lineage of Jesus upwards, after the manner of the Gentiles, instead of downwards, as Matthew had done; tracing it up to Adam, and thus showing that Jesus was the promised seed of the woman; and he marks the eras of his birth, and of the ministry-of-John, by the reigns of the Roman emperors. He also has introduced several things, not mentioned by the other evangelists, but highly encouraging to the Gentiles to turn to God in the hope of pardon and acceptance; of which description are the parables of the publican and pharisee, in the temple; the lost piece of sil-

---

[1] See Horne's Introd vol. iv. p. 252-259. [2] Acts xvi. 10, 11.

ver; and the prodigal son; and the fact of Christ's visit to Zaccheus the publican, and the pardon of the penitent thief.

§ 30. That Luke was a physician, appears not only from the testimony of Paul,[1] but from the internal marks in his Gospel, showing that he was both an acute observer, and had given particular and even professional attention to all our Savior's miracles of healing. Thus, the man whom Matthew and Mark describe simply as a leper, Luke describes as *full* of leprosy;[2] he, whom they mention as having *a* withered hand, Luke says had his *right* hand withered;[3] and of the maid, of whom the others say that Jesus took her by the hand and she arose, he adds, that *her spirit came to her again*.[4] He alone, with professional accuracy of observation, says that *virtue went out* of Jesus, and healed the sick;[5] he alone states the fact that the sleep of the disciples in Gethsemane was *induced by extreme sorrow;* and mentions the blood-like sweat of Jesus, as occasioned by the *intensity of his agony;* and he alone relates the miraculous healing of Malchus's ear.[6] That he was also a man of a liberal education, the comparative elegance of his writings sufficiently show.[7]

§ 31. The design of Luke's Gospel was to supersede the defective and inaccurate narratives then in circulation, and to deliver to Theophilus, to whom it is addressed, a full and authentic account of the life, doctrines, miracles, death and resurrection of our Savior. Who Theophilus was, the learned are not perfectly agreed; but the most probable opinion is that of Dr. Lardner, now generally adopted, that, as Luke wrote his Gospel in Greece, Theophilus was a man of rank in that country.[8] Either the relations subsisting between him and

---

[1] Col. iv. 14. Luke, the beloved physician.

[2] Luke v. 12; Matt. viii. 2; Mark i. 40.

[3] Luke vi. 6, Matt. xii. 10; Mark iii. 1.

[4] Luke viii. 55; Matt. ix. 25; Mark v. 42.   [5] Luke vi. 19.

[6] Luke xxii. 44, 45, 51.

[7] See Horne's Introd. vol. iv. pp. 260 – 272, where references may be found to earlier writers.

[8] See Lardner's Works, 8vo. vol. vi. pp 138, 139; 4to. vol iii pp. 203, 204, and other authors, cited in Horne's Introd. vol. iv. p. 267.

Luke, or the dignity and power of his rank, or both, induced the evangelist, who himself also "had perfect understanding of all things from the first," to devote the utmost care to the drawing up of a complete and authentic narrative of these great events. He does not affirm himself to have been an eyewitness; though his personal knowledge of some of the transactions may well be inferred from the "perfect understanding" which he says he possessed. Some of the learned seem to have drawn this inference as to them all, and to have placed him in the class of original witnesses, but this opinion, though maintained on strong and plausible grounds, is not generally adopted. If, then, he did not write from his own personal knowledge, the question is, what is the legal character of his testimony?

§ 32. If it were "the result of inquiries, made under competent public authority, concerning matters in which the public are concerned"[1] it would possess every legal attribute of an inquisition, and, as such, would be legally admissible in evidence in a court of justice. To entitle such results, however, to our full confidence, it is not necessary that they should be obtained under a legal commission; it is sufficient if the inquiry is gravely undertaken and pursued, by a person of competent intelligence, sagacity and integrity. The request of a person in authority, or a desire to serve the public, are, to all moral intents, as sufficient a motive as a legal commission.[2] Thus, we know that when complaint is made to the head of a department, of official misconduct or abuse, existing in some remote quarter, nothing is more common than to send some confidential person to the spot, to ascertain the facts and report them to the department; and this report is confidently adopted as the basis of its discretionary action, in the correction of the

[1] 2 Phillips on Evidence, 95, (9th edition)

[2] When Abbot, Archbishop of Canterbury, in shooting at deer with a crossbow, in Bramsil park, accidentally killed the keeper, King James I. by a letter dated Oct. 3, 1621, requested the Lord Keeper, the Lord Chief Justice, and others, to inquire into the circumstances and consider the case and "the scandal that may have risen thereupon," and to certify the King what it may amount to. Could there be any reasonable doubt of the truth of their report of the facts, thus ascertained? See Spelman's Posthumous Works, p. 121.

abuse, or the removal of the offender. Indeed, the result of any grave inquiry is equally certain to receive our confidence, though it may have been voluntarily undertaken, if the party making it had access to the means of complete and satisfactory information upon the subject.[1] If, therefore, Luke's Gospel were to be regarded only as the work of a contemporary historian, it would be entitled to our confidence. But it is more than this. It is the result of careful inquiry and examination, made by a person of science, intelligence and education, concerning subjects which he was perfectly competent to investigate, and as to many of which he was peculiarly skilled, they being cases of the cure of maladies; subjects, too, of which he already had the perfect knowledge of a contemporary, and perhaps an eye-witness, but beyond doubt, familiar with the parties concerned in the transactions, and belonging to the community in which the events transpired, which were in the mouths of all; and the narrative, moreover, drawn up for the especial use, and probably at the request, of a man of distinction, whom it would not be for the interest nor safety of the writer to deceive or mislead. Such a document certainly possesses all the moral attributes of an inquest of office, or of any other official investigation of facts, and as such is entitled, *in foro conscientiæ*, to be adduced as original, competent and satisfactory evidence of the matters it contains.

§ 33 JOHN, the last of the evangelists, was the son of Zebedee, a fisherman of the town of Bethsaida, on the sea of Galilee. His father appears to have been a respectable man

---

[1] The case of the ill-fated steamer President furnishes an example of this sort of inquiry. This vessel, it is well known, sailed from New York for London in the month of March, 1841, having on board many passengers, some of whom were highly connected. The ship was soon overtaken by a storm, after which she was never heard of. A few months afterwards a solemn inquiry was instituted by three gentlemen of respectability, one of whom was a British admiral, another was agent for the underwriters at Lloyd's, and the other a government packet agent, concerning the time, circumstances and causes of that disaster; the result of which was communicated to the public, under their hands. This document received universal confidence, and no further inquiry was made.

in his calling, owning his vessel and having hired servants.[1] His mother, too, was among those who followed Jesus and "ministered unto him;"[2] and to John himself, Jesus, when on the cross, confided the care and support of his own mother.[3] This disciple also seems to have been favorably known to the high priest, and to have influence in his family; by means of which he had the privilege of being present in his palace at the examination of his Master, and of introducing also Peter, his friend.[4] He was the youngest of the apostles; was eminently the object of our Lord's regard and confidence; was on various occasions admitted to free and intimate intercourse with him; and is described as "the disciple whom Jesus loved."[5] Hence he was present at several scenes, to which most of the others were not admitted. He alone, in company with Peter and James, was present at the resurrection of Jairus's daughter, at the transfiguration on the mount, and at the agony of our Savior in the garden of Gethsemane.[6] He was the only apostle who followed Jesus to the cross, he was the first of them at the sepulchre, and he was present at the several appearances of our Lord after his resurrection. These circumstances, together with his intimate friendship with the mother of Jesus, especially qualify him to give a circumstantial and authentic account of the life of his Master. After the ascension of Christ, and the effusion of the Holy Spirit on the day of Pentecost, John became one of the chief apostles of the circumcision, exercising his ministry in and near Jerusalem. From ecclesiastical history we learn that, after the death of Mary the mother of Jesus, he proceeded to Asia Minor, where he founded and presided over seven churches, in as many cities, but resided chiefly at Ephesus. Thence he was banished, in Domitian's reign, to the isle of Patmos, where he wrote his Revelation. On the accession of Nerva he was freed from exile, and returned to Ephesus, where he wrote his Gospel and Epistles, and died at the age of one hundred

---

[1] Mark i 20.
[2] Matt. xxvii. 55, 56 ; Mark xv 40, 41.
[3] John xix. 26, 27.
[4] John xviii. 15, 16.
[5] John xiii. 23
[6] Luke viii. 51 ; Matt. xvii. 1, and xxvi. 37.

years, about A. D. 100, in the third year of the emperor Trajan.[1]

§ 34. The learned are not agreed as to the time when the Gospel of John was written; some dating it as early as the year 68, others as late as the year 98; but it is generally conceded to have been written after all the others. That it could not have been the work of some Platonic Christian of a subsequent age, as some have without evidence asserted, is manifest from references to it by some of the early fathers, and from the concurring testimony of many other writers of the ancient Christian church.[2]

§ 35. That it was written either with especial reference to the Gentiles, or at a period when very many of them had become converts to Christianity, is inferred from the various explanations it contains, beyond the other Gospels, which could have been necessary only to persons unacquainted with Jewish names and customs.[3] And that it was written after all the others, and to supply their omissions, is concluded, not only from the uniform tradition and belief in the church, but from his studied omission of most of the transactions noticed by the others, and from his care to mention several incidents which they have not recorded. That their narratives were known to him, is too evident to admit of doubt; while his omission to repeat what they had already stated, or, where he does mention the same things, his relating them in a brief and cursory manner, affords incidental but strong testimony that he regarded their accounts as faithful and true.[4]

§ 36. Such is the brief history of the witnesses, whose narratives we are to compare and examine. That they had the best possible opportunities to know the truth of the facts which they narrate, can hardly admit of a doubt, since three of them, (Mark being understood, as we have seen, to give the testi-

---

[1] This account is abridged from Horne's Introd vol iv p. 286-288.
[2] Horne's Introd. vol. iv. p. 289, and authors there cited.
[3] See, among others, John i. 38, 41, and ii. 6, 13, and iv. 9, and xi. 55.
[4] See Horne's Introd. vol. iv. pp. 297, 298.

mony of Peter,) were intelligent personal attendants and intimate associates of Jesus during the whole period of his
ministry; and the fourth was a contemporary, familiarly
conversant with the eye-witnesses of the transactions which he
has recorded, and of which he also had perfect knowledge from
the beginning. It is equally apparent that they were accurate
observers. We may safely assume that they were men of ordinary accuracy, till the contrary is shown by an objector. It is
always to be presumed that men are honest, and of sound mind,
and of ordinary intelligence. This is not the judgment of mere
charity; it is also the uniform presumption of the law of the
land; a presumption which is allowed freely and fully to oper-
ate, until the contrary is proved by the party who denies the
applicability of this presumption to the particular case in question. Whenever an objection is raised in opposition to the
ordinary presumptions of the law, or to the ordinary experience
of mankind, the burden of proof is devolved on the objector,
by the common and ordinary rules of evidence and of practice
in courts. No lawyer would be permitted to argue to a jury
in disparagement of the intelligence or integrity of a witness,
against whom the case itself afforded no particle of testimony.
This is sufficient for our purpose in regard to these witnesses.
But more than this is evident, from the minuteness of their
narratives, and from their history. Matthew was trained, by his
calling, to habits of severe investigation and suspicious scrutiny; and Luke's profession demanded an exactness of observation equally close and searching.[1] If, then, the evangelists
were men of integrity and disposed to testify the truth, the facts
they relate may be taken as *proved*, since, as we have before
remarked, every matter which is the subject of moral evidence
is *proved*, when it is shown by competent and satisfactory
testimony.

§ 37. Any other supposition leads to the greatest absurdities. The great truths which the apostles declared, were, that

---

[1] It has been well remarked, that, of the evangelists chosen by Jesus, two,
Peter (or Mark) and John, were too unlearned to forge the story of his life,
and two, Matthew and Luke, were too learned to be deceived by imposture.

Christ had risen from the dead, and that only through repentance from sin, and faith in him, could men hope for salvation. This doctrine they asserted with one voice, everywhere, not only under the greatest discouragements, but in the face of the most appalling terrors that can be presented to the mind of man. Their master had recently perished as a malefactor, by the sentence of a public tribunal. His religion sought to overthrow the religions of the whole world. The laws of every country were against the teachings of his disciples. The interests and passions of all the rulers and great men in the world were against them. The fashion of the world was against them. Propagating this new faith, even in the most inoffensive and peaceful manner, they could expect nothing but contempt, opposition, revilings, bitter persecutions, stripes, imprisonments, torments and cruel deaths. Yet this faith they zealously did propagate; and all these miseries they endured undismayed, nay, rejoicing. As one after another was put to a miserable death, the survivors only prosecuted their work with increased vigor and resolution. The annals of military warfare afford scarcely an example of the like heroic constancy, patience and unblenching courage. They had every possible motive to review carefully the grounds of their faith, and the evidences of the great facts and truths which they asserted; and these motives were pressed upon their attention with the most melancholy and terrific frequency. It was therefore impossible that they could have persisted in affirming the truths they have narrated, had not Jesus actually risen from the dead, and had they not known this fact as certainly as they knew any other fact.[1] If it were morally pos-

[1] If the witnesses could be supposed to have been biased, this would not destroy their testimony to matters of fact ; it would only detract from the weight of their judgment in matters of opinion. The rule of law on this subject has been thus stated by Dr. Lushington : " When you examine the testimony of witnesses nearly connected with the parties, and there is nothing very peculiar tending to destroy their credit, when they depose to mere facts, their testimony is to be believed ; when they depose as to matter of opinion, it is to be received with suspicion." Dillon v. Dillon, 3 Curteis's Eccl. Rep. 96, 102.

sible for them to have been deceived in this matter, every human motive operated to lead them to discover and avow their error. To have persisted in so gross a falsehood, after it was known to them, was not only to encounter, for life, all the evils which man could inflict, from without, but to endure also the pangs of inward and conscious guilt; with no hope of future peace, no testimony of a good conscience, no expectation of honor or esteem among men, no hope of happiness in this life, or in the world to come.

, '§ 38. Such conduct in the apostles would moreover have been utterly irreconcilable with the fact, that they possessed the ordinary constitution of our common nature. Yet their lives do show them to have been men like all others of our race; swayed by the same motives, animated by the same hopes, affected by the same joys, subdued by the same sorrows, agitated by the same fears, and subject to the same passions, temptations and infirmities, as ourselves. And their writings show them to have been men of vigorous understandings. If then their testimony was not true, there was no possible motive for its fabrication.

§ 39. It would also have been irreconcilable with the fact that they were good men. But it is impossible to read their writings, and not feel that we are conversing with men eminently holy, and of tender consciences, with men acting under an abiding sense of the presence and omniscience of God, and of their accountability to him, living in his fear, and walking in his ways. Now, though, in a single instance, a good man may fall, when under strong temptations, yet he is not found persisting, for years, in deliberate falsehood, asserted with the most solemn appeals to God, without the slightest temptation or motive, and against all the opposing interests which reign in the human breast. If, on the contrary, they are supposed to have been bad men, it is incredible that such men should have chosen this form of imposture; enjoining, as it does, unfeigned repentance, the utter forsaking and abhorrence of all falsehood and of every other sin, the practice of daily self-denial, self-abasement and self-sacrifice, the crucifixion of the flesh with all its earthly appetites and desires, indifference to the honors, and hearty contempt of the vanities of the world; and inculcating perfect purity and holiness of heart and life, and intercourse of the soul with heaven. It is incredible, that bad men should invent false-hoods to promote the religion of the God of truth. The sup-position is suicidal. If they did believe in a future state of retribution, a heaven and a hell hereafter, they took the most certain course, if false witnesses, to secure the latter for their portion. And if, still being bad men, they did not believe in future punishment, how came they to invent falsehoods, the direct and certain tendency of which was to destroy all their prospects of worldly honor and happiness, and to ensure their misery in this life? From these absurdities there is no escape, but in the perfect conviction and admission that they were good men, testifying to that which they had carefully observed and considered, and well knew to be true.[1]

§ 40. This conclusion would be readily admitted by the objector, if the facts they relate were such as ordinarily occur in human experience. But they also relate events which were miraculous, or out of the ordinary course of human ex-perience, and on this circumstance an argument is founded against their credibility. Miracles, say the objectors, are impos-sible; and therefore the evangelists were either deceivers or deceived; and in either case their narratives are unworthy of belief. Spinosa's argument against the possibility of miracles, was founded on the broad and bold assumption that all things are governed by immutable laws, or fixed modes of motion and relation, termed the laws of nature, by which God him-self is of necessity bound. This erroneous assumption is the tortoise, on which stands the elephant that upholds his sys-tem of atheism. He does not inform us who made these im-mutable laws, nor whence they derive their binding force and irresistible operation   The argument supposes that the crea-tor of all things first made a code of laws, and then put it out

---

[1] This subject has been so fully treated by Dr. Paley, in his View of the Evidences of Christianity, Part I. Proposition I   that it is unnecessary to pursue it further in this place.

of his own power to change them. The scheme of Mr. Hume is
but another form of the same error. He deduces the existence of such immutable laws from the uniform course of
human experience. This, he affirms, is our only guide in
reasoning concerning matters of fact; and whatever is contrary to human experience, he pronounces incredible.[1] With-

---

[1] Mr. Hume's argument is thus refuted by Lord Brougham. "Here are
two answers, to which the doctrine proposed by Mr. Hume is exposed, and
either appears sufficient to shake it.

"*First*—Our belief in the uniformity of the laws of nature rests not
altogether upon our own experience. We believe no man ever was raised
from the dead,—not merely because we ourselves never saw it, for indeed
that would be a very limited ground of deduction; and our belief was fixed
on the subject long before we had any considerable experience,—fixed
chiefly by authority,—that is, by deference to other men's experience.
We found our confident belief in this negative position partly, perhaps
chiefly, upon the testimony of others; and at all events, our belief that in
times before our own the same position held good, must of necessity be
drawn from our trusting the relations of other men—that is, it depends upon
the evidence of testimony If, then, the existence of the law of nature is
proved, in great part at least, by such evidence, can we wholly reject the
like evidence when it comes to prove an exception to the rule—a deviation
from the law? The more numerous are the cases of the law being kept—
the more rare those of its being broken—the more scrupulous certainly
ought we to be in admitting the proofs of the breach. But that testimony
is capable of making good the proof there seems no doubt. In truth, the
degree of excellence and of strength to which testimony may arise seems almost indefinite. There is hardly any cogency which it is not capable by possible supposition of attaining. The endless multiplication of witnesses,—the
unbounded variety of their habits of thinking, their prejudices, their interests,—afford the means of conceiving the force of their testimony, aug-
mented *ad infinitum*, because these circumstances afford the means of dimin-
ishing indefinitely the chances of their being all mistaken, all misled, or all
combining to deceive us. Let any man try to calculate the chances of a
thousand persons who come from different quarters, and never saw each
other before, and who all vary in their habits, stations, opinions, interests,
—being mistaken or combining to deceive us, when they give the same account of an event as having happened before their eyes,—these chances are
many hundreds of thousands to one. And yet we can conceive them multiplied indefinitely; for one hundred thousand such witnesses may all in like
manner bear the same testimony; and they may all tell us their story within
twenty-four hours after the transaction, and in the next parish And yet,

out stopping to examine the correctness of this doctrine, as a
fundamental principle in the law of evidence, it is sufficient

according to Mr. Hume's argument, we are bound to disbelieve them all,
because they speak to a thing contrary to our own experience, and to the accounts which other witnesses' had formerly given us of the laws of nature,
and which our forefathers had handed down to us as derived from witnesses
who lived in the old time before them. It is unnecessary to add that no'
testimony of the witnesses, whom we are supposing to concur in their relation, contradicts any testimony of our own senses. If it did, the argument
would resemble Archbishop Tillotson's'upon the Real Presence, and our dis-
belief would be at once warranted.

   Secondly—This leads us to the next objection to which Mr. Hume's argument is liable, and which we have in part anticipated while illustrating the
first   He requires us to withhold our belief in circumstances which would
force every man of common understanding to lend his assent, and to act
upon the supposition of the story told being true. For, suppose either such
numbers of various witnesses as we have spoken of, or, what is perhaps
stronger, suppose a miracle reported to us, first by a number of relators, and
then by three or four of the very soundest judges and most incorruptibly
honest men we know,—men noted for their difficult belief of wonders, and,
above all, steady unbelievers in miracles, without any bias in favor of religion, but rather accustomed to doubt, if not disbelieve,—most people would
lend an easy belief to any miracle thus vouched. But let us add this circumstance, that a friend on his death-bed had been attended by us, and that
we had told him a fact known only to ourselves,—something that we had
secretly done the very moment before we told it to the dying man, and
which to no other being we had ever revealed,—and that the credible witnesses we are supposing, inform us that the deceased appeared to them, con-
versed with them, remained with them a day or two, accompanying them,
and to avouch the fact of his reappearance on this earth, communicated to
them the secret of which we had made him the sole depository the moment
before his death; —according to Mr. Hume, we are bound rather to believe,
not only that those credible witnesses deceive us, or that those sound and
unprejudiced men were themselves deceived, and fancied things without real
existence, but further, that they all hit by chance upon the discovery of a
real secret, known only to ourselves and the dead man. Mr. Hume's argument requires us to believe this as the lesser improbability of the two —
as less unlikely than the rising of one from the dead; and yet every one
must feel convinced, that were he placed in the situation we have been
figuring, he would not only lend his belief to the relation, but, if the relators accompanied it with a special warning from the deceased person to
avoid a certain contemplated act, he would, acting upon the belief of their

in this place to remark, that it contains this fallacy; it excludes
all knowledge derived by inference or deduction from facts,

story, take the warning, and avoid doing the forbidden deed   Mr. Hume's
argument makes no exception   This is its scope; and whether he chooses
to push it thus far or no, all miracles are of necessity denied by it, without
the least regard to the kind or the quantity of the proof on which they are
rested; and the testimony which we have supposed, accompanied by the test
or check we have supposed, would fall within the grasp of the argument
just as much and as clearly as any other miracle avouched by more ordinary
combinations of evidence.

The use of Mr. Hume's argument is this, and it is an important and a
valuable one.   It teaches us to sift closely and rigorously the evidence for
miraculous events.   It bids us remember that the probabilities are always,
and must always be incomparably greater against, than for, the truth of
these relations, because it is always far more likely that the testimony should
be mistaken or false, than that the general laws of nature should be suspended.   Further than this the doctrine cannot in soundness of reason be
carried.   It does not go the length of proving that those general laws cannot, by the force of human testimony, be shown to have been, in a particular
instance, and with a particular purpose, suspended." See his Discourse of
Natural Theology, Note 5, p. 210–214. (Ed. 1835.)

Laplace, in his Essai sur les Probabilities, maintains that, the more extraordinary the fact attested, the greater the probability of error or falsehood
in the attestor.   Simple good sense, he says, suggests this; and the calcu-
lation of probabilities confirms its suggestion.   There are some things, he
adds, so extraordinary, that nothing can balance their improbability.   The
position here laid down is, that the probability of error, or of the falsehood
of testimony, becomes *in proportion* greater, as the fact which is attested is
more extraordinary.   And hence a fact extraordinary in the highest possible
degree, becomes in the highest possible degree improbable, or so much so,
that nothing can counterbalance its improbability.

This argument has been made much use of, to discredit the evidence of miracles, and the truth of that divine religion which is attested by them   But however sound it may be, in one sense, this application of it is fallacious   The
fallacy lies in the meaning affixed to the term "extraordinary"   If Laplace means a fact extraordinary *under* its existing circumstances and relations, that is, a fact remaining extraordinary, notwithstanding all its circumstances, the position needs not here to be controverted.   But if the term
means extraordinary *in the abstract*, it is far from being universally true, or
affording a correct test of truth, or rule of evidence.   Thus, it is extraordinary that a man should leap fifteen feet at a bound; but not extraordinary
that a strong and active man should do it, under a sudden impulse to save
his life.   The former is improbable in the abstract; the latter is rendered

confining us to what we derive from experience alone, and thus
depriving us of any knowledge, or even rational belief, of the
existence or character of God.   Nay more, it goes to prove
that successive generations of men can make no advancement
in knowledge, but each must begin *de novo*, and be limited to
the results of its own experience   But if we may infer, from
what we see and know, that there is a Supreme Being, by
whom this world was created, we may certainly, and with

probable by the circumstances. So, things extraordinary, and therefore improbable under one hypothesis, become the reverse under another. Thus,
the occurrence of a violent storm at sea, and the utterance by Jesus of the
words, " Peace, be still," succeeded instantly by a perfect calm, are facts
which, taken separately from each other, are not in themselves extraordinary.   The connexion between the command of Jesus and the ensuing calm,
as cause and effect, would be extraordinary and improbable if he were a
mere man , but it becomes perfectly natural and probable, when his divine
power is considered.   Each of those facts is in its nature so simple and
obvious, that the most ignorant person is capable of observing it.   There
is nothing extraordinary in the facts themselves ; and the extraordinary coincidence, in which the miracle consists, becomes both intelligible and probable upon the hypothesis of the Christian   (See the Christian Observer for
Oct 1838, p 617) The theory of Laplace may, with the same propriety,
be applied to the creation of the world. That matter was created out
of nothing is extremely improbable, in the abstract, that is, if there is no
God , and therefore it is not to be believed. But if the existence of a
Supreme Being is conceded, the fact is perfectly credible.

Laplace was so fascinated with his theory, that he thought the calculus of
probabilities might be usefully employed in discovering the value of the
different methods resorted to, in those sciences which are in a great measure
conjectural, as medicine, agriculture, and political economy.   And he proposed that there should be kept, in every branch of the administration, an
• exact register of the trials made of different measures, and of the results,
whether good or bad, to which they have led. (See the Edinburgh Review, vol. xxiii. pp..335, 336.) Napoleon, who appointed him Minister of
the Interior, has thus described him · " A geometrician of the first class, he
did not reach mediocrity as a statesman. He never viewed any subject in
its true light , he was always occupied with subtleties ; his notions were all
problematic ; and he carried into the administration the spirit of the *infinitely
small* " See the Encyclopedia Brittanica, art Laplace, vol xii. p. 101.
Memoires Ecrits à Ste. Helena, i 3. The injurious effect of deductive
reasoning, upon the minds of those who addict themselves to this method
alone, to the exclusion of all other modes of arriving at the knowledge of

equal reason, believe him capable of works which *we* have never yet known him to perform. We may fairly conclude that the power which was originally put forth to create the world is still constantly and without ceasing exerted to sustain it; and that the experienced connexion between cause and effect is but the uniform and constantly active operation of the finger of God. Whether this uniformity of operation extends to things beyond the limits of our observation, is a point we cannot certainly know. Its existence in all things that ordinarily concern us may be supposed to be ordained as conducive to our happiness; and if the belief in a revelation of peace and mercy from God is conducive to the happiness of man, it is not irrational to suppose that he would depart from his ordinary course of action, in order to give it such attestations as should tend to secure that belief. "A miracle is improbable, when we can perceive no sufficient cause in reference to his creatures, why the Deity should vary his modes of operation; it ceases to be so, when such cause is assigned." [1]

§ 41. But the discussion of the subject of miracles, forms no part of the present design. Their credibility has been fully established, and the objections of skeptics most satisfactorily met and overthrown, by the ablest writers of our own day, whose works are easily accessible. [2] Thus much, however,

truth in fact, is shown with great clearness and success, by Mr. Whewell in the ninth of the Bridgewater Treatises, Book 3, ch 6. The calculus of probabilities has been applied by some writers, to judicial evidence; but its very slight value as a test, is clearly shewn in an able article on Presumptive Evidence, in the Law Magazine, vol. i. p. 28–32, (New Series.)

[1] See Mr. Norton's "Discourse on the latest form of Infidelity," p. 18.

[2] The arguments on this subject are stated in a condensed form, by Mr. Horne, in his Introduction to the Study of the Holy Scriptures, vol. i. ch. 4, sec. 2; in which he refers, among others, to Dr. Gregory's Letters on the Evidences of the Christian Revelation; Dr. Campbell's Dissertation on Miracles; Vince's Sermons on the Credibility of Miracles, Bishop Marsh's Lectures, part 6, lect. 30, Dr. Adams's Treatise in reply to Mr. Hume; Bishop Gleig's Dissertation on Miracles, (in the third volume of his edition of Stackhouse's History of the Bible, p. 240, &c.); Dr. Key's Norrisian Lectures, vol. i.

Among the more popular treatises on miracles, are Bogue's Essay on

may here be remarked; that in almost every miracle related by the evangelists, the facts, separately taken, were plain, intelligible, transpiring in public, and about which no person of ordinary observation would be likely to mistake. Persons blind or crippled, who applied to Jesus for relief, were known to have been crippled or blind for many years; they came to be cured; he spake to them; they went away whole. Lazarus had been dead and buried four days; Jesus called him to come forth from the grave; he immediately came forth, and was seen alive for a long time afterwards. In every case of healing, the previous condition of the sufferer was known to all; all saw his instantaneous restoration; and all witnessed the act of Jesus in touching him, and heard his words.[1] All these, separately considered, were facts, plain and simple in their nature, easily seen and fully comprehended by persons of common capacity and observation. If they were separately testified to, by witnesses of ordinary intelligence and integrity, in any court of justice, the jury would be bound to believe them; and a verdict, rendered contrary to the uncontradicted testimony of credible witnesses to any one of these plain facts, separately taken, would be liable to be set aside, as a verdict against evidence. If one credible witness testified to the fact, that Bartimeus was blind, according to the uniform course of administering justice, this fact would be taken as satisfactorily proved. So also, if his subsequent restoration to sight were the sole fact in question, this also would be deemed established, by the like evidence. Nor would the rule of evidence be at all different, if the fact to be proved were the declaration of Jesus, immediately preceding his restoration to sight, that his faith had made him whole. In each of these cases, each isolated fact was capable of being accurately observed, and certainly known; and the evidence demands our assent, precisely as the

the Divine Authority of the New Testament, ch. 5; Bishop Wilson's Evidences of Christianity, vol. i. lect 7; Bishop Sumner's Evidences, ch. 10; Gambier's Guide to the Study of Moral Evidence, ch. 5; Mr. Norton's Discourse on the latest form of Infidelity, and Dr. Dewey's Dudleian Lecture, delivered before Harvard University, in May, 1836.

[1] See Bishop Wilson's Evidences, lect. 7, p. 130.

like evidence upon any other indifferent subject. The connexion of the word or the act of Jesus with the restoration of
the blind, lame and dead, to sight, and health, and life, as
cause and effect, is a conclusion which our reason is compelled
to admit, from the uniformity of their concurrence, in such a
multitude of instances, as well as from the universal conviction of all, whether friends or foes, who beheld the miracles
which he wrought. Indeed, if the truth of one of the miracles is satisfactorily established, our belief cannot reasonably
be withheld from them all. This is the issue proposed by
Dr. Paley, in regard to the evidence of the death of Jesus upon
the cross, and his subsequent resurrection, the truth of which
he has established in an argument, incapable of refutation.

§ 42. The narratives of the evangelists, moreover, contain
in themselves abundant internal evidence that they are true.
The essential marks of difference between true narratives of
facts, and the creations of fiction, have already been adverted
to, in the preceding pages. It may here be added, that these
attributes of truth are strikingly apparent throughout the gospel histories, and that the absence of the others is equally remarkable. They allude, for example, to the existing manners
and customs, and to the circumstances of the times and of
their country, with the utmost minuteness of reference. And
these references are never formally made, nor with preface
and explanation, never multiplied and heaped upon each other,
nor brought together, as though introduced by design; but
they are scattered broad-cast and singly over every part of
the story, and so connect themselves with every incident related, as to render the detection of falsehood inevitable. This
minuteness, too, is not peculiar to any one of the historians,
but is common to them all. Though they wrote at different
periods, and without mutual concert, they all alike refer incidentally to the same state of affairs, and to the same contemporary and collateral circumstances. Their testimony, in this
view, stands on the same ground with that of four witnesses,
separately examined, before different commissioners, upon the
same interrogatories, and all adverting, incidentally, to the
same circumstances as surrounding and accompanying the

principal transaction, to which alone their attention is directed. And it is worthy of observation that these circumstances were at that time of a peculiar character. Hardly a state or kingdom in the world ever experienced so many vicissitudes in its government and political relations, as did Judea, during the period of the gospel history It was successively under the government of Herod the Great, of Archelaus, and of a Roman magistrate; it was a kingdom, a tetrarchate, and a province; and its affairs, its laws, and the administration of justice, were all involved in the confusion and uncertainty naturally to be expected from recent conquest. It would be difficult to select any place or period in the history of nations, for the time and scene of a fictitious history or an imposture, which would combine so many difficulties for the fabricator to surmount, so many contemporary writers to confront him with, and so many facilities for the detection of falsehood.[1]

§ 43. "Had the evangelists been false historians," says Dr. Chalmers, "they would not have committed themselves upon so many particulars. They would not have furnished the vigilant inquirers of that period with such an effectual instrument for bringing them into discredit with the people; nor foolishly supplied, in every page of their narrative, so many materials for a cross-examination, which would infallibly have disgraced them. Now, we of this age can institute the same cross-examination. We can compare the evangelical writers with contemporary authors, and verify a number of circumstances in the history, and government, and peculiar economy of the Jewish people. We therefore have it in our power to institute a cross-examination upon the writers of the New Testament; and the freedom and frequency of their allusions to these circumstances supply us with ample materials for it. The fact, that they are borne out in their minute and incidental allusions by the testimony of other historians, gives a strong weight of what has been called circumstantial evidence in their favor. As a specimen of the argument, let us confine our observations to the history of our Savior's trial, and exe-

---

[1] See Chalmers's Evidence, chap. iii.

cution, and burial. They brought him to Pontius Pilate. We know both from Tacitus and Josephus, that he was at that time governor of Judea. A sentence from him was necessary before they could proceed to the execution of Jesus; and we know that the power of life and death was usually vested in the Roman governor. Our Savior was treated with derision; and this we know to have been a customary practice at that time, previous to the execution of criminals, and during the time of it. Pilate scourged Jesus before he gave him up to be crucified. We know from ancient authors, that this was a very usual practice among the Romans. The account of an execution generally run in this form · he was stripped, whipped, and beheaded or executed. According to the evangelists, his accusation was written on the top of the cross; and we learn from Suetonius and others, that the crime of the person to be executed was affixed to the instrument of his punishment. According to the evangelists, this accusation was written in three different languages; and we know from Josephus that it was quite common in Jerusalem to have all public advertisements written in this manner. According to the evangelists, Jesus had to bear his cross; and we know from other sources of information, that this was the constant practice of these times. According to the evangelists, the body of Jesus was given up to be buried at the request of friends. We know that, unless the criminal was infamous, this was the law, or the custom with all Roman governors." [1]

§ 44. There is also a striking naturalness in the characters exhibited in the sacred historians, rarely if ever found in works of fiction, and probably nowhere else to be collected in a similar manner from fragmentary and incidental allusions and expressions, in the writings of different persons. Take, for example, that of Peter, as it may be gathered from the evangelists, and it will be hardly possible to conceive that four persons, writing at different times, could have concurred in the delineation of such a character, if it were not real; a character too, we must observe, which is nowhere expressly drawn, but is

[1] See Chalmers's Evidence, p. 76 - 78, Amer. ed.

shown only here and there, casually, in the subordinate parts of the main narrative. Thus disclosed, it is that of a confident, sanguine, and zealous man; sudden and impulsive, yet humble and ready to retract; honest and direct in his purposes; ardently loving his master, yet deficient in fortitude and firmness in his cause.[1] When Jesus put any question to the apostles, it was Peter who was foremost to reply;[2] and if they would inquire of Jesus, it was Peter who was readiest to speak.[3] He had the impetuous courage to cut off the ear of the high priest's servant, who came to arrest his master; and the weakness to dissemble before the Jews, in the matter of eating with Gentile converts.[4] It was he who ran with John to the sepulchre, on the first intelligence of the resurrection of Jesus, and with characteristic zeal rushed in, while John paused without the door.[5] He had the ardor to desire and the faith to attempt to walk on the water, at the command of his Lord; but as soon as he saw the wind boisterous, he was afraid.[6] He was the first to propose the election of another apostle in the place of Judas;[7] and he it was who courageously defended them all, on the day of Pentecost, when the multitude charged them with being filled with new wine.[8] He was forward to acknowledge Jesus to be the Messiah;[9] yet having afterwards endangered his own life by wounding the servant of the High Priest, he suddenly consulted his own safety by denying the same master, for whom, but a few hours before, he had declared himself ready to die.[10] We may safely affirm that the annals of fiction afford no example of a similar but not uncommon character, thus incidentally delineated.

§ 45. There are other internal marks of truth in the narratives of the evangelists, which, however, need here be only

[1] See Mark viii. 32; ix. 5; and xiv. 29; Matt. xvi. 22; and xvii. 5; Luke ix. 33; and xviii. 18; John xiii. 8; and xviii 15.

[2] Mark viii. 29, Matt. xvi. 16; Luke ix. 20.

[3] Matt xviii. 21; and xix. 27, John xiii. 36.

[4] Gal. ii. 11.   [5] John xx. 3 - 6.   [6] Matt xiv. 30.

[7] Acts i 15.   [8] Acts ii. 14.

[9] Matt xvi. 16; Mark viii. 29; Luke ix. 20, John vi. 69.

[10] Matt. xxvi. 33, 35, Mark xiv. 29.

alluded to, as they have been treated with great fulness and force by able writers, whose works are familiar to all.[1] Among these may be mentioned the nakedness of the narratives, the absence of all parade by the writers; about their own integrity, of all anxiety to be believed, or to impress others with a good opinion of themselves or their cause, of all marks of wonder, or of desire to excite astonishment at the greatness of the events they record, and of all appearance of design to exalt their Master. On the contrary, there is apparently the most perfect indifference on their part, whether they are believed or not; or rather, the evident consciousness that they were recording events well known to all, in their own country and times, and undoubtedly to be believed, like any other matter of public history, by readers in all other countries and ages. It is worthy, too, of especial observation, that though the evangelists record the unparalleled sufferings and cruel death of their beloved Lord, and this too, by the hands and with the consenting voices of those on whom he had conferred the greatest benefits, and their own persecutions and dangers, yet they have bestowed no epithets of harshness or even of just censure on the authors of all this wickedness, but have everywhere left the plain and unincumbered narrative to speak for itself, and the reader to pronounce his own sentence of condemnation; like true witnesses, who have nothing to gain or to lose by the event of the cause, they state the facts, and leave them to their fate. Their simplicity and artlessness, also, should not pass unnoticed, in readily stating even those things most disparaging to themselves. Their want of faith in their master, their dulness of apprehension of his teachings, their strifes for preeminence, their inclination to call fire from heaven upon their enemies, their desertion of their Lord in his hour of extreme peril; these, and many other incidents tending directly to their own dishonor, are nevertheless set down with

[1] See Paley's View of the Evidences of Christianity, part ii. chapters iii. iv. v vi. vii.; Ibid. part iii. ch. i.; Chalmers on the Evidence and Authority of the Christian Revelation, ch. iii. iv. viii.; Wilson's Evidences of Christianity. lect. vi ; Bogue's Essay on the Divine Authority of the New Testament. chap. iii. iv.

all the directness and sincerity of truth, as by men writing under the deepest sense of responsibility to God. Some of the more prominent instances of this class of proofs will be noticed hereafter, in their proper places, in the narratives themselves.

§ 46. Lastly, the great character they have portrayed is perfect. It is the character of a sinless Being; of one supremely wise and supremely good. It exhibits no error, no sinister intention, no imprudence, no ignorance, no evil passion, no impatience; in a word, no fault; but all is perfect uprightness, innocence, wisdom, goodness and truth. The mind of man has never conceived the idea of such a character, even for his gods; nor has history nor poetry shadowed it forth. The doctrines and precepts of Jesus are in strict accordance with the attributes of God, agreeably to the most exalted idea which we can form of them, either from reason or from revelation. They are strikingly adapted to the capacity of mankind, and yet are delivered with a simplicity and majesty wholly divine. He spake as never man spake. He spake with authority; yet addressed himself to the reason and the understanding of men; and he spake with wisdom, which men could neither gainsay nor resist. In his private life, he exhibits a character not merely of strict justice, but of overflowing benignity. He is temperate, without austerity; his meekness and humility are signal; his patience is invincible; truth and sincerity illustrate his whole conduct; every one of his virtues is regulated by consummate prudence; and he both wins the love of his friends, and extorts the wonder and admiration of his enemies.[1] He is represented in every variety of situation in life, from the height of worldly grandeur, amid the acclamations of an admiring multitude, to the deepest abyss of human degradation and woe, apparently deserted of God and man. Yet everywhere he is the same; displaying a character of unearthly perfection, symmetrical in all its proportions, and encircled with splendor more than human. Either the men of Galilee were men of superlative wisdom, of extensive knowl-

---

[1] See Bogue's Essay, chap. i. sect. 2, Newcome's Obs. part ii. ch. i. sec. 14.

edge and experience, and of deeper skill in the arts of deception, than any and all others, before or after them, or they
have truly stated the astonishing things which they saw and
heard.

By the light of the principles above stated, we now proceed
to a comparative view of the narratives of the Four Evangelists. For this purpose, we have arranged them in sections,
after the order of Professor Robinson's Greek Harmony of the
Gospels. But in adopting this order, we do not affect to decide
the question of the propriety of arrangement, between this
and the schemes of other Harmonists. The issue, to which
we address ourselves, is simply that of the veracity of the
witnesses whose testimony is before us; and therefore Newcome's, or some other of the modern Harmonies, would probably have served the purpose equally as well as this; but
this has been preferred, as being the latest and most generally in use. Such parts of the narratives as seemed to require
particular remark are explained or commented upon, in the
notes at the end of the several sections.

HARMONY OF THE GOSPELS.

PART I.

EVENTS

CONNECTED WITH THE

BIRTH AND CHILDHOOD OF JESUS.

TIME. About thirteen and a half years.

6

§ 1. Preface to

MATTHEW. | MARK.

§ 2. An Angel appears

Luke's Gospel.

LUKE.	JOHN.

CH. I. 1-4.

FORASMUCH as many have taken in hand to set forth in order a declaration of those things which are most surely believed among us,

2 Even as they delivered them unto us, which from the beginning were eye-witnesses, and ministers of the word ;

3 It seemed good to me also, having had perfect understanding of all things from the very first, to write unto thee in order, most excellent Theophilus,

4 That thou mightest know the certainty of those things wherein thou hast been instructed.

to Zacharias. *Jerusalem.*

CH. I. 5-25.

5 THERE was in the days of Herod the king of Judea, a certain priest named Zacharias, of the course of Abia : and his wife *was* of the daughters of Aaron, and her name *was* Elisabeth.

6 And they were both righteous before God, walking in all the commandments and ordinances of the Lord blameless.

7 And they had no child, because that Elisabeth was barren ; and they both were *now* well stricken in years.

8 And it came to pass, that, while he executed the priest's office before God in the order of his course,

9 According to the custom of the priest's office, his lot was to burn incense when he went into the temple of the Lord.

10 And the whole multitude of the people were praying without, at the time of incense.

11 And there appeared unto him an angel of the Lord, standing on the right side of the altar of incense.

12 And when Zacharias saw *him*, he was troubled, and fear fell upon him.

13 But the angel said unto him, Fear not, Zacharias : for thy prayer is heard ; and thy wife Elisabeth shall bear thee a son, and thou shalt call his name John.

14 And thou shalt have joy and

§ 3. An Angel appears

MATTHEW.	MARK.

to Zacharias. *Jerusalem.*

LUKE.	JOHN.

LUKE.
ch. i. 5–25.

gladness, and many shall rejoice at his birth.

15 For he shall be great in the sight of the Lord, and shall drink neither wine nor strong drink; and he shall be filled with the Holy Ghost, even from his mother's womb.

16 And many of the children of Israel shall he turn to the Lord their God.

17 And he shall go before him in the spirit and power of Elias,ᵃ to turn the hearts of the fathers to the children, and the disobedient to the wisdom of the just; to make ready a people prepared for the Lord.

18 And Zacharias said unto the angel, Whereby shall I know this? for I am an old man, and my wife well stricken in years.

19 And the angel, answering, said unto him, I am Gabriel, that stand in the presence of God; and am sent to speak unto thee, and to show thee these glad tidings.

20 And behold, thou shalt be dumb, and not able to speak, until the day that these things shall be performed, because thou believest not my words, which shall be fulfilled in their season.

21 And the people waited for Zacharias, and marvelled that he tarried so long in the temple.

22 And when he came out, he could not speak unto them: and they perceived that he had seen a vision in the temple; for he beckoned unto them, and remained speechless.

23 And it came to pass, that as soon as the days of his ministration were accomplished, he departed to his own house.

24 And after those days his wife Elisabeth conceived, and hid herself five months, saying,

25 Thus hath the Lord dealt with me in the days wherein he looked on *me*, to take away my reproach among men.

ᵃ Mal. 4, 5, 6.

§ 3. An Angel appears

MATTHEW.	MARK.

§ 4. Mary visits

to Mary. *Nazareth.*

LUKE.
CH. I. 26–38.

26 And in the sixth month the angel Gabriel was sent from God unto a city of Galilee, named Nazareth,

27 To a virgin espoused to a man whose name was Joseph, of the house of David ; and the virgin's name *was* Mary.

28 And the angel came in unto her, and said, Hail, *thou that art* highly favored, the Lord *is* with thee : blessed *art* thou among women.

29 And when she saw *him,* she was troubled at his saying, and cast in her mind what manner of salutation this should be.

30 And the angel said unto her, Fear not, Mary : for thou hast found favor with God.

31 And behold, thou shalt conceive in thy womb, and bring forth a son, and shalt call his name JESUS.

32 He shall be great, and shall be called the son of the Highest ; and the Lord God shall give unto him the throne of his father David.

33 And[a] he shall reign over the house of Jacob forever ; and of his kingdom there shall be no end.

34 Then said Mary unto the angel, How shall this be, seeing I know not a man ?

35 And the angel answered and said unto her, The Holy Ghost shall come upon thee, and the power of the Highest shall overshadow thee : therefore also that holy thing which shall be born of thee, shall be called the Son of God.

36 And behold, thy cousin Elisabeth, she hath also conceived a son in her old age ; and this is the sixth month with her who was called barren :

37 For with God nothing shall be impossible.

38 And Mary said, Behold the handmaid of the Lord, be it unto me according to thy word. And the angel departed from her.

JOHN.

Elisabeth. *Juttah.*

CH. I. 39–56.

39 And Mary arose in those days, and went into the hill-country with haste, into a city of Juda,

[a] Mic. iv. 7.

§ 4. Mary visits

MATTHEW.	MARK.

Elisabeth. *Juttah.*

LUKE.	JOHN.

LUKE.
CH. I. 39–56.

40 And entered into the house of Zacharias, and saluted Elisabeth.

41 And it came to pass, that when Elisabeth heard the salutation of Mary, the babe leaped in her womb : and Elisabeth was filled with the Holy Ghost.

42 And she spake out with a loud voice and said, Blessed *art* thou among women, and blessed *is* the fruit of thy womb.

43 And whence *is* this to me, that the mother of my lord should come to me ?

44 For lo, as soon as the voice of thy salutation sounded in mine ears, the babe leaped in my womb for joy.

45 And blessed *is* she that believed : for there shall be a performance of those things which were told her from the Lord.

46 And Mary said, My soul doth magnify the Lord,

47 And my spirit hath rejoiced in God my Savior.

48 For he hath regarded the low estate of his handmaiden : for behold, from henceforth all generations shall call me blessed.

49 For he that is mighty hath done to me great things ; and holy *is* his name.

50 And his mercy *is* on them that fear him, from generation to generation.

51 He hath shewed strength with his arm ; he hath scattered the proud in the imagination of their hearts.

52 He hath put down the mighty from *their* seats, and exalted them of low degree.

53 He hath filled the hungry with good things, and the rich he hath sent empty away.

54 He hath holpen his servant Israel, in remembrance of *his* mercy ;

55 As[a] he spake to our fathers, to Abraham, and to his seed, for ever.

56 And Mary abode with her about three months, and returned to her own house.

---

[a] Is. xli. 8, 9 ; Gen. xxii. 16, seq.

§ 5. The birth of

MATTHEW.	MARK.

John the Baptist.   *Juttah.*

LUKE.	JOHN.

LUKE.
CH. I. 57–80.

57 Now Elisabeth's full time came that she should be delivered; and she brought forth a son.

58 And her neighbors and her cousins heard how the Lord had shewed great mercy upon her; and they rejoiced with her.

59 And it came to pass, that on the eighth day they came to circumcise the child; and they called him Zacharias, after the name of his father.

60 And his mother answered and said, not *so;* but he shall be called John.

61 And they said unto her, There is none of thy kindred that is called by this name.

62 And they made signs to his father, how he would have him called.

63 And he asked for a writing-table, and wrote, saying, His name is John. And they marvelled all.

64 And his mouth was opened immediately, and his tongue loosed, and he spake, and praised God.

65 And fear came on all that dwelt round about them : and all these sayings were noised abroad throughout all the hill-country of Judea.

66 And all they that heard *them,* laid *them* up in their hearts, saying, What manner of child shall this be ! And the hand of the Lord was with him.

67 And his father Zacharias was filled with the Holy Ghost, and prophesied, saying,

68 Blessed *be* the Lord God of Israel ; for he hath visited and redeemed his people,

69 And hath raised up a horn of salvation for us, in the house of his servant David :

70 As he spake by the mouth of his holy prophets, which have been since the world began :

71 That we should be saved from our enemies, and from the hand of all that hate us ;

72 To perform the mercy *promised* to our fathers, and to remember his holy covenant ;

§ 5. The birth of

MATTHEW.	MARK.

§ 6. An Angel appears

CH. I. 18 – 25.

18 Now the birth of Jesus Christ was on this wise : When as his mother Mary was espoused to Joseph, before they came together, she was found with child of the Holy Ghost.

19 Then Joseph her husband, being a just *man*, and not willing to make her a public example, was minded to put her away privily.

20 But while he thought on these things, Behold, the angel of the Lord appeared unto him in a dream, saying, Joseph, thou son of David, fear not to take unto thee Mary thy wife ; for that which is conceived in her is of the Holy Ghost.

21 And she shall bring forth a son, and thou shalt call his name JESUS : for he shall save his people from their sins.

22 Now all this was done, that it

Matt. i. 19. *husband.*] There was commonly an interval of ten or twelve months, between the making of the contract of marriage and the time of its celebration. *Gen.* xxiv. 55 ; *Judg.* xiv. 8. During this period, though there was no intercourse between the bride and bridegroom, not even so much as an interchange of conversation, yet they were considered and spoken of as husband and wife. If, at the end of

John the Baptist. *Juttah.*

LUKE.	JOHN.
CH. I. 57–80.	

73 The oath which he sware to our father Abraham,[a]

74 That he would grant unto us, that we, being delivered out of the hand of our enemies, might serve him without fear,

75 In holiness and righteousness before him, all the days of our life.

76 And thou, child, shalt be called the Prophet of the Highest, for thou shalt go before the face of the Lord to prepare his ways ;

77 To give knowledge of salvation unto his people, by the remission of their sins,

78 Through the tender mercy of our God ; whereby the day-spring from on high hath visited us,

79 To give light to them that sit in darkness and *in* the shadow of death, to guide our feet into the way of peace.

80 And the child grew, and waxed strong in spirit, and was in the deserts till the day of his showing unto Israel.

to Joseph. *Nazareth.*

[a] Gen. xxii. 16, seq.

this probationary period, the bridegroom was unwilling to solemnize his engagements by the marriage of the bride, he was bound to give her a bill of divorce, as if she had been his wife. And if she, during the same period, had illicit intercourse with another man, she was liable to punishment, as an adulteress. JAHN's Archæol. § 154.

§ 6. An Angel appears

MATTHEW.	MARK.
CH. I. 18–25.	
might be fulfilled which was spoken of the Lord by the prophet, saying,	
23 Behold,[a] a virgin shall be with child, and shall bring forth a son, and they shall call his name Emmanuel, which being interpreted is, God with us.	
24 Then Joseph, being raised from sleep, did as the angel of the Lord had bidden him, and took unto him his wife :	
25 And knew her not till she had brought forth her first-born son : and he called his name JESUS.	

§ 7. The birth

a Is. vii. 14.

Luke ii. 1. *a decree.*] This decree was issued eleven years before it was carried into effect, the delay having been procured by Herod. This fact reconciles the evan-

to Joseph.   *Nazareth.*

LUKE.	JOHN.

of Jesus.   *Bethlehem.*

CH. II. 1-7.

AND it came to pass in those days, that there went out a decree from Cesar Augustus, that all the world should be taxed.

2 (And this taxing was first made when Cyrenius was governor of Syria.)

3 And all went to be taxed, every one into his own city.

4 And Joseph also went up from Galilee, out of the city of Nazareth, into Judea, unto the city of David, which is called Bethlehem, (because he was of the house and lineage of David,)

5 To be taxed with Mary his espoused wife, being great with child.

6 And so it was, that while they were there, the days were accomplished that she should be delivered.

7 And she brought forth her first-born son, and wrapped him in swaddling-clothes, and laid him in a manger; because there was no room for them in the inn.

gelist with the Roman historians, from whom it appears that Cyrenius was not governor when the decree was issued, though he held that office when the census was taken and the tax assessed. See TOWNSEND, *in loc.*

§ 8. An Angel appears

MATTHEW.	MARK.

§ 9. The circumcision of Jesus and

to the Shepherds.   *Near Bethlehem.*

LUKE.	JOHN.

CH. II. 8-20.

8 And there were in the same country shepherds abiding in the field, keeping watch over their flock by night.

9 And lo, the angel of the Lord came upon them, and the glory of the Lord shone round about them; and they were sore afraid.

10 And the angel said unto them, Fear not: for behold, I bring you good tidings of great joy, which shall be to all people.

11 For unto you is born this day, in the city of David, a Savior, which is Christ the Lord.

12 And this *shall be* a sign unto you; Ye shall find the babe wrapped in swaddling-clothes, lying in a manger.

13 And suddenly there was with the angel a multitude of the heavenly host praising God, and saying,

14 Glory to God in the highest, and on earth peace, good will toward men.

15 And it came to pass, as the angels were gone away from them into heaven, the shepherds said one to another, Let us now go even unto Bethlehem, and see this thing which is come to pass, which the Lord hath made known unto us.

16 And they came with haste, and found Mary and Joseph, and the babe lying in a manger.

17 And when they had seen *it*, they made known abroad the saying which was told them concerning this child.

18 And all they that heard *it*, wondered at those things which were told them by the shepherds.

19 But Mary kept all these things, and pondered *them* in her heart.

20 And the shepherds returned, glorifying and praising God for all the things that they had heard and seen, as it was told unto them.

his presentation in the temple.   *Bethlehem.   Jerusalem.*

CH. II. 21-38.

21 And when eight days were accomplished for the circumcising of the child,[a] his name was called JESUS,

a Gen. xvii. 12 ; Lev. xii. 3.

7

§ 9. The circumcision of Jesus and

MATTHEW.	MARK.

his presentation in the Temple.　*Bethlehem.*　*Jerusalem.*

LUKE.	JOHN.
CH. II. 21—38.	

which was so named of the angel before he was conceived in the womb.

22 And when the days of her purification according to the law of Moses were accomplished, they brought him to Jerusalem, to present *him* to the Lord;)

23 (As it is written in the law of the Lord,[a] Every male that openeth the womb shall be called holy to the Lord;)

24 And to offer a sacrifice according to that which is said in the law of the Lord,[b] A pair of turtle-doves, or two young pigeons.

25 And behold, there was a man in Jerusalem, whose name *was* Simeon; and the same man *was* just and devout, waiting for the consolation of Israel: and the Holy Ghost was upon him.

26 And it was revealed unto him by the Holy Ghost, that he should not see death, before he had seen the Lord's Christ.

27 And he came by the Spirit into the temple; and when the parents brought in the child Jesus, to do for him after the custom of the law,

28 Then took he him up in his arms, and blessed God, and said,

29 Lord, now lettest thou thy servant depart in peace, according to thy word:

30 For mine eyes have seen thy salvation,

31 Which thou hast prepared before the face of all people;

32 A light to lighten the Gentiles, and the glory of thy people Israel.

33 And Joseph and his mother marvelled at those things which were spoken of him.

34 And Simeon blessed them, and said unto Mary his mother, Behold, this child is[c] set for the fall and rising again of many in Israel; and for a sign which shall be spoken against,

35 (Yea, a sword shall pierce through thy own soul also;) that the thoughts of many hearts may be revealed.

[a] Ex. xiii. 2; Numb. viii. 16, 17.　　[b] Lev. xii. 6, 8.　　[c] Is. viii. 14.

§ 9. The circumcision of Jesus and

MATTHEW.	MARK.

§ 10. The Magi.

CH. II. 1-12.

Now when Jesus was born in Bethlehem of Judea in the days of Herod the king, behold, there came wise men from the east to Jerusalem,

2 Saying, Where is he that is born king of the Jews? for we have seen his star in the east, and are come to worship him.

3 When Herod the king had heard *these things,* he was troubled, and all Jerusalem with him.

4 And when he had gathered all the chief priests and scribes of the people together, he demanded of them where Christ should be born.

5 And they said unto him, in Bethlehem of Judea : for thus it is written by the prophet,

6 And ª thou Bethlehem, *in* the land of Juda, art not the least among the princes of Juda : for out of thee shall come a Governor, that shall rule my people Israel.

7 Then Herod, when he had privily called the wise men, inquired of them diligently what time the star appeared.

8 And he sent them to Bethlehem, and said Go, and search diligently for the young child ; and when ye have found *him,* bring me word again, that I may come and worship him also.

9 When they had heard the king, they departed ; and lo, the star, which

ª Mic. v. 2.

his presentation in the Temple. *Bethlehem.* *Jerusalem.*

LUKE.	JOHN.
CH. II. 21 – 38.	

36 And there was one Anna, a prophetess, the daughter of Phanuel, of the tribe of Aser: she was of a great age, and had lived with a husband seven years from her virginity.

37 And she *was* a widow of about fourscore and four years, which departed not from the temple, but served *God* with fastings and prayers night and day.

38 And she coming in that instant, gave thanks likewise unto the Lord, and spake of him to all them that looked for redemption in Jerusalem.

Jerusalem. *Bethlehem.*

§ 10. The Magi.

MATTHEW.	MARK.
CH. II. 1–12.	

they saw in the east, went before them, till it came and stood over where the young child was.

10 When they saw the star, they rejoiced with exceeding great joy.

11 And when they were come into the house, they saw the young child with Mary his mother, and fell down, and worshipped him: and when they had opened their treasures, they presented unto him gifts; gold, and frankincense, and myrrh.

12 And being warned of God in a dream that they should not return to Herod, they departed into their own country another way.

§ 11. The flight into Egypt. Herod's

CH. II. 13–23.

13 And when they were departed, behold, the angel of the Lord appeareth to Joseph in a dream, saying, Arise, and take the young child and his mother, and flee into Egypt, and be thou there until I bring thee word: for Herod will seek the young child to destroy him.

14 When he arose, he took the young child and his mother by night, and departed into Egypt:

15 And was there until the death of Herod: that it might be fulfilled which was spoken of the Lord by the prophet, saying,ᵃ Out of Egypt have I called my Son.

16 Then Herod, when he saw that he was mocked of the wise men, was exceeding wroth, and sent forth, and slew all the children that were in Bethlehem, and in all the coasts thereof, from two years old and under, according to the time which he had diligently inquired of the wise men.

17 Then was fulfilled that which was spoken by Jeremy the prophet, saying,

18 Inᵇ Rama was there a voice heard, lamentation, and weeping, and great mourning, Rachel weeping *for* her children, and would not be comforted, because they are not.

ᵃ Hos. xi. 1.

ᵇ Jer. xxxi. 15, and xl. 1

Jerusalem. Bethlehem.

LUKE.	JOHN.

cruelty. The return. *Bethlehem. Nazareth.*

CH. II. 39, 40.

§ 11. The flight into Egypt. Herod's

MATTHEW.	MARK.

MATTHEW.
CH. II. 13 – 23.

19 But, when Herod was dead, behold, an angel of the Lord appeareth in a dream to Joseph in Egypt,

20 Saying, Arise, and take the young child and his mother, and go into the land of Israel : for they are dead which sought the young child's life.

21 And he arose, and took the young child and his mother, and came into the land of Israel.

22 But when he heard that Archelaus did reign in Judea in the room of his father Herod, he was afraid to go thither : notwithstanding, being warned of God in a dream, he turned aside into the parts of Galilee :

23 And he came and dwelt in a city called Nazareth : that it might be fulfilled which was spoken by the prophets, He shall be called a Nazarene.[a]

§ 12. At twelve years of age, Jesus

---

[a] Is. xi. 1, and liii. 2 ; Zech. vi. 12 ; Rev. v. 5.

Matth. ii. 22, *he was afraid.*] The naked statement of this fact, without explanation, is a mark of the sincerity of the evangelist, for the value of which we are indebted to Josephus, who relates, (Ant. b. 17, ch. 9, § 3,) an instance of savage cruelty in Archelaus, immediately on his coming to the throne, in causing three thousand persons to be butchered in cold blood, at the first passover after Herod's death. Such an act, committed under such circumstances, must have been rapidly made known abroad, and inspired all persons with horror. Well, therefore, might Joseph fear to return. But Matthew's incidental allusion to the cause, is characteristic of a man intent only upon the statement of the main facts, and regardless of appearances or explanations. BLUNT, Veracity, &c. sect. ii. 3.

Luke ii. 42 ; *twelve years old.*] Jewish children were not obliged to the observances of the ceremonial law, until they attained to years of discretion, which, in males, was fixed by common consent at twelve years. On arriving at this age, they were taken to

cruelty.　The return.　*Bethlehem.*　*Nazareth.*

LUKE.	JOHN.
CH. II. 39, 40.	

39 And when they had performed all things according to the law of the Lord, they returned into Galilee, to their own city Nazareth.

40 And the child grew, and waxed strong in spirit, filled with wisdom ; and the grace of God was upon him.

goes to the Passover.　*Jerusalem.*

CH. II. 41–52.

41 Now his parents went to Jerusalem every year at the feast of the passover.

42 And when he was twelve years old, they went up to Jerusalem after the custom of the feast.

43 And when they had fulfilled the days, as they returned, the child Jesus tarried behind in Jerusalem ; and Joseph and his mother knew not *of it.*

44 But they, supposing him to have been in the company, went a day's journey ; and they sought him among *their* kinsfolk and acquaintance.

Jerusalem at the passover, of which they thenceforth participated, as "sons of commandment," being fully initiated into the doctrines and ceremonies of the Jewish church, probably after examination by the doctors. This accounts for the circumstance of his being found among them, both hearing, and asking them questions. Stackhouse, Hist. N. T. ch. i. ; Bloomfield, *in loc.*

Luke ii. 44 ; *in the company.*] All who came, not only from the same city, but from the same canton or district, made one company. They carried necessaries along with them, and tents for their lodging at night. Such companies they now call *caravans,* and in several places have houses fitted up for their reception, called *caravanseries.* This account of their manner of travelling furnishes a ready answer to the question, How could Joseph and Mary make a day's journey, without discovering, before night, that Jesus was not in the company ? In the day-time, we may reasonably presume, the travellers would mingle with different parties of their friends and acquaintance ; but in the evening, when they were about to encamp, every one would join the family to which he belonged. Campbell, *in loc.*

§ 12. At twelve years of age, Jesus

MATTHEW.	MARK.

§ 13. The

CH. I. 1 – 17.

THE book of the generation of Jesus Christ, the son of David, the son of Abraham.

2 Abraham begat Isaac ; and Isaac begat Jacob; and Jacob begat Judas and his brethren ;

3 And Judas begat Phares and Zara of Thamar ; and Phares begat Esrom ; and Esrom begat Aram ;

4 And Aram begat Aminadab ; and Aminadab begat Naasson ; and Naasson begat Salmon ;

goes to the Passover. *Jerusalem.*

LUKE.

CH. II. 41–52.

JOHN.

45 And when they found him not, they turned back again to Jerusalem, seeking him.

46 And it came to pass, that after three days they found him in the temple, sitting in the midst of the doctors, both hearing them, and asking them questions.

47 And all that heard him were astonished at his understanding and answers.

48 And when they saw him, they were amazed : and his mother said unto him, Son, why hast thou thus dealt with us? Behold, thy father and I have sought thee sorrowing.

49 And he said unto them, How is it that ye sought me? wist ye not that I must be about my Father's business?

50 And they understood not the saying which he spake unto them.

51 And he went down with them, and came to Nazareth, and was subject unto them : but his mother kept all these sayings in her heart.

52 And Jesus increased in wisdom and stature, and in favor with God and man.

Genealogies.

CH. III. 23–38, INVERTED.

38 *The son* of God, *the son* of Adam, *the son* of Seth, *the son* of Enos,

37 *The son* of Cainan, *the son* of Maleleel, *the son* of Jared, *the son* of Enoch, *the son* of Mathusala,

36 *The son* of Lamech, *the son* of Noe, *the son* of Sem, *the son* of Arphaxad, *the son* of Cainan,

35 *The son* of Sala, *the son* of Heber, *the son* of Phalec, *the son* of Ragau, *the son* of Saruch,

34 *The son* of Nachor, *the son* of Thara, *the son* of Abraham, *the son* of Isaac, *the son* of Jacob,

33 *The son* of Juda, *the son* of Phares, *the son* of Esrom, *the son* of Aram, *the son* of Aminadab,

32 *The son* of Naasson, *the son* of Salmon, *the son* of Booz, *the son* of Obed, *the son* of Jesse,

§ 13. The

MATTHEW.	MARK.
CH. I. 1 – 17.	

5 And Salmon begat Booz of Rachab ; and Booz begat Obed of Ruth ; and Obed begat Jesse ;

6 And Jesse begat David the king ; and David the king begat Solomon of her *that had been the wife* of Urias ;

7 And Solomon begat Roboam ; and Roboam begat Abia ; and Abia begat Asa ;

8 And Asa begat Josaphat ; and Josaphat begat Joram ; and Joram begat Ozias ;

9 And Ozias begat Joatham ; and Joatham begat Achaz ; and Achaz begat Ezekias ;

10 And Ezekias begat Manasses ; and Manasses begat Amon ; and Amon begat Josias ;

11 And Josias begat Jechonias and his brethren, about the time they were carried away to Babylon :

12 And after they were brought to Babylon, Jechonias begat Salathiel ; and Salathiel begat Zorobabel ;

13 And Zorobabel begat Abiud ; and Abiud begat Eliakim ; and Eliakim begat Azor ;

14 And Azor begat Sadoc ; and Sadoc begat Achim ; and Achim begat Eliud ;

15 And Eliud begat Eleazar ; and Eleazar begat Matthan ; and Matthan begat Jacob ;

16 And Jacob begat Joseph the husband of Mary, of whom was born Jesus, who is called Christ.

17 So all the generations from Abraham to David *are* fourteen generations ; and from David until the carrying away into Babylon *are* fourteen generations ; and from the carrying away into Babylon unto Christ *are* fourteen generations.

Genealogies.

LUKE.	JOHN.

CH. III. 23 – 38, INVERTED.

31 *The son* of David, *the son* of Nathan, *the son* of Mattatha, *the son* of Menan, *the son* of Melea,

30 *The son* of Eliakim, *the son* of Jonan, *the son* of Joseph, *the son* of Juda, *the son* of Simeon,
29 *The son* of Levi, *the son* of Matthat, *the son* of Jorim, *the son* of Eliezer, *the son* of Jose,
28 *The son* of Er, *the son* of Elmodam, *the son*, of Cosam, *the son* of Addi, *the son* of Melchi,
27 *The son* of Neri, *the son* of Salathiel, *the son* of Zorobabel, *the son* of Rhesa, *the son* of Joanna,
26 *The son* of Juda, *the son* of Joseph, *the son* of Semei, *the son* of Mattathias, *the son* of Maath,
25 *The son* of Nagge, *the son* of Esli, *the son* of Naum, *the son* of Amos, *the son* of Mattathias,
24 *The son* of Joseph, *the son* of Janna, *the son* of Melchi, *the son* of Levi, *the son* of Matthat,
23 *The son* of Heli, the son of Joseph, — And Jesus himself . . . being (as was supposed) —

Note.] See Appendix, No. I.

PART II.

ANNOUNCEMENT AND INTRODUCTION

OF

OUR LORD'S PUBLIC MINISTRY.

TIME.   About one year.

§ 14. The Ministry of

| MATTHEW. | MARK. |
| CH. III. 1–12. | CH. I. 1–8. |

THE beginning of the gospel of Jesus Christ the Son of God ;

2 As it is written in the prophets,ₐ Behold, I send my messenger before thy face, which shall prepare thy way before thee ;

IN those days came John the Baptist, preaching in the wilderness of Judea,

3 The voice of one crying in the wilderness, Prepare ye the way of the Lord, make his paths straight.

2 And saying, Repent ye ; for the kingdom of heaven is at hand.

3 For this is he that was spoken of by the prophet Esaias, saying, The voice of one crying in the wilderness, Prepare ye the way of the Lord, make his paths straight.

4 John did baptize in the wilderness, and preach the baptism of repentance, for the remission of sins.

5 And there went out unto him all the land of Judea, and they of Jerusalem, and were all baptized of him in the river of Jordan, confessing their sins.

4 And the same John had his raiment of camel's hair, and a leathern girdle about his loins ; and his meat was locusts and wild honey.

6 And John was clothed with camel's hair, and with a girdle of a skin about his loins ; and he did eat locusts and wild honey ;

5 Then went out to him Jerusalem, and all Judea, and all the region round about Jordan,

6 And were baptized of him in Jordan, confessing their sins.

7 But when he saw many of the Pharisees and Sadducees come to his baptism, he said unto them, O generation of vipers, who hath warned you to flee from the wrath to come ?

8 Bring forth therefore fruits meet for repentance :

9 And think not to say within yourselves, We have Abraham to *our* father : for I say unto you, that God is able of these stones to raise up children unto Abraham.

10 And now also the axe is laid unto the root of the trees : therefore every tree which bringeth not forth good fruit is hewn down, and cast into the fire.

ₐ Mal. iii. 1 ; Is. xl. 3.

Luke iii. 2, *high priests.*] In the New Testament, the same word is used for *the high priests,* and *the chief priests,* who were the heads of the twenty-four courses. So that the two persons whom the Roman governor considered as the chief of the priests, and whose names stood as such in those public registers which seem here referred to,

John the Baptist. *The Desert.* *The Jordan.*

LUKE.
CH. III. 1–18.

Now in the fifteenth year of the reign of Tiberius Cesar, Pontius Pilate being governor of Judea, and Herod being tetrarch of Galilee, and his brother Philip tetrarch of Iturea and of the region of Trachonitis, and Lysanias the tetrarch of Abilene,

2 Annas and Caiaphas being the high priests, the word of God came unto John the son of Zacharias in the wilderness.

3 And he came into all the country about Jordan, preaching the baptism of repentance, for the remission of sins ;

4 As it is written in the book of the words of Esaias the prophet, saying,[a] The voice of one crying in the wilderness, Prepare ye the way of the Lord, make his paths straight.

5 Every valley shall be filled, and every mountain and hill shall be brought low ; and the crooked shall be made straight, and the rough ways *shall be* made smooth ;

6 And all flesh shall see the salvation of God.

7 Then said he to the multitude that came forth to be baptized of him, O generation of vipers, who hath warned you to flee from the wrath to come ?

8 Bring forth therefore fruits worthy of repentance, and begin not to say within yourselves, We have Abraham to *our* father : for I say unto you, That God is able of these stones to raise up children unto Abraham.

9 And now also the axe is laid unto the root of the trees : every tree therefore which bringeth not forth good fruit, is hewn down, and cast into the fire.

10 And the people asked him, saying, What shall we do then ?

JOHN.

---

[a] Is. xl. 3, seq.

---

may be intended. An irregularity had arisen out of the confusion of the times : and the ruler or prince under the Romans, though a *chief* priest, was a distinct person from the *high* priest : Annas being the one, and Caiaphas the other. SCOTT, *in loc.* See also Campbell, *in loc.*

ᵇ

§ 14. The Ministry of

MATTHEW.	MARK.
CH. III. 1–12.	CH. I. 1–8.

11 I indeed baptize you with water unto repentance : but he that cometh after me is mightier than I, whose shoes I am not worthy to bear : he shall baptize you with the Holy Ghost, and *with* fire :

12 Whose fan *is* in his hand, and he will thoroughly purge his floor, and gather his wheat into the garner ; but he will burn up the chaff with unquenchable fire.

7 And preached, saying, There cometh one mightier than I after me, the latchet of whose shoes I am not worthy to stoop down and unloose.

8 I indeed have baptized you with water : but he shall baptize you with the Holy Ghost.

§ 15. The Baptism

CH. III. 13–17.	CH. I. 9–11.

13 Then cometh Jesus from Galilee to Jordan unto John, to be baptized of him.

14 But John forbade him, saying, I have need to be baptized of thee, and comest thou to me ?

15 And Jesus answering said unto him, Suffer *it to be so* now : for thus it becometh us to fulfil all righteousness. Then he suffered him.

16 And Jesus, when he was baptized, went up straightway out of the water : and lo, the heavens were opened unto him, and he saw the Spirit of God descending like a dove, and lighting upon him :

9 And it came to pass in those days, that Jesus came from Nazareth of Galilee, and was baptized of John in Jordan.

10 And straightway coming up out of the water, he saw the heavens opened, and the Spirit like a dove descending upon him :

11 And there came a voice from heaven *saying*, Thou art my be-

John the Baptist. *The Desert.　The Jordan.*

LUKE.	JOHN.
CH. III. 1–18.	

11 He answereth and saith unto them, He that hath two coats, let him impart to him that hath none ; and he that hath meat, let him do likewise.

12 Then came also publicans to be baptized, and said unto him, Master, what shall we do ?

13 And he said unto them, Exact no more than that which is appointed you.

14 And the soldiers likewise demanded of him, saying, And what shall we do ? And he said unto them, Do violence to no man, neither accuse *any* falsely ; and be content with your wages.

15 And as the people were in expectation, and all men mused in their hearts of John, whether, he were the Christ, or not ;

16 John answered, saying unto *them* all, I indeed baptize you with water ; but one mightier than I cometh, the latchet of whose shoes I am not worthy to unloose : he shall baptize you with the Holy Ghost, and with fire :

17 Whose fan *is* in his hand, and he will thoroughly purge his floor, and will gather the wheat into his garner; but the chaff he will burn with fire unquenchable.

18 And many other things in his exhortation preached he unto the people.

of Jesus.　The Jordan.

CH. III. 21–23.

21 Now, when all the people were baptized, it came to pass, that Jesus also being baptized,

and praying, the heaven was opened,

22 And the Holy Ghost descended in a bodily shape like a dove upon him,

§ 15. The Baptism

MATTHEW.	MARK.
CH. III. 13–17.	CH. I. 9–11.
17 And lo, a voice from heaven, saying, This is my beloved Son, in whom I am well pleased.	loved Son, in whom I am well pleased.

§ 16. The Temptation.

CH. IV. 1–11.	CH. I. 12–13.
THEN was Jesus led up of the Spirit into the wilderness to be tempted of the devil.	12 And immediately the Spirit driveth him into the wilderness.
2 And when he had fasted forty days and forty nights, he was afterward an hungered.	13 And he was there in the wilderness forty days tempted of Satan; and was with the wild beasts; and the angels ministered unto him.

3 And when the tempter came to him, he said, If thou be the Son of God, command that these stones be made bread.

4 But he answered and said, It is written[a] Man shall not live by bread alone, but by every word that proceedeth out of the mouth of God.

5 Then the devil taketh him up into the holy city, and setteth him on a pinnacle of the temple,

6 And saith unto him, If thou be the Son of God cast thyself down, for it is written[b] He shall give his angels charge concerning thee : and in *their* hands they shall bear thee up, lest at any time thou dash thy foot against a stone.

7 Jesus said unto him, It is written again,[c] Thou shalt not tempt the Lord thy God.

8 Again, the devil taketh him up into an exceeding high mountain and sheweth him all the kingdoms of the world, and the glory of them :

9 And saith unto him, All these things will I give thee, if thou wilt fall down and worship me.

10 Then saith Jesus unto him, Get thee hence, Satan : for it is written,[d]

[a] Deut. viii. 3.   [b] Deut. vi. 16.   [c] Ps. xci. 11.   [d] Deut. vi. 13.

Note.] There is a seeming discrepancy between Matthew and Luke, in the order of

of Jesus. *The Jordan.*

LUKE.	JOHN.

LUKE.
CH. III. 21–23.

and a voice came from heaven, which said, Thou art my beloved Son ; in thee I am well pleased.

23 And Jesus himself began to be about thirty years of age,

Desert of Judea.

CH. IV. 1–13.

AND Jesus, being full of the Holy Ghost, returned from Jordan, and was led by the Spirit into the wilderness,

2 Being forty days tempted of the devil. And in those days he did eat nothing : and when they were ended, he afterward hungered.

3 And the devil said unto him, If thou be the Son of God, command this stone that it be made bread.

4 And Jesus answered him, saying, It is written, That man shall not live by bread alone, but by every word of God.

9 And he brought him to Jerusalem, and set him on a pinnacle of the temple, and said unto him, If thou be the Son of God, cast thyself down from hence :

10 For it is written, He shall give his angels charge over thee, to keep thee :

11 And in *their* hands they shall bear thee up, lest at any time thou dash thy foot against a stone.

12 And Jesus answering, said unto him, It is said, Thou shalt not tempt the Lord thy God.

5 And the devil, taking him up into a high mountain, shewed unto him, all the kingdoms of the world in a moment of time.

6 And the devil said unto him, All this power will I give thee, and the glory of them : for that is delivered unto me, and to whomsoever I will, I give it.

7 If thou therefore wilt worship me, all shall be thine.

8 And Jesus answered and said

---

the temptations ; but Luke does not affirm the order , whereas Matthew uses particles, in *v.* 2 and 8, which seem to fix it as he has written NEWCOME.

§ 16. The Temptation.

MATTHEW.	MARK.
CH. IV. 1–11.	
Thou shalt worship the Lord thy God, and him only shalt thou serve.	
11 Then the devil leaveth him, and behold, angels came and ministered unto him.	

§ 17. Preface to

Desert of Judea.

LUKE.	JOHN.

CH. IV. 1 – 13.

unto him, Get thee behind me, Satan :
for it is written, Thou shalt worship
the Lord thy God, and him only shalt
thou serve.

13 And when the devil had ended
all the temptation, he departed from
him for a season.

John's Gospel.

CH. I. 1 – 18.

IN the beginning was the Word,
and the Word was with God, and the
Word was God.

2 The same was in the beginning
with God.

3 All things were made by him ;
and without him was not anything
made that was made.

4 In him was life ; and the life was
the light of men.

5 And the light shineth in darkness ; and the darkness comprehended
it not.

6 There was a man sent from God,
whose name *was* John.

7 The same came for a witness, to
bear witness of the Light, that all *men*
through him might believe.

8 He was not that Light, but *was
sent* to bear witness of that Light.

9 *That* was the true Light, which
lighteth every man that cometh into
the world.

10 He was in the world, and the
world was made by him, and the world
knew him not.

11 He came unto his own, and his
own received him not.

12 But as many as received him, to
them gave he power to become the
sons of God, *even* to them that believe
on his name :

13 Which were born, not of blood,
nor of the will of the flesh, nor of the
will of man, but of God.

14 And the Word was made flesh,
and dwelt among us, (and we beheld
his glory, the glory as of the only
begotten of the Father,) full of grace
and truth.

15 John bare witness of him, and
cried, saying, This was he of whom I
spake, He that cometh after me, is

§ 17. Preface to

MATTHEW.	MARK.

§ 18. Testimony of John the Baptist

John i. 21.] John means that he was not really Elias risen from the dead. But when Jesus says, (Matth. xvii. 12, and xi. 14.) that Elias was come already, he means that John had appeared *in the spirit and power of Elias.* Luke i. 17. Thus likewise,

John's Gospel.

LUKE.	JOHN.

JOHN.

CH. I. 1–18.

preferred before me ; for he was before me.

16 And of his fulness have all we received, and grace for grace.

17 For the law was given by Moses, *but* grace and truth came by Jesus Christ.

18 No man hath seen God at any time ; the only begotten Son, which is in the bosom of the Father, he hath declared *him*.

---

to Jesus.	*Bethany beyond Jordan.*

CH. I. 19–34.

19 And this is the record of John, when the Jews sent priests and Levites from Jerusalem, to ask him, Who art thou ?

20 And he confessed, and denied not ; but confessed, I am not the Christ.

21 And they asked him, What then ? Art thou Elias ? And he saith, I am not. Art thou that prophet ? And he answered, No.

22 Then said they unto him, Who art thou ? that we may give an answer to them that sent us. What sayest thou of thyself ?

23 He said,ᵃ I *am* the voice of one crying in the wilderness, Make straight the way of the Lord, as said the prophet Esaias.

24 And they which were sent were of the Pharisees.

25 And they asked him, and said unto him, Why baptizest thou then, if thou be not that Christ, nor Elias, neither that prophet ?

26 John answered them, saying, I baptize with water : but there standeth one among you, whom ye know not.

27 He it is, who coming after me, is preferred before me, whose shoe's latchet I am not worthy to unloose.

ₐ Is. xl. 3,

John here denies that he is one of the ancient prophets again appearing on earth : see Luke ix. 19 ; with which our Lord's assertion that he was an eminent prophet, Luke vii. 28, seems perfectly consistent. NEWCOME.

§ 18. Testimony of John the Baptist

MATTHEW.	MARK.

§ 19. Jesus gains

to Jesus.   *Bethany beyond Jordan.*

LUKE.	JOHN.
	CH. I. 19–34.

28 These things were done in Bethabara beyond Jordan, where John was baptizing.

29 The next day John seeth Jesus coming unto him, and saith, Behold the Lamb of God, which taketh away the sin of the world!

30 This is he of whom I said, After me cometh a man which is preferred before me ; for he was before me.

31 And I knew him not : but that he should be made manifest to Israel, therefore am I come baptizing with water.

32 And John bare record, saying, I saw the Spirit descending from heaven like a dove, and it abode upon him.

33 And I knew him not : but he that sent me to baptize with water, the same said unto me, Upon whom thou shalt see the Spirit descending and remaining on him, the same is he which baptizeth with the Holy Ghost.

34 And I saw and bare record, that this is the Son of God.

disciples.   *The Jordan.   Galilee.*

CH. I. 35–51.

35 Again the next day after, John stood, and two of his disciples ;

36 And looking upon Jesus as he walked, he saith, Behold the Lamb of God !

37 And the two disciples heard him speak, and they followed Jesus.

38 Then Jesus turned, and saw them following, and saith unto them, What seek ye ? They said unto him, Rabbi, (which is to say, being interpreted, Master,) where dwellest thou !

39 He saith unto them, Come and see. They came and saw where he dwelt, and abode with him that day : for it was about the tenth hour.

40 One of the two which heard John *speak*, and followed him, was Andrew, Simon Peter's brother.

41 He first findeth his own brother Simon, and saith unto him, We have found the Messias ; which is, being interpreted, the Christ.

§ 19. Jesus gains

MATTHEW.	MARK.

John i. 42.] Kings and princes very often changed the names of those who held
offices under them, particularly when they first attracted their notice and were taken
into their employ ; and when subsequently they were elevated to some new station,
and crowned with additional honors. Gen. xli. 45 ; and xvii. 5 ; and xxxii. 28 ;
and xxxv. 10 : 2 Kin. xxiii. 34, 35 ; and xxiv. 17 ; Dan. i. 6.   Hence a name (*a new
name*) occurs tropically, as a token of honor, in Phil. ii. 9 ; Heb. i. 4 ; Rev. ii. 17.
See also Mark iii. 17.   JAHN's Archæol. § 164.

disciples. *The Jordan. Galilee.*

LUKE.

JOHN.
CH. I. 35–51.

42 And he brought him to Jesus. And when Jesus beheld him, he said, Thou art Simon the son of Jona : thou shalt be called Cephas ; which is, by interpretation, a stone.

43 The day following Jesus would go forth into Galilee, and findeth Philip, and saith unto him, Follow me.

44 Now Philip was of Bethsaida, the city of Andrew and Peter.

45 Philip findeth Nathanael, and saith unto him, We have found him of whom Moses in the law, and the prophets, did write, Jesus of Nazareth the son of Joseph.

46 And Nathanael said unto him, Can there any good thing come out of Nazareth? Philip saith unto him, Come and see.

47 Jesus saw Nathanael coming to him, and saith of him, Behold an Israelite indeed, in whom is no guile !

48 Nathanael saith unto him, Whence knowest thou me? Jesus answered and said unto him, Before that Philip called thee, when thou wast under the fig-tree, I saw thee.

49 Nathanael answered and saith unto him, Rabbi, thou art the Son of God ; thou art the King of Israel.

50 Jesus answered and said unto him, Because I said unto thee, I saw thee under the fig-tree, believest thou? thou shalt see greater things than these.

51 And he saith unto him, Verily, verily, I say unto you, Hereafter ye shall see heaven open, and the angels of God ascending and descending upon the[a] Son of man.

[a] Gen. xxviii. 12.

John i. 45, *Nathanael.*] This apostle is supposed to be the same with *Bartholomew*, of whom John says nothing ; and the others make no mention of *Nathanael.* This seems to have been his proper name ; since the name of *Bartholomew* is not a proper name, but only signifies *the son of Ptolomy. Nathanael* is also ranked among the Apostles to whom Jesus showed himself. *John* xxi. 2 4. A. CLARKE, *in loc.*

§ 20. The Marriage

MATTHEW.	MARK.

at Cana of Galilee.

LUKE.

JOHN.

ch. ii. 1 – 12.

And the third day there was a mar-riage in Cana of Galilee; and the mother of Jesus was there.

2 And both Jesus was called, and his disciples, to the marriage.

3 And when they wanted wine, the mother of Jesus saith unto him, They have no wine.

4 Jesus saith unto her, Woman, what have I to do with thee ? mine hour is not yet come.

5 His mother saith unto the ser-vants, Whatsoever he saith unto you, do *it.*

6 And there were set there six water-pots of stone, after the manner of the purifying of the Jews, contain-ing two or three firkins apiece.

7 Jesus saith unto them, Fill the water-pots with water. And they filled them up to the brim.

8 And he saith unto them, Draw out now, and bear unto the governor of the feast. And they bare *it.*

9 When the ruler of the feast had tasted the water that was made wine, and knew not whence it was, (but the servants which drew the water knew,) the governor of the feast called the bridegroom,

10 And saith unto him, Every man at the beginning doth set forth good wine ; and when men have well drunk, then that which is worse : *but* thou has kept the good wine until now.

11 This beginning of miracles did Jesus in Cana of Galilee, and mani-fested forth his glory ; and his disci-ples believed on him.

12 After this he went down to Capernaum, he, and his mother, and his brethren, and his disciples ; and they continued there not many days.

PART III.

OUR LORD'S FIRST PASSOVER,

AND THE

SUBSEQUENT TRANSACTIONS

UNTIL THE SECOND.

Time. One year.

9

§ 21. At the Passover Jesus drives

MATTHEW.	MARK.

§ 22. Our Lord's discourse

the traders out of the Temple. *Jerusalem.*

LUKE.	JOHN.
	CH. II. 13–25.

13 And the Jews' passover was at hand, and Jesus went up to Jerusalem,

14 And found in the temple those that sold oxen, and sheep, and doves, and the changers of money, sitting:

15 And when he had made a scourge of small cords, he drove them all out of the temple, and the sheep, and the oxen; and poured out the changers' money, and overthrew the tables;

16 And said unto them that sold doves, Take these things hence: make not my Father's house an house of merchandise.

17 And his disciples remembered that it was written, The zeal of thine house hath eaten me up.

18 Then answered the Jews, and said unto him, What sign shewest thou unto us, seeing that thou doest these things?

19 Jesus answered and said unto them, Destroy this temple, and in three days I will raise it up.

20 Then said the Jews, Forty and six years was this temple in building, and wilt thou rear it up in three days?

21 But he spake of the temple of his body.

22 When therefore he was risen from the dead, his disciples remembered that he had said this unto them: and they believed the scripture, and the word which Jesus had said.

23 Now, when he was in Jerusalem at the passover, in the feast-*day*, many believed in his name, when they saw the miracles which he did.

24 But Jesus did not commit himself unto them, because he knew all *men*,

25 And needed not that any should testify of man: for he knew what was in man.

with Nicodemus. *Jerusalem.*

CH. III. 1–21.

THERE was a man of the Pharisees named Nicodemus, a ruler of the Jews:

2 The same came to Jesus by night,

Ps. lxix. 9.

§ 22. Our Lord's discourse

MATTHEW. MARK.

with Nicodemus. *Jerusalem.*

LUKE.

JOHN.
CH. III. 1–21.

and said unto him, Rabbi, we know that thou art a teacher come from God : for no man can do these miracles that thou doest, except God be with him.

3 Jesus answered and said unto him, Verily, verily, I say unto thee, Except a man be born again, he cannot see the kingdom of God.

4 Nicodemus saith unto him, How can a man be born when he is old ? can he enter the second time into his mother's womb, and be born ?

5 Jesus answered, Verily, verily, I say unto thee, Except a man be born of water, and *of* the Spirit, he cannot enter into the kingdom of God.

6 That which is born of the flesh, is flesh ; and that which is born of the Spirit, is spirit.

7 Marvel not that I said unto thee, Ye must be born again.

8 The wind bloweth where it listeth, and thou hearest the sound thereof, but canst not tell whence it cometh, and whither it goeth : so is every one that is born of the Spirit.

9 Nicodemus answered and said unto him, How can these things be ?

10 Jesus answered and said unto him, Art thou a master of Israel, and knowest not these things ?

11 Verily, verily, I say unto thee, We speak that we do know, and testify that we have seen ; and ye receive not our witness.

12 If I have told you earthly things, and ye believe not, how shall ye believe if I tell you *of* heavenly things ?

13 And no man hath ascended up to heaven, but he that came down from heaven, *even* the Son of man which is in heaven.

14 And as[a] Moses lifted up the serpent in the wilderness, even so must the Son of man be lifted up :

15 That whosoever believeth in him should not perish, but have eternal life.

16 For God so loved the world, that he gave his only begotten Son, that

---

[a] Numb. xxi. 8, seq.

§ 22. Our Lord's discourse

MATTHEW.	MARK.

§ 23. Jesus remains in Judea and baptizes.

with Nicodemus. *Jerusalem.*

LUKE.

JOHN.
CH. III. 1−21.

whosoever believeth in him, should not perish, but have everlasting life.

17 For God sent not his Son into the world to condemn the world, but that the world through him might be saved.

18 He that believeth on him, is not condemned: but he that believeth not, is condemned already, because he hath not believed in the name of the only begotten Son of God.

19 And this is the condemnation, that light is come into the world, and men loved darkness rather than light, because their deeds were evil.

20 For every one that doeth evil hateth the light, neither cometh to the light, lest his deeds should be reproved.

21 But he that doeth truth, cometh to the light, that his deeds may be made manifest, that they are wrought in God.

Further testimony of John the Baptist.

CH. III. 22−36.

22 After these things came Jesus and his disciples into the land of Judea; and there he tarried with them, and baptized.

23 And John also was baptizing in Ænon, near to Salim, because there was much water there: and they came, and were baptized.

24 For John was not yet cast into prison.

25 Then there arose a question between *some* of John's disciples and the Jews, about purifying.

26 And they came unto John and said unto him, Rabbi, he that was with thee beyond Jordan, to whom thou bearest witness, behold, the same baptizeth, and all *men* come to him.

27 John answered and said, A man can receive nothing, except it be given him from heaven.

28 Ye yourselves bear me witness, that I said, I am not the Christ, but that I am sent before him.

29 He that hath the bride, is the bridegroom: but the friend of the bridegroom, which standeth and hear-

§ 23. Jesus remains in Judea and baptizes.

MATTHEW.	MARK.

§ 24. Jesus departs into Galilee

CH. IV. 12.	CH. I. 14.
12 Now, when Jesus had heard that John was cast into prison, he departed into Galilee.	14 Now, after that John was put in prison, Jesus came into Galilee,
CH. XIV. 3–5.	CH. VI. 17–20.
3 For Herod had laid hold on John, and bound him, and put *him* in prison for Herodias' sake, his brother Philip's wife.	17 For Herod himself had sent forth and laid hold upon John, and bound him in prison for Herodias' sake, his brother Philip's wife : for he had married her.
4 For John said unto him, It is not lawful for thee to have her.	18 For John had said unto Herod, It is not lawful for thee to have thy brother's wife.
5 And when he would have put him to death, he feared the multitude, because they counted him as a prophet.	19 Therefore Herodias had a quarrel against him, and would have killed him ; but she could not :
	20 For Herod feared John, knowing that he was a just man and an holy, and observed him : and when he heard him, he did many things, and heard him gladly.

Further testimony of John the Baptist.

LUKE.	JOHN.
	CH. III. 22 – 36.
	eth him, rejoiceth greatly, because of the bridegroom's voice : this my joy therefore is fulfilled.
	30 He must increase, but I *must* decrease.
	31 He that cometh from above, is above all : he that is of the earth is earthly, and speaketh of the earth : he that cometh from heaven is above all.
	32 And what he hath seen and heard, that he testifieth ; and no man receiveth his testimony.
	33 He that hath received his testimony, hath set to his seal that God is true.
	34 For he whom God hath sent, speaketh the words of God : for God giveth not the Spirit by measure *unto him.*
	35 The Father loveth the Son, and hath given all things into his hand.
	36 He that believeth on the Son hath everlasting life : and he that believeth not the Son, shall not see life ; but the wrath of God abideth on him.

after John's imprisonment.

CH. IV. 14.	CH. IV. 1 – 3.
	WHEN therefore the Lord knew how the Pharisees had heard that Jesus made and baptized more disciples than John,
	2 (Though Jesus himself baptized not, but his disciples,)
14 And Jesus returned in the power of the Spirit into Galilee :	3 He left Judea, and departed again into Galilee.
CH. III. 19, 20.	
19 But Herod the tetrarch, being reproved by him for Herodias his brother Philip's wife, and for all the evils which Herod had done,	
20 Added yet this above all, that he shut up John in prison.	

§ 25. Our Lord's discourse with the Samaritan woman.

MATTHEW.	MARK.

Many Samaritans believe on him. *Shechem* or *Neapolis.*

LUKE.	JOHN.

JOHN.

CH. IV. 4–42.

4 And he must needs go through Samaria.

5 Then cometh he to a city of Samaria, which is called Sychar, near to the parcel of ground that Jacob gave to his son Joseph.

6 Now Jacob's well was there. Jesus therefore being wearied with *his* journey, sat thus on the well: *and* it was about the sixth hour.

7 There cometh a woman of Samaria to draw water; Jesus saith unto her, Give me to drink.

8 (For his disciples were gone away unto the city to buy meat.)

9 Then saith the woman of Samaria unto him, How is it that thou, being a Jew, askest drink of me, which am a woman of Samaria? for the Jews have no dealings with the Samaritans.

10 Jesus answered and said unto her, If thou knewest the gift of God, and who it is that saith to thee, Give me to drink; thou wouldest have asked of him, and he would have given thee living water.

11 The woman saith unto him, Sir, thou hast nothing to draw with, and the well is deep: from whence then hast thou that living water?

12 Art thou greater than our father Jacob, which gave us the well, and drank thereof himself, and his children, and his cattle?

13 Jesus answered and said unto her, Whosoever drinketh of this water, shall thirst again:

14 But whosoever drinketh of the water that I shall give him, shall never thirst; but the water that I shall give him, shall be in him a well of water springing up into everlasting life.

15 The woman saith unto him, Sir, give me this water, that I thirst not, neither come hither to draw.

16 Jesus saith unto her, Go call thy husband, and come hither.

17 The woman answered and said, I have no husband. Jesus said unto her, Thou hast well said, I have no husband:

18 For thou hast had five hus

§ 25. Our Lord's discourse with the Samaritan woman.

MATTHEW.	MARK.

LUKE.

JOHN.
CH. IV. 4 – 42.

bands, and he whom thou now hast, is not thy husband : in that saidst thou truly.

19 The woman saith unto him, Sir, I perceive that thou art a prophet.

20 Our fathers worshipped in this mountain ; and ye say, that in Jerusalem is the place where men ought to worship.

21 Jesus saith unto her, Woman, believe me, the hour cometh, when ye shall neither in this mountain, nor yet at Jerusalem, worship the Father.

22 Ye worship ye know not what : we know what we worship, for salvation is of the Jews.

23 But the hour cometh, and now is, when the true worshippers shall worship the Father in spirit and in truth : for the Father seeketh such to worship him.

24 God *is* a Spirit : and they that worship him, must worship *him* in spirit and in truth.

25 The woman saith unto him, I know that Messias cometh, which is called Christ ; when he is come, he will tell us all things.

26 Jesus saith unto her, I that speak unto thee am *he.*

27 And upon this came his disciples, and marvelled that he talked with the woman : yet no man said, What seekest thou ? or, Why talkest thou with her ?

28 The woman then left her waterpot, and went her way into the city, and saith to the men,

29 Come, see a man which told me all things that ever I did : is not this the Christ ?

30 Then they went out of the city, and came unto him.

31 In the mean while his disciples prayed him, saying, Master, eat.

32 But he said unto them, I have meat to eat that ye know not of.

33 Therefore said the disciples one to another, Hath any man brought him *aught* to eat ?

34 Jesus saith unto them, My meat is to do the will of him that sent me, and to finish his work.

§ 25. Our Lord's discourse with the Samaritan woman.

MATTHEW.	MARK.

§ 26. Jesus teaches

CH. IV. 17.	CH. I. 14, 15.
17 From that time Jesus began to preach, and to say, Repent : for the kingdom of heaven is at hand.	preaching the gospel of the kingdom of God,
	15 And saying, The time is fulfilled, and the kingdom of God is at hand ; repent ye, and believe the gospel.

§ 27. Jesus, again at Cana, heals the son

Many Samaritans believe on him. *Shechem* or *Neapolis.*

LUKE.	JOHN.
	CH. IV. 4–42.
	35 Say not ye, There are yet four months, and *then* cometh harvest? behold, I say unto you, Lift up your eyes, and look on the fields ; for they are white already to harvest.
	36 And he that reapeth receiveth wages, and gathereth fruit unto life eternal : that both he that soweth, and he that reapeth, may rejoice together.
	37 And herein is that saying true, One soweth, and another reapeth.
	38 I sent you to reap that whereon ye bestowed no labor : other men labored, and ye are entered into their labors.
	39 And many of the Samaritans of that city believed on him for the saying of the woman, which testified, He told me all that ever I did.
	40 So when the Samaritans were come unto him, they besought him that he would tarry with them : and he abode there two days.
	41 And many more believed, because of his own word ;
	42 And said unto the woman, Now we believe, not because of thy saying : for we have heard *him* ourselves, and know that this is indeed the Christ, the Saviour of the world.

publicly in Galilee.

CH. IV. 14, 15.	**CH. IV. 43–45.**
and there went out a fame of him through all the region round about.	43 Now, after two days he departed thence, and went into Galilee.
15 And he taught in their synagogues, being glorified of all.	44 For Jesus himself testified, that a prophet hath no honor in his own country.
	45 Then when he was come into Galilee, the Galileans received him, having seen all the things that he did at Jerusalem at the feast : for they also went unto the feast.

of a nobleman lying ill at Capernaum. *Cana of Galilee.*

CH. IV. 46–54.

46 So Jesus came again into Cana of Galilee, where he made the water wine. And there was a certain nobleman, whose son was sick at Capernaum.

47 When he heard that Jesus was

§ 27. Jesus, again at Cana, heals the son

MATTHEW.	MARK.

§ 28. Jesus is rejected at Nazareth,

of a nobleman lying ill at Capernaum.   *Cana of Galilee.*

LUKE.	JOHN.
	CH. IV. 46–54.

come out of Judea into Galilee, he went unto him, and besought him that he would come down, and heal his son : for he was at the point of death.

48 Then said Jesus unto him, Except ye see signs and wonders, ye will not believe.

49 The nobleman saith unto him, Sir, come down ere my child die.

50 Jesus saith unto him, Go thy way ; thy son liveth. And the man believed the word that Jesus had spoken unto him, and he went his way.

51 And as he was now going down, his servants met him, and told *him*, saying, Thy son liveth.

52 Then inquired he of them the hour when he began to amend. And they said unto him, Yesterday at the seventh hour the fever left him.

53 So the father knew that *it was* at the same hour, in the which Jesus said unto him, Thy son liveth : and himself believed, and his whole house.

54 This *is* again the second miracle *that* Jesus did, when he was come out of Judea into Galilee.

and fixes his abode at Capernaum.

CH. IV. 16–31.

16 And he came to Nazareth, where he had been brought up : and, as his custom was, he went into the synagogue on the sabbath-day, and stood up for to read.

17 And there was delivered unto him the book of the prophet Esaias. And when he had opened the book, he found the place where it was written,[a]

18 The Spirit of the Lord *is* upon me, because he hath anointed me to preach the gospel to the poor ; he hath sent me to heal the broken-hearted, to preach deliverance to the captives, and recovering of sight to the blind, to set at liberty them that are bruised,

' Is. lxi. 1, and lviii. 6.

10

§ 28. Jesus is rejected at Nazareth,

MATTHEW.	MARK.
CH. IV. 13–16.	

Luke iv. 20. *sat down.*] The service of the synagogue consisted of reading the scriptures, prayer, and preaching. The posture in which the latter was performed, whether in the synagogue or elsewhere, (see *Matth.* v. 1 ; *Luke* v. 3,) was sitting. Accordingly when our Savior had read the portion of scripture, in the synagogue at Nazareth, of which he was a member, having been brought up in that city, and then, instead of retiring to his place, *sat down* in the desk or pulpit, it is said "the eyes of all that were present were fastened upon him," because they perceived, by his posture, that he was about to preach to them. See also Acts xiii. 14, 15. JENNINGS, Ant. 375.

and fixes his abode at Capernaum.

LUKE.
CH. IV. 16 – 31.

19 To preach the acceptable year of the Lord.

20 And he closed the book, and he gave *it* again to the minister, and sat down. And the eyes of all them that were in the synagogue were fastened on him.

21 And he began to say unto them, This day is this scripture fulfilled in your ears.

22 And all bare him witness, and wondered at the gracious words which proceeded out of his mouth. And they said, Is not this Joseph's son ?

23 And he said unto them, Ye will surely say unto me this proverb, Physician, heal thyself : whatsoever we have heard done in Capernaum, do also here in thy country.

24 And he said, Verily, I say unto you, No prophet is accepted in his own country.

25 But I tell you of a truth, many widows were in Israel in the days of Elias, when the heaven was shut up three years and six months, when great famine was throughout all the land :

26 But unto none of them was Elias sent, save unto Sarepta, *a city* of Sidon, unto a woman *that was* a widow.[a]

27 And many lepers were in Israel in the time of Eliseus the prophet ; and none of them was cleansed, saving Naaman the Syrian.[b]

28 And all they in the synagogue, when they heard these things, were filled with wrath,

29 And rose up, and thrust him out of the city, and led him unto the brow of the hill, (whereon their city was built,) that they might cast him down headlong.

JOHN.

---

[a] 1 Kings xvii. 1, 9.   [b] 2 Kings v. 14.

Luke iv. 20. *to the minister.*] This word denotes only a subordinate officer, who attended the minister and obeyed his orders in what concerned the more servile part of the work. Among other things he had charge of the sacred books, and delivered them to those to whom he was commanded by his superiors to deliver them. After the reading was over, he deposited them in their proper place. CAMPBELL, *in loc.*

§ 28. Jesus is rejected at Nazareth,

MATTHEW.	MARK.
CH. IV. 13-16.	
13 And leaving Nazareth, he came and dwelt in Capernaum, which is upon the sea-coast, in the borders of Zabulon and Nephthalim ;	
14 That it might be fulfilled which was spoken by Esaias the prophet, saying,[a]	
15 The land of Zabulon, and the land of Nephthalim, *by* the way of the sea, beyond Jordan, Galilee of the Gentiles :	
16 The people which sat in darkness, saw great light ; and to them which sat in the region and shadow of death, light is sprung up.	

§ 29. The call of Simon Peter and Andrew, and of James

CH. IV. 18-22.	CH. I. 16-20.
18 And Jesus, walking by the sea of Galilee, saw two brethren, Simon called Peter, and Andrew his brother,	16 Now as he walked by the sea of Galilee, he saw Simon, and Andrew his brother,

[a] Is. ix. 1.

Matth. iv. 18. *walking.*] Matthew says that the disciples were called by Christ while walking by the sea, because that calling followed the walk by the sea. " We say that a thing was done by one walking in this or that place, because he took such a walk, whether he who did the act was then walking, or sitting or standing." Spanh. dub. lxxii. v. 2. This remark reconciles " *walking*," Matth. iv. 18. with " *stood*," Luke v. 1. A like remark may be made with respect to the passages placed parallel to Luke v. 6. Jesus is concisely represented as if he had at first seen Peter and Andrew casting a net into the sea, because they were employed thus in consequence of the interview.

Luke does not deny that more than Simon were seen, nor does he affirm that Simon

and fixes his abode at Capernaum.

LUKE.	JOHN.
ch. iv. 16 – 31.	
30 But he, passing through the midst of them, went his way,	
31 And came down to Capernaum, a city of Galilee,	

and John, with the miraculous draught of fishes. *Near Capernaum.*

ch. v. 1 – 11.

And it came to pass, that as the people pressed upon him to hear the word of God, he stood by the lake of Gennesaret,

2 And saw two ships standing by the lake : but the fishermen were gone out of them, and were washing *their* nets.

3 And he entered into one of the ships, which was Simon's, and prayed him that he would thrust out a little from the land. And he sat down, and taught the people out of the ship.

4 Now, when he had left speaking, he said unto Simon, Launch out into the deep, and let down your nets for a draught.

5 And Simon, answering, said unto him, Master, we have toiled all the night, and have taken nothing ; nevertheless, at thy word I will let down the net.

alone was seen. Indeed our Lord is said to have seen *two* ships by the lake. The calling of others besides Simon not only is not denied by Luke, but is sufficiently indicated in v. 11. The words of Matthew (*v.* 21) "going on from thence," are not to be understood as implying a great distance, but as relating to the neighboring shore. Matthew relates the principal fact, the calling and the following ; Luke has the accompanying circumstances. And there is a remarkable harmony between them. Matthew records the repairing of their nets by the fishermen ; Luke shows how they became broken,—by the great draught they had taken. What is related by Luke, is not denied by Matthew, but omitted only. Nothing, indeed, is more common than to find the omission of some supplied by the other Evangelists. Newcome.

§ 29. The call of Simon Peter and Andrew, and of James

MATTHEW.	MARK.
CH. IV. 18-22.	CH. I. 16-20.

casting a net into the sea; for they were fishers.	casting a net into the sea: for they were fishers.
19 And he saith unto them, Follow me, and I will make you fishers of men.	17 And Jesus said unto them, Come ye after me, and I will make you to become fishers of men.
20 And they straightway left *their* nets, and followed him.	18 And straightway they forsook their nets, and followed him.
21 And going on from thence, he saw other two brethren, James *the son* of Zebedee, and John his brother, in a ship with Zebedee their father, mending their nets: and he called them.	19 And when he had gone a little farther thence, he saw James the *son* of Zebedee, and John his brother, who also were in the ship mending their nets.
22 And they immediately left the ship, and their father, and followed him.	20 And straightway he called them: and they left their father Zebedee in the ship with the hired servants, and went after him.

§ 30. The healing of a demoniac

	CH. I. 21-28.
	21 And they went into Capernaum; and straightway on the Sabbath-day he entered into the synagogue and taught.
	22 And they were astonished at his doctrine: for he taught them as one that had authority, and not as the scribes.
	23 And there was in their synagogue a man with an unclean spirit; and he cried out,
	24 Saying, Let *us* alone; what have we to do with thee, thou Jesus of Nazareth! art thou come to de-

---

Matth. iv. 21, *with Zebedee their father.*] The death of Zebedee is nowhere mentioned in the gospels; yet an undesigned coincidence, and proof of the veracity of the Evangelists, is evident by comparing this place with others, in which his death is tacitly alluded to. Thus, in Chap. viii. 21, it is related that "another of his *disciples* said

and John, with the miraculous draught of fishes. *Near Capernaum.*

LUKE.	JOHN.
CH. v. 1-11.	

6 And when they had this done, they enclosed a great multitude of fishes : and their net brake.

7 And they beckoned unto *their* partners, which were in the other ship, that they should come and help them. And they came, and filled both the ships, so that they began to sink.

8 When Simon Peter saw *it*, he fell down at Jesus' knees, saying, Depart from me ; for I am a sinful man, O Lord.

9 For he was astonished, and all that were with him, at the draught of the fishes which they had taken :

10 And so *was* also James and John the sons of Zebedee, which were partners with Simon. And Jesus said unto Simon, Fear not : from henceforth thou shalt catch men.

11 And when they had brought their ships to land, they forsook all, and followed him.

in the Synagogue. *Capernaum.*

CH. IV. 31-37.

and taught them on the Sabbath-days.

32 And they were astonished at his doctrine : for his word was with power.

33 And in the synagogue there was a man which had a spirit of an unclean devil ; and he cried out with a loud voice,

34 Saying, Let *us* alone ; what have we to do with thee, *thou* Jesus

---

unto him, Lord, suffer me first to go and *bury my father ;* " and in Chap. xx. 20, it is said, " Then came to him the *mother of Zebedee's children*, with her sons, worshipping him." &c. See also Chap. xxvii. 55. BLUNT, Veracity of the Gospels, Sec. I. 2. See note on Mark vi. 3 ; Post, § 55.

§ 30. The healing of a demoniac

MATTHEW.	MARK.
	CH. I. 21–28.
	stroy us! I know thee who thou art, the Holy One of God.
	25 And Jesus rebuked him, saying, Hold thy peace, and come out of him.
	26 And when the unclean spirit had torn him, and cried with a loud voice, he came out of him.
	27 And they were all amazed, insomuch that they questioned among themselves, saying, What thing is this! what new doctrine is this! for with authority commandeth he even the unclean spirits, and they do obey him.
	28 And immediately his fame spread abroad throughout all the region round about Galilee.

§ 31. The healing of Peter's wife's mother

CH. VIII. 14–17.	CH. I. 29–34.
	29 And forthwith, when they were come out of the synagogue, they entered into the house of Simon and Andrew, with James and John.
14 And when Jesus was come into Peter's house, he saw his wife's mother laid, and sick of a fever.	30 But Simon's wife's mother lay sick of a fever; and anon they tell him of her.
15 And he touched her hand, and the fever left her : and she arose, and ministered unto them.	31 And he came and took her by the hand, and lifted her up ; and immediately the fever left her, and she ministered unto them.
16 When the even was come, they brought unto him many that were possessed with devils : and he cast out the spirits with *his* word, and healed all that were sick ;	32 And at even when the sun did set, they brought unto him all that were diseased, and them that were possessed with devils.
17 That it might be fulfilled which was spoken by Esaias the prophet, saying,[a] Himself took our infirmities, and bare *our* sicknesses.	33 And all the city was gathered together at the door.
	34 And he healed many that were sick of divers diseases, and cast out many devils ; and suffered not the devils to speak, because they knew him.

§ 32. Jesus with his disciples

CH. IV. 23–25.	CH. I. 35–39.
	35 And in the morning, rising up a great while before day, he went out

[a] Is. liii. 4.

Mark i. 26. *torn him.*] There is no inconsistency between this place, and the last clause of Luke iv. 35. The word translated *torn*, signifies to move, agitate, convulse. It occurs only twice in the Septuagint. In 2. Sam. xxii. 8, the Hebrew signifies to be shaken, *ut in terræ motu.* In Jer. iv. 19, it is applied to commotion of mind. Here,

in the Synagogue. *Capernaum.*

LUKE.	JOHN.
CH. IV. 31–37.	

of Nazareth? art thou come to destroy us? I know thee who thou art, the Holy One of God.

35 And Jesus rebuked him, saying, Hold thy peace, and come out of him. And when the devil had thrown him in the midst, he came out of him, and hurt him not.

36 And they were all amazed, and spake among themselves, saying, What a word *is* this! for with authority and power he commandeth the unclean spirits, and they come out.

37 And the fame of him went out into every place of the country round about.

and many others. *Capernaum.*

CH. IV. 38–41.

38 And he arose out of the synagogue, and entered into Simon's house. And Simon's wife's mother was taken with a great fever; and they besought him for her.

39 And he stood over her, and rebuked the fever; and it left her: and immediately she arose and ministered unto them.

40 Now, when the sun was setting, all they that had any sick with divers diseases, brought them unto him: and he laid his hands on every one of them, and healed them.

41 And devils also came out of many, crying out, and saying, Thou art Christ the Son of God. And he, rebuking *them*, suffered them not to speak: for they knew that he was Christ.

goes from Capernaum throughout Galilee.

CH. IV. 42–44.

42 And when it was day, he departed, and went into a desert place;

the demoniac was violently agitated; but the agitation left no lasting bad effect; he was restored to perfect health and soundness. Newcome.

Luke iv. 42. *when it was day.*] This clause may be rendered " when the day was coming on," and thus be reconciled with the words of Mark, who says it was a great while before day, namely, before broad day-light. Scott, *in loc.*

§ 32. Jesus with his disciples

MATTHEW.	MARK.
CH. IV. 23–25.	CH. I. 35–39.
	and departed into a solitary place, and there prayed.
	36 And Simon, and they that were with him, followed after him.
	37 And when they had found him, they said unto him, All *men* seek for thee.
	38 And he said unto them, Let us go into the next towns, that I may
23 And Jesus went about all Galilee, teaching in their synagogues, and preaching the gospel of the kingdom, and healing all manner of sickness, and all manner of disease among the people.	preach there also : for therefore came I forth.
	39 And he preached in their synagogues throughout all Galilee, and cast out devils.
24 And his fame went throughout all Syria : and they brought unto him all sick people that were taken with divers diseases and torments, and those which were possessed with devils, and those which were lunatic, and those that had the palsy ; and he healed them.	
25 And there followed him great multitudes of people from Galilee, and *from* Decapolis, and *from* Jerusalem, and *from* Judea, and *from* beyond Jordan.	

§ 33. The healing

CH. VIII. 2–4.	CH. I. 40–45.
2 And behold, there came a leper and worshipped him, saying, Lord, if thou wilt, thou canst make me clean.	40 And there came a leper to him, beseeching him, and kneeling down to him, and saying unto him, If thou wilt, thou canst make me clean.
3 And Jesus put forth *his* hand, and touched him, saying, I will ; be thou clean. And immediately his leprosy was cleansed.	41 And Jesus, moved with compassion, put forth *his* hand, and touched him, and saith unto him, I will ; be thou clean.
	42 And as soon as he had spoken, immediately the leprosy departed from him, and he was cleansed.
4 And Jesus saith unto him, See thou tell no man : but go thy way,	43 And he straitly charged him, and forthwith sent him away ;

Matth. viii. 4. *tell no man.*] "The miraculous cure of the leprosy was thought by the Jews to be characteristic of the Messiah ; and therefore there was peculiar reason for enjoining this man silence." *Benson's Life of Christ, p.* 340. NEWCOME. For the consequences of a premature full manifestation of himself as the Messiah, by awakening the jealousy of the Roman government, might, humanly speaking, have impeded his ministry. Yet there was great propriety in the private exhibition, to the priesthood, of full proof that he was the Messiah ; after which, their obstinacy in rejecting him was inexcusable. In this, and divers other instances our Lord mani-

goes from Capernaum throughout Galilee.

LUKE.	JOHN.
CH. IV. 42–44.	
and the people sought him, and came unto him, and stayed him, that he should not depart from them.	
43 And he said unto them, I must preach the kingdom of God to other cities also, for therefore am I sent.	
44 And he preached in the synagogues of Galilee.	

of a leper. *Galilee.*

CH. V. 12–16.

12 And it came to pass, when he was in a certain city, behold, a man full of leprosy : who, seeing Jesus, fell on *his* face, and besought him, saying, Lord, if thou wilt, thou canst make me clean.

13 And he put forth *his* hand and touched him, saying, I will : Be thou clean. And immediately the leprosy departed from him.

14 And he charged him to tell no man : but go, and shew thyself to the

fested his intent not to be generally known to the Jews as their Messiah, till the consummation of his ministry. A general announcement of his divine character at the outset would have been productive of no good ; on the contrary it would have excited the malice of the Scribes, Pharisees and Herodians against him ; would have favored the conceit of the Jews that he was to be their temporal king ; would have awakened the jealousy of the Roman government ; and in the natural course of things, would have prevented him from giving the many miraculous proofs which he gave of his ministry, and thus laying solid foundations for faith in his divine mission ; would have

§ 33. The healing

MATTHEW.	MARK.
CH. VIII. 2 – 4.	CH. I. 40 – 45.
shew thyself to the priest, and offer the gift that Moses commanded, for a testimony unto them.[a]	44 And saith unto him, See thou say nothing to any man ; but go thy way, shew thyself to the priest, and offer for thy cleansing those things which Moses commanded, for a testimony unto them.
	45 But he went out, and began to publish *it* much, and to blaze abroad the matter, insomuch that Jesus could no more openly enter into the city, but was without in desert places : and they came to him from every quarter.

§ 34. The healing

CH. IX. 2 – 8.	CH. II. 1 – 12.
	AND again he entered into Capernaum, after *some* days ; and it was noised that he was in the house.
	2 And straightway many were gathered together, insomuch that there was no room to receive *them*, no, not so much as about the door : and he preached the word unto them.
2 And behold, they brought to him a man sick of the palsy, lying on a bed : and Jesus, seeing their faith, said unto the sick of the palsy, Son, be of good cheer ; thy sins be forgiven thee.	3 And they come unto him, bringing one sick of the palsy, which was borne of four.
	4 And when they could not come nigh unto him for the press, they uncovered the roof where he was : and when they had broken *it* up, they let down the bed wherein the sick of the palsy lay.
	5 When Jesus saw their faith, he said unto the sick of the palsy, Son, thy sins be forgiven thee.
3 And behold, certain of the scribes said within themselves, This *man* blasphemeth.	6 But there were certain of the scribes sitting there, and reasoning in their hearts,
	7 Why doth this *man* thus speak blasphemies ? who can forgive sins but God only ?
4 And Jesus, knowing their thoughts, said, Wherefore think ye evil in your hearts ?	8 And immediately, when Jesus perceived in his spirit, that they so reasoned within themselves, he said unto them, Why reason ye these things in your hearts ?

[a] Lev. xiv. 2, seq.

exposed him and his religion to the charge of ostentation, vanity, and love of power and display ; and would have deprived the world of that example which he gave, of meekness, humility and patient suffering and self-denial. According to human experience, an early assumption of regal splendor, supported by the miracles he wrought,

of a leper. *Galilee.*

LUKE.	JOHN.
CH. V. 12–16.	
priest, and offer for thy cleansing, according as Moses commanded, for a testimony unto them.	
15 But so much the more went there a fame abroad of him: and great multitudes came together to hear and to be healed by him of their infirmities.	
16 And he withdrew himself into the wilderness, and prayed.	

of a paralytic. *Capernaum.*

CH. V. 17–26.

17 And it came to pass on a certain day, as he was teaching, that there were Pharisees and doctors of the law sitting by, which were come out of every town of Galilee, and Judea, and Jerusalem : and the power of the Lord was *present* to heal them.

18 And behold, men brought in a bed a man which was taken with a palsy : and they sought *means* to bring him in, and to lay *him* before him.

19 And when they could not find by what *way* they might bring him in, because of the multitude, they went upon the house-top, and let him down through the tiling with *his* couch, into the midst before Jesus.

20 And when he saw their faith, he said unto him, Man, thy sins are forgiven thee.

21 And the scribes and the Pharisees began to reason, saying, Who is this which speaketh blasphemies? Who can forgive sins but God alone?

22 But when Jesus perceived their thoughts, he, answering, said unto them, What reason ye in your hearts?

would have been successful, and carried him to the throne instead of the cross ; but it would have deprived the world of the great object of his mission. A sufficient number were enlightened to attest his miracles and proclaim his religion, and enough were left in their ignorance, to condemn and crucify him. See A. CLARKE, and SCOTT, *in lo.*

§ 34. The healing

MATTHEW.	MARK.
CH. IX. 1-8.	CH. II. 1-12.
5 For whether is easier to say, *Thy* sins be forgiven thee ; or to say, Arise, and walk ?	9 Whether is it easier to say to the sick of the palsy, *Thy* sins be forgiven thee ; or to say, Arise, and take up thy bed, and walk ?
6 But that ye may know that the Son of man hath power on earth to forgive sins, (then saith he to the sick of the palsy,) Arise, take up thy bed, and go unto thy house.	10 But that ye may know that the Son of man hath power on earth to forgive sins, (he saith to the sick of the palsy,)
7 And he arose, and departed to his house.	11 I say unto thee, Arise, and take up thy bed, and go thy way into thy house.
8 But when the multitude saw *it*, they marvelled, and glorified God, which had given such power unto men.	12 And immediately he arose, took up the bed, and went forth before them all ; insomuch that they were all amazed, and glorified God, saying, We never saw it on this fashion.

§ 35. The call

CH. IX. 9.	CH. II. 13, 14.
9 And as Jesus passed forth from thence, he saw a man named Matthew, sitting at the receipt of custom : and he saith unto him, Follow me. And he arose, and followed him.	13 And he went forth again by the sea-side ; and all the multitude resorted unto him, and he taught them.
	14 And as he passed by, he saw Levi the *son* of Alpheus, sitting at the receipt of custom, and said unto him, Follow me. And he arose, and followed him.

Mark ii. 14, *Levi*.] When a Jew became a Roman citizen, he usually assumed a Roman name. It is therefore supposed that Levi was the original Hebrew, and

of a paralytic. *Capernaum.*

LUKE.	JOHN.

CH. v. 17–26.

23 Whether is easier, to say, Thy sins be forgiven thee ; or to say, Rise up and walk?

24 But that ye may know that the Son of man hath power upon earth to forgive sins, (he said unto the sick of the palsy,) I say unto thee, Arise, and take up thy couch, and go unto thine house.

25 And immediately he arose up before them, and took up that whereon he lay, and departed to his own house, glorifying God.

26 And they were all amazed, and they glorified God, and were filled with fear, saying, We have seen strange things to-day.

of Matthew. *Capernaum.*

CH. v. 27, 28.

27 And after these things he went forth, and saw a publican named Levi, sitting at the receipt of custom : and he said unto him, Follow me.

28 And he left all, rose up, and followed him.

Matthew the assumed Roman name of this evangelist. STOWE's Introd. 120. See, also, HARMER's Obs. vol. iv. p. 330 ; Obs. 94.

PART IV.

———— .

OUR LORD'S SECOND PASSOVER,

AND THE

SUBSEQUENT TRANSACTIONS

UNTIL THE THIRD

————

TIME. One year.

11

§ 36. The pool of Bethesda ; the healing of the infirm man ;

MATTHEW.	MARK.

LUKE.

JOHN.
ch. v. 1–47.

AFTER this there was a feast of the Jews: and Jesus went up to Jerusalem.

2 Now there is at Jerusalem, by the sheep *market*, a pool, which is called in the Hebrew tongue, Bethesda, having five porches.

3 In these lay a great multitude of impotent folk, of blind, halt, withered, waiting for the moving of the water.

4 For an angel went down at a certain season into the pool, and troubled the water: whosoever then first after the troubling of the water stepped in, was made whole of whatsoever disease he had.

5 And a certain man was there, which had an infirmity thirty and eight years.

6 When Jesus saw him lie, and knew that he had been now a long time *in that case*, he saith unto him, Wilt thou be made whole?

7 The impotent man answered him, Sir, I have no man, when the water is troubled, to put me into the pool: but while I am coming, another steppeth down before me.

8 Jesus saith unto him, Rise, take up thy bed, and walk.

9 And immediately the man was made whole, and took up his bed, and walked: and on the same day was the sabbath.

10 The Jews therefore said unto him that was cured, It is the sabbathday; it is not lawful for thee to carry *thy* bed.

11 He answered them, He that made me whole, the same said unto me, Take up thy bed, and walk.

12 Then asked they him, What man is that which said unto thee, Take up thy bed, and walk?

13 And he that was healed wist not who it was: for Jesus had conveyed himself away, a multitude being in *that* place.

14 Afterward Jesus findeth him in the temple, and said unto him, Behold, thou art made whole; sin no more, lest a worse thing come unto thee.

§ 36. The pool of Bethesda ; the healing of the infirm man ;

MATTHEW.	MARK.

and our Lord's subsequent discourse.   *Jerusalem.*

LUKE.

JOHN.
CH. v. 1–47.

15 The man departed, and told the Jews that it was Jesus which had made him whole.

16 And therefore did the Jews persecute Jesus, and sought to slay him, because he had done these things on the sabbath-day.

17 But Jesus answered them, My Father worketh hitherto, and I work.

18 Therefore the Jews sought the more to kill him, because he not only had broken the sabbath, but said also, that God was his Father, making himself equal with God.

19 Then answered Jesus, and said unto them, Verily, verily, I say unto you, The Son can do nothing of himself, but what he seeth the Father do : for what things soever he doeth, these also doeth the Son likewise.

20 For the Father loveth the Son, and sheweth him all things that himself doeth : and he will shew him greater works than these, that ye may marvel.

21 For as the Father raiseth up the dead, and quickeneth *them;* even so the Son quickeneth whom he will.

22 For the Father judgeth no man ; but hath committed all judgment unto the Son :

23 That all *men* should honor the Son, even as they honor the Father. He that honoreth not the Son, honoreth not the Father which hath sent him.

24 Verily, verily, I say unto you, He that heareth my word, and believeth on him that sent me, hath everlasting life, and shall not come into condemnation ; but is passed from death unto life.

25 Verily, verily, I say unto you, The hour is coming, and now is, when the dead shall hear the voice of the Son of God : and they that hear shall live.

26 For as the Father hath life in himself, so hath he given to the Son to have life in himself ;

27 And hath given him authority to execute judgment also, because he is the Son of man.

28 Marvel not at this : for the hour is coming, in the which all that are in the graves shall hear his voice,

§ 36. The pool of Bethesda; the healing of the infirm man;

MATTHEW.	MARK.

John v. 37, *heard his voice.*] Spanheim, dub. evang. ii. 185, doubts how the latter part of this verse is reconcilable with Matthew iii. 17, and the parallel verses. But the voice from heaven was not God's *immediate* voice; but uttered at his command,

and our Lord's subsequent discourse. *Jerusalem.*

LUKE.	JOHN.
	CH. v. 1–47.

JOHN.

CH. v. 1–47.

29 And shall come forth ; they that have done good, unto the resurrection of life ; and they that have done evil, unto the resurrection of damnation.

30 I can of mine own self do nothing : as I hear, I judge : and my judgment is just ; because I seek not mine own will, but the will of the Father which hath sent me.

31 If I bear witness of myself, my witness is not true.

32 There is another that beareth witness of me, and I know that the witness which he witnesseth of me is true.

33 Ye sent unto John, and he bare witness unto the truth.

34 But I receive not testimony from man : but these things I say, that ye might be saved.

35 He was a burning and a shining light : and ye were willing for a season to rejoice in his light.

36 But I have greater witness than *that* of John : for the works which the Father hath given me to finish, the same works that I do, bear witness of me, that the Father hath sent me.

37 And the Father himself which hath sent me, hath borne witness of me. Ye have neither heard his voice at any time, nor seen his shape.

38 And ye have not his word abiding in you : for whom he hath sent, him ye believe not.

39 Search the scriptures ; for in them ye think ye have eternal life : And they are they which testify of me.

40 And ye will not come to me, that ye might have life.

41 I receive not honor from men.

42 But I know you, that ye have not the love of God in you.

43 I am come in my Father's name, and ye receive me not : if another shall come in his own name, him ye will receive.

44 How can ye believe, which receive honor one of another, and seek not the honor that *cometh* from God only ?

and in his person. See Deut. iv. 33 ; Ex. xx. 1, 2 ; Comp. Hebr. ii. 2 ; Gal. iii. 19 ; Acts vii. 53. NEWCOME.

§ 36. The pool of Bethesda ; the healing of the infirm man ;

MATTHEW.	MARK.

§ 37. The disciples pluck ears of grain

CH. XII. 1—8.	CH. II. 23—28.
AT that time Jesus went on the sabbath-day through the corn, and his disciples were a hungered, and began to pluck the ears of corn, and to eat.[a]	23 And it came to pass, that he went through the corn-fields on the sabbath-day ; and his disciples began, as they went, to pluck the ears of corn.
2 But when the Pharisees saw *it*, they said unto him, Behold, thy disciples do that which is not lawful to do upon the sabbath-day.	24 And the Pharisees said unto him, Behold, why do they on the sabbath-day that which is not lawful ?
3 But he said unto them, Have ye not read what David did when he was a hungered, and they that were with him ;	25 And he said unto them, Have ye never read what David did,[d] when he had need, and was a hungered, he and they that were with him ?
4 How he entered into the house of God, and did eat the shew-bread, which was not lawful for him to eat, neither for them which were with him, but only for the priests ?	26 How he went into the house of God, in the days of Abiathar the high priest, and did eat the shew-bread, which is not lawful to eat, but for the priests, and gave also to them which were with him ?
5 Or have ye not read in the law how that on the sabbath-days the priests in the temple profane the sabbath, and are blameless ?[b]	
6 But I say unto you, that in this place is *one* greater than the temple.	
7 But if ye had known what *this* meaneth,[c] I will have mercy, and not sacrifice, ye would not have condemned the guiltless.	27 And he said unto them, The sabbath was made for man, and not man for the sabbath :
8 For the Son of man is Lord even of the sabbath-day.	28 Therefore, the Son of man is Lord also of the sabbath.

a Deut. xxiii. 25.	b Numb. xxviii. 9, 10 ; xviii. 19.
c 1 Sam. xxi. 1 -7.	d Hos. vi. 6.

Matth. xii. 2, *to do upon the Sabbath day*.] The act of plucking the ears of corn by the hand, in another's field, was expressly permitted, by the law of Moses, Deut. xxiii. 23 ; but it was considered so far a species of reaping as to be servile work, and therefore not lawful to be done on the Sabbath. CAMPBELL, *in loc.*

Mark ii. 26, *Abiathar.*] It appears from 1 Sam. xxi. 1, that Abimelech was the

and our Lord's subsequent discourse. *Jerusalem.*

LUKE.	JOHN.
	CH. V. 1—47.
	45 Do not think that I will accuse you to the Father : there is *one* that accuseth you, *even* Moses, in whom ye trust.
	46 For had ye believed Moses, ye would have believed me : for he wrote of me.
	47 But if ye believe not his writings, how shall ye believe my words ?

on the Sabbath. *On the way to Galilee?*

CH. VI. 1—5.

AND it came to pass on the second sabbath after the first, that he went through the corn-fields ; and his disciples plucked the ears of corn, and did eat, rubbing *them* in *their* hands.

2 And certain of the Pharisees said unto them, Why do ye that which is not lawful to do on the sabbath-days?

3 And Jesus, answering them, said, Have ye not read so much as this, what David did, when himself was a hungered, and they which were with him ;

4 How he went into the house of God, and did take and eat the shew-bread, and gave also to them that were with him, which it is not lawful to eat but for the priests alone ?

5 And he said unto them, That the Son of man is Lord also of the sabbath.

high priest at the time referred to ; but Abiathar his son was the *chief* priest under him, and probably superintended the tabernacle and its stated concerns. Abimelech was soon after slain ; and Abiathar succeeded him in that office, and continued in it about forty years, until after the death of David. This circumstance, and his great eminence, above his father, may account for the use of his name rather than his father's, as illustrating the times of David and Saul. See SCOTT, *in loc.*

§ 38. The healing of the withered hand

MATTHEW.	MARK.
CH. XII. 9–14.	CH. III. 1–6.
9 And when he was departed thence, he went into their synagogue.	AND he entered again into the synagogue ; and there was a man there which had a withered hand.
10 And behold, there was a man which had *his* hand withered. And they asked him, saying, Is it lawful to heal on the sabbath-days ? that they might accuse him.	2 And they watched him, whether he would heal him on the sabbath-day ; that they might accuse him.
11 And he said unto them, What man shall there be among you, that shall have one sheep, and if it fall into a pit on the sabbath-day, will he not lay hold on it, and lift *it* out ?	3 And he saith unto the man which had the withered hand, Stand forth.
12 How much then is a man better than a sheep ? wherefore it is lawful to do well on the sabbath-days.	4 And he saith unto them, Is it lawful to do good on the sabbath-days, or to do evil ? to save life, or to kill ? But they held their peace.
13 Then saith he to the man, Stretch forth thy hand. And he stretched *it* forth ; and *it* was restored whole, like as the other.	5 And when he had looked round about on them with anger, being grieved for the hardness of their hearts, he saith unto the man, Stretch forth thy hand. And he stretched *it* out : and his hand was restored whole as the other.
14 Then the Pharisees went out, and held a council against him, how they might destroy him.	6 And the Pharisees went forth, and straightway took counsel with the Herodians against him, how they might destroy him.

§ 39. Jesus arrives at the sea of Tiberias,

CH. XII. 15–21.	CH. III. 7–12.
15 But when Jesus knew *it*, he withdrew himself from thence : and great multitudes followed him, and he healed them all.	7 But Jesus withdrew himself with his disciples to the sea : and a great multitude from Galilee followed him, and from Judea,
16 And charged them that they should not make him known :	8 And from Jerusalem, and from Idumea, and *from* beyond Jordan ; and they about Tyre and Sidon, a great multitude, when they had heard what great things he did, came unto him.
17 That it might be fulfilled which was spoken by Esaias the prophet,[a] saying,	
18 Behold my servant, whom I have chosen ; my beloved, in whom my soul is well pleased : I will put my Spirit upon him, and he shall shew judgment to the Gentiles.	9 And he spake to his disciples, that a small ship should wait on him, because of the multitude, lest they should throng him.
19 He shall not strive, nor cry ; neither shall any man hear his voice in the streets.	10 For he had healed many ; insomuch that they pressed upon him for to touch him, as many as had plagues.
20 A bruised reed shall he not break, and smoking flax, shall he not	11 And unclean spirits, when they saw him, fell down before him, and cried, saying, Thou art the Son of God.

[a] Is. xlii. 1, seq. ; Is. xi. 10.

Matth. xii. 20, *smoking flax.*] There may be an allusion, in these words of the prophet, to an Eastern custom, for those who were grievously afflicted to come to the sovereign for relief or redress, having pots of fire, or of burning straw, or other com-

on the Sabbath.   *Galilee.*

LUKE.	JOHN.
CH. VI. 6 – 11.	

LUKE.

CH. VI. 6 – 11.

6 And it came to pass also on another sabbath, that he entered into the synagogue, and taught : and there was a man whose right hand was withered :

7 And the scribes and Pharisees watched him, whether he would heal on the sabbath-day ; that they might find an accusation against him.

8 But he knew their thoughts, and said to the man which had the withered hand, Rise up, and stand forth in the midst.   And he arose, and stood forth.

9 Then said Jesus unto them, I will ask you one thing ; Is it lawful on the sabbath-days to do good, or to do evil ? to save life, or to destroy *it?*

10 And looking round about upon them all, he said unto the man, Stretch forth thy hand.   And he did so : and his hand was restored whole as the other.

11 And they were filled with madness ; and communed one with another what they might do to Jesus.

---

and is followed by multitudes.   *Lake of Galilee.*

---

bustible on their heads, in token of their extreme trouble.   Not one of these, the prophet seems to intimate, should go away without redress ; he will certainly remove the cause of their complaints, and render truth and justice victorious over falsehood and oppression.   3 CALM. 394.

§ 39. Jesus arrives at the sea of Tiberias,

MATTHEW. CH. XII. 15-21.	MARK.
quench, till he send forth judgment unto victory. 21 And in his name shall the Gentiles trust.	12 And he straitly charged them, that they should not make him known.

§ 40. Jesus withdraws to the Mountain and chooses the Twelve ;

CH. X. 2-4.	CH. III. 13-19.
	13 And he goeth up into a mountain, and calleth *unto him* whom he would : and they came unto him. 14 And he ordained twelve, that they should be with him, and that he might send them forth to preach. 15 And to have power to heal sicknesses, and to cast out devils.
2 Now the names of the twelve apostles are these ; The first, Simon, who is called Peter, and Andrew his brother ; James *the son* of Zebedee, and John his brother ; 3 Philip, and Bartholomew ; Thomas, and Matthew the publican ; James *the son* of Alpheus, and Lebbeus, whose surname was Thaddeus ; 4 Simon the Canaanite, and Judas Iscariot, who also betrayed him.	16 And Simon he surnamed Peter. 17 And James the *son* of Zebedee, and John the brother of James, (and he surnamed them Boanerges, which is, The sons of thunder,) 18 And Andrew, and Philip, and Bartholomew, and Matthew, and Thomas, and James the *son* of Alpheus, and Thaddeus, and Simon the Canaanite, 19 And Judas Iscariot, which also betrayed him : and they went into a house.

Matth. x. 3, *Thomas and Matthew.*] It appears from Mark vi. 7, that the apostles were sent forth by *two and two* to preach ; and this accounts for their being here and in the parallel places named in couples. Luke mentions Matthew first, as being regarded as the senior of Thomas, his companion ; but Matthew modestly places his own name last. Mark is less observant of the order of the names, but he alone states that they were thus associated. The others give the names in couples, but state no reason for it. This is not the method of false witnesses ; such incidental corroborations belong only to the narratives of truth.

Matth. x. 3, *Lebbeus.*] Thaddeus, Theudas and Judas (or Jude) are probably names of the same signification, the Greek termination being added to different forms of a Hebrew verb. " The Canaanite," Matth. x. 4, is the same with " Zelotes " in Luke. " Cognomen erat Chald. quod Lucas reddidit Zelotem," Wetstein. Thus, Thomas is rendered Didymus, or, the twin ; Cephas, Peter ; and Silas, Tertius. Some suppose that this name had been given to Simon on account of his religious zeal ; or, because he had been of a Jewish sect called Zealots, who were addicted to the Pharisees, and justified themselves by the example of Phinehas, for punishing offenders without waiting for the sentence of the magistrate. NEWCOME.

" Between Matthew (x. 2,) and Mark (iii. 16,) we observe a strict correspondence, but the catalogue in St. Luke (vi. 14,) differs from both the first-mentioned writers, in two particulars. 1, ' Simon the Canaanite,' of Matthew and Mark is introduced as ' Simon called Zelotes.' Now if any difference was admitted in this place, we might expect it to extend no farther than to the order of the names, or the addition of a surname ; as, for instance, Matthew calls the ' Thaddeus ' of Mark also ' Lebbeus ;' but here we have one surname changed for another. It is indeed easy to conceive, that Simon might have been commonly distinguished by either appellative, but this we can

and is followed by multitudes. *Lake of Galilee.*

LUKE.	JOHN.

multitudes follow him. *Near Capernaum.*

CH. VI. 12—19.

12 And it came to pass in those days, that he went out into a mountain to pray, and continued all night in prayer to God.

13 And when it was day, he called *unto him* his disciples : and of them he chose twelve, whom also he named Apostles ;

14 Simon (whom he also named Peter) and Andrew his brother, James and John, Philip and Bartholomew,

15 Matthew and Thomas, James the *son* of Alpheus, and Simon called Zelotes,

16 And Judas *the brother* of James, and Judas Iscariot, which also was the traitor.

17 And he came down with them, and stood in the plain ; and the company of his disciples, and a great mul-

---

only conjecture ; neither Evangelist adds a word to explain the point. 2, The other discrepancy, however, appears more serious. The Lebbeus or Thaddeus of St. Matthew and Mark, is entirely omitted in the list of St. Luke, who substitutes 'Judas the brother of James.' Here is certainly a marked difference, for it would not seem very probable, that the Apostle in question, passed by three distinct names. Nor could this be a mere oversight in St. Luke, for, in Acts i. 13, where a catalogue of the eleven is inserted, he mentions this individual in exactly the same manner. Are we to suppose then that the Evangelist commits a deliberate error in this particular ? We have distinct and satisfactory witnesses to prove that there really was an Apostle, besides Iscariot, who bore the name of Judas. Both Matthew (xiii. 55,) and Mark (vi. 3,) concur in speaking of James and Jude as the near relations of Christ, and part of this statement is incidentally confirmed by St. Paul, who calls James 'the Lord's brother.' (Gal. i. 19.) But farther, St. John (xiv. 22,) presents us with a remark made by 'Judas not Iscariot ;' evidently one of the Apostles ; and St. Jude himself, in the first verse of his Epistle, styles himself 'the brother of James.' There is thus amply sufficient evidence, that all the Gospel writers acknowledge an Apostle of this name, though St. Matthew, with his usual simplicity, familiarly mentions him by two of his appellations, omitting that of Judas, and St. Mark sees no occasion to depart from his language, in a matter of such general notoriety. Luke, on the other hand, usually studious of accuracy, distinguishes this Apostle by the name generally current in the Church, when his Gospel was written. This variation then may, upon the whole, convince us how undesignedly the writers of Scripture confirm each other's statements ; yet can this only be the result of a minute examination upon our part, and upon the probability of this, a cautious writer would hardly stake his reputation for truth or exactness." See ROBERTS's "Light shining out of Darkness," p. 91 - 93.

§ 40. Jesus withdraws to the Mountain and chooses the Twelve;

MATTHEW.	MARK.

§ 41. The Sermon

CH. V. VI. VII. VIII. 1.

AND seeing the multitudes, he went up into a mountain : and when he was set, his disciples came unto him.

2 And he opened his mouth, and taught them, saying,

3 Blessed *are* the poor in spirit : for theirs is the kingdom of heaven.

4 Blessed *are* they that mourn : for they shall be comforted.

5 Blessed *are* the meek : for they shall inherit the earth.

6 Blessed *are* they which do hunger and thirst after righteousness : for they shall be filled.

7 Blessed *are* the merciful : for they shall obtain mercy.

8 Blessed *are* the pure in heart : for they shall see God.

9 Blessed *are* the peace-makers : for they shall be called the children of God.

10 Blessed *are* they which are persecuted for righteousness' sake : for theirs is the kingdom of heaven.

11 Blessed *are* ye when *men* shall revile you, and persecute *you*, and shall say all manner of evil against you falsely, for my sake.

12 Rejoice, and be exceeding glad : for great *is* your reward in heaven : for so persecuted they the prophets which were before you.

Matth. v. 1, *into a mountain.*] It may be objected that Matthew, in saying that this discourse was delivered sitting on a mountain, is contradicted by Luke, who says, that Jesus was standing on a plain. Luke vi. 17. But Dr. Clarke, on this latter place, has suggested that Jesus " being pressed with great multitudes of people, might retire from them again to the top of the hill." And Dr. Priestley observes that " Matthew's saying that Jesus was *sat down* after he had gone up the mountain, and Luke's saying that he *stood* on the plain, when he healed the sick before the discourse, are no inconsistencies." Harm. p. 83.

multitudes follow him. *Near Capernaum.*

LUKE.	JOHN.

LUKE.

CH. VI. 12–19.

titude of people out of all Judea and
Jerusalem, and from the sea-coast of
Tyre and Sidon, which came to hear
him, and to be healed of their diseases ;

18 And they that were vexed with
unclean spirits : and they were healed.

19 And the whole multitude sought
to touch him ; for there went virtue
out of him, and healed *them* all.

on the Mount. *Near Capernaum.*

CH. VI. 20–49.

20 And he lifted up his eyes on his
disciples, and said, Blessed *be ye* poor ;
for yours is the kingdom of God.

21 Blessed *are ye* that hunger now :
for ye shall be filled. Blessed *are ye*
that weep now : for ye shall laugh.

22 Blessed are ye when men shall
hate you, and when they shall separate you *from their company*, and
shall reproach *you*, and cast out your
name as evil, for the Son of man's
sake.

23 Rejoice ye in that day, and leap
for joy : for behold, your reward *is*
great in heaven : for in the like manner did their fathers unto the prophets.

24 But wo unto you that are rich !
for ye have received your consolation.

25 Wo unto you that are full ! for
ye shall hunger. Wo unto you that
laugh now ! for ye shall mourn and
weep.

26 Wo unto you, when all men
shall speak well of you ! for so did
their fathers to the false prophets.

The whole picture is striking. Jesus ascends a mountain, employs the night in
prayer, and having thus solemnly invoked the divine blessing, authoritatively separates
the twelve apostles from the mass of his disciples. He descends, and heals, in the
plain, all among a great multitude, collected from various parts by the fame of his
miraculous power. Having thus created attention, he satisfies the desire of the people
to hear his doctrine ; and retiring first to the mountain whence he came, that his atten-
tive hearers might follow him, and might better arrange themselves before him. Sacro
digna silentio Mirantur *omnes* dicere. *Hor.* NEWCOME.

§ 41. The Sermon

MATTHEW.

CH. V. VI. VII. VIII. 1.

13 Ye are the salt of the earth : but if the salt have lost his savour, wherewith shall it be salted? it is thenceforth good for nothing, but to be cast out, and to be trodden under foot of men.

14 Ye are the light of the world. A city that is set on a hill cannot be hid.

15 Neither do men light a candle, and put it under a bushel, but on a candlestick : and it giveth light unto all that are in the house.

16 Let your light so shine before men, that they may see your good works, and glorify your Father which is in heaven.

17 Think not that I am come to destroy the law, or the prophets : I am not come to destroy, but to fulfil.

18 For verily, I say unto you, Till heaven and earth pass, one jot or one tittle shall in no wise pass from the law, till all be fulfilled.

19 Whosoever therefore shall break one of these least commandments, and shall teach men so, he shall be called the least in the kingdom of heaven : but whosoever shall do, and teach *them*, the same shall be called great in the kingdom of heaven.

20 For I say unto you, That except your righteousness shall exceed *the righteousness* of the scribes and Pharisees, ye shall in no case enter into the kingdom of heaven.

21 Ye have heard that it was said by them of old time, Thou shalt not kill ; and whosoever shall kill, shall be in danger of the judgment :

22 But I say unto you, That whosoever is angry with his brother without a cause, shall be in danger of the judgment : and whosoever shall say to his brother, Raca, shall be in danger of the council : but whosoever shall say, Thou fool, shall be in danger of hell-fire.

23 Therefore, if thou bring thy gift to the altar, and there rememberest that thy brother hath aught against thee,

24 Leave there thy gift before the altar, and go thy way ; first be recon-

MARK.

on the Mount. *Near Capernaum.*

LUKE.	JOHN.

§ 41. The Sermon

MATTHEW.
CH. V. VI. VII. VIII. 1.

ciled to thy brother, and then come and offer thy gift.

25 Agree with thine adversary quickly, while thou art in the way with him ; lest at any time the adversary deliver thee to the judge, and the judge deliver thee to the officer, and thou be cast into prison.

26 Verily, I say unto thee, Thou shalt by no means come out thence, till thou hast paid the uttermost farthing.

27 Ye have heard that it was said by them of old time, Thou shalt not commit adultery :

28 But I say unto you, That whosoever looketh on a woman to lust after her, hath committed adultery with her already in his heart.

29 And if thy right eye offend thee, pluck it out, and cast *it* from thee : for it is profitable for thee that one of thy members should perish, and not *that* thy whole body should be cast into hell.

30 And if thy right hand offend thee, cut it off, and cast *it* from thee : for it is profitable for thee that one of thy members should perish, and not *that* thy whole body should be cast into hell.

31 It hath been said, Whosoever shall put away his wife, let him give her a writing of divorcement :

32 But I say unto you, That whosoever shall put away his wife, saving for the cause of fornication, causeth her to commit adultery : and whosoever shall marry her that is divorced, committeth adultery.

33 Again, ye have heard that it hath been said by them of old time, Thou shalt not forswear thyself, but shalt perform unto the Lord thine oaths :

34 But I say unto you, Swear not at all : neither by heaven ; for it is God's throne :

35 Nor by the earth ; for it is his footstool : neither by Jerusalem ; for it is the city of the great King :

36 Neither shalt thou swear by thy head ; because thou canst not make one hair white or black.

37 But let your communication be,

MARK.

on the Mount. *Near Capernaum.*

LUKE.	JOHN.

§ 41. The Sermon

MATTHEW.

CH. V. VI. VII. VIII. 1.

Yea, yea; Nay, nay : for whatsoever *is* more than these cometh of evil.

38 Ye have heard that it hath been said, An eye for an eye, and a tooth for a tooth.

39 But I say unto you, That ye resist not evil : but whosoever shall smite thee on thy right cheek, turn to him the other also.

40 And if any man will sue thee at the law, and take away thy coat, let him have *thy* cloak also.

41 And whosoever shall compel thee to go a mile, go with him twain.

42 Give to him that asketh thee, and from him that would borrow of thee, turn not thou away.

43 Ye have heard that it hath been said, Thou shalt love thy neighbor, and hate thine enemy :

44 But I say unto you, Love your enemies, bless them that curse you, do good to them that hate you, and pray for them which despitefully use you, and persecute you ;

45 That ye may be the children of your Father which is in heaven : for he maketh his sun to rise on the evil and on the good, and sendeth rain on the just and on the unjust.

46 For if ye love them which love you, what reward have ye ? do not even the publicans the same ?

47 And if ye salute your brethren only, what do ye more *than others?* do not even the publicans so ?

48 Be ye therefore perfect, even as your Father which is in heaven is perfect.

CH. VI.

TAKE heed that ye do not your alms before men, to be seen of them : otherwise ye have no reward of your Father which is in heaven.

2 Therefore, when thou doest *thine* alms, do not sound a trumpet before thee, as the hypocrites do, in the synagogues, and in the streets, that they

MARK.

Matth. v. 41, *shall compel thee.*] The Greek word here employed is said to be derived from the Persians, among whom the king's messengers or posts were called *Angari.* These had the royal authority for pressing horses, ships, and even men, to assist them in the business on which they were sent. The word therefore signifies,

on the Mount. *Near Capernaum.*

LUKE.
CH. VI. 20–41.

LUKE.	JOHN.

JOHN.

27 But I say unto you which hear, Love your enemies, do good to them which hate you,

28 Bless them that curse you, and pray for them which despitefully use you.

29 And unto him that smiteth thee on the *one* cheek, offer also the other; and him that taketh away thy cloak, forbid not *to take thy* coat also.

30 Give to every man that asketh of thee; and of him that taketh away thy goods ask *them* not again.

31 And as ye would that men should do to you, do ye also to them likewise.

32 For if ye love them which love you, what thank have ye? for sinners also love those that love them.

33 And if ye do good to them which do good to you, what thank have ye? for sinners also do even the same.

34 And if ye lend *to them* of whom ye hope to receive, what thank have ye? for sinners also lend to sinners, to receive as much again.

35 But love ye your enemies, and do good, and lend, hoping for nothing again; and your reward shall be great, and ye shall be the children of the Highest: for he is kind unto the unthankful and *to* the evil.

36 Be ye therefore merciful, as your Father also is merciful.

---

to be compelled by violence to do any particular service, especially of the public kind, by the king's authority. And the sentiment is a lesson of patience and gentleness under severe exactions from man. *Lightfoot, apud* A. CLARKE, *in loc.* Sir J. CHARDIN's Travels, Vol. i. p. 238, 257.

§ 41. The Sermon

MATTHEW.	MARK.

MATTHEW.
CH. V. VI. VII. VIII. 1.

may have glory of men. Verily, I say unto you, They have their reward.

3 But when thou doest alms, let not thy left hand know what thy right hand doeth;

4 That thine alms may be in secret: and thy Father which seeth in secret, himself shall reward thee openly.

5 And when thou prayest, thou shalt not be as the hypocrites *are;* for they love to pray standing in the synagogues, and in the corners of the streets, that they may be seen of men. Verily, I say unto you, They have their reward.

6 But thou, when thou prayest, enter into thy closet, and when thou hast shut thy door, pray to thy Father which is in secret; and thy Father, which seeth in secret, shall reward thee openly.

7 But when ye pray, use not vain repetitions, as the heathen *do:* for they think that they shall be heard for their much speaking.

8 Be not ye therefore like unto them: for your Father knoweth what things ye have need of before ye ask him.

9 After this manner therefore pray ye: Our Father which art in heaven, Hallowed be thy name.

10 Thy kingdom come. Thy will be done in earth as *it is* in heaven.

11 Give us this day our daily bread.

12 And forgive us our debts, as we forgive our debtors.

13 And lead us not into temptation, but deliver us from evil. For thine is the kingdom, and the power, and the glory, for ever. Amen.

14 For, if ye forgive men their trespasses, your heavenly Father will also forgive you:

15 But, if ye forgive not men their trespasses, neither will your Father forgive your trespasses.

16 Moreover, when ye fast, be not as the hypocrites, of a sad countenance: for they disfigure their faces, that they may appear unto men to fast. Verily, I say unto you, They have their reward.

17 But thou, when thou fastest,

on the Mount. *Near Capernaum.*

LUKE.	JOHN.

§ 41. The Sermon

MATTHEW.

CH. V. VI. VII. VIII. **1.**

est, anoint thy head, and wash thy face ;

18 That thou appear not unto men to fast, but unto thy Father, which is in secret : and thy Father, which seeth in secret, shall reward thee openly.

19 Lay not up for yourselves treasures upon earth, where moth and rust doth corrupt, and where thieves break through and steal :

20 But lay up for yourselves treasures in heaven, where neither moth nor rust doth corrupt, and where thieves do not break through nor steal.

21 For where your treasure is, there will your heart be also.

22 The light of the body is the eye : if therefore thine eye be single, thy whole body shall be full of light.

23 But if thine eye be evil, thy whole body shall be full of darkness. If therefore the light that is in thee be darkness, how great *is* that darkness !

24 No man can serve two masters : for either he will hate the one, and love the other ; or else he will hold to the one, and despise the other. Ye cannot serve God and mammon.

25 Therefore I say unto you, Take no thought for your life, what ye shall eat, or what ye shall drink ; nor yet for your body, what ye shall put on. Is not the life more than meat, and the body than raiment ?

26 Behold the fowls of the air : for they sow not, neither do they reap, nor gather into barns ; yet your heavenly Father feedeth them. Are ye not much better than they ?

27 Which of you by taking thought can add one cubit unto his stature ?

28 And why take ye thought for raiment ? Consider the lilies of the field how they grow ; they toil not, neither do they spin ;

29 And yet I say unto you, That even Solomon, in all his glory, was not arrayed like one of these.

30 Wherefore, if God so clothe the grass of the field, which to-day is, and to-morrow is cast into the oven, *shall he* not much more *clothe* you, O ye of little faith ?

MARK.

on the Mount. *Near Capernaum.*

LUKE. JOHN.

§ 41. The Sermon

MATTHEW.	MARK.

MATTHEW.
CH. V. VI. VII. VIII. 1.

31 Therefore take no thought, saying, What shall we eat? or, what shall we drink? or, wherewithal shall we be clothed?

32 (For after all these things do the Gentiles seek) for your heavenly Father knoweth that ye have need of all these things.

33 But seek ye first the kingdom of God, and his righteousness, and all these things shall be added unto you.

34 Take therefore no thought for the morrow: for the morrow shall take thought for the things of itself. Sufficient unto the day is the evil thereof.

CH. VII.

JUDGE not, that ye be not judged.

2 For with what judgment ye judge, ye shall be judged: and with what measure ye mete, it shall be measured to you again.

3 And why beholdest thou the mote that is in thy brother's eye, but considerest not the beam that is in thine own eye?

4 Or how wilt thou say to thy brother, Let me pull out the mote out of thine eye; and behold, a beam is in thine own eye?

5 Thou hypocrite, first cast out the beam out of thine own eye; and then shalt thou see clearly to cast out the mote out of thy brother's eye.

6 Give not that which is holy unto the dogs, neither cast ye your pearls before swine, lest they trample them under their feet, and turn again and rend you.

7 Ask, and it shall be given you; seek, and ye shall find; knock, and it shall be opened unto you:

8 For every one that asketh, receiveth; and he that seeketh, findeth; and to him that knocketh, it shall be opened.

9 Or what man is there of you, whom if his son ask bread, will he give him a stone?

10 Or if he ask a fish, will he give him a serpent?

11 If ye then being evil know how to give good gifts unto your children, how much more shall your Father which is in heaven give good things to them that ask him?

on the Mount. *Near Capernaum.*

LUKE.	JOHN.
ch. vi. 20–49.	

37 Judge not, and ye shall not be judged : condemn not, and ye shall not be condemned : forgive, and ye shall be forgiven :

38 Give, and it shall be given unto you ; good measure, pressed down, and shaken together, and running over, shall men give into your bosom. For with the same measure that ye mete withal, it shall be measured to you again.

39 And he spake a parable unto them ; Can the blind lead the blind? shall they not both fall into the ditch?

40 The disciple is not above his master : but every one that is perfect, shall be as his master.

41 And why beholdest thou the mote that is in thy brother's eye, but perceivest not the beam that is in thine own eye?

42 Either how canst thou say to thy brother, Brother, let me pull out the mote that is in thine eye, when thou thyself beholdest not the beam that is in thine own eye? Thou hypocrite, cast out first the beam out of thine own eye, and then shalt thou see clearly to pull out the mote that is thy brother's eye.

43 For a good tree bringeth not forth corrupt fruit ; neither doth a corrupt tree bring forth good fruit.

44 For every tree is known by his own fruit : for of thorns men do not gather figs, nor of a bramble-bush gather they grapes.

45 A good man out of the good

§ 41. The Sermon

MATTHEW.

CH. V. VI. VII. VIII. 1.

12 Therefore all things whatsoever ye would that men should do to you, do ye even so to them : for this is the law and the prophets.

13 Enter ye in at the strait gate ; for wide *is* the gate, and broad *is* the way, that leadeth to destruction, and many there be which go in thereat :

14 Because, strait *is* the gate, and narrow *is* the way, which leadeth unto life, and few there be that find it.

15 Beware of false prophets, which come to you in sheep's clothing, but inwardly they are ravening wolves.

16 Ye shall know them by their fruits : Do men gather grapes of thorns, or figs of thistles?

17 Even so every good tree bringeth forth good fruit ; but a corrupt tree bringeth forth evil fruit.

18 A good tree cannot bring forth evil fruit, neither *can* a corrupt tree bring forth good fruit.

19 Every tree that bringeth not forth good fruit is hewn down, and cast into the fire.

20 Wherefore, by their fruits ye shall know them.

21 Not every one that saith unto me, Lord, Lord, shall enter into the kingdom of heaven ; but he that doeth the will of my Father which is in heaven.

22 Many will say to me in that day, Lord, Lord, have we not prophesied in thy name? and in thy name have cast out devils? and in thy name done many wonderful works?

23 And then will I profess unto them, I never knew you : depart from me, ye that work iniquity.

24 Therefore, whosoever heareth these sayings of mine, and doeth them, I will liken him unto a wise man, which built his house upon a rock :

25 And the rain descended, and the floods came, and the winds blew, and beat upon that house ; and it fell not : for it was founded upon a rock.

26 And every one that heareth these sayings of mine, and doeth them not, shall be likened unto a foolish man, which built his house upon the sand :

MARK.

on the Mount. *Near Capernaum.*

LUKE.	JOHN.
CH. VI. 20—49.	

treasure of his heart, bringeth forth that which is good ; and an evil man, out of the evil treasure of his heart, bringeth forth that which is evil: for of the abundance of the heart his mouth speaketh.

46 And why call ye me Lord, Lord, and do not the things which I say ?

47 Whosoever cometh to me, and heareth my sayings, and doeth them, I will shew you to whom he is like.

48 He is like a man which built a house, and digged deep, and laid the foundation on a rock : and when the flood arose, the stream beat vehemently upon that house, and could not shake it : for it was founded upon a rock.

49 But he that heareth and doeth not, is like a man that without a foundation built a house upon the earth,

§ 41. The Sermon

MATTHEW.	MARK.
CH. V. VI. VII. VIII. 1.	
27 And the rain descended, and the floods came, and the winds blew, and beat upon that house; and it fell: and great was the fall of it.	
28 And it came to pass when Jesus had ended these sayings, the people were astonished at his doctrine.	
29 For he taught them as *one* having authority, and not as the scribes.	
CH. VIII.	
WHEN he was come down from the mountain, great multitudes followed him.	

§ 42. The healing

CH. VIII. 5 – 13.

5 And when Jesus was entered into Capernaum, there came unto him a centurion, beseeching him,

6 And saying, Lord, my servant lieth at home sick of the palsy, grievously tormented.

7 And Jesus saith unto him, I will come and heal him.

8 The centurion answered and said, Lord, I am not worthy that thou shouldest come under my roof: but speak the word only, and my servant shall be healed.

9 For I am a man under authority, having soldiers under me: and I say to this *man*, Go, and he goeth; and to another, Come, and he cometh; and to my servant, Do this, and he doeth *it*.

10 When Jesus heard *it*, he marvelled, and said to them that followed, Verily I say unto you, I have not found so great faith, no, not in Israel.

11 And I say unto you, That many shall come from the east and west, and shall sit down with Abraham, and Isaac, and Jacob, in the kingdom of heaven:

12 But the children of the kingdom shall be cast out into outer darkness:

Matth. viii. 5, *came unto him*.] Calvin says that Matthew, being more brief, introduces the centurion himself as speaking; and that Luke expresses more at large his sending by his friends; but that the sense of both is the same. *Harm.* p. 124.

(Toinard quotes Exod. xviii. 6, where the words related as *spoken* by Jethro, were evidently a message *sent* by him to Moses. *Harm.* 147.)

on the Mount. *Near Capernaum.*

LUKE.	JOHN.
CH. VI. 20—49.	
against which the stream did beat vehemently, and immediately it fell, and the ruin of that house was great.	

of the centurion's servant. *Capernaum.*

CH. VII. 1—10.

Now, when he had ended all his sayings in the audience of the people, he entered into Capernaum,

2 And a certain centurion's servant, who was dear unto him, was sick, and ready to die.

3 And when he heard of Jesus, he sent unto him the elders of the Jews, beseeching him that he would come and heal his servant.

4 And when they came to Jesus, they besought him instantly, saying, That he was worthy for whom he should do this :

5 For he loveth our nation, and he hath built us a synagogue.

6 Then Jesus went with them. And when he was now not far from the house, the centurion sent friends to him, saying unto him, Lord, trouble not thyself: for I am not worthy that thou shouldest enter under my roof;

7 Wherefore neither thought I myself worthy to come unto thee; but say in a word, and my servant shall be healed.

8 For I also am a man set under authority, having under me soldiers, and I say unto one, Go, and he goeth; and to another, Come, and he cometh; and to my servant, Do this, and he doeth *it.*

Considering then the sameness of the scene, of the person, of the words and of the transaction, I cannot but conclude with Grotius, that the miracle is one and the same, related in general by Matthew, and with greater accuracy by Luke. NEWCOME.

§ 42. The healing

MATTHEW.	MARK.
CH. VIII. 5 – 13.	
there shall be weeping and gnashing of teeth.	
13 And Jesus said unto the centurion, Go thy way; and as thou hast believed, *so* be it done unto thee. And his servant was healed in the self-same hour.	

§ 43. The raising

§ 44. John the Baptist, in prison,

CH. XI. 2 – 19.	
2 Now when John had heard in the prison the works of Christ, he sent two of his disciples,	
3 And said unto him, Art thou he that should come, or do we look for another?	

Matth. xi. 3, *he that should come.*] The nature of our Lord's ministry, as it now appeared, so unlike what John as a Jew expected, may have surprised and perplexed him. And his own misfortune, coming upon this disappointment and perplexity, would increase his doubt and embarrassment. His faith was shaken ;—the ques-

of the centurion's servant. *Capernaum.*

LUKE.
CH. VII. 1 – 10.

9 When Jesus heard these things, he marvelled at him, and turned him about and said unto the people that followed him, I say unto you, I have not found so great faith, no, not in Israel.

10 And they that were sent, returning to the house, found the servant whole that had been sick.

JOHN.

of the widow's son. *Nain.*

CH. VII. 11 – 17.

11 And it came to pass the day after, that he went into a city called Nain : and many of his disciples went with him, and much people.

12 Now, when he came nigh to the gate of the city, behold, there was a dead man carried out, the only son of his mother, and she was a widow : and much people of the city was with her.

13 And when the Lord saw her, he had compassion on her, and said unto her, Weep not.

14 And he came and touched the bier : and they that bare *him* stood still. And he said, Young man, I say unto thee, Arise.

15 And he that was dead sat up, and began to speak : and he delivered him to his mother.

16 And there came a fear on all : and they glorified God, saying, That a great prophet is risen up among us ; and, That God hath visited his people.

17 And this rumor of him went forth throughout all Judea, and throughout all the region round about.

sends disciples to Jesus. *Galilee. Capernaum!*

CH. VII. 18 – 35.

18 And the disciples of John shewed him of all these things.

19 And John calling *unto him* two of his disciples, sent *them* to Jesus, saying, Art thou he that should come? or look we for another?

tion implies no more ;—and he sent that his doubts might be removed, and his faith confirmed. Jesus therefore merely referred John to the miracles which he was doing, and the prophecies which spake of him, and which were fulfilled by those miracles. Bp. Sumner, *in loc.*

13

§ 44. John the Baptist, in prison,

MATTHEW.
CH. XI. 2 – 19.

MARK.

4 Jesus answered and said unto them, Go and shew John again those things which ye do hear and see:

5 The blind receive their sight, and the lame walk, the lepers are cleansed, and the deaf hear, the dead are raised up, and the poor have the gospel preached to them.[a]

6 And blessed is *he* whosoever shall not be offended in me.

7 And as they departed, Jesus began to say unto the multitudes concerning John, What went ye out into the wilderness to see? A reed shaken with the wind?

8 But what went ye out for to see? A man clothed in soft raiment? Behold, they that wear soft *clothing* are in kings' houses.

9 But what went ye out for to see? A prophet? yea, I say unto you, and more than a prophet.

10 For this is *he* of whom it is written,[b] Behold, I send my messenger before thy face, which shall prepare thy way before thee.

11 Verily, I say unto you, Among them that are born of women, there hath not risen a greater than John the Baptist: notwithstanding, he that is least in the kingdom of heaven, is greater than he.

12 And from the days of John the Baptist, until now, the kingdom of heaven suffereth violence, and the violent take it by force.

13 For all the prophets and the law prophesied until John.

14 And if ye will receive *it*, this is Elias which was for to come.[c]

15 He that hath ears to hear, let him hear.

16 But whereunto shall I liken this generation? It is like unto children sitting in the markets, and calling unto their fellows,

[a] Is. xxxv. 5, seq.   [b] Mal. iii. 1.   [c] Mal. iv. 5.

LUKE.
CH. VII. 18 – 35.

JOHN.

20 When the men were come unto him, they said, John Baptist hath sent us unto thee, saying, Art thou he that should come? or look we for another?

21 And in that same hour he cured many of *their* infirmities, and plagues, and of evil spirits; and unto many *that were* blind he gave sight.

22 Then Jesus answering, said unto them, Go your way, and tell John what things ye have seen and heard; how that the blind see, the lame walk, the lepers are cleansed, the deaf hear, the dead are raised, to the poor the gospel is preached.

23 And blessed is *he,* whosoever shall not be offended in me.

24 And when the messengers of John were departed, he began to speak unto the people concerning John, What went ye out into the wilderness for to see? A reed shaken with the wind?

25 But what went ye out for to see? A man clothed in soft raiment? Behold, they which are gorgeously apparelled, and live delicately, are in kings' courts.

26 But what went ye out for to see? A prophet? Yea, I say unto you, and much more than a prophet.

27 This is *he,* of whom it is written, Behold, I send my messenger before thy face, which shall prepare thy way before thee.

28 For I say unto you, Among those that are born of women, there is not a greater prophet than John the Baptist: but he that is least in the kingdom of God, is greater than he.

29 And all the people that heard *him,* and the publicans, justified God, being baptized with the baptism of John.

30 But the Pharisees and lawyers rejected the counsel of God against themselves, being not baptized of him.

31 And the Lord said, Whereunto then shall I liken the men of this generation? and to what are they like?

32 They are like unto children sitting in the market-place, and calling one to another, and saying, We have

§ 44. John the Baptist, in prison,

MATTHEW.	MARK.
CH. XI. 2–19.	

17 And saying, We have piped unto you, and ye have not danced; we have mourned unto you, and ye have not lamented.

18 For John came neither eating nor drinking, and they say, He hath a devil.

19 The Son of man came eating and drinking, and they say, Behold a man gluttonous, and a wine-bibber, a friend of publicans and sinners. But Wisdom is justified of her children.

§ 45. Reflections of Jesus

CH. XI. 20–30.

20 Then began he to upbraid the cities wherein most of his mighty works were done, because they repented not.

21 Wo unto thee, Chorazin! wo unto thee, Bethsaida! for if the mighty works which were done in you had been done in Tyre and Sidon, they would have repented long ago in sackcloth and ashes.

22 But I say unto you, It shall be more tolerable for Tyre and Sidon at the day of judgment, than for you.

23 And thou, Capernaum, which art exalted unto heaven, shalt be brought down to hell: for if the mighty works which have been done in thee, had been done in Sodom, it would have remained until this day.

24 But I say unto you, That it shall be more tolerable for the land of Sodom, in the day of judgment, than for thee.

25 At that time Jesus answered and said, I thank thee, O Father, Lord of heaven and earth, because thou hast hid these things from the wise and prudent, and hast revealed them unto babes.

26 Even so, Father, for so it seemed good in thy sight.

27 All things are delivered unto me of my Father; and no man knoweth the Son, but the Father; neither knoweth any man the Father, save the Son, and *he* to whomsoever the Son will reveal *him*.

28 Come unto me, all *ye* that labor,

sends disciples to Jesus. *Galilee.* *Capernaum?*

LUKE.
CH. VII. 18–35.

piped unto you, and ye have not danced ; we have mourned to you, and ye have not wept.

33 For John the Baptist came neither eating bread, nor drinking wine ; and ye say, He hath a devil.

34 The Son of man is come eating and drinking ; and ye say, Behold a gluttonous man, and a wine-bibber, a friend of publicans and sinners !

35 But Wisdom is justified of all her children.

JOHN.

on appealing to his mighty works. *Capernaum.*

§ 45. Reflections of Jesus

MATTHEW.	MARK.
CH. XI. 20 – 30.	
and are heavy laden, and I will give you rest.	
29 Take my yoke upon you, and learn of me : for I am meek and lowly in heart ; and ye shall find rest unto your souls.	
30 For my yoke *is* easy, and my burden is light.	

§ 46. While sitting at meat with a Pharisee,

on appealing to his mighty works. *Capernaum.*

LUKE.	JOHN.

Jesus is anointed by a woman who had been a sinner. *Capernaum!*

CH. VII. 36–50.

36 And one of the Pharisees desired him that he would eat with him. And he went into the Pharisee's house, and sat down to meat.

37 And behold, a woman in the city, which was a sinner, when she knew that *Jesus* sat at meat in the Pharisee's house, brought an alabaster-box of ointment,

38 And stood at his feet behind *him* weeping, and began to wash his feet with tears, and did wipe *them* with the hairs of her head, and kissed his feet, and anointed *them* with the ointment.

39 Now, when the Pharisee which had bidden him, saw *it*, he spake within himself, saying, This man, if he were a prophet, would have known who, and what manner of woman *this is* that toucheth him: for she is a sinner.

40 And Jesus answering, said unto him, Simon, I have somewhat to say unto thee. And he saith, Master, say on.

41 There was a certain creditor, which had two debtors : the one owed five hundred pence, and the other fifty.

42 And when they had nothing to pay, he frankly forgave them both. Tell me, therefore, which of them will love him most?

43 Simon answered and said, I suppose that *he*, to whom he forgave most. And he said unto him, Thou hast rightly judged.

44 And he turned to the woman, and said unto Simon, Seest thou this woman? I entered into thine house, thou gavest me no water for my feet : but she hath washed my feet with tears, and wiped *them* with the hairs of her head.

§ 46. While sitting at meat with a Pharisee,

MATTHEW.	MARK.

§ 47. Jesus, with the Twelve,

§ 48. The healing of a demoniac.

CH. XII. 22–37.	CH. III. 19–30
	19 —— and they went into a house.
	20 And the multitude cometh together again, so that they could not so much as eat bread.
	21 And when his friends heard *of it*, they went out to lay hold on him : for they said, He is beside himself.
22 Then was brought unto him one possessed with a devil, blind and dumb ; and he healed him, insomuch that the blind and dumb, both spake and saw.	

Matth. xii. 22.] We here learn that the demoniac was both blind and dumb.

Jesus is anointed by a woman who had been a sinner.   *Capernaum?*

LUKE.	JOHN.
CH. VII. 36–50.	

LUKE.

CH. VII. 36–50.

45 Thou gavest me no kiss : but this woman, since the time I came in, hath not ceased to kiss my feet.

46 My head with oil thou didst not anoint : but this woman hath anointed my feet with ointment.

47 Wherefore I say unto thee, Her sins which are many, are forgiven ; for she loved much : but to whom little is forgiven, *the same* loveth little.

48 And he said unto her, Thy sins are forgiven.

49 And they that sat at meat with him, began to say within themselves, Who is this that forgiveth sins also?

50 And he said to the woman, Thy faith hath saved thee ; go in peace.

makes a second circuit in Galilee.

CH. VIII. 1–3.

AND it came to pass afterward, that he went throughout every city and village, preaching and shewing the the glad tidings of the kingdom of God : and the twelve *were* with him.

2 And certain women, which had been healed of evil spirits and infirmities, Mary called Magdalene, out of whom went seven devils,

3 And Joanna the wife of Chuza, Herod's steward, and Susanna, and many others, which ministered unto him of their substance.

The Scribes and Pharisees blaspheme.   *Galilee.*

CH. XI. 14, 15, 17–23.

14 And he was casting out a devil, and it was dumb. And it came to pass when the devil was gone out, the dumb spake ; and the people wondered.

St. Luke omits the former circumstance, but does not contradict it.   NEWCOME.

§ 48. The healing of a demoniac.

MATTHEW.	MARK.
CH. XII. 22–37.	CH. III. 19–30.

MATTHEW.
CH. XII. 22–37.

23 And all the people were amazed, and said, Is not this the son of David?

24 But when the Pharisees heard *it* they said, This *fellow* doth not cast out devils, but by Beelzebub the prince of the devils.

25 And Jesus knew their thoughts, and said unto them, Every kingdom divided against itself, is brought to desolation; and every city or house divided against itself, shall not stand.

26 And if Satan cast out Satan, he is divided against himself; how shall then his kingdom stand?

27 And if I by Beelzebub cast out devils, by whom do your children cast *them* out? therefore they shall be your judges.

28 But if I cast out devils by the Spirit of God, then the kingdom of God is come unto you.

29 Or else, how can one enter into a strong man's house, and spoil his goods, except he first bind the strong man? and then he will spoil his house.

30 He that is not with me is against me; and he that gathereth not with me, scattereth abroad.

31 Wherefore I say unto you, All manner of sin and blasphemy shall be forgiven unto men: but the blasphemy *against* the *Holy* Ghost shall not be forgiven unto men.

32 And whosoever speaketh a word against the Son of man, it shall be forgiven him: but whosoever speaketh against the Holy Ghost, it shall not be forgiven him, neither in this world, neither in the *world* to come.

33 Either make the tree good, and his fruit good; or else make the tree corrupt, and his fruit corrupt: for the tree is known by *his* fruit.

34 O generation of vipers, how can ye, being evil, speak good things? for out of the abundance of the heart the mouth speaketh.

MARK.
CH. III. 19–30.

22 And the scribes which came down from Jerusalem, said, He hath Beelzebub, and by the prince of the devils casteth he out devils.

23 And he called them *unto him*, and said unto them in parables, How can Satan cast out Satan?

24 And if a kingdom be divided against itself, that kingdom cannot stand.

25 And if a house be divided against itself, that house cannot stand.

26 And if Satan rise up against himself, and be divided, he cannot stand, but hath an end.

27 No man can enter into a strong man's house, and spoil his goods, except he will first bind the strong man; and then he will spoil his house.

28 Verily, I say unto you, All sins shall be forgiven unto the sons of men, and blasphemies wherewith soever they shall blaspheme:

29 But he that shall blaspheme against the Holy Ghost hath never forgiveness, but is in danger of eternal damnation:

30 Because they said, he hath an unclean spirit.

Matth. xii. 23, *the people were amazed.*] An accurate reader will observe that Matth. xii. 22, and Luke xi. 14, show the general occasion of the blasphemy against Jesus; and that Matth. xii. 23, shows the particular occasion of it, the multitude alarming the Jewish rulers by their question whether Jesus were the Christ. No cause for the absurd and impious insinuation of the Scribes and Pharisees is assigned by St. Mark: however, he suggests an important circumstance, that they came from

The Scribes and Pharisees blaspheme.   *Galilee.*

LUKE.	JOHN.
CH. XI. 14, 15, 17—23.	

15 But some of them said, He casteth out devils through Beelzebub, the chief of the devils.

17 But he, knowing their thoughts, said unto them, Every kingdom divided against itself, is brought to desolation ; and a house *divided* against a house, falleth.

18 If Satan also be divided against himself, how shall his kingdom stand ? because ye say that I cast out devils through Beelzebub.

19 And if I by Beelzebub cast out devils, by whom do your sons cast *them* out ? therefore shall they be your judges.

20 But if I with the finger of God cast out devils, no doubt the kingdom of God is come upon you.

21 When a strong man armed keepeth his palace, his goods are in peace :

22 But when a stronger than he shall come upon him, and overcome him, he taketh from him all his armour, wherein he trusted, and divideth his spoils.

23 He that is not with me, is against me : and he that gathereth not with me scattereth.

Jerusalem to watch the conduct of Jesus.   The latter part of Luke viii. 19, shows that his relations were not able to enter the house on account of the press.   Thus one Evangelist is wonderfully supplemental to another by notations of time, place, and other circumstances ; and the strictest propriety and agreement result from diligently comparing them.   NEWCOME.

§ 48. The healing of a demoniac.

MATTHEW.	MARK.
CH. XII. 22–37.	
35 A good man, out of the good treasure of the heart, bringeth forth good things : and an evil man, out of the evil treasure, bringeth forth evil things.	
36 But I say unto you, That every idle word that men shall speak, they shall give account thereof in the day of judgment.	
37 For by thy words thou shalt be justified, and by thy words thou shalt be condemned.	

§ 49. The Scribes and Pharisees seek a sign.

CH. XII. 38–45.

38 Then certain of the scribes and of the Pharisees answered, saying, Master, we would see a sign from thee.

39 But he answered and said to them, An evil and adulterous generation seeketh after a sign, and there shall no sign be given to it, but the sign of the prophet Jonas.

40 For as Jonas was three days and three nights in the whale's belly,[a] so shall the Son of man be three days and three nights in the heart of the earth.

41 The men of Nineveh shall rise in judgment with this generation, and shall condemn it : because they repented at the preaching of Jonas ;[b] and behold, a greater than Jonas is here.

42 The queen of the south shall rise up in the judgment with this generation, and shall condemn it : for she came from the uttermost parts of the earth to hear the wisdom of Solomon ;[c] and behold, a greater than Solomon is here.

---

[a] Jonah i. 17.   [b] Jonah iii. 4, 5.   [c] 1 Kin. x. 1 seq.

Matth. xii. 39, *shall no sign be given.*] The writer of a false narrative would either have omitted to mention the request for a sign, or would have related that it was com-

The Scribes and Pharisees blaspheme. *Galilee.*

LUKE.	JOHN.

Our Lord's reflections. *Galilee.*

cH. xɪ. 16, 24 – 36.

16 And others tempting *him*, sought of him a sign from heaven.

29 And when the people were gathered thick together, he began to say, This is an evil generation : they seek a sign , and there shall no sign be given it, but the sign of Jonas the prophet.

30 For as Jonas was a sign unto the Ninevites, so shall also the Son of man be to this generation.

31 The queen of the south shall rise up in the judgment with the men of this generation, and condemn them : for she came from the utmost parts of the earth, to hear the wisdom of Solomon ; and behold, a greater than Solomon *is* here.

32 The men of Nineveh shall rise up in the judgment with this generation, and shall condemn it : for they repented at the preaching of Jonas ; and behold, a greater than Jonas *is* here.

33 No man when he hath lighted a candle, putteth *it* in a secret place, neither under a bushel, but on a candlestick, that they which come in may see the light.

34 The light of the body is the eye : therefore when thine eye is single, thy whole body also is full of light ; but when *thine eye* is evil, thy body also *is* full of darkness.

35 Take heed therefore, that the light which is in thee be not darkness.

plied with. He would never have exposed his Master to the suspicion of a want of power. See also, Matth. xvi. 1.

§ 49. The Scribes and Pharisees seek a sign.

MATTHEW.	MARK.
CH. XII. 38–45.	

43 When the unclean spirit is gone out of a man, he walketh through dry places, seeking rest, and findeth none.

44 Then he saith, I will return into my house from whence I came out; and when he is come, he findeth *it* empty, swept, and garnished.

45 Then goeth he, and taketh with himself seven other spirits more wicked than himself, and they enter in and dwell there : and the last *state* of that man is worse than the first. Even so shall it be also unto this wicked generation.

§ 50. The true disciples of Christ

CH. XII. 46–50.	CH. III. 31–35.

46 While he yet talked to the people, behold, *his* mother and his brethren stood without, desiring to speak with him.

47 Then one said unto him, Behold, thy mother and thy brethren stand without, desiring to speak with thee.

48 But he answered and said unto him that told him, Who is my mother? and who are my brethren?

49 And he stretched forth his hand toward his disciples, and said, Behold my mother and my brethren!

50 For whosoever shall do the will of my Father which is in heaven, the same is my brother, and sister, and mother.

31 There came then his brethren and his mother, and standing without, sent unto him, calling him.

32 And the multitude sat about him ; and they said unto him, Behold, thy mother and thy brethren without seek for thee.

33 And he answered them, saying, Who is my mother, or my brethren?

34 And he looked round about on them which sat about him, and said, Behold, my mother and my brethren!

35 For whosoever shall do the will of God, the same is my brother, and my sister, and mother.

§ 51. At a Pharisee's table,

Our Lord's reflections. *Galilee.*

LUKE.	JOHN.
CH. XI. 16, 24—36.	

36 If thy whole body therefore *be* full of light, having no part dark, the whole shall be full of light ; as when the bright shining of a candle doth give thee light.

24 When the unclean spirit is gone out of a man, he walketh through dry places, seeking rest : and finding none, he saith, I will return unto my house whence I came out.

25 And when he cometh, he findeth *it* swept and garnished.

26 Then goeth he, and taketh *to him* seven other spirits more wicked than himself ; and they enter in, and dwell there : and the last *state* of that man is worse than the first.

27 And it came to pass, as he spake these things, a certain woman of the company lifted up her voice, and said unto him, Blessed *is* the womb that bare thee, and the paps which thou hast sucked.

28 But he said, Yea, rather blessed *are* they that hear the word of God, and keep it.

his nearest relatives. *Galilee.*

CH. VIII. 19—21.

19 Then came to him *his* mother and his brethren, and could not come at him for the press.

20 And it was told him *by certain*, which said, Thy mother and thy brethren stand without, desiring to see thee.

21 And he answered and said unto them, My mother and my brethren are these which hear the word of God, and do it.

Jesus denounces woes against the Pharisees and others. *Galilee.*

CH. XI. 37—54.

37 And as he spake, a certain Pharisee besought him to dine with him : and he went in and sat down to meat.

§ 51. At a Pharisee's table,

MATTHEW.	MARK.

Luke xi. 38, *had not first washed.*] This omission may seem inconsistent with the character of Jesus, who appears to have generally complied with all the innocent usages of his countrymen ; and of course it may be adduced as an objection against the veracity of the Evangelist. Luke simply records the fact, however it may seem to make against the character of his Master, or his own veracity. But Mark, vii. 3-9,

Jesus denounces woes against the Pharisees and others. *Galilee.*

LUKE.
CH. XI. 37–54.

38 And when the Pharisee saw *it*, he marvelled that he had not first washed before dinner.

39 And the Lord said unto him, Now do ye Pharisees make clean the outside of the cup and the platter; but your inward part is full of ravening and wickedness.

40 *Ye* fools, did not he that made that which is without, make that which is within also ?

41 But rather give alms of such things as ye have; and behold, all things are clean unto you.

42 But wo unto you, Pharisees ! for ye tithe mint, and rue, and all manner of herbs, and pass over judgment and the love of God : these ought ye to have done, and not to leave the other undone.

43 Wo unto you, Pharisees ! for ye love the uppermost seats in the synagogues, and greetings in the markets.

44 Wo unto you, scribes and Pharisees, hypocrites ! for ye are as graves which appear not, and the men that walk over *them* are not aware *of them.*

45 Then answered one of the lawyers, and said unto him, Master, thus saying, thou reproachest us also.

46 And he said, Wo unto you also, *ye* lawyers ! for ye lade men with burdens grievous to be borne, and ye yourselves touch not the burdens with one of your fingers.

47 Wo unto you ! for ye build the sepulchres of the prophets, and your fathers killed them.

48 Truly ye bear witness, that ye allow the deeds of your fathers : for they indeed killed them, and ye build their sepulchres.

49 Therefore also said the wisdom of God, I will send them prophets and apostles, and *some* of them they shall slay and persecute :

50 That the blood of all the pro-

JOHN.

---

in a manner equally incidental and without design, discloses the truth that this washing was superstitious, and connected with the dangerous error of placing the traditions of the elders on equal footing with the commands of God. Where there was danger of his practice being misinterpreted, our Lord withheld his compliance, even in things indifferent. See Bp. SUMNER on Luke, Lect. 41.

§ 51. At a Pharisee's table,

MATTHEW.	MARK.

§ 52. Jesus discourses to his disciples

Jesus denounces woes against the Pharisees and others.   *Galilee.*

LUKE.
CH. XI. 37–54.

phets, which was shed from the foundation of the world, may be required of this generation ;

51 From the blood of Abel[a] unto the blood of Zacharias, which perished between the altar and the temple : verily, I say unto you, It shall be required of this generation.

52 Wo unto you, lawyers ! for ye have taken away the key of knowledge : ye entered not in yourselves, and them that were entering in ye hindered.

53 And as he said these things unto them, the scribes and the Pharisees began to urge *him* vehemently, and to provoke him to speak of many things ;

54 Laying wait for him, and seeking to catch something out of his mouth, that they might accuse him.

JOHN.

and the multitude.   *Galilee.*

CH. XII. 1–59.

In the mean time, when there were gathered together an innumerable multitude of people, insomuch that they trode one upon another, he began to say unto his disciples first of all, Beware ye of the leaven of the Pharisees, which is hypocrisy.

2 For there is nothing covered, that shall not be revealed ; neither hid, that shall not be known.

3 Therefore, whatsoever ye have spoken in darkness, shall be heard in the light ; and that which ye have spoken in the ear in closets, shall be proclaimed upon the house-tops.

4 And I say unto you, my friends, Be not afraid of them that kill the body, and after that, have no more that they can do.

5 But I will forewarn you whom ye shall fear ; Fear him, which, after he hath killed, hath power to cast into hell ; yea, I say unto you, Fear him.

6 Are not five sparrows sold for two farthings, and not one of them is forgotten before God ?

7 But even the very hairs of your head are all numbered. Fear not therefore : ye are of more value than many sparrows.

[a] Gen. iv. 3 ; 2 Chron. xxiv. 20, seq.

§ 52. Jesus discourses to his disciples

MATTHEW.	MARK.

and the multitude. *Galilee.*

LUKE.

CH. XII. 1 – 59.

8 Also I say unto you, Whosoever shall confess me before men, him shall the Son of man also confess before the angels of God.

9 But he that denieth me before men, shall be denied before the angels of God.

10 And whosoever shall speak a word against the Son of man, it shall be forgiven him : but unto him that blasphemeth against the Holy Ghost, it shall not be forgiven.

11 And when they bring you unto the synagogues, and *unto* magistrates, and powers, take ye no thought how or what thing ye shall answer, or what ye shall say :

12 For the Holy Ghost shall teach you in the same hour what ye ought to say.

13 And one of the company said unto him, Master, speak to my brother, that he divide the inheritance with me.

14 And he said unto him, Man, who made me a judge, or a divider over you ?

15 And he said unto them, Take heed, and beware of covetousness : for a man's life consisteth not in the abundance of the things which he possesseth.

16 And he spake a parable unto them, saying, The ground of a certain rich man brought forth plentifully :

17 And he thought within himself, saying, What shall I do, because I have no room where to bestow my fruits ?

18 And he said, This will I do : I will pull down my barns, and build greater ; and there will I bestow all my fruits and my goods.

19 And I will say to my soul, Soul, thou hast much goods laid up for many years ; take thine ease, eat, drink, *and* be merry.

20 But God said unto him, *Thou* fool, this night thy soul shall be required of thee : then whose shall those things be, which thou hast provided ?

21 So *is* he that layeth up treasure for himself, and is not rich toward God.

JOHN.

§ 52. Jesus discourses to his disciples

MATTHEW.	MARK.

and the multitude.   *Galilee.*

LUKE.	JOHN.

LUKE.
CH. XII. 1 – 59.

22 And he said unto his disciples, Therefore I say unto you, Take no thought for your life, what ye shall eat; neither for the body, what ye shall put on.

23 The life is more than meat, and the body *is more* than raiment.

24 Consider the ravens : for they neither sow nor reap : which neither have store-house, nor barn ; and God feedeth them. How much more are ye better than the fowls !

25 And which of you with taking thought can add to his stature one cubit ?

26 If ye then be not able to do that thing which is least, why take ye thought for the rest !

27 Consider the lilies how they grow : they toil not, they spin not ; and yet I say unto you, that Solomon in all his glory was not arrayed like one of these.

28 If then God so clothe the grass, which is to-day in the field, and to-morrow is cast into the oven ; how much more *will he clothe* you, O ye of little faith ?

29 And seek not ye what ye shall eat, or what ye shall drink, neither be ye of doubtful mind.

30 For all these things do the nations of the world seek after : and your Father knoweth that ye have need of these things.

31 But rather seek ye the kingdom of God, and all these things shall be added unto you.

32 Fear not, little flock ; for it is your Father's good pleasure to give you the kingdom.

33 Sell that ye have, and give alms : provide yourselves bags which wax not old, a treasure in the heavens that faileth not, where no thief approacheth, neither moth corrupteth.

34 For where your treasure is, there will your heart be also.

35 Let your loins be girded about, and *your* lights burning ;

36 And ye yourselves like unto men that wait for their lord, when he will return from the wedding ; that,

§ 52. Jesus discourses to his disciples

MATTHEW.	MARK.

and the multitude.   *Galilee.*

LUKE.
CH. XII. 1 – 59.

when he cometh and knocketh, they may open unto him immediately.

37 Blessed *are* those servants, whom the lord when he cometh shall find watching : verily, I say unto you, that he shall gird himself, and make them to sit down to meat, and will come forth and serve them.

38 And if he shall come in the second watch, or come in the third watch, and find *them* so, blessed are those servants.

39 And this know, that if the good man of the house had known what hour the thief would come, he would have watched, and not have suffered his house to be broken through.

40 Be ye therefore ready also : for the Son of man cometh at an hour when ye think not.

41 Then Peter said unto him, Lord, speakest thou this parable unto us, or even to all ?

42 And the Lord said, Who then is that faithful and wise steward, whom *his* lord shall make ruler over his household, to give *them their* portion of meat in due season ?

43 Blessed *is* that servant, whom his lord when he cometh shall find so doing.

44 Of a truth I say unto you, That he will make him ruler over all that he hath.

45 But and if that servant say in his heart, My lord delayeth his coming ; and shall begin to beat the menservants, and maidens, and to eat and drink, and to be drunken ;

46 The lord of that servant will come in a day when he looketh not for *him*, and at an hour when he is not aware, and will cut him in sunder, and will appoint him his portion with the unbelievers.

47 And that servant which knew his lord's will, and prepared not *himself*, neither did according to his will, shall be beaten with many *stripes*.

48 But he that knew not, and did commit things worthy of stripes, shall be beaten with few *stripes*. For unto whomsoever much is given, of him

JOHN.

§ 52. Jesus discourses to his disciples

MATTHEW.	MARK.

§ 53. The slaughter of certain Galileans.

and the multitude. *Galilee.*

LUKE.
CH. XII. 1–59.

shall be much required ; and to whom men have committed much, of him they will ask the more.

49 I am come to send fire on the earth, and what will I, if it be already kindled ?

50 But I have a baptism to be baptized with ; and how am I straitened till it be accomplished !

51 Suppose ye that I am come to give peace on earth ? I tell you, Nay ; but rather division :

52 For from henceforth there shall be five in one house divided, three against two, and two against three.

53 The father shall be divided against the son, and the son against the father ; the mother against the daughter, and the daughter against the mother ; the mother-in-law against her daughter-in-law, and the daughter-in-law against her mother-in-law.

54 And he said also to the people, When ye see a cloud rise out of the west, straightway ye say, There cometh a shower ; and so it is.

55 And when *ye see* the south wind blow, ye say, There will be heat ; and it cometh to pass.

56 *Ye* hypocrites, ye can discern the face of the sky, and of the earth ; but how is it, that ye do not discern this time ?

57 Yea, and why even of yourselves judge ye not what is right ?

58 When thou goest with thine adversary to the magistrate, *as thou art* in the way, give diligence that thou mayest be delivered from him ; lest he hale thee to the judge, and the judge deliver thee to the officer, and the officer cast thee into prison.

59 I tell thee, thou shalt not depart thence, till thou hast paid the very last mite.

JOHN.

Parable of the barren fig-tree. *Galilee.*

CH. XIII. 1–9.

THERE were present at that season some that told him of the Galileans, whose blood Pilate had mingled with their sacrifices.

2 And Jesus answering, said unto them, Suppose ye that these Galileans

§ 53. The slaughter of certain Galileans.

MATTHEW.	MARK.

§ 54. The parable

CH. XIII. 1–23.	CH. IV. 1–25.
THE same day went Jesus out of the house, and sat by the sea-side.	AND he began again to teach by the sea-side : and there was gathered unto him a great multitude, so that he entered into a ship, and sat in the sea ; and the whole multitude was by the sea, on the land.
2 And great multitudes were gathered together unto him, so that he went into a ship, and sat ; and the whole multitude stood on the shore.	
3 And he spake many things unto them in parables, saying, Behold, a sower went forth to sow ;	2 And he taught them many things by parables, and said unto them in his doctrine,
	3 Hearken ; Behold, there went out a sower to sow.
4 And when he sowed, some *seeds* fell by the way-side, and the fowls came and devoured them up :	4 And it came to pass as he sowed, some fell by the way-side, and the fowls of the air came and devoured it up.
5 Some fell upon stony places, where they had not much earth : and forthwith they sprung up, because they had no deepness of earth :	5 And some fell on stony ground, where it had not much earth ; and immediately it sprang up, because it had no depth of earth :
6 And when the sun was up, they were scorched ; and because they had no root, they withered away.	6 But when the sun was up it was scorched ; and because it had no root, it withered away.
7 And some fell among thorns ; and the thorns sprung up, and choked them :	7 And some fell among thorns, and the thorns grew up, and choked it, and it yielded no fruit.
8 But other fell into good ground,	8 And other fell on good ground,

Parable of the barren fig-tree. *Galilee.*

LUKE.	JOHN.
CH. XIII. 1 – 9.	

were sinners above all the Galileans,
because they suffered such things?

3 I tell you, Nay; but, except ye
repent, ye shall all likewise perish.

4 Or those eighteen, upon whom
the tower in Siloam fell, and slew
them, think ye that they were sinners
above all men that dwelt in Jerusalem?

5 I tell you, Nay; but, except ye
repent, ye shall all likewise perish.

6 He spake also this parable: A
certain *man* had a fig-tree planted
in his vineyard; and he came and
sought fruit thereon, and found none.

7 Then said he unto the dresser of
his vineyard, Behold, these three
years I come seeking fruit on this fig-
tree, and find none: cut it down;
why cumbereth it the ground?

8 And he answering, said unto him,
Lord, let it alone this year also, till I
shall dig about it, and dung *it :*

9 And if it bear fruit, *well :* and if
not, *then* after that thou shalt cut it
down.

of the sower. *Lake of Galilee.* *Near Capernaum?*

CH. VIII. 4 – 18.

4 And when much people were
gathered together, and were come to
him out of every city, he spake by a
parable:

5 A sower went out to sow his
seed: and as he sowed, some fell by
the way-side; and it was trodden
down, and the fowls of the air devoured it.

6 And some fell upon a rock; and
as soon as it was sprung up, it withered away, because it lacked moisture.

7 And some fell among thorns; and
the thorns sprang up with it, and
choked it.

8 And other fell on good ground,

§ 54. The parable

MATTHEW.	MARK.
CH. XIII. 1-23.	CH. IV. 1-25.

and brought forth fruit, some a hundred-fold, some sixty-fold, some thirty-fold.

9 Who hath ears to hear, let him hear.

10 And the disciples came, and said unto him, Why speakest thou unto them in parables?

11 He answered and said unto them, Because it is given unto you to know the mysteries of the kingdom of heaven, but to them it is not given.

12 For whosoever hath, to him shall be given, and he shall have more abundance : but whosoever hath not, from him shall be taken away even that he hath.

13 Therefore speak I to them in parables : because they seeing, see not ; and hearing, they hear not ; neither do they understand.

14 And in them is fulfilled the prophecy of Esaias,[a] which saith, By hearing ye shall hear, and shall not understand ; and seeing ye shall see, and shall not perceive :

15 For this people's heart is waxed gross, and *their* ears are dull of hearing, and their eyes they have closed ; lest at any time they should see with *their* eyes, and hear with *their* ears, and should understand with *their* heart, and should be converted, and I should heal them.

16 But blessed *are* your eyes, for they see : and your ears, for they hear.

17 For, verily I say unto you, That many prophets and righteous *men* have desired to see *those things* which ye see, and have not seen *them ;* and to hear *those things* which ye hear, and have not heard *them.*

18 Hear ye therefore the parable of the sower.

19 When any one heareth the word of the kingdom, and understandeth *it* not, then cometh the wicked *one,* and catcheth away that which was sown in his heart. This is he which received seed by the way-side.

and did yield fruit that sprang up, and increased, and brought forth, some thirty, and some sixty, and some a hundred.

9 And he said unto them, He that hath ears to hear, let him hear.

10 And when he was alone, they that were about him, with the twelve, asked of him the parable.

11 And he said unto them, Unto you it is given to know the mystery of the kingdom of God : but unto them that are without, all *these* things are done in parables :

12 That seeing they may see, and not perceive ; and hearing they may hear, and not understand ; lest at any time they should be converted, and *their* sins should be forgiven them.

13 And he said unto them, Know ye not this parable? and how then will ye know all parables?

14 The sower soweth the word.

15 And these are they by the way-side, where the word is sown ; but when they have heard, Satan cometh immediately, and taketh away the word that was sown in their hearts.

[a] Is. vi. 9, 10.

of the sower.   Lake of Galilee.   Near Capernaum?

LUKE.	JOHN.

LUKE.

CH. VIII. 4-18.

and sprang up, and bare fruit a hundred-fold. And when he had said these things, he cried, He that hath ears to hear, let him hear.

9 And his disciples asked him, saying, What might this parable be?

10 And he said, Unto you it is given to know the mysteries of the kingdom of God : but to others in parables ; that seeing they might not see, and hearing they might not understand.

11 Now the parable is this : The seed is the word of God.

12 Those by the way-side, are they that hear : then cometh the devil, and taketh away the word out of their hearts, lest they should believe and be saved.

13 They on the rock *are they*, which, when they hear, receive the word with joy ; and these have no

MATTHEW.
CH. XIII. 1-23.

20 But he that received the seed into stony places, the same is he that heareth the word, and anon with joy receiveth it ;

21 Yet hath he not root in himself, but dureth for a while : for when tribulation or persecution ariseth because of the word, by and by he is offended.

22 He also that received seed among the thorns is he that heareth the word ; and the care of this world, and the deceitfulness of riches, choke the word, and he becometh unfruitful.

23 But he that received seed into the good ground is he that heareth the word, and understandeth *it ;* which also beareth fruit, and bringeth forth, some a hundred-fold, some sixty, some thirty.

MARK.
CH. IV. 1-25.

16 And these are they likewise which are sown on stony ground ; who, when they have heard the word, immediately receive it with gladness ;

17 And have no root in themselves, and so endure but for a time : afterward, when affliction or persecution ariseth for the word's sake, immediately they are offended.

18 And these are they which are sown among thorns ; such as hear the word,

19 And the cares of this world, and the deceitfulness of riches, and the lusts of other things entering in, choke the word, and it becometh unfruitful.

20 And these are they which are sown on good ground ; such as hear the word, and receive *it,* and bring forth fruit, some thirty-fold, some sixty, and some a hundred.

21 And he said unto them, Is a candle brought to be put under a bushel, or under a bed ? and not to be set on a candlestick ?

22 For there is nothing hid, which shall not be manifested ; neither was any thing kept secret, but that it should come abroad.

23 If any man have ears to hear, let him hear.

24 And he said unto them, Take heed what ye hear : With what measure ye mete, it shall be measured to you : and unto you that hear shall more be given.

25 For he that hath, to him shall be given : and he that hath not, from him shall be taken even that which he hath.

§ 55. Parable of the tares.

CH. XIII. 24-53.

24 Another parable put he forth unto them, saying, The kingdom of heaven is likened unto a man which sowed good seed in his field :

25 But while men slept, his enemy came and sowed tares among the wheat, and went his way.

26 But when the blade was sprung up, and brought forth fruit, then appeared the tares also.

CH. IV. 26-34.

of the sower.   *Lake of Galilee.   Near Capernaum?*

LUKE.	JOHN.
CH. VIII. 4–18.	

root, which for a while believe, and in time of temptation fall away.

14 And that which fell among thorns, are they, which, when they have heard, go forth, and are choked with cares, and riches, and pleasures of *this* life, and bring no fruit to perfection.

15 But that on the good ground are they, which, in an honest and good heart, having heard the word, keep *it*, and bring forth fruit with patience.

16 No man, when he hath lighted a candle, covereth it with a vessel, or putteth *it* under a bed ; but setteth *it* on a candlestick, that they which enter in may see the light.

17 For nothing is secret, that shall not be made manifest ; neither *anything* hid, that shall not be known, and come abroad.

18 Take heed therefore how ye hear : for whosoever hath, to him shall be given : and whosoever hath not, from him shall be taken even that which he seemeth to have.

Other parables.   *Near Capernaum?*

15

§ 55. Parable of the tares.

MATTHEW.	MARK.
CH. XIII. 24–53.	CH. IV. 26–34.

27 So the servants of the house-holder came and said unto him, Sir, didst not thou sow good seed in thy field? from whence then hath it tares?

28 He said unto them, An enemy hath done this. The servant said unto him, Wilt thou then that we go and gather them up?

29 But he said, Nay; lest while ye gather up the tares, ye root up also the wheat with them.

30 Let both grow together until the harvest: and in the time of harvest I will say to the reapers, Gather ye together first the tares, and bind them in bundles to burn them: but gather the wheat into my barn.

31 Another parable put he forth unto them, saying, The kingdom of heaven is like to a grain of mustard-seed, which a man took, and sowed in his field:

32 Which indeed is the least of all seeds: but when it is grown, it is the greatest among herbs, and becometh a tree, so that the birds of the air come and lodge in the branches thereof.

33 Another parable spake he unto them; The kingdom of heaven is like unto leaven, which a woman took, and hid in three measures of meal, till the whole was leavened.

34 All these things spake Jesus unto the multitude in parables; and without a parable spake he not unto them:

35 That it might be fulfilled which was spoken by the prophet,[a] saying, I will open my mouth in parables; I will utter things which have been kept secret from the foundation of the world.

36 Then Jesus sent the multitude away, and went into the house: and his disciples came unto him, saying, Declare unto us the parable of the tares of the field.

37 He answered and said unto them, He that soweth the good seed is the Son of man;

38 The field is the world; the good seed are the children of the kingom;

26 And he said, So is the kingdom of God, as if a man should cast seed into the ground;

27 And should sleep, and rise night and day, and the seed should spring and grow up, he knoweth not how.

28 For the earth bringeth forth fruit of herself; first the blade, then the ear, after that the full corn in the ear.

29 But when the fruit is brought forth, immediately he putteth in the sickle, because the harvest is come.

30 And he said, Whereunto shall we liken the kingdom of God? or with what comparison shall we compare it?

31 It is like a grain of mustard-seed, which when it is sown in the earth, is less than all the seeds that be in the earth:

32 But when it is sown, it groweth up, and becometh greater than all herbs, and shooteth out great branches; so that the fowls of the air may lodge under the shadow of it.

33 And with many such parables spake he the word unto them, as they were able to hear it.

34 But without a parable spake he not unto them: and when they were alone, he expounded all things to his disciples.

[a] Ps. lxxviii. 2.

Other parables. *Near Capernaum?*

LUKE.	JOHN.

§ 55. Parable of the tares.

MATTHEW.	MARK.
CH. XIII. 24–53.	

but the tares are the children of the wicked *one;*

39 The enemy that sowed them is the devil; the harvest is the end of the world; and the reapers are the angels.

40 As therefore the tares are gathered and burned in the fire; so shall it be in the end of this world.

41 The Son of man shall send forth his angels, and they shall gather out of his kingdom all things that offend, and them which do iniquity;

42 And shall cast them into a furnace of fire: there shall be wailing and gnashing of teeth.

43 Then shall the righteous shine forth as the sun in the kingdom of their Father. Who hath ears to hear, let him hear.

44 Again, The kingdom of heaven is like unto treasure hid in a field; the which when a man hath found, he hideth, and for joy thereof goeth and selleth all that he hath, and buyeth that field.

45 Again, The kingdom of heaven is like unto a merchant-man seeking goodly pearls:

46 Who, when he had found one pearl of great price, went and sold all that he had, and bought it.

47 Again, The kingdom of heaven is like unto a net, that was cast into the sea, and gathered of every kind:

48 Which, when it was full, they drew to shore, and sat down, and gathered the good into vessels, but cast the bad away.

49 So shall it be at the end of the world: the angels shall come forth, and sever the wicked from among the just,

50 And shall cast them into the furnace of fire: there shall be wailing and gnashing of teeth.

51 Jesus saith unto them, Have ye understood all these things? They say unto him, Yea, Lord.

52 Then said he unto them, Therefore every scribe *which is* instructed unto the kingdom of heaven, is like unto a man *that is* a householder,

Other parables. *Near Capernaum ?*

LUKE.   JOHN.

§ 55. Parable of the tares.

MATTHEW.	MARK.
CH. XIII. 24 – 53.	
which bringeth forth out of his treasure *things* new and old.	
53 And it came to pass, *that* when Jesus had finished these parables, he departed thence.	

§ 56. Jesus directs to cross the lake. Incidents.

CH. VIII. 18 – 27.	CH. IV. 35 – 41.
18 Now when Jesus saw great multitudes about him, he gave commandment to depart unto the other side.	35 And the same day, when the even was come, he saith unto them, Let us pass over unto the other side.
19 And a certain scribe came, and said unto him, Master, I will follow thee whithersoever thou goest.	
20 And Jesus saith unto him, The foxes have holes, and the birds of the air *have* nests; but the Son of man hath not where to lay *his* head.	
21 And another of his disciples said unto him, Lord, suffer me first to go and bury my father.	
22 But Jesus said unto him, Follow me; and let the dead bury their dead.	
23 And when he was entered into a ship, his disciples followed him.	36 And when they had sent away the multitude, they took him even as he was in the ship. And there were also with him other little ships.
24 And behold, there arose a great tempest in the sea, insomuch that the ship was covered with the waves: but he was asleep.	37 And there arose a great storm of wind, and the waves beat into the ship, so that it was now full.
25 And his disciples came to *him*, and awoke him, saying, Lord, save us: we perish.	38 And he was in the hinder part of the ship, asleep on a pillow: and they awake him, and say unto him, Master, carest thou not that we perish?
26 And he saith unto them, Why are ye fearful, O ye of little faith? Then he arose, and rebuked the winds and the sea; and there was a great calm.	39 And he arose, and rebuked the wind, and said unto the sea, Peace, be still: and the wind ceased, and there was a great calm.
	40 And he said unto them, Why are ye so fearful? how is it that ye have no faith?

Other parables. *Near Capernaum?*

LUKE.	JOHN.

The tempest stilled. *Lake of Galilee.*

CH. VIII. 22 – 25.

CH. IX. 57 – 62.

22 Now it came to pass on a certain day, that he went into a ship with his disciples : and he said unto them, Let us go over unto the other side of the lake.

CH. IX.

57 And it came to pass, that as they went in the way, a certain *man* said unto him, Lord, I will follow thee whithersoever thou goest.

58 And Jesus said unto him, Foxes have holes, and birds of the air *have* nests ; but the Son of man hath not where to lay *his* head.

59 And he said unto another, Follow me. But he said, Lord, suffer me first to go and bury my father.

60 Jesus said unto him, Let the dead bury their dead : but go thou and preach the kingdom of God.

61 And another also said, Lord, I will follow thee ; but let me first go bid them farewell which are at home at my house.

62 And Jesus said unto him, No man having put his hand to the plough, and looking back, is fit for the kingdom of God.

CH. VIII.

22 And they launched forth.

23 But as they sailed, he fell asleep: and there came down a storm of wind on the lake ; and they were filled *with water*, and were in jeopardy.

24 And they came to him, and awoke him, saying, Master, Master, we perish. Then he .arose, and rebuked the wind, and the raging of the water : and they ceased, and there was a calm.

25 And he said unto them, Where is your faith ? And they being afraid,

§ 56. Jesus directs to cross the lake. Incidents.

MATTHEW. CH. VIII. 18 – 27.	MARK. CH. IV. 35 – 41.
27 But the men marvelled, saying, What manner of man is this, that even the winds and the sea obey him!	41 And they feared exceedingly, and said one to another, What manner of man is this, that even the wind and the sea obey him?

§ 57. The two demoniacs

CH. VIII. 28 – 34. CH. IX. 1.	CH. V. 1 – 21.
28 And when he was come to the other side, into the country of the Gergesenes, there met him two possessed with devils, coming out of the tombs, exceeding fierce, so that no man might pass by that way.	AND they came over unto the other side of the sea, into the country of the Gadarenes. 2 And when he was come out of the ship, immediately there met him out of the tombs a man with an unclean spirit, 3 Who had *his* dwelling among the tombs ; and no man could bind him, no, not with chains : 4 Because that he had been often bound with fetters and chains, and the chains had been plucked asunder by him, and the fetters broken in pieces : neither could any *man* tame him. 5 And always, night and day, he was in the mountains, and in the tombs, crying, and cutting himself with stones. 6 But when he saw Jesus afar off, he ran and worshipped him, 7 And cried with a loud voice, and said, What have I to do with thee, Jesus, *thou* Son of the most high God? I adjure thee by God, that thou torment me not. 8 (For he said unto him, Come out of the man, *thou* unclean spirit.)
29 And behold, they cried out,	9 And he asked him, What *is* thy

Matth. viii. 28, *Gergesenes.*] This is made consistent with the other Evangelists, by reading "Gadarenes." If Gergasa was subordinate to Gadara, the metropolis of Perea, as Cellamies and Reland judge, and St. Mark did not write in Judea, what wonder that he chose the more general name, which was best known in the world? But Cellarius from Eusebius takes notice that some esteemed Gergasi, so Eusebius writes it, and Gadara two names of the same city ; and this he thinks was the sentiment of the Syriac translator. To this Sir Richard Ellis most inclines, in his Fortuita Sacra. Townson, p. 72.

The tempest stilled.　*Lake of Galilee.*

LUKE.	JOHN.
CH. VIII. 22–25. CH. IX. 57–62. wondered, saying one to another, What manner of man is this! for he commandeth even the winds and water, and they obey him.	

of Gadara.　*S. E. coast of the Lake of Galilee.*

CH. VIII. 26–40.

26 And they arrived at the country
of the Gadarenes, which is over
against Galilee.

27 And when he went forth to land,
there met him out of the city a certain man, which had devils long time,
and ware no clothes, neither abode in
any house, but in the tombs.

28 When he saw Jesus, he cried
out, and fell down before him, and
with a loud voice said, What have I
to do with thee, Jesus, *thou* Son of
God most high? I beseech thee torment me not.

29 (For he had commanded the
unclean spirit to come out of the man.
For oftentimes it had caught him:
and he was kept bound with chains,
and in fetters; and he brake the bands,
and was driven of the devil into the
wilderness.)

30 And Jesus asked him, saying,

In Matthew mention is made of two demoniacs; in Mark and Luke of one only.
Here Le Clerc's maxim is undoubtedly true: Qui plura narrat, pauciora complectitur:
qui pauciora memorat, plura non negat. *Harm.* p. 524.

We may collect a reason from the Gospels themselves, why Mark and Luke mention only one demoniac; because, one only being grateful for the miracle, his cure
only was recorded by the two Evangelists, who mention this gratitude, and who
are more intent on inculcating the moral, than on magnifying our Lord's power.
NEWCOME.

§ 57. The two demoniacs

MATTHEW.	MARK.
CH. VIII. 28–34.	CH. V. 1–21.
CH. IX. 1.	

saying, What have we to do with thee, Jesus, thou Son of God? art thou come hither to torment us before the time?

30 And there was a good way off from them a herd of many swine, feeding.

31 So the devils besought him, saying, If thou cast us out, suffer us to go away into the herd of swine.

32 And he said unto them, Go. And when they were come out, they went into the herd of swine: and behold, the whole herd of swine ran violently down a steep place into the sea, and perished in the waters.

33 And they that kept them, fled, and went their ways into the city, and told everything; and what was befallen to the possessed of the devils.

34 And behold, the whole city came out to meet Jesus: and when they saw him, they besought him that he would depart out of their coasts.

CH. IX.

AND he entered into a ship, and passed over, and came into his own city.

name? And he answered, saying, My name is Legion: for we are many.

10 And he besought him much that he would not send them away out of the country.

11 Now there was there nigh unto the mountains a great herd of swine feeding.

12 And all the devils besought him, saying, Send us into the swine, that we may enter into them.

13 And forthwith Jesus gave them leave. And the unclean spirits went out, and entered into the swine: and the herd ran violently down a steep place into the sea, (they were about two thousand) and were choked in the sea.

14 And they that fed the swine fled, and told it in the city, and in the country. And they went out to see what it was that was done.

15 And they come to Jesus, and see him that was possessed with the devil, and had the legion, sitting, and clothed, and in his right mind: and they were afraid.

16 And they that saw it told them how it befell to him that was possessed with the devil, and also concerning the swine.

17 And they began to pray him to depart out of their coasts.

18 And when he was come into the ship, he that had been possessed with the devil prayed him that he might be with him.

19 Howbeit Jesus suffered him not, but saith unto him, Go home to thy

---

Matth. viii. 30, *a good way off.*] There is no contradiction here between Matth. and Mark. The demoniacs met Jesus on the shore, as he came out of the ship. Luke viii. 27. The swine were within sight, on the ascending ground, Luke viii. 32, at the side of the mountain, Mark v. 11, which was at some distance from the shore where they stood. Matth. viii. 30.

Mark v. 11, *herd of swine.*] Since swine were held in abhorrence by the Jews, how happened a herd of them to be feeding by the sea of Tiberias? The answer shows the accuracy of the Evangelist and his intimate knowledge of the local circumstances of Judea; for it appears from Josephus, Antiq. xvii. 11, 4, that *Gadara* was a *Grecian city*, the inhabitants of which, therefore, were not Jews. BLUNT, Veracity, &c. sect. ii. 6.

of Gadara. *S. E. coast of the Lake of Galilee.*

LUKE.	JOHN.
CH. VIII. 26 – 40.	

What is thy name? And he said, Legion: because many devils were entered into him.

31 And they besought him, that he would not command them to go out into the deep.

32 And there was there a herd of many swine feeding on the mountain : and they besought him that he would suffer them to enter into them. And he suffered them.

33 Then went the devils out of the man, and entered into the swine : and the herd ran violently down a steep place into the lake, and were choked.

34 When they that fed *them* saw what was done, they fled, and went and told *it* in the city and in the country.

35 Then they went out to see what was done ; and came to Jesus, and found the man out of whom the devils were departed, sitting at the feet of Jesus, clothed, and in his right mind : and they were afraid.

36 They also which saw *it*, told them by what means he that was possessed of the devils was healed.

37 Then the whole multitude of the country of the Gadarenes round about, besought him to depart from them ; for they were taken with great fear. And he went up into the ship, and returned back again.

38 Now, the man out of whom the devils were departed, besought him that he might be with him. But Jesus sent him away, saying,

---

Luke viii. 35, *sitting at the feet of Jesus*.] Here is a reference to an Eastern custom, which affords internal evidence of the truth of the narrative. The master sat on a higher seat, and the scholars sat at his feet. Sitting at the feet, was the posture of a learner ; and indicated the reverence and submission due to the teacher. Thus Moses says of the people, to whom God gave the law from mount Sinai, — "they sat down at thy feet." Deut. xxxiii. 3. Isaiah, speaking of Abraham, who was taught of God, says "he called him to his foot." Is. xli. 2. Mary "sat at Jesus's feet and heard his words." Luke x. 39. Paul was brought up "at the feet of Gamaliel ; " Acts xxii. 3 ; studied law with him. And the restored maniac sat down at Jesus's feet, in the posture of a humble learner, desiring no other wisdom than to be taught of him.

§ 57. The two demoniacs

MATTHEW.	MARK.
	CH. V. 1–21.
	friends, and tell them how great things the Lord hath done for thee, and hath had compassion on thee.
	20 And he departed, and began to publish in Decapolis how great things Jesus had done for him. And all *men* did marvel.
	21 And when Jesus was passed over again by ship unto the other side, much people gathered unto him : and he was nigh unto the sea.

§ 58. Levi's feast.

CH. IX. 10–17.	CH. II. 15–22.
10 And it came to pass, as Jesus sat at meat in the house, behold, many publicans and sinners came and sat down with him and his disciples.	15 And it came to pass, that as Jesus sat at meat in his house, many publicans and sinners sat also together with Jesus and his disciples ; for there were many, and they followed him.
11 And when the Pharisees saw *it*, they said unto his disciples, Why eateth your Master with publicans and sinners ?	16 And when the scribes and Pharisees saw him eat with publicans and sinners, they said unto his disciples, How is it that he eateth and drinketh with publicans and sinners ?
12 But when Jesus heard *that*, he said unto them, They that be whole need not a physician, but they that are sick.	17 When Jesus heard *it*, he saith unto them, They that are whole, have no need of the physician, but they that are sick : I came not to call the righteous, but sinners to repentance.
13 But go ye and learn what *that* meaneth,[a] I will have mercy, and not sacrifice : for I am not come to call the righteous, but sinners to repentance.	18 And the disciples of John, and of the Pharisees, used to fast : and they come, and say unto him, Why do the disciples of John, and of the Pharisees fast, but thy disciples fast not ?
14 Then came to him the disciples of John, saying, Why do we and the Pharisees fast oft, but thy disciples fast not ?	
15 And Jesus said unto them, Can the children of the bride-chamber mourn, as long as the bridegroom is with them ? but the days will come, when the bridegroom shall be taken from them, and then shall they fast.	19 And Jesus said unto them, Can the children of the bride-chamber fast, while the bridegroom is with them ? As long as they have the bridegroom with them, they cannot fast.
	20 But the days will come, when the bridegroom shall be taken away from them, and then shall they fast in those days.
16 No man putteth a piece of new cloth unto an old garment : for that	21 No man also seweth a piece of new cloth on an old garment : else

[a] Hos. vi. 6 ; 1 Sam. xv. 22.

Matth. ix. 10, *in the house*.] Both Mark and Luke state that this was in Matthew's own house ; and Luke calls it a great feast, made in honor of Jesus. The omission of

of Gadara. S. E. coast of the Lake of Galilee.

LUKE.	JOHN.
CH. VIII. 26—40.	

39 Return to thine own house, and shew how great things God hath done unto thee.   And he went his way and published throughout the whole city, how great things Jesus had done unto him.

40 And it came to pass, that, when Jesus was returned, the people *gladly* received him : for they were all waiting for him.

Capernaum.

CH. V. 29—39.

29 And Levi made him a great feast in his own house ; and there was a great company of publicans, and of others that sat down with them.

30 But their scribes and Pharisees murmured against his disciples, saying, Why do ye eat and drink with publicans and sinners ?

31 And Jesus answering, said unto them, They that are whole need not a physician ; but they that are sick.

32 I came not to call the righteous, but sinners to repentance.

33 And they said unto him, Why do the disciples of John fast often, and make prayers, and likewise *the disciples* of the Pharisees ; but thine eat and drink ?

34 And he said unto them, Can ye make the children of the bride-chamber fast while the bridegroom is with them?

35 But the days will come, when the bridegroom shall be taken away from them, and then shall they fast in those days.

36 And he spake also a parable unto them : No man putteth a piece of a new garment upon an old : if other-

---

this fact by Matthew, not only shows his modesty and humility, but adds much to the weight of evidence in his favor, both as a man, and as a witness. See BLUNT's Veracity of the Gospels, Sect, i. 4.

§ 58. Levi's feast.

MATTHEW.
CH. IX. 10 – 17.
which is put in to fill it up, taketh
from the garment, and the rent is
made worse.

17 Neither do men put new wine
into old bottles : else the bottles break,
and the wine runneth out, and the
bottles perish : but they put new wine
into new bottles, and both are preserved.

MARK.
CH. II. 15 – 22.
the new piece that filled it up, taketh
away from the old, and the rent is
made worse.

22 And no man putteth new wine
into old bottles : else the new wine
doth burst the bottles, and the wine is
spilled, and the bottles will be marred :
but new wine must be put into new
bottles.

§ 59. The raising of Jairus's daughter.

CH. IX. 18 – 26.
18 While he spake these things
unto them, behold, there came a certain ruler, and worshipped him, saying, My daughter is even now dead :
but come and lay thy hand upon her,
and she shall live.

19 And Jesus arose, and followed
him, and so did his disciples.

20 (And behold, a woman which
was diseased with an issue of blood
twelve years, came behind him, and
touched the hem of his garment.

21 For she said within herself, If I
may but touch his garment, I shall be
whole.

22 But Jesus turned him about, and
when he saw her, he said, Daughter,
be of good comfort : thy faith hath
made thee whole. And the woman
was made whole from that hour.)

CH. V. 22 – 43.
22 And behold, there cometh one
of the rulers of the synagogue, Jairus
by name ; and when he saw him, he
fell at his feet,

23 And besought him greatly, saying, My little daughter lieth at the
point of death : I pray thee, come and
lay thy hands on her, that she may
be healed ; and she shall live.

24 And Jesus went with him ; and
much people followed him, and
thronged him.

25 And a certain woman which had
an issue of blood twelve years,

26 And had suffered many things
of many physicians, and had spent all
that she had, and was nothing bettered,
but rather grew worse,

27 When she had heard of Jesus,
came in the press behind, and touched
his garment :

28 For she said, If I may touch but
his clothes, I shall be whole.

29 And straightway the fountain of
her blood was dried up ; and she felt
in her body that she was healed of
that plague.

30 And Jesus, immediately knowing in himself that virtue had gone
out of him, turned him about in the
press, and said, Who touched my
clothes ?

31 And his disciples said unto him,
Thou seest the multitude thronging
thee, and sayest thou, Who touched
me ?

32 And he looked round about to
see her that had done this thing.

Capernaum.

LUKE.	JOHN.

LUKE.
CH. V.　29 – 39.

wise, then both the new maketh a rent,
and the piece that was *taken* out of the
new, agreeth not with the old.

37 And no man putteth new wine
into old bottles ; else the new wine
will burst the bottles, and be spilled,
and the bottles shall perish.

38 But new wine must be put into
new bottles, and both are preserved.

39 No man also having drunk old
wine, straightway desireth new : for
he saith, The old is better.

The woman with a bloody flux.　*Capernaum.*

CH. VIII.　41 – 56.

41 And behold, there came a man
named Jairus, and he was a ruler of
the synagogue : and he fell down at
Jesus' feet, and besought him that
he would come into his house :

42 For he had one only daughter,
about twelve years of age, and she
lay a-dying. But as he went, the people thronged him.

43 And a woman having an issue
of blood twelve years, which had spent
all her living upon physicians, neither
could be healed of any,

44 Came behind *him* and touched
the border of his garment : and immediately her issue of blood stanched.

45 And Jesus said, Who touched
me? When all denied, Peter, and
they that were with him, said, Master, the multitude throng thee, and
press *thee*, and sayest thou, Who
touched me?

46 And Jesus said, Somebody hath
touched me : for I perceive that virtue
is gone out of me.

§ 59. The raising of Jairus's daughter.

MATTHEW.	MARK.
CH. IX.　18–26.	CH. V.　22–43.

MATTHEW. CH. IX. 18–26.	MARK. CH. V. 22–43.
	33 But the woman, fearing and trembling, knowing what was done in her, came and fell down before him, and told him all the truth.
	34 And he said unto her, Daughter, thy faith hath made thee whole ; go in peace, and be whole of thy plague.
	35 While he yet spake, there came from the ruler of the synagogue's *house certain* which said, Thy daughter is dead : why troublest thou the Master any further ?
	36 As soon as Jesus heard the word that was spoken, he saith unto the ruler of the synagogue, Be not afraid, only believe.
	37 And he suffered no man to follow him, save Peter, and James, and John the brother of James.
23 And when Jesus came into the ruler's house, and saw the minstrels and the people making a noise,	38 And he cometh to the house of the ruler of the synagogue, and seeth the tumult, and them that wept and wailed greatly.
24 He said unto them, Give place : for the maid is not dead, but sleepeth. And they laughed him to scorn.	39 And when he was come in, he saith unto them, Why make ye this ado, and weep? the damsel is not
25 But when the people were put forth, he went in, and took her by the hand, and the maid arose.	dead, but sleepeth.
26 And the fame hereof went abroad into all that land.	40 And they laughed him to scorn. But, when he had put them all out, he taketh the father and the mother of the damsel, and them that were with him, and entereth in where the damsel was lying.
	41 And he took the damsel by the hand, and said unto her, Talitha-cumi : which is, being interpreted, Damsel, (I say unto thee) arise.
	42 And straightway the damsel arose, and walked ; for she was *of the age* of twelve years. And they were astonished with a great astonishment.
	43 And he charged them straitly that no man should know it ; and commanded that something should be given her to eat.

§ 60.　Two blind men healed,

CH. IX.　27–34.
27 And when Jesus departed thence, two blind men followed him, crying, and saying, *Thou* son of David, have mercy on us.

The woman with a bloody flux.   *Capernaum.*

LUKE.
CH. VIII. 41–56.

47 And when the woman saw that she was not hid, she came trembling, and falling down before him, she declared unto him before all the people for what cause she had touched him, and how she was healed immediately.

48 And he said unto her, Daughter, be of good comfort : thy faith hath made thee whole ; go in peace.

49 While he yet spake, there cometh one from the ruler of the synagogue's *house,* saying to him, Thy daughter is dead : trouble not the Master.

50 But when Jesus heard *it,* he answered him, saying, Fear not : believe only, and she shall be made whole.

51 And when he came into the house, he suffered no man to go in, save Peter, and James, and John, and the father and the mother of the maiden.

52 And all wept and bewailed her : but he said, Weep not : she is not dead, but sleepeth.

53 And they laughed him to scorn, knowing that she was dead.

54 And he put them all out, and took her by the hand, and called, saying, Maid, arise.

55 And her spirit came again, and she arose straightway : and he commanded to give her meat.

56 And her parents were astonished : but he charged them that they should tell no man what was done.

JOHN.

and a dumb spirit cast out.   *Capernaum.*

§ 60. Two blind men healed,

MATTHEW.	MARK.

MATTHEW.

CH. IX. 27 – 34.

28 And when he was come into the house, the blind men came to him : and Jesus saith unto them, Believe ye that I am able to do this? They said unto him, Yea, Lord.

29 Then touched he their eyes, saying, According to your faith, be it unto you.

30 And their eyes were opened ; and Jesus straitly charged them, saying, See *that* no man know *it.*

31 But they, when they were departed, spread abroad his fame in all that country.

32 As they went out, behold, they brought to him a dumb man possessed with a devil.

33 And when the devil was cast out, the dumb spake : and the multitudes marvelled, saying, It was never so seen in Israel.

34 But the Pharisees said, He casteth out devils, through the prince of the devils.

§ 61. Jesus again at Nazareth,

CH. XIII. 54 – 58.	CH. VI. 1 – 6.

CH. XIII.   54 – 58.

54 And when he was come into his own country, he taught them in their synagogue, insomuch that they were astonished, and said, Whence hath this *man* this wisdom, and *these* mighty works?

55 Is not this the carpenter's son? is not his mother called Mary? and his brethren, James, and Joses, and Simon, and Judas?

56 And his sisters, are they not all with us? Whence then hath this *man* all these things?

57 And they were offended in him. But Jesus said unto them, A prophet is not without honor, save in his own country, and in his own house.

58 And he did not many mighty works there, because of their unbelief.

CH. VI.   1 – 6.

AND he went out from thence, and came into his own country ; and his disciples follow him.

2 And when the sabbath-day was come, he began to teach in the synagogue : and many hearing *him* were astonished, saying, From whence hath this *man* these things? and what wisdom *is* this which is given unto him, that even such mighty works are wrought by his hands?

3 Is not this the carpenter, the son of Mary, the brother of James, and Joses, and of Juda, and Simon? and are not his sisters here with us? And they were offended at him.

4 But Jesus said unto them, A prophet is not without honor, but in his own country, and among his own kin, and in his own house.

5 And he could there do no mighty work, save that he laid his hands upon a few sick folk, and healed *them.*

6 And he marvelled because of their unbelief.

Mark vi. 3, *son of Mary.*] Neither of the Evangelists expressly mentions the death of Joseph ; yet from all four of them it may indirectly be inferred to have happened

and a dumb spirit cast out.   *Capernaum.*

LUKE.	JOHN.

and again rejected.

while Jesus was yet alive. Comp. Luke viii. 19, John ii. 12, and xix. 25 -27. Such harmony as this could not have been the effect of concert. See BLUNT's Veracity, &c. Sect. i. 7.

§ 62. A third circuit in Galilee.

MATTHEW.	MARK.

MATTHEW.
CH. IX. 35–38. CH. X. 1, 5–42.
CH. XI. 1.

35 And Jesus went about all the cities and villages, teaching in their synagogues, and preaching the gospel of the kingdom, and healing every sickness, and every disease among the people.

36 But when he saw the multitudes, he was moved with compassion on them, because they fainted, and were scattered abroad, as sheep having no shepherd.

37 Then saith he unto his disciples, The harvest truly *is* plenteous, but the laborers *are* few.

38 Pray ye therefore the Lord of the harvest, that he will send forth laborers into his harvest.

CH. X.

AND when he had called unto *him* his twelve disciples, he gave them power *against* unclean spirits, to cast them out, and to heal all manner of sickness, and all manner of disease.

5 These twelve Jesus sent forth, and commanded them, saying, Go not into the way of the Gentiles, and into *any* city of the Samaritans enter ye not.

6 But go rather to the lost sheep of the house of Israel.

7 And as ye go, preach, saying, The kingdom of heaven is at hand.

8 Heal the sick, cleanse the lepers, raise the dead, cast out devils : freely ye have received, freely give.

9 Provide neither gold, nor silver, nor brass in your purses ;

10 Nor scrip for *your* journey, neither two coats, neither shoes, nor yet staves : (for the workman is worthy of his meat.)

11 And into whatsoever city or town ye shall enter, inquire who in it is worthy ; and there abide till ye go thence.

12 And when ye come into a house, salute it.

MARK.
CH. VI. 6–13.

7 And he called *unto him* the twelve, and began to send them forth by two and two, and gave them power over unclean spirits ;

8 And commanded them that they should take nothing for *their* journey, save a staff only ; no scrip, no bread, no money in *their* purse :

9 But *be* shod with sandals ; and not put on two coats.

10 And he said unto them, In what place soever ye enter into a house, there abide till ye depart from that place.

Matth. x. 10, *shoes.*] Commentators have noted two inconsistent circumstances in this section. In Matthew, *shoes* are forbidden ; in Mark the apostles are commanded to be shod with *sandals*. But the true solution seems to be this, that the Apostles

The Twelve instructed and sent forth. *Galilee.*

LUKE.	JOHN.
CH. IX. 1 – 6.	

THEN he called his twelve disciples together, and gave them power and authority over all devils, and to cure diseases.

2 And he sent them to preach the kingdom of God, and to heal the sick.

3 And he said unto them, Take nothing for *your* journey, neither staves, nor scrip, neither bread, neither money ; neither have two coats apiece.

4 And whatsoever house ye enter into, there abide, and thence depart.

5 And whosoever will not receive you, when ye go out of that city, shake off the very dust from your feet for a testimony against them.

should not furnish themselves with *spare* garments, and should wear the simplest covering for their feet. " Non vult ullis rebus studiose comparatis onerari." BEZA. See NEWCOME, in loc.

§ 62. A third circuit in Galilee.

MATTHEW.
CH. IX. 35–38.   CH. X. 1, 5–42.
CH. XI. 1.

13 And if the house be worthy, let your peace come upon it : but if it be not worthy, let your peace return to you.

14 And whosoever shall not receive you, nor hear your words, when ye depart out of that house, or city, shake off the dust of your feet.

15 Verily, I say unto you, It shall be more tolerable for the land of Sodom and Gomorrah, in the day of judgment, than for that city.

16 Behold, I send you forth as sheep in the midst of wolves : be ye therefore wise as serpents, and harmless as doves.

17 But beware of men : for they will deliver you up to the councils, and they will scourge you in their synagogues.

18 And ye shall be brought before governors and kings for my sake, for a testimony against them and the Gentiles.

19 But when they deliver you up, take no thought how or what ye shall speak, for it shall be given you in that same hour what ye shall speak.

20 For it is not ye that speak, but the Spirit of your Father which speaketh in you.

21 And the brother shall deliver up the brother to death, and the father the child : and the children shall rise up against *their* parents, and cause them to be put to death.

22 And ye shall be hated of all *men* for my name's sake : but he that endureth to the end shall be saved.

23 But when they persecute you in this city, flee ye into another : for verily I say unto you, Ye shall not have gone over the cities of Israel till the Son of man be come.

24 The disciple is not above *his* master, nor the servant above his lord.

25 It is enough for the disciple that he be as his master, and the servant as his lord : if they have called the master of the house Beelzebub, how

MARK.
CH. VI. 6–13.

11 And whosoever shall not receive you, nor hear you, when ye depart thence, shake off the dust under your feet, for a testimony against them. Verily, I say unto you, it shall be more tolerable for Sodom and Gomorrah in the day of judgment, than for that city.

The Twelve instructed and sent forth.   *Galilee.*

| LUKE. | JOHN. |

MATTHEW.

CH. IX. 35–38. CH. X. 1, 5–42.
CH. XI. 1.

much more *shall they call* them of his household !

26 Fear them not therefore : for there is nothing covered, that shall not be revealed ; and hid, that shall not be known.

27 What I tell you in darkness, *that* speak ye in light : and what ye hear in the ear, *that* preach ye upon the house-tops.

28 And fear not them which kill the body, but are not able to kill the soul : but rather fear him which is able to destroy both soul and body in hell.

29 Are not two sparrows sold for a farthing? and one of them shall not fall on the ground without your Father.

30 But the very hairs of your head are all numbered.

31 Fear ye not therefore, ye are of more value than many sparrows.

32 Whosoever therefore shall confess me before men, him will I confess also before my Father which is in heaven.

33 But whosoever shall deny me before men, him will I also deny before my Father which is in heaven.

34 Think not that I am come to send peace on earth ; I came not to send peace, but a sword.

35 For I am come to set a man at variance against his father, and the daughter against her mother, and the daughter-in-law against her mother-in-law.

36 And a man's foes *shall be* they of his own household.[a]

37 He that loveth father or mother more than me, is not worthy of me : and he that loveth son or daughter more than me, is not worthy of me.

38 And he that taketh not his cross, and followeth after me, is not worthy of me.

39 He that findeth his life shall lose it : and he that loseth his life for my sake, shall find it.

MARK.

[a] Mic. vii. 6.

The Twelve instructed and sent forth. *Galilee.*

LUKE.	JOHN.

§ 62. A third circuit in Galilee.

MATTHEW.	MARK.
CH. IX. 35–38. CH. X. 1, 5–42.	CH. VI. 6, 13.
CH. XI. 1.	

40 He that receiveth you, receiveth me ; and he that receiveth me, receiveth him that sent me.

41 He that receiveth a prophet in the name of a prophet, shall receive a prophet's reward ; and he that receiveth a righteous man in the name of a righteous man, shall receive a righteous man's reward.

42 And whosoever shall give to drink unto one of these little ones, a cup of cold *water* only, in the name of a disciple, verily, I say unto you, he shall in no wise lose his reward.

CH. XI.

AND it came to pass when Jesus had made an end of commanding his twelve disciples, he departed thence to teach and to preach in their cities.

6   And he went round about the villages teaching.

12 And they went out, and preached that men should repent.

13 And they cast out many devils, and anointed with oil many that were sick, and healed *them.*

---

§ 63. Herod holds Jesus to be John the Baptist,

CH. XIV. 1, 2, 6–12.	CH. VI. 14–16, 21–29.

AT that time Herod the tetrarch heard of the fame of Jesus,

2 And said unto his servants, This is John the Baptist ; he is risen from the dead ; and therefore mighty works do shew forth themselves in him.

14 And king Herod heard *of him,* (for his name was spread abroad,) and he said, That John the Baptist was risen from the dead, and therefore mighty works do shew forth themselves in him.

15 Others said, That it is Elias. And others said, That it is a prophet, or as one of the prophets.

16 But when Herod heard *thereof,* he said, It is John, whom I beheaded : he is risen from the dead.

6 But when Herod's birth-day was kept, the daughter of Herodias danced before them, and pleased Herod.

21 And when a convenient day was come, that Herod on his birthday made a supper to his lords, high captains, and chief *estates* of Galilee :

22 And when the daughter of the said Herodias came in, and danced, and pleased Herod, and them that sat with him, the king said unto the damsel, Ask of me whatsoever thou wilt, and I will give *it* thee.

7 Whereupon he promised with an oath to give her whatsoever she would ask.

23 And he sware unto her, What-

Matth. xiv. 2, *unto his servants.*] Matthew alone mentions, and without any apparent reason for such minuteness, that Herod addressed his remark to his *servants.* Luke, in the parallel passage, says he *heard of all that was done by him ;* but by re-

The Twelve instructed and sent forth.

LUKE.	JOHN.
6 And they departed, and went through the towns, preaching the gospel, and healing everywhere.	

whom he had just before beheaded.　*Galilee ? Perea.*

| CH. IX. 7–9.
7 Now Herod the tetrarch heard of all that was done by him: and he was perplexed, because that it was said of some, that John was risen from the dead ;
8 And of some, that Elias had appeared ; and of others, that one of the old prophets was risen again.
9 And Herod said, John have I beheaded ; but who is this of whom I hear such things ? And he desired to see him. | |

ferring to Luke viii. 3, and to Acts xiii. 1, we find that Christ had followers from among the household of this very prince, with whom Herod was likely to converse on a subject in which they were better informed than himself. BLUNT, Veracity, &c., sec. i, 8.

§ 63. Herod holds Jesus to be John the Baptist,

MATTHEW.	MARK.
CH. XIV. 1, 2, 6 – 12.	CH. VI. 14 – 16, 21 – 29.
	soever thou shalt ask of me, I will give *it* thee, unto the half of my kingdom.
	24 And she went forth, and said unto her mother, What shall I ask? And she said, The head of John the Baptist.
8 And she, being before instructed of her mother, said, Give me here John Baptist's head in a charger.	25 And she came in straightway with haste unto the king, and asked, saying, I will that thou give me, by and by, in a charger, the head of John the Baptist.
9 And the king was sorry : nevertheless for the oath's sake, and them which sat with him at meat, he commanded *it* to be given *her*.	26 And the king was exceeding sorry ; yet for his oath's sake, and for their sakes which sat with him, he would not reject her.
10 And he sent, and beheaded John in the prison.	27 And immediately the king sent an executioner, and commanded his head to be brought : and he went and beheaded him in the prison ;
11 And his head was brought in a charger, and given to the damsel : and she brought *it* to her mother.	28 And brought his head in a charger, and gave it to the damsel ; and the damsel gave it to her mother.
12 And his disciples came, and took up the body, and buried it, and went and told Jesus.	29 And when his disciples heard *of it*, they came and took up his corpse, and laid it in a tomb.

§ 64. The Twelve return. Jesus retires with them across the lake.

CH. XIV. 13 – 21.	CH. VI. 30 – 44.
13 When Jesus heard *of it*, he departed thence by ship into a desert place apart : and when the people had heard *thereof*, they followed him on foot out of the cities.	30 And the apostles gathered themselves together unto Jesus, and told him all things, both what they had done, and what they had taught.
14 And Jesus went forth, and saw a great multitude, and was moved with compassion toward them, and he healed their sick.	31 And he said unto them, Come ye yourselves apart into a desert place, and rest a while : for there were many coming and going, and they had no leisure so much as to eat.
	32 And they departed into a desert place by ship privately.
	33 And the people saw them departing, and many knew him, and ran afoot thither out of all cities, and

---

Mark vi. 31, *many coming and going*.] Mark incidentally mentions the great multitude coming and going, and the purpose of Jesus to withdraw *awhile*. The occasion of this great multitude of *travellers* is stated in the like incidental manner by John, [vi. 4,] that the *passover* was nigh at hand ; and hence, if Jesus withdrew awhile, the throng would be drawn off towards Jerusalem. These undesigned coincidences tend to verify both the narratives. BLUNT. Veracity, &c. sect. i. 13.

John v. *saith unto Philip*.] Why Jesus addressed this question to Philip, and why John mentioned so unimportant a fact, is not here explained. Nor does Luke indicate any reason for his own statement of the place where this miracle was wrought, namely,

whom he had just before beheaded.   *Galilee? Perea.*

LUKE.	JOHN.

Five thousand are fed.   *Capernaum.   N. E. coast of the lake.*

CH. IX. 10 – 17.	CH. VI. 1 – 14.
10 And the apostles, when they were returned, told him all that they had done. And he took them, and went aside privately into a desert place, belonging to the city called Bethsaida.	AFTER these things Jesus went over the sea of Galilee, which is *the sea* of Tiberias.
11 And the people, when they knew *it*, followed him: and he received them, and spake unto them of the kingdom of God, and healed them that had need of healing.	2 And a great multitude followed him, because they saw his miracles which he did on them that were diseased.
	3 And Jesus went up into a mountain, and there he sat with his disciples.
	4 And the passover, a feast of the Jews, was nigh.

near Bethsaida. But John, in another place, (ch. i. 44,) with apparently as little reason, gratuitously states that Philip was of Bethsaida ; and this fact renders both the others intelligible and significant. Jesus, intending to furnish bread for the multitude by a miracle, first asked Philip, who belonged to the city and was perfectly acquainted with the neighborhood, whether bread could be procured there. His answer amounts to saying that it was not possible. These slight circumstances, thus collected together, constitute very cogent evidence of the veracity of the narrative, and evince the reality of the miracle itself. See BLUNT, Veracity, &c. sect. i. 13.

§ 64. The Twelve return. Jesus retires with them across the lake.

MATTHEW. CH. XIV. 13–21.	MARK. CH. VI. 30–44.
	outwent them, and came together unto him. 34 And Jesus, when he came out, saw much people, and was moved with compassion toward them, because they were as sheep not having a shepherd : and he began to teach them many things.
15 And when it was evening his disciples came to him, saying, This is a desert place, and the time is now past ; send the multitude away, that they may go into the villages, and buy themselves victuals.	35 And when the day was now far spent, his disciples came unto him, and said, This is a desert place, and now the time is far passed : 36 Send them away, that they may go into the country round about, and into the villages, and buy themselves bread : for they have nothing to eat.
16 But Jesus said unto them, They need not depart ; give ye them to eat. 17 And they say unto him, We have here but five loaves, and two fishes. 18 He said, Bring them hither to me.	37 He answered and said unto them, Give ye them to eat. And they say unto him, Shall we go and buy two hundred pennyworth of bread, and give them to eat? 38 He saith unto them, How many loaves have ye? go and see. And when they knew, they say, Five, and two fishes.
19 And he commanded the multitude to sit down on the grass, and took the five loaves, and the two fishes, and looking up to heaven, he blessed, and brake, and gave the loaves to *his* disciples, and the disciples to the multitude.	39 And he commanded them to make all sit down by companies upon the green grass. 40 And they sat down in ranks, by hundreds, and by fifties. 41 And when he had taken the five loaves, and the two fishes, he looked up to heaven, and blessed, and brake the loaves, and gave *them* to his disciples to set before them ; and the two fishes divided he among them all.
20 And they did all eat, and were filled : and they took up of the fragments that remained twelve baskets full. 21 And they that had eaten were about five thousand men, besides women and children.	42 And they did all eat, and were filled. 43 And they took up twelve baskets full of the fragments, and of the fishes. 44 And they that did eat of the loaves, were about five thousand men.

§ 65. Jesus walks upon the water.

CH. XIV. 22–36.	CH. VI. 45–56.
22 And straightway Jesus constrained his disciples to get into a ship, and to go before him unto the	45 And straightway he constrained his disciples to get into the ship, and to go to the other side before unto

Luke ix. 14, *by fifties.*] In Luke, Jesus commands that the people should be made to sit down by *fifties.* In Mark it is said that they sat down by *hundreds and by fifties.*

Five thousand are fed.   Capernaum.   N. E. coast of the lake.

LUKE.
CH. IX. 10–17.

JOHN.
CH. VI. 1–14.

5 When Jesus then lifted up *his* eyes, and saw a great company come unto him, he saith unto Philip, Whence shall we buy bread that these may eat?

6 (And this he said to prove him: for he himself knew what he would do.)

12 And when the day began to wear away, then came the twelve, and said unto him, Send the multitude away, that they may go into the towns and country round about, and lodge, and get victuals: for we are here in a desert place.

7 Philip answered him, Two hundred pennyworth of bread is not sufficient for them, that every one of them may take a little.

8 One of his disciples, Andrew, Simon Peter's brother, saith unto him,

9 There is a lad here, which hath five barley-loaves, and two small fishes: but what are they among so many?

13 But he said unto them, Give ye them to eat. And they said, We have no more but five loaves and two fishes; except we should go and buy meat for all this people.

14 (For they were about five thousand men.) And he said to his disciples, Make them sit down by fifties in a company.

15 And they did so, and made them all sit down.

10 And Jesus said, Make the men sit down. (Now there was much grass in the place.) So the men sat down in number about five thousand.

11 And Jesus took the loaves; and when he had given thanks, he distributed to the disciples, and the disciples to them that were set down; and likewise of the fishes, as much as they would.

12 When they were filled, he said unto his disciples, Gather up the fragments that remain, that nothing be lost.

16 Then he took the five loaves, and the two fishes, and looking up to heaven, he blessed them, and brake, and gave to the disciples to set before the multitude.

13 Therefore they gathered *them* together, and filled twelve baskets with the fragments of the five barley-loaves, which remained over and above unto them that had eaten.

17 And they did eat, and were all filled: and there was taken up of fragments that remained to them twelve baskets.

14 Then those men, when they had seen the miracle that Jesus did, said, This is of a truth that Prophet that should come into the world.

Lake of Galilee.   Gennesaret.

CH. VI. 15–21.

15 When Jesus therefore perceived that they would come and take him by force, to make him a king, he de-

Piscator, and Pearce, in a dissertation at the end of his comment on St. Paul's Epistles, say that they sat an hundred in front, and fifty deep; which very satisfactorily solves the seeming variation. NEWCOME.

§ 65. Jesus walks upon the water.

MATTHEW.
CH. XIV. 22–36.

other side, while he sent the multitudes away.

23 And when he had sent the multitudes away, he went up into a mountain apart to pray: and when the evening was come, he was there alone.

24 But the ship was now in the midst of the sea, tossed with waves: for the wind was contrary.

25 And in the fourth watch of the night Jesus went unto them, walking on the sea.

26 And when the disciples saw him walking on the sea, they were troubled, saying, It is a spirit; and they cried out for fear.

27 But straightway Jesus spake unto them, saying, Be of good cheer; it is I; be not afraid.

28 And Peter answered him and said, Lord, if it be thou, bid me come unto thee on the water.

29 And he said, Come. And when Peter was come down out of the ship, he walked on the water, to go to Jesus.

30 But when he saw the wind boisterous, he was afraid; and beginning to sink, he cried, saying, Lord, save me.

31 And immediately Jesus stretched forth *his* hand, and caught him, and said unto him, O thou of little faith, wherefore didst thou doubt?

32 And when they were come into the ship, the wind ceased.

33 Then they that were in the ship came and worshipped him, saying, Of a truth thou art the Son of God.

34 And when they were gone over, they came into the land of Gennesaret.

35 And when the men of that place had knowledge of him, they sent out into all that country round about, and brought unto him all that were diseased;

36 And besought him that they might only touch the hem of his garment: and as many as touched were made perfectly whole.

MARK.
CH. VI. 45–56.

Bethsaida, while he sent away the people.

46 And when he had sent them away, he departed into a mountain to pray.

47 And when even was come, the ship was in the midst of the sea, and he alone on the land.

48 And he saw them toiling in rowing; for the wind was contrary unto them: and about the fourth watch of the night he cometh unto them, walking upon the sea, and would have passed by them.

49 But when they saw him walking upon the sea, they supposed it had been a spirit, and cried out.

50 (For they all saw him, and were troubled.) And immediately he talked with them, and saith unto them, Be of good cheer: it is I; be not afraid.

51 And he went up unto them into the ship; and the wind ceased; and they were sore amazed in themselves beyond measure, and wondered.

52 For they considered not *the miracle* of the loaves; for their heart was hardened.

53 And when they had passed over, they came into the land of Gennesaret, and drew to the shore.

54 And when they were come out of the ship, straightway they knew him,

55 And ran through that whole region round about, and began to carry about in beds those that were sick, where they heard he was.

56 And whithersoever he entered, into villages, or cities, or country, they laid the sick in the streets, and besought him that they might touch, if it were but the border of his garment: and as many as touched him were made whole.

Lake of Galilee.   Gennesaret.

LUKE. | JOHN.

JOHN.

CH. VI. 15—21.

parted again into a mountain himself alone.

16 And when even was *now* come, his disciples went down unto the sea,

17 And entered into a ship, and went over the sea toward Capernaum. And it was now dark, and Jesus was not come to them.

18 And the sea arose by reason of a great wind that blew.

19 So when they had rowed about five and twenty or thirty furlongs, they see Jesus walking on the sea, and drawing nigh unto the ship: and they were afraid.

20 But he saith unto them, It is I; be not afraid.

21 Then they willingly received him into the ship: and immediately the ship was at the land whither they went.

§ 66. Our Lord's discourse in the Synagogue at Capernaum.

MATTHEW.	MARK.

John vi. 25, *Rabbi, when camest thou hither?*] This seemingly idle inquiry becomes important as a note of veracity in the narrator, when compared with the account of Matthew. John indeed tells us, v. 18, that the wind blew a gale, but he does not state from what quarter. He also says that there were boats from Tiberias, near the place where the miracle of bread was wrought, v. 23, but this does not at all explain the inquiry of the people how Jesus came to Capernaum. But Matthew states that "the wind was contrary," that is, west, Matth. xiv. 22. This fact, and the geographical position of the places, explains the whole. The miracle was wrought near Bethsaida,

Many disciples turn back. Peter's profession of faith. *Capernaum.*

LUKE.	JOHN.
	CH. VI. 22–71. CH. VII. 1.

22 The day following, when the people which stood on the other side of the sea saw that there was none other boat there, save that one whereinto his disciples were entered, and that Jesus went not with his disciples into the boat, but *that* his disciples were gone away alone;

23 (Howbeit there came other boats from Tiberias nigh unto the place where they did eat bread, after that the Lord had given thanks :)

24 When the people therefore saw that Jesus was not there, neither his disciples, they also took shipping, and came to Capernaum, seeking for Jesus.

25 And when they had found him on the other side of the sea, they said unto him, Rabbi, when camest thou hither?

26 Jesus answered them and said, Verily, verily, I say unto you, Ye seek me, not because ye saw the miracles, but because ye did eat of the loaves, and were filled.

27 Labor not for the meat which perisheth, but for that meat which endureth unto everlasting life, which the Son of man shall give unto you : for him hath God the Father sealed.

28 Then said they unto him, What shall we do, that we might work the works of God?

29 Jesus answered and said unto them, This is the work of God, that ye believe on him whom he hath sent.

30 They said therefore unto him, What sign shewest thou then, that we may see, and believe thee? what dost thou work?

31 Our fathers did eat manna in the

---

on the east side of the lake. The people saw the disciples take the only boat which was there, and depart for Capernaum, which was on the west side of the lake, and saw that Jesus was not with them. In the night it blew a tempest from the west. In the morning, the storm being over, the people crossed over to Capernaum and found Jesus already there. Well might they ask him, with astonishment, how he came thither. For though there were boats over from Tiberias, which was also on the west side of the lake, yet he could not have returned in one of them, for the wind would not have permitted them to cross the lake. BLUNT, Veracity of the Gospels, sect. i. 17.

§ 66. Our Lord's discourse in the Synagogue at Capernaum.

MATTHEW.	MARK.

Many disciples turn back.   Peter's profession of faith.   *Capernaum.*

LUKE.

JOHN.

cx. vi. 22 – 71. ch. vii. 1.

desert ; as it is written,[a] He gave them bread from heaven to eat.

32 Then Jesus said unto them, Verily, verily, I say unto you, Moses gave you not that bread from heaven ; but my Father giveth you the true bread from heaven.

33 For the bread of God is he which cometh down from heaven, and giveth life unto the world.

34 Then said they unto him, Lord, evermore give us this bread.

35 And Jesus said unto them, I am the bread of life : he that cometh to me, shall never hunger ; and he that believeth on me, shall never thirst.

36 But I said unto you, That ye also have seen me, and believe not.

37 All that the Father giveth me, shall come to me ; and him that cometh to me, I will in no wise cast out.

38 For I came down from heaven, not to do mine own will, but the will of him that sent me.

39 And this is the Father's will which hath sent me, that of all which he hath given me, I should lose nothing, but should raise it up again at the last day.

40 And this is the will of him that sent me, that every one which seeth the Son, and believeth on him, may have everlasting life : and I will raise him up at the last day.

41 The Jews then murmured at him, because he said, I am the bread which came down from heaven.

42 And they said, Is not this Jesus the son of Joseph, whose father and mother we know ? how is it then that he saith, I came down from heaven ?

43 Jesus therefore answered and said unto them, Murmur not among yourselves.

44 No man can come to me, except the Father which hath sent me draw him : and I will raise him up at the last day.

45 It is written in the prophets,[b] And they shall be all taught of God. Every man therefore that hath heard,

---

[a] Ps. lxxviii. 24.   Ex. xvi. 15.   [b] Isa. liv. 13.   Jer. xxxi. 33, seq.

§ 66. Our Lord's discourse in the Synagogue at Capernaum.

MATTHEW.	MARK.

Many disciples turn back.　Peter's profession of faith.　*Capernaum.*

LUKE.

JOHN.

CH. VI. 22–71.　CH. VII. 1.

and hath learned of the Father, cometh unto me.

46 Not that any man hath seen the Father, save he which is of God, he hath seen the Father.

47 Verily, verily, I say unto you, He that believeth on me hath everlasting life.

48 I am that bread of life.[a]

49 Your fathers did eat manna in the wilderness, and are dead.

50 This is the bread which cometh down from heaven, that a man may eat thereof, and not die.

51 I am the living bread which came down from heaven : if any man eat of this bread, he shall live for ever : and the bread that I will give is my flesh, which I will give for the life of the world.

52 The Jews therefore strove among themselves, saying, How can this man give us *his* flesh to eat ?

53 Then Jesus said unto them, Verily, verily, I say unto you, Except ye eat the flesh of the Son of man, and drink his blood, ye have no life in you.

54 Whoso eateth my flesh, and drinketh my blood, hath eternal life ; and I will raise him up at the last day.

55 For my flesh is meat indeed, and my blood is drink indeed.

56 He that eateth my flesh, and drinketh my blood, dwelleth in me, and I in him.

57 As the living Father hath sent me, and I live by the Father : so he that eateth me, even he shall live by me.

58 This is that bread which came down from heaven : not as your fathers did eat manna, and are dead : he that eateth of this bread shall live for ever.

59 These things said he in the synagogue, as he taught in Capernaum.

60 Many therefore of his disciples, when they had heard *this*, said, This is a hard saying ; who can hear it ?

[a] Ex. xvi. 15.

§ 66. Our Lord's discourse in the Synagogue at Capernaum.

MATTHEW.	MARK.

John vi. 66, *went back.*] The truth of the Gospels has been argued from the *confessions* they contain. On this verse Paley asks, "Was it the part of a writer, who dealt in suppression and disguise, to put down *this* anecdote?" *Evid.* 255.

John vi. 70, *a devil.*] The admission of *Judas Iscariot* into the domestic and confidential circle of our Lord, was the result of profound and even of divine wisdom. It showed that Jesus was willing to throw open his most secret actions, discourses, and

Many disciples turn back.   Peter's profession of faith.   *Capernaum.*

LUKE.

JOHN.

CH. VI. 22 – 71.   CH. VII. 1.

61 When Jesus knew in himself that his disciples murmured at it, he said unto them, Doth this offend you?

62 *What* and if ye shall see the Son of man ascend up where he was before?

63 It is the Spirit that quickeneth; the flesh profiteth nothing : the words that I speak unto you, *they* are spirit, and *they* are life.

64 But there are some of you that believe not. For Jesus knew from the beginning who they were that believed not, and who should betray him.

65 And he said, Therefore said I unto you, that no man can come unto me, except it were given unto him of my Father.

66 From that *time* many of his disciples went back, and walked no more with him.

67 Then said Jesus unto the twelve, Will ye also go away?

68 Then Simon Peter answered him, Lord, to whom shall we go? thou hast the words of eternal life.

69 And we believe, and are sure that thou art that Christ, the Son of the living God.

70 Jesus answered them, Have not I chosen you twelve, and one of you is a devil?

71 He spake of Judas Iscariot *the son* of Simon: for he it was that should betray him, being one of the twelve.

CH. VII.

AFTER these things Jesus walked in Galilee : for he would not walk in Jewry, because the Jews sought to kill him.

views, not merely to his devoted friends, but to a sagacious and hardened enemy. If Judas had ever discovered the least fault in the character or conduct of Jesus, he certainly would have disclosed it ; — he would not have publicly confessed that he had betrayed innocent blood, and have sunk down in insupportable anguish and despair. See TAPPAN's Lect. on Eccl. Hist. ii.

PART V.

FROM OUR LORD'S THIRD PASSOVER,

UNTIL HIS

FINAL DEPARTURE FROM GALILEE,

AT THE

FESTIVAL OF TABERNACLES.

TIME. SIX months.

§ 67. Our Lord justifies his Disciples for eating with

MATTHEW.	MARK.
CH. XV. 1 – 20.	CH. VII. 1 – 23.

THEN came to Jesus scribes and Pharisees, which were of Jerusalem, saying,

2 Why do thy disciples transgress the tradition of the elders? for they wash not their hands when they eat bread.

THEN came together unto him the Pharisees, and certain of the scribes, which came from Jerusalem.

2 And when they saw some of his disciples eat bread with defiled (that is to say, with unwashen) hands, they found fault.

3 For the Pharisees, and all the Jews, except they wash *their* hands oft, eat not, holding the tradition of the elders.

4 And *when they come* from the market, except they wash, they eat not. And many other things there be, which they have received to hold, *as* the washing of cups, and pots, and brazen vessels, and tables.

5 Then the Pharisees and scribes asked him, Why walk not thy disciples according to the tradition of the elders, but eat bread with unwashen hands?

3 But he answered and said unto them, Why do ye also trangress the commandment of God by your tradition?

4 For God commanded,[a] saying, Honour thy father and mother: and, He that curseth father or mother, let him die the death.

5 But ye say, Whosoever shall say to *his* father or *his* mother, *It is* a gift, by whatsoever thou mightest be profited by me;

6 And honour not his father or his mother, *he shall be free.* Thus have ye made the commandment of God of none effect by your tradition.

7 *Ye* hypocrites, well did Esaias prophesy of you,[b] saying,

8 This people draweth nigh unto me with their mouth, and honoureth me with *their* lips; but their heart is far from me.

9 But in vain they do worship me, teaching *for* doctrines the commandments of men.

6 He answered and said unto them, Well hath Esaias prophesied of you hypocrites, as it is written, This people honoureth me with *their* lips, but their heart is far from me.

7 Howbeit, in vain do they worship me, teaching *for* doctrines the commandments of men.

8 For, laying aside the commandment of God, ye hold the tradition of men, *as* the washing of pots and cups: and many other such like things ye do.

9 And he said unto them, Full well ye reject the commandment of God, that ye may keep your own tradition.

10 For Moses said, Honour thy father and thy mother; and, Whoso curseth father or mother, let him die the death:

11 But ye say, If a man shall say to his father or mother, *It is* Corban, that is to say, a gift, by whatsoever thou mightest be profited by me; *he shall be free.*

[a] Ex. xx. 12. Ex. xxi. 17. Deut. v. 16.   [b] Is. xxix. 13.

Matth. xv. 2, *the tradition of the elders.*] See Appendix No. 2.

Mark vii. 3, 4.] Matthew was not only a Jew himself, but it is evident, from the whole structure of his Gospel, especially from his numerous references to the Old Tes-

unwashen hands.   Pharisaic traditions.   *Capernaum.*

LUKE.	JOHN.

tament, that he wrote for Jewish readers. *Paley.* But the explanation here given by Mark is an additional evidence of the fact asserted by Jerome and Clement of Alexandria, that he wrote at Rome, for the benefit chiefly of the converts of that nation.

§ 67. Our Lord justifies his Disciples for eating with

MATTHEW.	MARK.
CH. XV. 1–20.	CH. VII. 1–23.

MARK. CH. VII. 1–23.

12 And ye suffer him no more to do aught for his father or his mother ;

13 Making the word of God of none effect through your tradition, which ye have delivered : and many such like things do ye.

MATTHEW (left column):

10 And he called the multitude, and said unto them, Hear, and understand :

11 Not that which goeth into the mouth defileth a man ; but that which cometh out of the mouth, this defileth a man.

12 Then came his disciples, and said unto him, Knowest thou that the Pharisees were offended after they heard this saying ?

13 But he answered and said, Every plant, which my heavenly Father hath not planted, shall be rooted up.

14 Let them alone : they be blind leaders of the blind. And if the blind lead the blind, both shall fall into the ditch.

15 Then answered Peter and said unto him, Declare unto us this parable.

16 And Jesus said, Are ye also yet without understanding ?

17 Do not ye yet understand, that whatsoever entereth in at the mouth goeth into the belly, and is cast out into the draught?

18 But those things which proceed out of the mouth come forth from the heart ; and they defile the man.

19 For out of the heart proceed evil thoughts, murders, adulteries, fornications, thefts, false witness, blasphemies :

20 These are *the things* which defile a man : but to eat with unwashen hands defileth not a man.

MARK (right column):

14 And when he had called all the people *unto him*, he said unto them, Hearken unto me every one *of you,* and understand.

15 There is nothing from without a man, that entering into him, can defile him: but the things which come out of him, those are they that defile the man.

16 If any man have ears to hear, let him hear.

17 And when he was entered into the house from the people, his disciples asked him concerning the parable.

18 And he saith unto them, Are ye so without understanding also? Do ye not perceive, that whatsoever thing from without entereth into the man, *it* cannot defile him :

19 Because it entereth not into his heart, but into the belly, and goeth out into the draught, purging all meats ?

20 And he said, That which cometh out of the man, that defileth the man.

21 For from within, out of the heart of men, proceed evil thoughts, adulteries, fornications, murders,

22 Thefts, covetousness, wickedness, deceit, lasciviousness, an evil eye, blasphemy, pride, foolishness ;

23 All these evil things come from within, and defile the man.

§ 68. The daughter of a Syrophenician woman

CH. XV. 21–28.	CH. VII. 24–30.

21 Then Jesus went thence, and departed into the coasts of Tyre and Sidon.

24 And from thence he arose, and went into the borders of Tyre and Sidon, and entered into a house, and

unwashen hands.   Pharisaic traditions.   *Capernaum.*

LUKE.	JOHN.

is healed.   *Region of Tyre and Sidon.*

§ 68. The daughter of a Syrophenician woman

MATTHEW.
CH. XV. 21 – 28.

22 And behold, a woman of Canaan came out of the same coasts, and cried unto him, saying, Have mercy on me, O Lord, *thou* son of David; my daughter is grievously vexed with a devil.

23 But he answered her not a word. And his disciples came and besought him, saying, Send her away; for she crieth after us.

24 But he answered and said, I am not sent but unto the lost sheep of the house of Israel.

25 Then came she and worshipped him, saying, Lord, help me.

26 But he answered and said, It is not meet to take the children's bread and to cast *it* to dogs.

27 And she said, Truth, Lord: yet the dogs eat of the crumbs which fall from their master's table.

28 Then Jesus answered and said unto her, O woman, great *is* thy faith: be it unto thee even as thou wilt. And her daughter was made whole from that very hour.

MARK.
CH. VII. 24 – 30.

would have no man know *it*: but he could not be hid.

25 For a *certain* woman, whose young daughter had an unclean spirit, heard of him, and came and fell at his feet:

26 (The woman was a Greek, a Syrophenician by nation,) and she besought him that he would cast forth the devil out of her daughter.

27 But Jesus said unto her, Let the children first be filled: for it is not meet to take the children's bread, and to cast it unto the dogs.

28 And she answered and said unto him, Yes, Lord: yet the dogs under the table eat of the children's crumbs.

29 And he said unto her, For this saying, go thy way; the devil is gone out of thy daughter.

30 And when she was come to her house, she found the devil gone out, and her daughter laid upon the bed.

§ 69. A deaf and dumb man healed; also many others.

CH. XV. 29 – 38.

29 And Jesus departed from thence, and came nigh unto the sea of Galilee; and went up into a mountain, and sat down there.

30 And great multitudes came unto him, having with them *those that were* lame, blind, dumb, maimed, and many others, and cast them down at Jesus' feet; and he healed them:

CH. VII. 31 – 37.   CH. VIII. 1 – 9.

31 And again departing from the coasts of Tyre and Sidon, he came unto the sea of Galilee, through the midst of the coasts of Decapolis.

32 And they bring unto him one that was deaf, and had an impediment in his speech; and they beseech him to put his hand upon him.

33 And he took him aside from the multitude, and put his fingers into his ears, and he spit, and touched his tongue:

34 And looking up to heaven, he sighed, and saith unto him, Ephphatha, that is, Be opened.

35 And straightway his ears were

Mark vii. 26, *Syrophenician.*] Mark designates the woman by the country where she dwelt; Matthew calls her a woman of Canaan, because of the people to whom she belonged. Thus they do not contradict each other. The treatment of this woman by our Lord has been the subject of remark, as evasive and insincere. But it was far otherwise. He had a twofold object; to call the attention of his disciples to the fact of her being a foreigner, in order to show them that his ministry, though primarily and chiefly to the Jews, was in truth designed for the benefit of the Gentiles also; and to

is healed. *Region of Tyre and Sidon.*

LUKE.	JOHN.

Four thousand are fed. *The Decapolis.*

draw out, as it were, the great faith of the woman, in order to teach them the effect of faithful and persevering supplication. To attain these objects, he took the direct and most obvious method. In this instance also, as in those of the centurion, (Matth. viii. 5–13,) and of the Samaritan leper, (Luke xvii. 16–18,) he indicated that the gospel would be more readily received by the Gentiles than by the Jews. See A. CLARKE, *in loc.* NEWCOME, Obs. on our Lord, p. 165.

§ 69. A deaf and dumb man healed ; also many others.

MATTHEW.	MARK.
CH. XV. 29 – 38.	CH. VII. 24 – 37. CH. VIII. 1–9.

MARK (CH. VII. 24–37):
opened, and the string of his tongue was loosed, and he spake plain.

36 And he charged them that they should tell no man : but the more he charged them, so much the more a great deal they published *it ;*

31 Insomuch that the multitude wondered, when they saw the dumb to speak, the maimed to be whole, the lame to walk, and the blind to see : and they glorified the God of Israel.

37 And were beyond measure astonished, saying, He hath done all things well ; he maketh both the deaf to hear, and the dumb to speak.

CH. VIII.

32 Then Jesus called his disciples *unto him*, and said, I have compassion on the multitude, because they continue with me now three days, and have nothing to eat: and I will not send them away fasting, lest they faint in the way.

IN those days the multitude being very great, and having nothing to eat, Jesus called his disciples *unto him*, and saith unto them,

2 I have compassion on the multitude, because they have now been with me three days, and have nothing to eat :

3 And if I send them away fasting to their own houses, they will faint by the way : for divers of them came from far.

33 And his disciples say unto him, Whence should we have so much bread in the wilderness, as to fill so great a multitude ?

4 And his disciples answered him, From whence can a man satisfy these *men* with bread here in the wilderness ?

34 And Jesus saith unto them, How many loaves have ye ? And they said, Seven, and a few little fishes.

5 And he asked them, How many loaves have ye ? And they said, Seven.

35 And he commanded the multitude to sit down on the ground.

36 And he took the seven loaves and the fishes, and gave thanks, and brake *them*, and gave to his disciples, and the disciples to the multitude.

6 And he commanded the people to sit down on the ground : and he took the seven loaves, and gave thanks, and brake, and gave to his disciples to set before *them ;* and they did set *them* before the people.

7 And they had a few small fishes : and he blessed, and commanded to set them also before *them.*

37 And they did all eat, and were filled : and they took up of the broken *meat* that was left seven baskets full.

8 So they did eat, and were filled : and they took up of the broken *meat* that was left, seven baskets.

38 And they that did eat were four thousand men, besides women and children.

9 And they that had eaten were about four thousand : and he sent them away.

§ 70. The Pharisees and Sadducees again

CH. XV. 39. CH. XVI. 1 – 4.	CH. VIII. 10 – 12.

39 And he sent away the multitude, and took ship, and came into the coasts of Magdala.

10 And straightway he entered into a ship with his disciples, and came into the parts of Dalmanutha.

Matth. xv. 39, *Magdala.*] Cellarius and Lightfoot think that Dalmanutha and Magdala were neighboring towns. See Calmet, voc. Dalmanutha. It is probable that

Four thousand are fed. *The Decapolis.*

LUKE.	JOHN.

require a sign. *Near Magdala.*

Dalmanutha and Magdala were in Gaulanitis, towards the southeast part of the lake. See Matth. xv. 21 ; Mark vii. 24. NEWCOME.

§ 70. The Pharisees and Sadducees again

MATTHEW.	MARK.
CH. XVI. 1–4.	CH. VIII. 10–12.
THE Pharisees also with the Sadducees came, and, tempting, desired him that he would show them a sign from heaven.	11 And the Pharisees came forth, and began to question with him, seeking of him a sign from heaven, tempting him.
2 He answered and said unto them, When it is evening, ye say, It will be fair weather: for the sky is red.	
3 And in the morning, It will be foul weather to-day: for the sky is red and lowering. O ye hypocrites, ye can discern the face of the sky; but can ye not discern the signs of the times?	
4 A wicked and adulterous generation seeketh after a sign; and there shall no sign be given unto it, but the sign of the prophet Jonas.	12 And he sighed deeply in his spirit, and saith, Why doth this generation seek after a sign? Verily I say unto you, There shall no sign be given unto this generation.

§ 71. The disciples cautioned against the leaven

CH. XVI. 4–12.	CH. VIII. 13–21.
4 And he left them, and departed.	13 And he left them, and entering into the ship again, departed to the other side.
5 And when his disciples were come to the other side, they had forgotten to take bread.	14 Now the disciples had forgotten to take bread, neither had they in the ship with them more than one loaf.
6 Then Jesus said unto them, Take heed and beware of the leaven of the Pharisees and of the Sadducees.	15 And he charged them, saying, Take heed, beware of the leaven of the Pharisees, and of the leaven of Herod.
7 And they reasoned among themselves, saying, It is because we have taken no bread.	16 And they reasoned among themselves, saying, It is because we have no bread.
8 Which when Jesus perceived, he said unto them, O ye of little faith, why reason ye among yourselves, because ye have brought no bread?	17 And when Jesus knew it, he saith unto them, Why reason ye, because ye have no bread? perceive ye not yet, neither understand? have ye your heart yet hardened?
	18 Having eyes, see ye not? and having ears, hear ye not? and do ye not remember?
9 Do ye not yet understand, neither remember the five loaves of the five thousand, and how many baskets ye took up?	19 When I brake the five loaves among five thousand, how many baskets full of fragments took ye up? They say unto him, Twelve.
10 Neither the seven loaves of the four thousand, and how many baskets ye took up?	20 And when the seven among four thousand, how many baskets full of fragments took ye up? And they said, Seven.

Matth. xvi. 9, 10.] Our Lord's words, Matth. xvi. 9, 10, and Mark viii. 19, 20, are the same in substance, though differently modified. The evangelists are not scrupulous in adhering to the precise words used by Christ. They often record them in a

require a sign. *Near Magdala.*

LUKE.	JOHN.

of the Pharisees, &c.   *N. E. coast of the lake of Galilee.*

general manner, non numerantes, sed tanquam appendentes ; regarding their purport, and not superstitiously detailing them. However, in this place, after uttering what Matthew relates, Jesus *may* have asked the questions recorded by Mark. Nᴇᴡᴄᴏᴍᴇ.

§ 71. The disciples cautioned against the leaven

MATTHEW.	MARK.
CH. XVI. 4 – 12.	CH. VIII. 13 – 21.
11 How is it that ye do not under-stand that I spake *it* not to you con-cerning bread, that ye should beware of the leaven of the Pharisees and of the Sadducees?	21 And he said unto them, How is it that ye do not understand?
12 Then understood they how that he bade *them* not beware of the leaven of bread, but of the doctrine of the Pharisees and of the Sadducees.	

§ 72. A blind man healed.

CH. VIII. 22 – 26.

22 And he cometh to Bethsaida ; and they bring a blind man unto him, and besought him to touch him.

23 And he took the blind man by the hand, and led him out of the town ; and when he had spit on his eyes, and put his hands upon him, he asked him if he saw aught.

24 And he looked up, and said, I see men as trees walking.

25 After that, he put *his* hands again upon his eyes, and made him look up : and he was restored, and saw every man clearly.

26 And he sent him away to his house, saying, Neither go into the town, nor tell *it* to any in the town.

§ 73. Peter and the others again profess their

CH. XVI. 13 – 20.	CH. VIII. 27 – 30.
13 When Jesus came into the coasts of Cesarea Philippi, he asked his disciples, saying, Whom do men say that I, the Son of man, am ?	27 And Jesus went out, and his disciples, into the towns of Cesarea Philippi : and by the way he asked his disciples, saying unto them, Whom do men say that I am ?
14 And they said, Some *say that thou art* John the Baptist : some, Elias ; and others, Jeremias, or one of the prophets.	28 And they answered, John the Baptist : but some *say*, Elias ; and others, One of the prophets.
15 He saith unto them, But whom say ye that I am ?	29 And he saith unto them, But whom say ye that I am ? And Peter
16 And Simon Peter answered and said, Thou art the Christ, the Son of the living God.	answereth and saith unto him, Thou art the Christ.
17 And Jesus answered and said unto him, Blessed art thou, Simon	

Mark viii. 23, *out of the town.*] The notice of this circumstance affords a proof of the veracity of the evangelist ; for he barely states a fact having no apparent connec-tion with any other in his narrative. The reason of it is found in facts stated by the

of the Pharisees, &c. N. E. coast of the lake of Galilee.

LUKE.	JOHN.

Bethsaida. (Julias.)

faith in Christ. *Region of Cesarea Philippi.*

CH. IX. 18-21.

18 And it came to pass, as he was alone praying, his disciples were with him; and he asked them, saying, Whom say the people that I am?

19 They, answering, said, John the Baptist; but some *say*, Elias; and others *say*, That one of the old prophets is risen again.

20 He said unto them, But whom say ye that I am? Peter, answering, said, The Christ of God.

other evangelists. The people of Bethsaida had already witnessed the miracles of our Lord, but these only served to increase their rage against him; and they were therefore abandoned to the consequences of their unbelief. Matth. xi. 21.

§ 73. Peter and the others again profess their

MATTHEW.	MARK.
CH. XVI. 13–20.	CH. VIII. 27–30.

MATTHEW.
CH. XVI. 13–20.

Bar-jona: for flesh and blood hath not revealed *it* unto thee, but my Father which is in heaven.

18 And I say also unto thee, That thou art Peter, and upon this rock I will build my church : and the gates of hell shall not prevail against it.

19 And I will give unto thee the keys of the kingdom of heaven : and whatsoever thou shalt bind on earth, shall be bound in heaven ; and whatsoever thou shalt loose on earth, shall be loosed in heaven.

20 Then charged he his disciples that they should tell no man that he was Jesus the Christ.

MARK.
CH. VIII. 27–30.

30 And he charged them that they should tell no man of him.

---

§ 74. Our Lord foretells his own death and resurrection,

CH. XVI. 21–28.

21 From that time forth began Jesus to shew unto his disciples, how that he must go unto Jerusalem, and suffer many things of the elders, and chief priests, and scribes, and be killed, and be raised again the third day.

22 Then Peter took him, and began to rebuke him, saying, Be it far from thee, Lord : this shall not be unto thee.

23 But he turned, and said unto Peter, Get thee behind me, Satan ; thou art an offence unto me : for thou savourest not the things that be of God, but those that be of men.

24 Then said Jesus unto his disciples, If any *man* will come after me, let him deny himself, and take up his cross, and follow me.

CH. VIII. 31–38. CH. IX. 1.

31 And he began to teach them, that the Son of man must suffer many things, and be rejected of the elders, and of the chief priests, and scribes, and be killed, and after three days rise again.

32 And he spake that saying openly. And Peter took him, and began to rebuke him.

33 But when he had turned about, and looked on his disciples, he rebuked Peter, saying, Get thee behind me, Satan : for thou savourest not the things that be of God, but the things that be of men.

34 And when he had called the people *unto him*, with his disciples also, he said unto them, Whosoever will come after me, let him deny himself, and take up his cross, and follow me.

Matth. xvi. 21, *the third day.*] The phrase *three days and three nights* is equivalent to *three days*, three natural days of twenty-four hours. Gen. i. 5 ; Dan. viii. 14. Comp. Gen. vii. 4. 17.

(It is a received rule among the Jews, *that a part of a day is put for the whole;* so that whatsoever is done in any part of the day, is properly said to be done that day. 1 Kings xx. 29 ; Esth. iv. 16. "When eight days were accomplished for the circumcision of the child," &c. Yet the day of his birth and of his circumcision were two of these eight days. *Whitby*, quoted by SCOTT, on Matth. xii. 40.)

Grotius establishes this way of reckoning the *parts* of the first and third days for *two* days, by Aben Ezra on Lev. xii. 3.

faith in Christ. *Region of Cæsarea Philippi.*

LUKE.	JOHN.
CH. IX. 18–21.	

21 And he straitly charged them, and commanded *them* to tell no man that thing.

and the trials of his followers. *Region of Cæsarea Philippi.*

CH. IX. 22–27.

22 Saying, The Son of man must suffer many things, and be rejected of the elders, and chief priests, and scribes, and be slain, and be raised the third day.

23 And he said *to them* all, If any *man* will come after me, let him deny himself, and take up his cross daily, and follow me.

(In proof that the phrase "*after three days*," is sometimes equivalent to "*on the third day*," compare Deut. xiv. 28 with xxvi. 12 ; 1 Sam. xx. 12 with v. 19 ; 2 Chron. x. 5 with v. 12 ; Matth. xxvi. 2 with xxvii. 63, 64 ; Luke ii. 21 with i. 59.)

St. Luke omits our Lord's sharp reproof of Peter, and the occasion of it ; though he records the discourse in consequence of it. Le Clerc's 12th canon is "Qui pauciora habet, non negat plura dicta aut facta ; modo ne ulla sit exclusionis nota." Perhaps the disciple and companion of that apostle who had withstood Peter to his face, Gal. ii. 11, willingly made this omission, as he omits some aggravating circumstances in Peter's denial of Christ, Luke xxii. 60, though he carefully records the greatness of his sorrow, *v.* 62. NEWCOME.

§ 74. Our Lord foretells his own death and resurrection,

MATTHEW.	MARK.
CH. XVI. 21–28.	CH. VIII. 31–38.　CH. IX. 1.
25 For whosoever will save his life, shall lose it: and whosoever will lose his life for my sake, shall find it.	35 For whosoever will save his life, shall lose it; but whosoever shall lose his life for my sake and the gospel's, the same shall save it.
26 For what is a man profited, if he shall gain the whole world, and lose his own soul? or what shall a man give in exchange for his soul?	36 For what shall it profit a man, if he shall gain the whole world, and lose his own soul?
	37 Or what shall a man give in exchange for his soul?
	38 Whosoever therefore shall be ashamed of me, and of my words, in this adulterous and sinful generation,
27 For the Son of man shall come in the glory of his Father, with his angels; and then he shall reward every man according to his works.	of him also shall the Son of man be ashamed, when he cometh in the glory of his Father with the holy angels.
	CH. IX.
28 Verily I say unto you, There be some standing here, which shall not taste of death, till they see the Son of man coming in his kingdom.	AND he said unto them, Verily, I say unto you, That there be some of them that stand here which shall not taste of death, till they have seen the kingdom of God come with power.

§ 75. The Transfiguration.　Our Lord's subsequent discourse

CH. XVII. 1–13.	CH. IX. 2–13.
AND after six days, Jesus taketh Peter, James, and John his brother, and bringeth them up into a high mountain apart,	2 And after six days, Jesus taketh *with him* Peter, and James, and John, and leadeth them up into a high mountain apart by themselves; and he was transfigured before them.
2 And was transfigured before them: and his face did shine as the sun, and his raiment was white as the light.	3 And his raiment became shining, exceeding white as snow; so as no fuller on earth can white them.
3 And behold, there appeared unto them Moses and Elias talking with him.	4 And there appeared unto them Elias, with Moses: and they were talking with Jesus.
4 Then answered Peter, and said unto Jesus, Lord, it is good for us to be here: if thou wilt, let us make here three tabernacles; one for thee, and one for Moses, and one for Elias.	5 And Peter answered and said to Jesus, Master, it is good for us to be here: and let us make three tabernacles; one for thee, and one for Moses, and one for Elias.
	6 For he wist not what to say: for they were sore afraid.

Matth. xvii. 1, *after six days.*] It has been shown, § 74, that "*after six days*" may signify on the sixth day. But we are not hence to conclude that the phrase has *always* such a signification. Here it means six days complete, after the discourse recorded in § 74. The eight days mentioned by St. Luke include that of Peter's reproof and of the transfiguration; which two days Matthew and Mark exclude. Macknight furnishes us with the following apposite reference to Tacitus; Hist. i. 29. Piso

and the trials of his followers.　*Region of Cesarea Philippi.*

LUKE.	JOHN.
CH. IX. 22–27.	

24 For whosoever will save his life, shall lose it : but whosoever will lose his life for my sake, the same shall save it.

25 For what is a man advantaged, if he gain the whole world, and lose himself, or be cast away ?

26 For whosoever shall be ashamed of me, and of my words, of him shall the Son of man be ashamed, when he shall come in his own glory, and *in his* Father's, and of the holy angels.

27 But I tell you of a truth, there be some standing here which shall not taste of death till they see the kingdom of God.

with the three disciples.　*Region of Cesarea Philippi.*

CH. IX. 28–36.

28 And it came to pass, about an eight days after these sayings, he took Peter, and John, and James, and went up into a mountain to pray.

29 And as he prayed, the fashion of his countenance was altered, and his raiment *was* white *and* glistering.

30 And behold, there talked with him two men, which were Moses and Elias :

31 Who appeared in glory, and spake of his decease which he should accomplish at Jerusalem.

32 But Peter and they that were with him were heavy with sleep : and when they were awake, they saw his glory, and the two men that stood with him.

33 And it came to pass, as they departed from him, Peter said unto

says, *Sextus dies* agitur — ex quo — Cæsar adscitus sum ; and yet, § 48 of the same book, Tacitus speaks of Piso as *quatriduo* Cæsar.

Grotius on Matth. xvii. 1, has another solution ; Quod Lucas dicit, tale est quale cum vulgò dicimus *post septimanam circiter.* Nam Judæos *octo dies* appellasse id quod ab uno sabbato est ad alterum apparet, Joan, 20 26, &c. NEWCOME.

§ 75. The Transfiguration. Our Lord's subsequent discourse

MATTHEW.	MARK.
CH. XVII. 1–13.	CH. IX. 2–13.

5 While he yet spake, behold, a bright cloud overshadowed them : and behold, a voice out of the cloud, which said, This is my beloved Son, in whom I am well pleased : hear ye him.

6 And when the disciples heard *it*, they fell on their face, and were sore afraid.

7 And Jesus came and touched them, and said, Arise, and be not afraid.

8 And when they had lifted up their eyes, they saw no man, save Jesus only.

9 And as they came down from the mountain, Jesus charged them, saying, Tell the vision to no man, until the Son of man be risen again from the dead.

10 And his disciples asked him, saying, Why then say the scribes, that Elias must first come ?

11 And Jesus answered and said unto them, Elias truly shall first come, and restore all things :

12 But I say unto you, That Elias is come already, and they knew him not, but have done unto him whatsoever they listed : likewise shall also the Son of man suffer of them.

13 Then the disciples understood that he spake unto them of John the Baptist.

—

7 And there was a cloud that overshadowed them : and a voice came out of the cloud, saying, This is my beloved Son : hear him.

8 And suddenly, when they had looked round about, they saw no man any more, save Jesus only with themselves.

9 And as they came down from the mountain, he charged them that they should tell no man what things they had seen, till the Son of man were risen from the dead.

10 And they kept that saying with themselves, questioning one with another what the rising from the dead should mean.

11 And they asked him, saying, Why say the scribes that Elias must first come ?

12 And he answered and told them, Elias verily cometh first, and restoreth all things ; and how it is written of the Son of man, that he must suffer many things, and be set at naught.

13 But I say unto you, That Elias is indeed come, and they have done unto him whatsoever they listed, as it is written of him.

§ 76. The healing of a demoniac, whom the disciples

CH. XVII. 14–21.	CH. IX. 14–29.

14 And when they were come to the multitude, there came to him a

14 And when he came to *his* disciples, he saw a great multitude about

---

Luke ix. 36, *told no man.*] It is remarkable that Luke assigns no reason for this extraordinary silence ; leaving his narrative in this place imperfect and obscure, which

with the three disciples.   *Region of Cesarea Philippi.*

LUKE.
CH. IX.   28–36.

Jesus, Master, it is good for us to be here: and let us make three tabernacles; one for thee, and one for Moses, and one for Elias: not knowing what he said.

34 While he thus spake, there came a cloud, and overshadowed them: and they feared as they entered into the cloud.

35 And there came a voice out of the cloud, saying, This is my beloved Son: hear him.

36 And when the voice was past, Jesus was found alone. And they kept *it* close, and told no man in those days any of those things which they had seen.

JOHN.

could not heal.   *Region of Cesarea Philippi.*

CH. IX.   37–43.

37 And it came to pass, that on the next day, when they were come

an impostor would not have done. It is explained by the command of Jesus, related only by Matthew and Mark.

§ 76. The healing of a demoniac, whom the disciples

MATTHEW.	MARK.
CH. XVII. 14–21.	CH. IX. 14–29.

certain man kneeling down to him, and saying,	them, and the scribes questioning with them.
15 Lord, have mercy on my son; for he is lunatic, and sore vexed, for oft-times he falleth into the fire, and oft into the water.	15 And straightway all the people, when they beheld him, were greatly amazed, and, running to *him*, saluted him.
16 And I brought him to thy disciples, and they could not cure him.	16 And he asked the scribes, What question ye with them?
	17 And one of the multitude answered and said, Master, I have brought unto thee my son, which hath a dumb spirit;
	18 And wheresoever he taketh him, he teareth him; and he foameth and gnasheth with his teeth, and pineth away; and I spake to thy disciples that they should cast him out, and they could not.
17 Then Jesus answered and said, O faithless and perverse generation, how long shall I be with you? how long shall I suffer you? Bring him hither to me.	19 He answereth him, and saith, O faithless generation, how long shall I be with you? how long shall I suffer you? Bring him unto me.
	20 And they brought him unto him: and when he saw him, straightway the spirit tare him; and he fell on the ground, and wallowed, foaming.
	21 And he asked his father, How long is it ago since this came unto him? And he said, Of a child.
	22 And oft-times it hath cast him into the fire, and into the waters to destroy him: but if thou canst do any thing, have compassion on us, and help us.
	23 Jesus said unto him, If thou canst believe, all things *are* possible to him that believeth.
	24 And straightway the father of the child cried out, and said with tears, Lord, I believe; help thou mine unbelief.
	25 When Jesus saw that the people came running together, he rebuked the foul spirit, saying unto him, *Thou* dumb and deaf spirit, I charge thee, come out of him, and enter no more into him.
	26 And *the spirit* cried, and rent him sore, and came out of him: and he was as one dead; insomuch that many said, He is dead.
18 And Jesus rebuked the devil, and he departed out of him: and the child was cured from that very hour.	27 But Jesus took him by the hand, and lifted him up; and he arose.

could not heal.   *Region of Cesarea Philippi.*

LUKE.	JOHN.
CH. IX. 37–43.	

down from the hill, much people met him.

38 And behold, a man of the company cried out, saying, Master, I beseech thee look upon my son : for he is mine only child.

39 And lo, a spirit taketh him, and he suddenly crieth out ; and it teareth him that he foameth again, and, bruising him, hardly departeth from him.

40 And I besought thy disciples to cast him out, and they could not.

41 And Jesus, answering, said, O faithless and perverse generation, how long shall I be with you, and suffer you? Bring thy son hither.

42 And as he was yet a coming, the devil threw him down, and tare *him*. And Jesus rebuked the unclean spirit, and healed the child, and delivered him again to his father.

43 And they were all amazed at the mighty power of God.

§ 76. The healing of a demoniac, whom the disciples

MATTHEW.	MARK.
CH. XVII. 14–21.	CH. IX. 14–29.
19 Then came the disciples to Jesus apart, and said, Why could not we cast him out?	28 And when he was come into the house, his disciples asked him privately, Why could not we cast him out?
20 And Jesus said unto them, Because of your unbelief: for verily I say unto you, if ye have faith as a grain of mustard-seed, ye shall say unto this mountain, Remove hence to yonder place; and it shall remove; and nothing shall be impossible unto you.	29 And he said unto them, This kind can come forth by nothing, but by prayer and fasting.
21 Howbeit, this kind goeth not out, but by prayer and fasting.	

§ 77. Jesus again foretells his own death and resurrection.

CH. XVII. 22, 23.	CH. IX. 30–32.
	30 And they departed thence, and passed through Galilee; and he would not that any man should know it.
22 And while they abode in Galilee, Jesus said unto them, The Son of man shall be betrayed into the hands of men:	31 For he taught his disciples, and said unto them, The Son of man is delivered into the hands of men, and they shall kill him; and after that he is killed, he shall rise the third day.
23 And they shall kill him, and the third day he shall be raised again. And they were exceeding sorry.	32 But they understood not that saying, and were afraid to ask him.

§ 78. The tribute-money

CH. XVII. 24–27.	CH. IX. 33.
24 And when they were come to Capernaum, they that received tribute-money, came to Peter, and said, Doth not your Master pay tribute?	33 And he came to Capernaum:
25 He saith, Yes. And when he was come into the house, Jesus prevented him, saying, What thinkest thou, Simon? of whom do the kings of the earth take custom or tribute? of their own children, or of strangers?	
26 Peter saith unto him, Of strangers. Jesus saith unto him, Then are the children free.	
27 Notwithstanding, lest we should offend them, go thou to the sea, and cast a hook, and take up the fish that first cometh up: and when thou hast opened his mouth, thou shalt find a piece of money: that take, and give unto them for me and thee.	

could not heal.   *Region of Cesarea Philippi.*

LUKE.	JOHN.

[See § 74.]   Galilee.

CH. IX. 43–45.

43   But while they wondered every one at all things which Jesus did, he said unto his disciples,

44 Let these sayings sink down into your ears : for the Son of man shall be delivered into the hands of men.

45 But they understood not this saying, and it was hid from them, that they perceived it not : and they feared to ask him of that saying.

miraculously provided.   *Capernaum.*

§ 79. The disciples contend who should be the greatest. Jesus

MATTHEW.	MARK.
CH. XVIII. 1–35.	CH. IX. 33–50.

MATTHEW. CH. XVIII. 1–35.

AT the same time came the disciples unto Jesus, saying, Who is the greatest in the kingdom of heaven?

2 And Jesus called a little child unto him, and set him in the midst of them,

3 And said, Verily, I say unto you, Except ye be converted, and become as little children, ye shall not enter into the kingdom of heaven.

4 Whosoever therefore shall humble himself as this little child, the same is greatest in the kingdom of heaven.

5 And whoso shall receive one such little child in my name, receiveth me.

6 But whoso shall offend one of these little ones which believe in me, it were better for him that a millstone were hanged about his neck, and *that* he were drowned in the depth of the sea.

7 Wo unto the world because of offences! for it must needs be that offences come; but wo to that man by whom the offence cometh:

8 Wherefore, if thy hand or thy foot offend thee, cut them off, and cast *them* from thee; it is better for thee to enter into life halt or maimed, rather than having two hands or two feet, to be cast into everlasting fire.

9 And if thine eye offend thee, pluck it out, and cast *it* from thee: it is better for thee to enter into life with one eye, rather than having two eyes, to be cast into hell-fire.

10 Take heed that ye despise not one of these little ones: for I say

MARK. CH. IX. 33–50.

33 And being in the house, he asked them, What was it that ye disputed among yourselves by the way?

34 But they held their peace: for by the way they had disputed among themselves, who *should be* the greatest.

35 And he sat down, and called the twelve, and saith unto them, If any man desire to be first, *the same* shall be last of all, and servant of all.

36 And he took a child, and set him in the midst of them: and when he had taken him in his arms, he said unto them,

37 Whosoever shall receive one of such children in my name, receiveth me: and whosoever shall receive me, receiveth not me, but him that sent me.

38 And John answered him, saying, Master, we saw one casting out devils in thy name, and he followeth not us; and we forbade him, because he followeth not us.

39 But Jesus said, Forbid him not: for there is no man which shall do a miracle in my name, that can lightly speak evil of me.

40 For he that is not against us, is on our part.

41 For whosoever shall give you a cup of water to drink in my name, because ye belong to Christ, verily I say unto you, he shall not lose his reward.

42 And whosoever shall offend one of *these* little ones that believe in me, it is better for him that a millstone were hanged about his neck, and he were cast into the sea.

43 And if thy hand offend thee, cut it off: It is better for thee to enter into life maimed, than having two hands to go into hell, into the fire that never shall be quenched:

44 Where their worm dieth not, and the fire is not quenched.

Luke ix. 49, *one casting out devils.*] The twelve apostles and the seventy disciples were commissioned and sent forth *at different times.* Hence the person here alluded to may, for aught that appears, have been one of the seventy, not personally known to John and to those who were were with him. *Letters on Evil Spirits,* p. 39.

Mark ix. 40. Luke ix. 50.] Here Jesus says, He that is not against us is for us;

exhorts to humility, forbearance, and brotherly love. *Capernaum.*

LUKE.	JOHN.
CH. IX. 46 – 50.	

46 Then there arose a reasoning among them, which of them should be greatest.

47 And Jesus perceiving the thought of their heart, took a child, and set him by him,

48 And said unto them, Whosoever shall receive this child in my name, receiveth me; and whosoever shall receive me, receiveth him that sent me: for he that is least among you all, the same shall be great.

49 And John answered and said, Master, we saw one casting out devils in thy name; and we forbade him, because he followeth not with us.

50 And Jesus said unto him, Forbid *him* not: for he that is not against us, is for us.

but in Matth. xii. 30, he says, He that is not with me is against me. Grotius regards both as proverbial sayings; — Proverbia in utramque partem usurpata, veritatem suam habent pro materia cui aptantur; — and alludes to similar forms in Prov. xxvi. 4, 5. NEWCOME.

§ 79. The disciples contend who should be the greatest. Jesus

MATTHEW.
CH. XVIII. 1 – 35.

unto you, That in heaven their angels do always behold the face of my Father which is in heaven.

11 For the Son of man is come to save that which was lost.

12 How think ye? If a man have a hundred sheep, and one of them be gone astray, doth he not leave the ninety and nine, and goeth into the mountains, and seeketh that which is gone astray?

13 And if so be that he find it, verily I say unto you, he rejoiceth more of that *sheep*, than of the ninety and nine which went not astray.

14 Even so it is not the will of your Father which is in heaven, that one of these little ones should perish.

15 Moreover, if thy brother shall trespass against thee, go and tell him his fault between thee and him alone : if he shall hear thee, thou hast gained thy brother.

16 But if he will not hear *thee, then* take with thee one or two more, that in the mouth of two or three witnesses every word may be established.

17 And if he shall neglect to hear them, tell *it* unto the church : but if he neglect to hear the church, let him be unto thee as a heathen man and a publican.

18 Verily, I say unto you, Whatsoever ye shall bind on earth, shall be bound in heaven : and whatsoever ye shall loose on earth, shall be loosed in heaven.

19 Again I say unto you, That if two of you shall agree on earth, as touching any thing that they shall ask, it shall be done for them of my Father which is in heaven.

20 For where two or three are gathered together in my name, there am I in the midst of them.

21 Then came Peter to him, and said, Lord, how oft shall my brother sin against me, and I forgive him? till seven times?

22 Jesus saith unto him, I say not unto thee, Until seven times : but, Until seventy times seven.

23 Therefore is the kingdom of heaven likened unto a certain king

MARK.
CH. IX. 33 – 50.

45 And if thy foot offend thee, cut it off : it is better for thee to enter halt into life, than having two feet to be cast into hell, into the fire that never shall be quenched :

46 Where their worm dieth not, and the fire is not quenched.

47 And if thine eye offend thee, pluck it out : it is better for thee to enter into the kingdom of God with one eye, than having two eyes, to be cast into hell-fire :

48 Where their worm dieth not, and the fire is not quenched.

49 For every one shall be salted with fire, and every sacrifice shall be salted with salt.

50 Salt *is* good : but if the salt have lost his saltness, wherewith will ye season it? Have salt in yourselves, and have peace one with another.

exhorts to humility, forbearance, and brotherly love.   *Capernaum.*

LUKE.   JOHN.

§ 79. The disciples contend who should be the greatest.   Jesus

MATTHEW.
CH. XVIII. 1 – 35.

which would take account of his servants.

24 And when he had begun to
reckon, one was brought unto him
which owed him ten thousand talents.

25 But forasmuch as he had not to
pay, his lord commanded him to be
sold, and his wife and children, and
all that he had, and payment to be
made.

26 The servant therefore fell down,
and worshipped him, saying, Lord,
have patience with me, and I will pay
thee all.

27 Then the lord of that servant
was moved with compassion, and
loosed him, and forgave him the debt.

28 But the same servant went out,
and found one of his fellow-servants,
which owed him a hundred pence:
and he laid hands on him, and took
him by the throat, saying, Pay me
that thou owest.

29 And his fellow-servant fell down
at his feet, and besought him, saying,
Have patience with me, and I will
pay thee all.

30 And he would not : but went
and cast him into prison, till he should
pay the debt.

31 So when his fellow-servants saw
what was done, they were very sorry,
and came and told unto their lord all
that was done.

32 Then his lord, after that he had
called him, said unto him, O thou
wicked servant, I forgave thee all
that debt, because thou desiredst me :

33 Shouldest not thou also have
had compassion on thy fellow-servant,
even as I had pity on thee ?

34 And his lord was wroth, and
delivered him to the tormentors, till
he should pay all that was due unto
him.

35 So likewise shall my heavenly
Father do also unto you, if ye from
your hearts forgive not every one his
brother their trespasses.

MARK.

§ 80. The Seventy instructed, and sent out.

exhorts to humility, forbearance, and brotherly love.   *Capernaum.*

LUKE.	JOHN.

Capernaum.

CH. X. 1−16.

AFTER these things, the Lord appointed other seventy also, and sent

§ 80. The Seventy instructed, and sent out.

MATTHEW.	MARK.

Capernaum.

LUKE.
CH. X. 1–16.

them two and two before his face into every city, and place, whither he himself would come.

2 Therefore said he unto them, The harvest truly *is* great, but the labourers *are* few : pray ye therefore the Lord of the harvest, that he would send forth labourers into his harvest.

3 Go your ways : behold, I send you forth as lambs among wolves.

4 Carry neither purse, nor scrip, nor shoes : and salute no man by the way.[a]

5 And into whatsoever house ye enter, first say, Peace *be* to this house.

6 And if the son of peace be there, your peace shall rest upon it : if not, it shall turn to you again.

7 And in the same house remain, eating and drinking such things as they give : for the labourer *is* worthy of his hire. Go not from house to house.

8 And into whatsoever city ye enter, and they receive you, eat such things as are set before you.

9 And heal the sick that are therein, and say unto them, The kingdom of God is come nigh unto you.

10 But into whatsoever city ye enter, and they receive you not, go your ways out into the streets of the same, and say,

11 Even the very dust of your city which cleaveth on us, we do wipe off against you : notwithstanding, be ye sure of this, that the kingdom of God is come nigh unto you.

12 But I say unto you, That it shall be more tolerable in that day for Sodom than for that city.

13 Wo unto thee, Chorazin! wo unto thee, Bethsaida ! for if the mighty works had been done in Tyre and Sidon, which have been done in you, they had a great while ago repented, sitting in sackcloth and ashes.

14 But it shall be more tolerable for Tyre and Sidon at the judgment, than for you.

15 And thou, Capernaum, which

JOHN.

[a] 2 Kings iv. 29.

§ 80. The Seventy instructed, and sent out.

MATTHEW.	MARK.

§ 81. Jesus goes up to the feast of tabernacles. His final

§ 82. Ten lepers cleansed.

Luke ix. 53, *did not receive him.*] This was near the passover; when Jesus, going to celebrate it at Jerusalem, plainly indicated that men ought to worship *there*; contrary to the practice of the Samaritans, who, in opposition to the Holy City, had set up a temple at Gerazim. Hence the cause of their hostility to him as well as to all others travelling in that direction *at that season.* This account perfectly harmonizes

Capernaum.

LUKE.	JOHN.
ch. x. 1–16.	

art exalted to heaven, shalt be thrust down to hell.

16 He that heareth you, heareth me; and he that despiseth you, despiseth me; and he that despiseth me, despiseth him that sent me.

---

departure from Galilee.   Incidents in Samaria.

ch. ix. 51–56.	ch. vii. 2–10.

51 And it came to pass, when the time was come that he should be received up, he steadfastly set his face to go to Jerusalem,

52 And sent messengers before his face: and they went and entered into a village of the Samaritans, to make ready for him.

53 And they did not receive him, because his face was as though he would go to Jerusalem.

54 And when his disciples James and John saw *this*, they said, Lord, wilt thou that we command fire to come down from heaven, and consume them, even as Elias did?

55 But he turned, and rebuked them, and said, Ye know not what manner of spirit ye are of.

56 For the Son of man is not come to destroy men's lives, but to save *them*. And they went to another village.

2 Now the Jews' feast of tabernacles was at hand.

3 His brethren therefore said unto him, Depart hence, and go into Judea, that thy disciples also may see the works that thou doest.

4 For *there is* no man *that* doeth any thing in secret, and he himself seeketh to be known openly. If thou do these things, shew thyself to the world.

5 (For neither did his brethren believe *in* him.)

6 Then Jesus said unto them, My time is not yet come: but your time is always ready.

7 The world cannot hate you; but me it hateth, because I testify of it, that the works thereof are evil.

8 Go ye up unto this feast: I go not up yet unto this feast; for my time is not yet full come.

9 When he had said these words unto them, he abode *still* in Galilee.

10 But when his brethren were gone up, then went he also up unto the feast, not openly, but as it were in secret.

Samaria.

ch. xvii. 11–19.	

11 And it came to pass, as he went to Jerusalem, that he passed through the midst of Samaria and Galilee.

12 And as he entered into a certain village, there met him ten men that were lepers, which stood afar off:

13 And they lifted up *their* voices,

---

with the respectful deportment of the Samaritans towards him at the time of his interview with the woman at Jacob's well, John iv. 1 — 42; for he was then coming *from* Judea, and it was not the season of resorting thither for any purposes of devotion. John iv. 35. Blunt, Veracity, &c., sect. i. 16.

§ 82. Ten lepers cleansed.

MATTHEW.	MARK.

Samaria.

LUKE.
CH. XVII. 11 – 19.

and said, Jesus, Master, have mercy on us.

14 And when he saw *them*, he said unto them, Go shew yourselves unto the priests. And it came to pass, that, as they went, they were cleansed.

15 And one of them, when he saw that he was healed, turned back, and with a loud voice glorified God,

16 And fell down on *his* face at his feet, giving him thanks : and he was a Samaritan.

17 And Jesus answering, said, Were there not ten cleansed? but where *are* the nine!

18 There are not found that returned to give glory to God, save this stranger.

19 And he said unto him, Arise, go thy way : thy faith hath made thee whole.

JOHN.

PART VI.

THE FESTIVAL OF TABERNACLES

AND THE

SUBSEQUENT TRANSACTIONS,

UNTIL

OUR LORD'S ARRIVAL AT BETHANY,

SIX DAYS BEFORE THE FOURTH PASSOVER.

TIME. SIX months, less one week.

§ 83. Jesus at the festival of Tabernacles.

MATTHEW.	MARK.

His public teaching. *Jerusalem.*

LUKE.

JOHN.

CH. VII. 11–53. CH. VIII. 1.

11 Then the Jews sought him at the feast, and said, Where is he?

12 And there was much murmuring among the people concerning him: for some said, He is a good man: others said, Nay; but he deceiveth the people.

13 Howbeit, no man spake openly of him, for fear of the Jews.

14 Now, about the midst of the feast, Jesus went up into the temple and taught.

15 And the Jews marvelled, saying, How knoweth this man letters, having never learned?

16 Jesus answered them, and said, My doctrine is not mine, but his that sent me.

17 If any man will do his will, he shall know of the doctrine, whether it be of God, or *whether* I speak of myself.

18 He that speaketh of himself, seeketh his own glory: but he that seeketh his glory that sent him, the same is true, and no unrighteousness is in him.

19 Did not Moses give you the law, and *yet* none of you keepeth the law? Why go ye about to kill me?

20 The people answered and said, Thou hast a devil: who goeth about to kill thee?

21 Jesus answered and said unto them, I have done one work, and ye all marvel.

22 Moses therefore gave unto you circumcision, (not because it is of Moses, but of the fathers;) and ye on the sabbath-day circumcise a man.[a]

23 If a man on the sabbath-day receive circumcision, that the law of Moses should not be broken; are ye angry at me, because I have made a man every whit whole on the sabbath-day?

24 Judge not according to the appearance, but judge righteous judgment.

25 Then said some of them of Jerusalem, Is not this he whom they seek to kill?

[a] Lev. xii. 3.

20

§ 83. Jesus at the festival of Tabernacles.

MATTHEW.	MARK.

His public teaching. *Jerusalem.*

LUKE.   JOHN.
                                  ch. vii. 11 – 53. ch. viii. 1.

26 But lo, he speaketh boldly, and they say nothing unto him. Do the rulers know indeed that this is the very Christ ?

27 Howbeit, we know this man, whence he is: but when Christ cometh, no man knoweth whence he is.

28 Then cried Jesus in the temple, as he taught, saying, Ye both know me, and ye know whence I am : and I am not come of myself, but he that sent me is true, whom ye know not.

29 But I know him; for I am from him, and he hath sent me.

30 Then they sought to take him : but no man laid hands on him, because his hour was not yet come.

31 And many of the people believed on him, and said, When Christ cometh, will he do more miracles than these which this *man* hath done?

32 The Pharisees heard that the people murmured such things concerning him : and the Pharisees and the chief priests sent officers to take him.

33 Then said Jesus unto them, Yet a little while am I with you, and *then* I go unto him that sent me.

34 Ye shall seek me, and shall not find *me:* and where I am, *thither* ye cannot come.

35 Then said the Jews among themselves, Whither will he go, that we shall not find him? will he go unto the dispersed among the Gentiles, and teach the Gentiles?

36 What *manner of* saying is this that he said, Ye shall seek me, and shall not find *me :* and where I am, *thither* ye cannot come?

37 In the last day, that great *day* of the feast, Jesus stood and cried, saying, If any man thirst, let him come unto me, and drink.

38 He that believeth on me, as the scripture hath said,[a] out of his belly shall flow rivers of living water.

39 (But this spake he of the Spirit, which they that believe on him should

[a] Isa. lv. 1 and lviii. 11, and xliv. 3.   Zech. xiii. 1, and xiv. 8.

§ 83. Jesus at the festival of Tabernacles.

MATTHEW.	MARK.

John viii. 1, *to the Mount of Olives.*] It is apparent, from various incidental allusions in the Evangelists, that it was the habit of our Lord at this period to spend his days in Jerusalem, in teaching the people and healing the sick, and his nights in the mount of Olives, in prayer. Yet it is nowhere directly asserted; and the manner in

His public teaching. *Jerusalem.*

LUKE.	JOHN.

JOHN.

CH. VII. 11–53. CH. VIII. 1.

receive, for the Holy Ghost was not yet *given*, because that Jesus was not yet glorified.)

40 Many of the people therefore, when they heard this saying, said, Of a truth this is the Prophet.

41 Others said, This is the Christ. But some said, Shall Christ come out of Galilee?

42 Hath not the scripture said,[a] That Christ cometh of the seed of David, and out of the town of Bethlehem, where David was?

43 So there was a division among the people because of him.

44 And some of them would have taken him; but no man laid hands on him.

45 Then came the officers to the chief priests and Pharisees; and they said unto them, Why have ye not brought him?

46 The officers answered, Never man spake like this man.

47 Then answered them the Pharisees, Are ye also deceived?

48 Have any of the rulers, or of the Pharisees believed on him?

49 But this people who knoweth not the law are cursed.

50 Nicodemus saith unto them, (he that came to Jesus by night, being one of them,)

51 Doth our law judge *any* man before it hear him, and know what he doeth?

52 They answered, and said unto him, Art thou also of Galilee: Search, and look: for out of Galilee ariseth no prophet.

53 And every man went unto his own house.

CH. VIII.

JESUS went unto the mount of Olives:

[a] Ps. lxxxix. 4, and cxxxii. 11.   Mic. v. 2.

which it is slightly mentioned or alluded to by the sacred writers, is worthy of particular notice, as a proof of their veracity, never met with, in works of fiction, Compare Matth. xxiv. 3, and xxvi. 30; Mark xiii. 3, and xiv. 26; Luke vi. 12, and xxi. 37, 38, and xxii. 39; John viii. 1, 2, and xviii. 1.

§ 84. The woman taken in

MATTHEW.	MARK.

§ 85. Further public teaching of our Lord. · He reproves the

John viii. 5, *should be stoned.*] The Romans, in settling the provincial government of Judea, which they had conquered, deprived the Jewish tribunals of the power of inflicting capital punishments. John xviii. 31. See Appendix, No. IV. The law of Moses, however, condemned adulterers to be stoned to death. "This woman had been caught in the very fact. Jesus must therefore determine against the law, which inflicted death; or against the Romans, who suffered them not to put any body to death, and who would still less have permitted it for such a crime as adultery, which was not capital among them. — If *he* condemned not the adulteress *to death* when he

adultery. *Jerusalem.*

LUKE.

JOHN.
CH. VIII. 2–11.

2 And early in the morning he came again into the temple, and all the people came unto him; and he sat down and taught them.

3 And the scribes and Pharisees brought unto him a woman taken in adultery : and when they had set her in the midst,

4 They say unto him, Master, this woman was taken in adultery, in the very act.

5 Now Moses in the law[a] commanded us, that such should be stoned : but what sayest thou ?

6 This they said, tempting him, that they might have to accuse him. But Jesus stooped down, and with *his* finger wrote on the ground, *as though he heard them not.*

7 So when they continued asking him, he lifted up himself, and said unto them, He that is without sin among you, let him first cast a stone at her.

8 And again he stooped down, and wrote on the ground.

9 And they which heard *it*, being convicted by their *own* conscience, went out one by one, beginning at the eldest, *even* unto the last : and Jesus was left alone, and the woman standing in the midst.

10 When Jesus had lifted up himself, and saw none but the woman, he said unto her, Woman, where are those thine accusers ? hath no man condemned thee ?

11 She said, No man, Lord. And Jesus said unto her, Neither do I condemn thee : go, and sin no more.

unbelieving Jews, and escapes from their hands. *Jerusalem.*

CH. VIII. 12–59.

12 Then spake Jesus again unto them, saying, I am the light of the

---

a Lev. xx. 10.   Deut. xxii. 21.

---

was alone with her, he hereby teaches us to submit to the civil laws of the places where we live." BASNAGE, *Hist. Jud.* lib. v. c. xx. § 2.

John viii. 7, *let him first cast a stone.*] When one was condemned to death, those witnesses, whose evidence decided the sentence, inflicted the first blows, in order to add the last degree of certainty to their evidence. DUPIN, Trial of Jesus, p. 7.

§ 85. Further public teaching of our Lord. He reproves the

MATTHEW.	MARK.

John viii. 14, *ye cannot tell.*] John vii. 28, is consistent with John viii. 14. " Ye both know my transactions among you, and whence, as a man, I derive my descent ; (ch. vi. 42,) and yet there is a sense in which ye know not whence I am, as I came not," &c. *Kαι* is used in the same manner, Matth. ix. 19. *And yet wisdom,* &c.

unbelieving Jews, and escapes from their hands.   *Jerusalem.*

LUKE.	JOHN.

JOHN.
CH. VIII. 12‒59.

world : he that followeth me shall not walk in darkness, but shall have the light of life.

13 The Pharisees therefore said unto him, Thou bearest record of thyself; thy record is not true.

14 Jesus answered and said unto them, Though I bear record of myself, *yet* my record is true : for I know whence I came, and whither I go : but ye cannot tell whence I come, and whither I go.

15 Ye judge after the flesh, I judge no man.

16 And yet if I judge, my judgment is true : for I am not alone, but I and the Father that sent me.

17 It is also written in your law, that the testimony of two men is true.[a]

18 I am one that bear witness of myself; and the Father that sent me, beareth witness of me.

19 Then said they unto him, Where is thy Father? Jesus answered, Ye neither know me, nor my Father: if ye had known me, ye should have known my Father also.

20 These words spake Jesus in the treasury, as he taught in the temple : and no man laid hands on him, for his hour was not yet come.

21 Then said Jesus again unto them, I go my way, and ye shall seek me, and shall die in your sins : whither I go, ye cannot come.

22 Then said the Jews, Will he kill himself? because he saith, Whither I go, ye cannot come.

23 And he said unto them, Ye are from beneath ; I am from above : ye are of this world ; I am not of this world.

24 I said therefore unto you, that ye shall die in your sins : for if ye believe not that I am *he*, ye shall die in your sins.

[a] Deut. xvii. 6, and xix. 15.

See also John ix. 30. In this latter sense (ch. viii. 14,) the Jews knew not whence Jesus came, knew not his divine mission, and that he would return to the Father at his ascension. NEWCOME.

§ 85. Further public teaching of our Lord.   He reproves the

MATTHEW.	MARK.

John viii. 30, *many believed on him.*] The Jews who are said to have believed on Jesus, (John viii. 30,) are not the same with those whom our Lord accuses of seeking to kill him, ver. 40, nor with those who insulted him, ver. 48, &c., although these are

unbelieving Jews, and escapes from their hands. *Jerusalem.*

| LUKE. | JOHN. |

JOHN.
CH. VIII. 12 – 59.

25 Then said they unto him, Who art thou? And Jesus saith unto them, Even *the same* that I said unto you from the beginning.

26 I have many things to say, and to judge of you : but he that sent me, is true ; and I speak to the world those things which I have heard of him.

27 They understood not that he spake to them of the Father.

28 Then said Jesus unto them, When ye have lifted up the Son of man, then shall ye know that I am *he*, and *that* I do nothing of myself ; but as my Father hath taught me, I speak these things.

29 And he that sent me is with me : the Father hath not left me alone ; for I do always those things that please him.

30 As he spake these words, many believed on him.

31 Then said Jesus to those Jews which believed on him, If ye continue in my word, *then* are ye my disciples indeed ;

32 And ye shall know the truth, and the truth shall make you free.

33 They answered him, We be Abraham's seed, and were never in bondage to any man : how sayest thou, Ye shall be made free?

34 Jesus answered them, Verily, verily, I say unto you, Whosoever committeth sin, is the servant of sin.

35 And the servant abideth not in the house for ever, *but* the Son abideth ever.

36 If the Son therefore shall make you free, ye shall be free indeed.

37 I know that ye are Abraham's seed ; but ye seek to kill me, because my word hath no place in you.

38 I speak that which I have seen with my Father : and ye do that which ye have seen with your father.

39 They answered and said unto him, Abraham is our father. Jesus

not distinguished from the others in the narrative of John, who always mentions the Jews indiscriminately as speaking with Jesus. Cler. Harm. 528. NEWCOMB.

§ 85. Further public teaching of our Lord. He reproves the

MATTHEW.	MARK.

unbelieving Jews, and escapes from their hands.　*Jerusalem.*

LUKE.	JOHN.

JOHN.

CH. VIII. 12–59.

saith unto them, If ye were Abraham's children, ye would do the works of Abraham.

40 But now ye seek to kill me, a man that hath told you the truth, which I have heard of God : this did not Abraham.

41 Ye do the deeds of your father. Then said they to him, We be not born of fornication ; we have one Father, *even* God.

42 Jesus said unto them, If God were your Father, ye would love me : for I proceeded forth and came from God ; neither came I of myself, but he sent me.

43 Why do ye not understand my speech ? *even* because ye cannot hear my word.

44 Ye are of *your* father the devil, and the lusts of your father ye will do : he was a murderer from the beginning, and abode not in the truth ; because there is no truth in him. When he speaketh a lie, he speaketh of his own : for he is a liar, and the father of it.

45 And because I tell you the truth, ye believe me not.

46 Which of you convinceth me of sin ? And if I say the truth, why do ye not believe me ?

47 He that is of God, heareth God's words : ye therefore hear *them* not, because ye are not of God.

48 Then answered the Jews, and said unto him, Say we not well that thou art a Samaritan, and hast a devil ?

49 Jesus answered, I have not a devil ; but I honour my Father, and ye do dishonour me.

50 And I seek not mine own glory : there is one that seeketh and judgeth.

51 Verily, verily, I say unto you, if a man keep my saying, he shall never see death.

52 Then said the Jews unto him, Now we know that thou hast a devil. Abraham is dead, and the prophets ; and thou sayest, If a man keep my saying, he shall never taste of death.

§ 85. Further public teaching of Our Lord. He reproves the

MATTHEW.	MARK.

§ 86. A lawyer instructed. Love to our neighbor defined.

unbelieving Jews, and escapes from their hands. *Jerusalem.*

LUKE.	JOHN.
	CH. VIII. 12–59.
	53 Art thou greater than our father Abraham, which is dead! and the prophets are dead: whom makest thou thyself?
	54 Jesus answered, If I honor myself, my honour is nothing: it is my Father that honoureth me, of whom ye say, that he is your God.
	55 Yet ye have not known him; but I know him: and if I should say, I know him not, I shall be a liar like unto you: but I know him, and keep his saying.
	56 Your father Abraham rejoiced to see my day: and he saw *it*, and was glad.
	57 Then said the Jews unto him, Thou art not yet fifty years old, and hast thou seen Abraham?
	58 Jesus said unto them, Verily, verily, I say unto you, Before Abraham was, I am.
	59 Then took they up stones to cast at him: but Jesus hid himself, and went out of the temple, going through the midst of them, and so passed by.

Parable of the Good Samaritan. *Near Jerusalem.*

CH. X. 25–37.

25 And behold, a certain lawyer stood up, and tempted him, saying, Master, what shall I do to inherit eternal life?

26 He said unto him, What is written in the law? how readest thou?

27 And he answering said, Thou shalt love the Lord thy God with all thy heart, and with all thy soul, and with all thy strength, and with all thy mind; and thy neighbour as thyself.[a]

28 And he said unto him, Thou hast answered right: this do, and thou shalt live.

29 But he, willing to justify himself, said unto Jesus, And who is my neighbour?

30 And Jesus answering, said, A

[a] Deut. vi. 5. Lev. xix. 18, and xviii. 5.

§ 86. A lawyer instructed. Love to our neighbor defined.

MATTHEW.	MARK.

§ 87. Jesus in the house of Martha

Luke x. 30, *down.*] A note of minute accuracy in the historian, Jericho being situ-

Parable of the Good Samaritan. *Near Jerusalem.*

LUKE.	JOHN.
CH. x. 25 – 37.	

certain *man* went down from Jerusalem to Jericho, and fell among thieves, which stripped him of his raiment, and wounded *him*, and departed, leaving *him* half dead.

31 And by chance there came down a certain priest that way; and when he saw him, he passed by on the other side.

32 And likewise a Levite, when he was at the place, came and looked *on him*, and passed by on the other side.

33 But a certain Samaritan, as he journeyed, came where he was: and when he saw him, he had compassion *on him*,

34 And went to *him*, and bound up his wounds, pouring in oil and wine, and set him on his own beast, and brought him to an inn, and took care of him.

35 And on the morrow, when he departed, he took out two pence, and gave *them* to the host, and said unto him, Take care of him: and whatsoever thou spendest more, when I come again, I will repay thee.

36 Which now of these three, thinkest thou, was neighbour unto him that fell among the thieves?

37 And he said, He that shewed mercy on him. Then said Jesus unto him, Go, and do thou likewise.

and Mary. *Bethany.*

CH. x. 38 – 42.

38 Now it came to pass, as they went, that he entered into a certain village: and a certain woman, named Martha, received him into her house.

39 And she had a sister called Mary, which also sat at Jesus' feet, and heard his word.

40 But Martha was cumbered about much serving, and came to him, and said, Lord, dost thou not care that my sister hath left me to serve alone? bid her therefore that she help me.

41 And Jesus answered, and said

ated in the plain or valley of Jordan, and Jerusalem being among the mountains of Judea.

§ 87. Jesus in the house of Martha

MATTHEW.	MARK.

§ 88. The disciples again taught

Luke xi. 5, *at midnight.*] An incidental and very natural allusion to the well-known custom of that country. For in those hot regions, men travel in the cool of the

and Mary. *Bethany.*

LUKE.	JOHN.
ch. x. 38 – 42.	
unto her, Martha, Martha, thou art careful, and troubled about many things :	
42 But one thing is needful ; and Mary hath chosen that good part, which shall not be taken away from her.	

how to pray. *Near Jerusalem.*

ch. xi. 1 – 13.	
And it came to pass, that as he was praying in a certain place, when he ceased, one of his disciples said unto him, Lord, teach us to pray, as John also taught his disciples.	
2 And he said unto them, When ye pray, say, Our Father which art in heaven, Hallowed be thy name. Thy kingdom come. Thy will be done, as in heaven, so in earth.	
3 Give us day by day our daily bread.	
4 And forgive us our sins ; for we also forgive every one that is indebted to us. And lead us not into temptation ; but deliver us from evil.	
5 And he said unto them, Which of you shall have a friend, and shall go unto him at midnight, and say unto him, Friend, lend me three loaves :	
6 For a friend of mine in his journey is come to me, and I have nothing to set before him ?	
7 And he from within shall answer and say, Trouble me not : the door is now shut, and my children are with me in bed ; I cannot rise and give thee.	
8 I say unto you, Though he will not rise and give him, because he is his friend, yet because of his importunity he will rise and give him as many as he needeth.	
9 And I say unto you, Ask, and it shall be given you ; seek, and ye shall find ; knock, and it shall be opened unto you.	
10 For every one that asketh receiveth ; and he that seeketh findeth ;	

evening and night, and rest in the daytime ; looking for refreshment, if they are not among total strangers, to the hospitality of friends.

§ 88. The disciples again taught

MATTHEW.	MARK.

§ 89. The Seventy return.

LUKE.	JOHN.

CH. XI. 1 – 13.

and to him that knocketh, it shall be opened.

11 If a son shall ask bread of any of you that is a father, will he give him a stone? or if *he ask* a fish, will he for a fish give him a serpent?

12 Or if he shall ask an egg, will he offer him a scorpion?

13 If ye then, being evil, know how to give good gifts unto your children, how much more shall *your* heavenly Father give the Holy Spirit to them that ask him?

Jerusalem?

CH. X. 17 – 24.

17 And the seventy returned again with joy, saying, Lord, even the devils are subject unto us through thy name.

18 And he said unto them, I beheld Satan as lightning fall from heaven.

19 Behold, I give unto you power to tread on serpents and scorpions, and over all the power of the enemy: and nothing shall by any means hurt you.

20 Notwithstanding, in this rejoice not, that the spirits are subject unto you; but rather rejoice, because your names are written in heaven.

21 In that hour Jesus rejoiced in spirit, and said, I thank thee, O Father, Lord of heaven and earth, that thou hast hid these things from the wise and prudent, and hast revealed them unto babes: even so, Father; for so it seemed good in thy sight.

22 All things are delivered to me of my Father: and no man knoweth who the Son is, but the Father; and who the Father is, but the Son, and *he* to whom the Son will reveal *him*.

23 And he turned him unto *his* disciples, and said privately, Blessed *are* the eyes which see the things that ye see.

24 For I tell you, That many prophets and kings have desired to see those things which ye see, and have not seen *them;* and to hear those things which ye hear, and have not heard *them.*

§ 90. A man born blind is healed on the Sabbath.

MATTHEW.	MARK.

Our Lord's subsequent discourses. *Jerusalem.*

LUKE.　　　　　　　　JOHN.

CH. IX. 1–41.　CH. X. 1–21.

AND as *Jesus* passed by, he saw a man which was blind from *his* birth.

2 And his disciples asked him, saying, Master, who did sin, this man, or his parents, that he was born blind?

3 Jesus answered, Neither hath this man sinned, nor his parents: but that the works of God should be made manifest in him.

4 I must work the works of him that sent me, while it is day: the night cometh, when no man can work.

5 As long as I am in the world, I am the light of the world.

6 When he had thus spoken, he spat on the ground, and made clay of the spittle, and he anointed the eyes of the blind man with the clay,

7 And said unto him, Go, wash in the pool of Siloam, (which is by interpretation, Sent.) He went his way therefore, and washed, and came seeing.

8 The neighbours therefore, and they which before had seen him that he was blind, said, Is not this he that sat and begged?

9 Some said, This is he: others *said*, He is like him: *but* he said, I am *he*.

10 Therefore said they unto him, How were thine eyes opened?

11 He answered and said, A man that is called Jesus, made clay, and anointed mine eyes, and said unto me, Go to the pool of Siloam, and wash; and I went and washed, and I received sight.

12 Then said they unto him, Where is he? He said, I know not.

13 They brought to the Pharisees him that aforetime was blind.

14 And it was the sabbath-day when Jesus made the clay, and opened his eyes.

15 Then again the Pharisees also asked him how he had received his sight. He said unto them, He put clay upon mine eyes, and I washed, and do see.

16 Therefore said some of the Pharisees, This man is not of God, because he keepeth not the sabbath-

§ 90. A man born blind is healed on the Sabbath.

MATTHEW.	MARK.

Our Lord's subsequent discourses.　*Jerusalem.*

LUKE.	JOHN.
	CH. IX. 1–41.　CH. X. 1–21.

day. Others said, How can a man
that is a sinner do such miracles?
And there was a division among
them.

17 They say unto the blind man
again, What sayest thou of him, that
he hath opened thine eyes? He said,
He is a prophet.

18 But the Jews did not believe
concerning him, that he had been
blind, and received his sight, until
they called the parents of him that
had received his sight.

19 And they asked them, saying,
Is this your son, who ye say was
born blind? How then doth he now
see?

20 His parents answered them and
said, We know that this is our son,
and that he was born blind:

21 But by what means he now
seeth, we know not; or who hath
opened his eyes, we know not: he is
of age; ask him: he shall speak for
himself.

22 These *words* spake his parents,
because they feared the Jews: for
the Jews had agreed already, that if
any man did confess that he was
Christ, he should be put out of the
synagogue.

23 Therefore said his parents, He
is of age; ask him.

24 Then again called they the man
that was blind, and said unto him,
Give God the praise: we know that
this man is a sinner.

25 He answered and said, Whether
he be a sinner *or no*, I know not:
one thing I know, that, whereas I
was blind, now I see.

26 Then said they to him again,
What did he to thee? how opened he
thine eyes?

27 He answered them, I have told
you already, and ye did not hear:
wherefore would ye hear *it* again?
will ye also be his disciples?

28 Then they reviled him, and said,
Thou art his disciple; but we are
Moses' disciples.

29 We know that God spake unto
Moses; *as for* this *fellow*, we know
not from whence he is.

§ 90. A man born blind is healed on the Sabbath.

MATTHEW.	MARK.

Our Lord's subsequent discourses. *Jerusalem.*

LUKE.

JOHN.

CH. IX. 1–41. CH. X. 1–21.

30 The man answered and said unto them, Why, herein is a marvellous thing, that ye know not from whence he is, and *yet* he hath opened mine eyes.

31 Now we know that God heareth not sinners: but if any man be a worshipper of God, and doeth his will, him he heareth.

32 Since the world began was it not heard that any man opened the eyes of one that was born blind.

33 If this man were not of God, he could do nothing.

34 They answered and said unto him, Thou wast altogether born in sins, and dost] thou teach us? And they cast him out.

35 Jesus heard that they had cast him out: and when he had found him, he said unto him, Dost thou believe on the Son of God?

36 He answered and said, Who is he, Lord, that I might believe on him?

37 And Jesus said unto him, Thou hast both seen him, and it is he that talketh with thee.

38 And he said, Lord, I believe. And he worshipped him.

39 And Jesus said, For judgment I am come into this world; that they which see not might see; and that they which see might be made blind.

40 And *some* of the Pharisees which were with him heard these words, and said unto him, Are we blind also?

41 Jesus said unto them, If ye were blind, ye should have no sin: but now ye say, We see; therefore your sin remaineth.

CH. X.

VERILY, verily, I say unto you, He that entereth not by the door into the sheepfold, but climbeth up some other way, the same is a thief and a robber.

2 But he that entereth in by the door is the shepherd of the sheep.

3 To him the porter openeth; and the sheep hear his voice: and he calleth his own sheep by name, and leadeth them out.

4 And when he putteth forth his

§ 90. A man born blind is healed on the Sabbath.

MATTHEW.	MARK.

Our Lord's subsequent discourses. *Jerusalem.*

LUKE.

JOHN.

ch. ix. 1 – 41. ch. x. 1 – 21.

own sheep, he goeth before them, and the sheep follow him : for they know his voice.

5 And a stranger will they not follow, but will flee from him : for they know not the voice of strangers.

6 This parable spake Jesus unto them : but they understood not what things they were which he spake unto them.

7 Then said Jesus unto them again, Verily, verily, I say unto you, I am the door of the sheep.

8 All that ever came before me are thieves and robbers : but the sheep did not hear them.

9 I am the door : by me if any man enter in, he shall be saved, and shall go in and out, and find pasture.

10 The thief cometh not, but for to steal, and to kill, and to destroy : I am come that they might have life, and that they might have *it* more abundantly.

11 I am the good shepherd : the good shepherd giveth his life for the sheep.

12 But he that is a hireling, and not the shepherd, whose own the sheep are not, seeth the wolf coming, and leaveth the sheep, and fleeth; and the wolf catcheth them, and scattereth the sheep.

13 The hireling fleeth, because he is a hireling, and careth not for the sheep.

14 I am the good shepherd, and know my *sheep*, and am known of mine.

15 As the Father knoweth me, even so know I the Father : and I lay down my life for the sheep.

16 And other sheep I have, which are not of this fold : them also I must bring, and they shall hear my voice ; and there shall be one fold, *and* one shepherd.

17 Therefore doth my Father love me, because I lay down my life, that I might take it again.

18 No man taketh it from me, but I lay it down of myself. I have power to lay it down, and I have power to

§ 90. A man born blind is healed on the Sabbath.

MATTHEW.	MARK.

§ 91. Jesus at Jerusalem at the feast of dedication.

Our Lord's subsequent discourses. *Jerusalem.*

LUKE.	JOHN.
	CH. IX. 1–41. CH. X. 1–21.
	take it again. This commandment have I received of my Father.
	19 There was a division therefore again among the Jews for these sayings.
	20 And many of them said, He hath a devil, and is mad; why hear ye him?
	21 Others said, These are not the words of him that hath a devil. Can a devil open the eyes of the blind?

He retires beyond Jordan.   *Jerusalem.*   *Bethany beyond Jordan.*

CH. X. 22–42.

22 And it was at Jerusalem the feast of the dedication, and it was winter.

23 And Jesus walked in the temple in Solomon's porch.

24 Then came the Jews round about him, and said unto him, How long dost thou make us to doubt? If thou be the Christ, tell us plainly.

25 Jesus answered them, I told you, and ye believed not: the works that I do in my Father's name, they bear witness of me.

26 But ye believe not, because ye are not of my sheep, as I said unto you.

27 My sheep hear my voice, and I know them, and they follow me:

28 And I give unto them eternal life; and they shall never perish, neither shall any pluck them out of my hand.

29 My Father, which gave *them* me, is greater than all; and none is able to pluck *them* out of my Father's hand.

30 I and *my* Father are one.

31 Then the Jews took up stones again to stone him.

32 Jesus answered them, Many good works have I shewed you from my Father; for which of those works do ye stone me?

33 The Jews answered him, saying, For a good work we stone thee not; but for blasphemy, and because that thou, being a man, makest thyself God.

§ 91. Jesus at Jerusalem at the feast of dedication.

MATTHEW.	MARK.

§ 92. The raising of Lazarus.

He retires beyond Jordan. *Jerusalem.* *Bethany beyond Jordan.*

LUKE.

JOHN.
CH. X. 22–42.

34 Jesus answered them, Is it not written in your law, I said, Ye are gods? [a]

35 If he called them gods, unto whom the word of God came, and the scripture cannot be broken;

36 Say ye of him whom the Father hath sanctified, and sent into the world, Thou blasphemest; because I said, I am the Son of God?

37 If I do not the works of my Father, believe me not.

38 But if I do, though ye believe not me, believe the works: that ye may know and believe that the Father *is* in me, and I in him.

39 Therefore they sought again to take him; but he escaped out of their hand,

40 And went away again beyond Jordan, into the place where John at first baptized; and there he abode.

41 And many resorted unto him, and said, John did no miracle; but all things that John spake of this man were true.

42 And many believed on him there.

Bethany.

CH. XI. 1–46.

Now a certain *man* was sick, *named* Lazarus, of Bethany, the town of Mary and her sister Martha.

2 (It was *that* Mary which anointed the Lord with ointment, and wiped his feet with her hair, whose brother Lazarus was sick.)

3 Therefore his sisters sent unto him, saying, Lord, behold, he whom thou lovest is sick.

4 When Jesus heard *that*, he said, This sickness is not unto death, but for the glory of God, that the Son of God might be glorified thereby.

5 Now Jesus loved Martha, and her sister, and Lazarus.

6 When he had heard therefore that he was sick, he abode two days still in the same place where he was.

7 Then after that saith he to *his* disciples, Let us go into Judea again.

---

[a] Ps. lxxxii. 6. Ex. xxii. 7, seq.

22

§ 92. The raising of Lazarus.

MATTHEW.	MARK.

Bethany.

LUKE.	JOHN.

JOHN.
CH. XI. 1-46.

8 *His* disciples say unto him, Master, the Jews of late sought to stone thee ; and goest thou thither again?

9 Jesus answered, Are there not twelve hours in the day? If any man walk in the day, he stumbleth not, because he seeth the light of this world.

10 But if a man walk in the night, he stumbleth, because there is no light in him.

11 These things said he : and after that he saith unto them, Our friend Lazarus sleepeth ; but I go that I may awake him out of sleep.

12 Then said his disciples, Lord, if he sleep, he shall do well.

13 Howbeit Jesus spake of his death : but they thought that he had spoken of taking of rest in sleep.

14 Then said Jesus unto them plainly, Lazarus is dead.

15 And I am glad for your sakes that I was not there, to the intent ye may believe ; nevertheless, let us go unto him.

16 Then said Thomas, which is called Didymus, unto his fellow-disciples, Let us also go, that we may die with him.

17 Then when Jesus came, he found that he had *lain* in the grave four days already.

18 (Now Bethany was nigh unto Jerusalem, about fifteen furlongs off:)

19 And many of the Jews came to Martha and Mary, to comfort them concerning their brother.

20 Then Martha, as soon as she heard that Jesus was coming, went and met him : but Mary sat *still* in the house.

21 Then said Martha unto Jesus, Lord, if thou hadst been here, my brother had not died.

22 But I know that even now, whatsoever thou wilt ask of God, God will give *it* thee.

23 Jesus saith unto her, Thy brother shall rise again.

24 Martha saith unto him, I know that he shall rise again in the resurrection at the last day.

25 Jesus said unto her, I am the

§ 92. The raising of Lazarus.

MATTHEW.	MARK.

Bethany.

LUKE.

JOHN.

CH. XI. 1–46.

resurrection, and the life : he that believeth in me, though he were dead,
yet shall he live :

26 And whosoever liveth, and believeth in me, shall never die. Believest thou this ?

27 She saith unto him, Yea, Lord :
I believe that thou art the Christ, the
Son of God, which should come into
the world.

28 And when she had so said, she
went her way, and called Mary her
sister secretly, saying, The master is
come, and calleth for thee.

29 As soon as she heard *that*, she
arose quickly, and came unto him.

30 Now Jesus was not yet come
into the town, but was in that place
where Martha met him.

31 The Jews then which were
with her in the house, and comforted
her, when they saw Mary that she
rose up hastily, and went out, followed her, saying, She goeth unto
the grave to weep there.

32 Then when Mary was come
where Jesus was, and saw him, she
fell down at his feet, saying unto him,
Lord, if thou hadst been here, my
brother had not died.

33 When Jesus therefore saw her
weeping, and the Jews also weeping
which came with her, he groaned in
the spirit, and was troubled,

34 And said, Where have ye laid
him ? They say unto him, Lord,
come and see.

35 Jesus wept.

36 Then said the Jews, Behold
how he loved him !

37 And some of them said, Could
not this man, which opened the eyes
of the blind, have caused that even
this man should not have died ?

38 Jesus therefore again groaning
in himself, cometh to the grave. It
was a cave, and a stone lay upon it.

39 Jesus said, Take ye away the
stone. Martha, the sister of him that
was dead, saith unto him, Lord, by
this time he stinketh : for he hath
been *dead* four days.

40 Jesus saith unto her, Said I not

§ 92. The raising of Lazarus.

MATTHEW.	MARK.

§ 93. The counsel of Caiaphas against Jesus.   He

Bethany.

.LUKE.

JOHN.

CH. XI. 1–46.

unto thee, that if thou wouldest believe, thou shouldest see the glory of
God?

41 Then they took away the stone
from the place where the dead was
laid. And Jesus lifted up *his* eyes,
and said, Father, I thank thee that
thou hast heard me:

42 And I knew that thou hearest
me always: but because of the people which stand by, I said *it*, that
they may believe that thou hast sent
me.

43 And when he thus had spoken,
he cried with a loud voice, Lazarus,
come forth.

44 And he that was dead came
forth, bound hand and foot with grave-
clothes: and his face was bound about
with a napkin. Jesus saith unto them,
Loose him, and let him go.

45 Then many of the Jews which
came to Mary, and had seen the
things which Jesus did, believed on
him.

46 But some of them went their
ways to the Pharisees, and told them
what things Jesus had done.

retires from Jerusalem.   *Jerusalem.   Ephraim.*

CH. XI. 47–54.

47 Then gathered the chief priests
and the Pharisees a council, and said,
What do we? for this man doeth
many miracles.

48 If we let him thus alone, all
men will believe on him: and the
Romans shall come, and take away
both our place and nation.

49 And one of them, *named* Caiaphas, being the high priest that same
year, said unto them, Ye know nothing at all,

50 Nor consider that it is expedient
for us, that one man should die for the
people, and that the whole nation
perish not.

51 And this spake he not of himself: but being high priest that year,
he prophesied that Jesus should die
for that nation;

52 And not for that nation only,
but that also he should gather together

§ 93. The counsel of Caiaphas against Jesus.   He

MATTHEW.	MARK.

§ 94. Jesus, beyond Jordan, is followed by multitudes.   The healing

CH. XIX. 1, 2.	CH. X. 1.
AND it came to pass, *that* when Jesus had finished these sayings, he departed from Galilee, and came into the coasts of Judea, beyond Jordan :	AND he arose from thence, and cometh into the coasts of Judea, by the farther side of Jordan : and the people resort unto him again ; and, as
2 And great multitudes followed him, and he healed them there.	he was wont, he taught them again.

retires from Jerusalem. Jerusalem. Ephraim.

LUKE.	JOHN.
	CH. XI. 47–54.

in one the children of God that were scattered abroad.

53 Then from that day forth they took counsel together for to put him to death.

54 Jesus therefore walked no more openly among the Jews; but went thence unto a country near to the wilderness, into a city called Ephraim, and there continued with his disciples.

of the infirm woman on the Sabbath. Valley of Jordan. Perea.

CH. XIII. 10–21.

10 And he was teaching in one of the synagogues on the sabbath.

11 And behold, there was a woman which had a spirit of infirmity eighteen years, and was bowed together, and could in no wise lift up *herself*.

12 And when Jesus saw her, he called *her to him*, and said unto her, Woman, thou art loosed from thine infirmity.

13 And he laid *his* hands on her: and immediately she was made straight, and glorified God.

14 And the ruler of the synagogue answered with indignation, because that Jesus had healed on the sabbath-day, and said unto the people, There are six days in which men ought to work: in them therefore come and be healed, and not on the sabbath-day.

15 The Lord then answered him, and said, *Thou* hypocrite, doth not each one of you on the sabbath loose his ox or *his* ass from the stall, and lead *him* away to watering?

16 And ought not this woman, being a daughter of Abraham, whom Satan hath bound, lo, these eighteen years, be loosed from this bond on the sabbath-day?

17 And when he had said these things, all his adversaries were ashamed: and all the people rejoiced for all the glorious things that were done by him.

18 Then said he, Unto what is the kingdom of God like? and whereunto shall I resemble it?

49 It is like a grain of mustard-

§ 94. Jesus, beyond Jordan, is followed by multitudes. The healing

MATTHEW.	MARK.

§ 95. Our Lord goes teaching and journeying towards Jerusalem.

LUKE.
CH. XIII. 10–21.

seed, which a man took, and cast into his garden, and it grew, and waxed a great tree; and the fowls of the air lodged in the branches of it.

20 And again he said, Whereunto shall I liken the kingdom of God?

21 It is like leaven, which a woman took and hid in three measures of meal, till the whole was leavened.

JOHN.

He is warned against Herod. *Perea.*

CH. XIII. 22–35.

22 And he went through the cities and villages, teaching, and journeying toward Jerusalem.

23 Then said one unto him, Lord, are there few that be saved? And he said unto them,

24 Strive to enter in at the strait gate: for many, I say unto you, will seek to enter in, and shall not be able.

25 When once the Master of the house is risen up, and hath shut to the door, and ye begin to stand without, and to knock at the door, saying, Lord, Lord, open unto us; and he shall answer and say unto you, I know you not whence ye are:

26 Then shall ye begin to say, We have eaten and drunk in thy presence, and thou hast taught in our streets.

27 But he shall say, I tell you, I know you not whence ye are; depart from me, all *ye* workers of iniquity.

28 There shall be weeping and gnashing of teeth, when ye shall see Abraham, and Isaac, and Jacob, and all the prophets, in the kingdom of God, and you *yourselves* thrust out.

29 And they shall come from the east, and *from* the west, and from the north, and *from* the south, and shall sit down in the kingdom of God.

30 And behold, there are last, which shall be first; and there are first, which shall be last.

31 The same day there came certain of the Pharisees, saying unto him, Get thee out, and depart hence; for Herod will kill thee.

32 And he said unto them, Go ye

§ 95. Our Lord goes teaching and journeying towards Jerusalem.

MATTHEW.	MARK.

§ 96. Our Lord dines with a chief Pharisee

He is warned against Herod. *Perea.*

LUKE.
ch. xiii. 22–35.

and tell that fox, Behold, I cast out devils, and I do cures to-day and to-morrow, and the third *day* I shall be perfected.

33 Nevertheless, I must work to-day and to-morrow, and the *day* following : for it cannot be that a prophet perish out of Jerusalem.

34 O Jerusalem, Jerusalem, which killest the prophets, and stonest them that are sent unto thee; how often would I have gathered thy children together, as a hen *doth gather* her brood under *her* wings, and ye would not!

35 Behold, your house is left unto you desolate.[a] And verily, I say unto you, Ye shall not see me, until *the time* come when ye shall say, Blessed *is* he that cometh in the name of the Lord.

JOHN.

on the Sabbath. Incidents. *Perea.*

ch. xiv. 1–24.

AND it came to pass, as he went into the house of one of the chief Pharisees to eat bread on the sabbath-day, that they watched him.

2 And behold, there was a certain man before him which had the dropsy.

3 And Jesus answering, spake unto the lawyers and Pharisees, saying, Is it lawful to heal on the sabbath-day?

4 And they held their peace. And he took *him*, and healed him, and let him go :

5 And answered them, saying, Which of you shall have an ass or an ox fallen into a pit, and will not straightway pull him out on the sabbath-day?

6 And they could not answer him again to these things.

7 And he put forth a parable to those which were bidden, when he marked how they chose out the chief rooms; saying unto them,

8 When thou art bidden of any *man* to a wedding, sit not down in the highest room, lest a more honourable man than thou be bidden of him;

[a] Ps. lxix. 25. Jer. xii. 7, and xxii. 5.

§ 96. Our Lord dines with a chief Pharisee

MATTHEW.	MARK.

LUKE.

CH. XIV. 1–24.

9 And he that bade thee and him come and say to thee, Give this man place ; and thou begin with shame to take the lowest room.

10 But when thou art bidden, go and sit down in the lowest room ; that when he that bade thee cometh, he may say unto thee, Friend, go up higher : then shalt thou have worship in the presence of them that sit at meat with thee.

11 For whosoever exalteth himself shall be abased, and he that humbleth himself shall be exalted.

12 Then said he also to him that bade him, When thou makest a dinner or a supper, call not thy friends, nor thy brethren, neither thy kinsmen, nor *thy* rich neighbours ; lest they also bid thee again, and a recompense be made thee.

13 But when thou makest a feast, call the poor, the maimed, the lame, the blind ;

14 And thou shalt be blessed : for they cannot recompense thee : for thou shalt be recompensed at the resurrection of the just.

15 And when one of them that sat at meat with him heard these things, he said unto him, Blessed *is* he that shall eat bread in the kingdom of God.

16 Then said he unto him, A certain man made a great supper, and bade many :

17 And sent his servant at suppertime, to say to them that were bidden, Come, for all things are now ready.

18 And they all with one *consent* began to make excuse. The first said unto him, I have bought a piece of ground, and I must needs go and see it : I pray thee have me excused.

19 And another said, I have bought five yoke of oxen, and I go to prove them : I pray thee have me excused.

20 And another said, I have married a wife : and therefore I cannot come.

21 So that servant came, and shewed his lord these things. Then

JOHN.

§ 96. Our Lord dines with a chief Pharisee

MATTHEW.	MARK.

§ 97. What is required of true

on the Sabbath. Incidents. *Perea.*

LUKE.	JOHN.
CH. XIV. 1–24.	

the master of the house being angry, said to his servant, Go out quickly into the streets and lanes of the city, and bring in hither the poor, and the maimed, and the halt, and the blind.

22 And the servant said, Lord, it is done as thou hast commanded, and yet there is room.

23 And the lord said unto the servant, Go out into the highways and hedges, and compel *them* to come in, that my house may be filled.

24 For I say unto you, that none of those men which were bidden, shall taste of my supper.

disciples. *Perea.*

CH. XIV. 25–35.

25 And there went great multitudes with him : and he turned, and said unto them,

26 If any *man* come to me, and hate not his father, and mother, and wife, and children, and brethren, and sisters, yea, and his own life also, he cannot be my disciple.

27 And whosoever doth not bear his cross, and come after me, cannot be my disciple.

28 For which of you, intending to build a tower, sitteth not down first, and counteth the cost, whether he have *sufficient* to finish *it?*

29 Lest haply after he hath laid the foundation, and is not able to finish *it*, all that behold *it* begin to mock him,

30 Saying, This man began to build, and was not able to finish.

31 Or what king going, to make war against another king, sitteth not down first, and consulteth whether he be able with ten thousand to meet him that cometh against him with twenty thousand?

32 Or else, while the other is yet a great way off, he sendeth an ambassage, and desireth conditions of peace.

33 So likewise, whosoever he be of you that forsaketh not all that he hath, he cannot be my disciple.

23

§ 97. What is required of true

MATTHEW.	MARK.

§ 98. Parables of the lost Sheep, etc.

disciples. *Perea.*

LUKE.	JOHN.
CH. XIV. 25–35.	

34 Salt *is* good: but if the salt have lost his savour, wherewith shall it be seasoned?

35 It is neither fit for the land, nor yet for the dunghill; *but* men cast it out. He that hath ears to hear, let him hear.

and of the Prodigal Son. *Perea.*

CH. XV. 1–32.

THEN drew near unto him all the publicans and sinners for to hear him.

2 And the Pharisees and scribes murmured, saying, This man receiveth sinners, and eateth with them.

3 And he spake this parable unto them, saying,

4 What man of you having a hundred sheep, if he lose one of them, doth not leave the ninety and nine in the wilderness, and go after that which is lost, until he find it?

5 And when he hath found it, he layeth *it* on his shoulders, rejoicing.

6 And when he cometh home, he calleth together *his* friends and neighbours, saying unto them, Rejoice with me; for I have found my sheep which was lost.

7 I say unto you, that likewise joy shall be in heaven over one sinner that repenteth, more than over ninety and nine just persons which need no repentance.

8 Either what woman having ten pieces of silver, if she lose one piece, doth not light a candle, and sweep the house, and seek diligently till she find *it?*

9 And when she hath found *it*, she calleth *her* friends and *her* neighbours together, saying, Rejoice with me; for I have found the piece which I had lost.

10 Likewise, I say unto you, There is joy in the presence of the angels of God over one sinner that repenteth.

11 And he said, A certain man had two sons:

12 And the younger of them said to *his* father, Father, give me the portion of goods that falleth *to me.* And he divided unto them *his* living.

§ 98. Parables of the lost Sheep, etc.

MATTHEW.	MARK.

and of the Prodigal Son.　*Perea.*

LUKE.　　　　　　　　　　JOHN.

ch. xv.　1–32.

13 And not many days after, the younger son gathered all together, and took his journey into a far country, and there wasted his substance with riotous living.

14 And when he had spent all, there arose a mighty famine in that land ; and he began to be in want.

15 And he went and joined himself to a citizen of that country ; and he sent him into his fields to feed swine.

16 And he would fain have filled his belly with the husks that the swine did eat ; and no man gave unto him.

17 And when he came to himself, he said, How many hired servants of my father's have bread enough and to spare, and I perish with hunger !

18 I will arise and go to my father, and will say unto him, Father, I have sinned against heaven, and before thee,

19 And am no more worthy to be called thy son : make me as one of thy hired servants.

20 And he arose, and came to his father. But when he was yet a great way off, his father saw him, and had compassion, and ran, and fell on his neck, and kissed him.

21 And the son said unto him, Father, I have sinned against Heaven, and in thy sight, and am no more worthy to be called thy son.

22 But the father said to his servants, Bring forth the best robe, and put *it* on him ; and put a ring on his hand, and shoes on *his* feet :

23 And bring hither the fatted calf, and kill *it ;* and let us eat, and be merry :

24 For this my son was dead, and is alive again ; he was lost, and is found. And they began to be merry.

25 Now his elder son was in the field : and as he came and drew nigh to the house, he heard music and dancing.

26 And he called one of the servants, and asked what these things meant.

27 And he said unto him, Thy

§ 98. Parables of the lost Sheep, etc.

MATTHEW.	MARK.

§ 99. Parable of the Unjust

and of the Prodigal Son. *Perea.*

LUKE.	JOHN.

LUKE.
CH. XV. 1–32.

brother is come ; and thy father hath killed the fatted calf, because he hath received him safe and sound.

28 And he was angry, and would not go in ; therefore came his father out, and entreated him.

29 And he, answering, said to *his* father, Lo, these many years do I serve thee, neither transgressed I at any time thy commandment ; and yet thou never gavest me a kid, that I might make merry with my friends :

30 But as soon as this thy son was come, which hath devoured thy living with harlots, thou hast killed for him the fatted calf.

31 And he said unto him, Son, thou art ever with me ; and all that I have is thine.

32 It was meet that we should make merry, and be glad : for this thy brother was dead, and is alive *again* ; and was lost, and is found.

Steward. *Perea.*

CH. XVI. 1–13.

AND he said also unto his disciples, There was a certain rich man which had a steward ; and the same was accused unto him that he had wasted his goods.

2 And he called him, and said unto him, How is it that I hear this of thee ? give an account of thy stewardship : for thou mayest be no longer steward.

3 Then the steward said within himself, What shall I do ? for my lord taketh away from me the stewardship : I cannot dig ; to beg I am ashamed.

4 I am resolved what to do, that when I am put out of the stewardship, they may receive me into their houses.

5 So he called every one of his lord's debtors *unto him*, and said unto the first, How much owest thou unto my lord ?

6 And he said, A hundred measures of oil. And he said unto him, Take thy bill, and sit down quickly, and write fifty.

7 Then said he to another, And

§ 99. Parable of the Unjust

MATTHEW.	MARK.

§ 100. The Pharisees reproved. Parable of

Steward. *Perea.*

LUKE.	JOHN.
ch. xvi. 1 – 13.	

how much owest thou? And he said,
A hundred measures of wheat. And
he said unto him, Take thy bill, and
write four-score.

8 And the lord commended the
unjust steward, because he had done
wisely : for the children of this world
are in their generation wiser than the
children of light.

9 And I say unto you, Make to
yourselves friends of the mammon of
unrighteousness ; that when ye fail,
they may receive you into everlasting
habitations.

10 He that is faithful in that which
is least, is faithful also in much ; and
he that is unjust in the least, is unjust
also in much.

11 If therefore ye have not been
faithful in the unrighteous mammon,
who will commit to your trust the true
riches?

12 And if ye have not been faithful
in that which is another man's, who
shall give you that which is your own?

13 No servant can serve two masters : for either he will hate the one,
and love the other ; or else he will
hold to the one, and despise the other.
Ye cannot serve God and mammon.

the Rich Man and Lazarus. *Perea.*

ch. xvi. 14 – 31.

14 And the Pharisees also, who
were covetous, heard all these things,
and they derided him.

15 And he said unto them, Ye are
they which justify yourselves before
men ; but God knoweth your hearts :
for that which is highly esteemed
among men, is abomination in the
sight of God.

16 The law and the prophets *were*
until John : since that time the kingdom of God is preached, and every
man presseth into it.

17 And it is easier for heaven and
earth to pass, than one tittle of the
law to fail.

18 Whosoever putteth away his
wife, and marrieth another, committeth adultery ; and whosoever marrieth
her that is put away from *her* husband,
committeth adultery.

§ 100. The Pharisees reproved. Parable of

MATTHEW.   MARK.

the Rich Man and Lazarus. *Perea.*

LUKE.	JOHN.

LUKE.
CH. XVI. 14–31.

19 There was a certain rich man, which was clothed in purple and fine linen and fared sumptuously every day:

20 And there was a certain beggar named Lazarus, which was laid at his gate, full of sores,

21 And desiring to be fed with the crumbs which fell from the rich man's table: moreover, the dogs came and licked his sores.

22 And it came to pass, that the beggar died, and was carried by the angels into Abraham's bosom. The rich man also died, and was buried:

23 And in hell he lifted up his eyes, being in torments, and seeth Abraham afar off, and Lazarus in his bosom.

24 And he cried, and said, Father Abraham, have mercy on me, and send Lazarus, that he may dip the tip of his finger in water, and cool my tongue: for I am tormented in this flame.

25 But Abraham said, Son, remember that thou in thy lifetime receivedst thy good things, and likewise Lazarus evil things: but now he is comforted, and thou art tormented.

26 And besides all this, between us and you there is a great gulf fixed: so that they which would pass from hence to you, cannot; neither can they pass to us, that *would come* from thence.

27 Then he said, I pray thee therefore, father, that thou wouldest send him to my father's house:

28 For I have five brethren; that he may testify unto them, lest they also come into this place of torment.

29 Abraham saith unto him, They have Moses and the prophets, let them hear them.

30 And he said, Nay, father Abraham: but if one went unto them from the dead, they will repent.

31 And he said unto him, If they hear not Moses and the prophets, neither will they be persuaded, though one rose from the dead.

§ 101. Jesus inculcates forbearance,

MATTHEW.	MARK.

§ 102. Christ's coming will be

faith, humility. *Perea.*

LUKE.	JOHN.

LUKE.

CH. XVII. 1 – 10.

THEN said he unto his disciples, It is impossible but that offences will come : but wo *unto him* through whom they come !

2 It were better for him that a millstone were hanged about his neck, and he cast into the sea, than that he should offend one of these little ones.

3 Take heed to yourselves : If thy brother trespass against thee, rebuke him ; and if he repent, forgive him.

4 And if he trespass against thee seven times in a day, and seven times in a day turn again to thee, saying, I repent ; thou shalt forgive him.

5 And the apostles said unto the Lord, Increase our faith.

6 And the Lord said, If ye had faith as a grain of mustard-seed, ye might say unto this sycamine-tree, Be thou plucked up by the root, and be thou planted in the sea ; and it should obey you.

7 But which of you having a servant ploughing, or feeding cattle, will say unto him by and by, when he is come from the field, Go and sit down to meat ?

8 And will not rather say unto him, Make ready wherewith I may sup, and gird thyself, and serve me, till I have eaten and drunken ; and afterward thou shalt eat and drink ?

9 Doth he thank that servant, because he did the things that were commanded him ? I trow not.

10 So likewise ye, when ye shall have done all those things which are commanded you, say, We are unprofitable servants : we have done that which was our duty to do.

sudden. *Perea.*

CH. XVII. 20 – 37.

20 And when he was demanded of the Pharisees, when the kingdom of God should come, he answered them and said, The kingdom of God cometh not with observation.

21 Neither shall they say, Lo here ! or, Lo there ! for behold, the kingdom of God is within you.

22 And he said unto the disciples,

§ 102. Christ's coming will be

MATTHEW.	MARK.

sudden. *Perea.*

LUKE.	JOHN.

LUKE.
CH. XVII. 20-37.

The days will come, when ye shall desire to see one of the days of the Son of man, and ye shall not see *it*.

23 And they shall say to you, See here! or, See there! go not after *them*, nor follow *them*.

24 For as the lightning that lighteneth out of the one *part* under heaven, shineth unto the other *part* under heaven ; so shall also the Son of man be in his day.

25 But first must he suffer many things, and be rejected of this generation.

26 And as it was in the days of Noe, so 'shall it be also in the days of the Son of man.

27 They did eat, they drank, they married wives, they were given in marriage, until the day that Noe entered into the ark, and the flood came, and destroyed them all.[a]

28 Likewise also as it was in the days of Lot : they did eat, they drank, they bought, they sold, they planted, they builded ;

29 But the same day that Lot went out of Sodom, it rained fire and brimstone from heaven, and destroyed *them* all :[b]

30 Even thus shall it be in the day when the Son of man is revealed.

31 In that day, he which shall be upon the house-top, and his stuff in the house, let him not come down to take it away : and he that is in the field, let him likewise not return back.

32 Remember Lot's wife.[c]

33 Whosoever shall seek to save his life, shall lose it ; and whosoever shall lose his life, shall preserve it.

34 I tell you, in that night there shall be two *men* in one bed ; the one shall be taken, and the other shall be left.

35 Two *women* shall be grinding together ; the one shall be taken, and the other left.

36 Two *men* shall be in the field ; the one shall be taken, and the other left.

---

[a] Gen. vii. 4, 7.   [b] Gen. xix. 15, seq.   [c] Gen. xix. 26.

§ 102. Christ's coming will be

MATTHEW.	MARK.

§ 103. Parables. The importunate Widow.

sudden. *Perea.*

LUKE.	JOHN.
CH. XVII. 20–37.	

37 And they answered and said unto him, Where, Lord? And he said unto them, Wheresoever the body *is*, thither will the eagles be gathered together.

The Pharisee and Publican. *Perea.*

CH. XVIII. 1–14.

AND he spake a parable unto them *to this end*, that men ought always *to* pray, and not to faint;

2 Saying, There was in a city a judge, which feared not God, neither regarded man.

3 And there was a widow in that city; and she came unto him, saying, Avenge me of mine adversary.

4 And he would not for a while: but afterward he said within himself, Though I fear not God, nor regard man;

5 Yet, because this widow troubleth me, I will avenge her, lest by her continual coming she weary me.

6 And the Lord said, Hear what the unjust judge saith.

7 And shall not God avenge his own elect, which cry day and night unto him, though he bear long with them?

8 I tell you that he will avenge them speedily. Nevertheless, when the Son of man cometh, shall he find faith on the earth?

9 And he spake this parable unto certain which trusted in themselves that they were righteous, and despised others:

10 Two men went up into the temple to pray; the one a Pharisee, and the other a publican.

11 The Pharisee stood and prayed thus with himself, God, I thank thee, that I am not as other men *are*, extortioners, unjust, adulterers, or even as this publican.

12 I fast twice in the week, I give tithes of all that I possess.

13 And the publican, standing afar off, would not lift up so much as *his* eyes unto heaven, but smote upon his breast, saying, God be merciful to me a sinner.

24

§ 103. Parables. The importunate Widow.

MATTHEW.	MARK.

§ 104. Precepts respecting divorce.

CH. XIX. 3–12.	CH. X. 2–12.
3 The Pharisees also came unto him, tempting him, and saying unto him, Is it lawful for a man to put away his wife for every cause?	2 And the Pharisees came to him, and asked him, Is it lawful for a man to put away *his* wife? tempting him.
4 And he answered and said unto them, Have ye not read,[a] that he which made *them* at the beginning, made them male and female,	3 And he answered and said unto them, What did Moses command you?
5 And said,[b] For this cause shall a man leave father and mother, and shall cleave to his wife: and they twain shall be one flesh?	4 And they said, Moses suffered to write a bill of divorcement, and to put *her* away.
6 Wherefore they are no more twain, but one flesh. What therefore God hath joined together, let not man put asunder.	5 And Jesus answered and said unto them, For the hardness of your heart, he wrote you this precept:
7 They say unto him, Why did Moses then command to give a writing of divorcement, and to put her away?[c]	6 But from the beginning of the creation, God made them male and female.
8 He saith unto them, Moses, because of the hardness of your hearts, suffered you to put away your wives: but from the beginning it was not so.	7 For this cause shall a man leave his father and mother, and cleave to his wife;
9 And I say unto you, Whosoever shall put away his wife, except *it be* for fornication, and shall marry another, committeth adultery: and whoso marrieth her which is put away, doth commit adultery.	8 And they twain shall be one flesh: so then they are no more twain, but one flesh.
10 His disciples say unto him, If the case of the man be so with *his* wife, it is not good to marry.	9 What, therefore, God hath joined together, let not man put asunder.
11 But he said unto them, All *men* cannot receive this saying, save *they* to whom it is given.	10 And in the house his disciples asked him again of the same *matter*.
	11 And he saith unto them, Whosoever shall put away his wife, and marry another, committeth adultery against her.
	12 And if a woman shall put away her husband, and be married to another, she committeth adultery.

a Gen. i. 27.   b Gen. ii. 24.   c Deut. xxiv. 1.

Matth. xix. 1–12.] The two Evangelists go on to relate our Lord's observations about divorce and marriage; they agree in substance, which is sufficient; though they differ in the form of the dialogue, neither adhering scrupulously to the exact manner in which the words passed, though we may learn it, by comparing both. Thus Matth. v. 9, reduces to a plain assertion, what Mark informs us was a reply to an inquiry made by the disciples apart. Or, we may suppose with Le Clerc, that this assertion was first advanced to the Pharisees, and then repeated to the disciples. NEWCOME.

The Pharisee and Publican. *Perea.*

LUKE.	JOHN.
CH. XVIII. 1–14.	
14 I tell you, this man went down to his house justified *rather* than the other: for every one that exalteth himself shall be abased; and he that humbleth himself shall be exalted.	

Perea.

Mark x. 12, *put away her husband.*] The practice of divorcing the husband, un-warranted by the law, had been introduced, as Josephus informs us, (Antiq. XV. vii. 10,) by Salome, sister of Herod the Great, who sent a bill of divorce to her husband Costobarus; which bad example was afterwards followed by Herodias and others. CAMPBELL. This natural allusion to an existing illegal custom is in perfect harmony with the whole history, it being true; but it seldom if ever has a parallel in the annals of forgery.

§ 104. Precepts respecting divorce.

MATTHEW.	MARK.
CH. XIX. 3-12.	

12 For there are some eunuchs, which were so born from *their* mother's womb: and there are some eunuchs, which were made eunuchs of men: and there be eunuchs, which have made themselves eunuchs for the kingdom of heaven's sake. He that is able to receive *it*, let him receive *it*.

---

§ 105. Jesus receives and blesses little

CH. XIX. 13-15.	CH. X. 13-16.

13 Then were there brought unto him little children, that he should put *his* hands on them, and pray: and the disciples rebuked them.

13 And they brought young children to him, that he should touch them; and *his* disciples rebuked those that brought *them.*

14 But when Jesus saw *it*, he was much displeased, and said unto them,

14 But Jesus said, Suffer little children, and forbid them not, to come unto me: for of such is the kingdom of heaven.

Suffer the little children to come unto me, and forbid them not: for of such is the kingdom of God.

15 Verily I say unto you, Whosoever shall not receive the kingdom of God as a little child, he shall not enter therein.

15 And he laid *his* hands on them, and departed thence.

16 And he took them up in his arms; put *his* hands upon them, and blessed them.

---

§ 106. The rich young man. Parable of the

CH. XIX. 16-30. CH. XX. 1-16.	CH. X. 17-31.

16 And behold, one came and said unto him, Good Master, what good thing shall I do that I may have eternal life?

17 And when he was gone forth into the way, there came one running, and kneeled to him, and asked him, Good Master, what shall I do that I may inherit eternal life?

17 And he said unto him, Why callest thou me good? *there is* none good but one, *that is,* God: but if thou wilt enter into life, keep the commandments.

18 And Jesus said unto him, Why callest thou me good? *there is* none good, but one, *that is* God.

18 He saith unto him, Which? Jesus said, Thou shalt do no murder, Thou shalt not commit adultery, Thou shalt not steal, Thou shalt not bear false witness,

19 Thou knowest the commandments, Do not commit adultery, Do not kill, Do not steal, Do not bear false witness, Defraud not, Honour thy father and mother.

19 Honour thy father and *thy* mother: and, Thou shalt love thy neighbour as thyself.[a]

20 The young man saith unto him, All these things have I kept from my youth up: what lack I yet?

20 And he answered and said unto him, Master, all these have I observed from my youth.

[a] Ex. xx. 12, seq. Lev. xix. 18.

Perea.

*LUKE.	JOHN.

children. *Perea.*

CH. XVIII. 15–17.

15 And they brought unto him also infants, that he would touch them: but when *his* disciples saw *it*, they rebuked them.

16 But Jesus called them *unto him*, and said, Suffer little children to come unto me, and forbid them not: for of such is the kingdom of God.

17 Verily, I say unto you, Whosoever shall not receive the kingdom of God as a little child, shall in no wise enter therein.

Laborers in the Vineyard. *Perea.*

CH. XVIII. 18–30.

18 And a certain ruler asked him, saying, Good Master, what shall I do to inherit eternal life?

19 And Jesus said unto him, Why callest thou me good? none *is* good, save one, *that is* God.

20 Thou knowest the commandments, Do not commit adultery, Do not kill, Do not steal, Do not bear false witness, Honour thy father and thy mother.

21 And he said, All these have I kept from my youth up.

§ 106. The rich young man.   Parable of the

MATTHEW.
CH. XIX. 16–30.   CH. XX. 1–16.

21 Jesus said unto him, If thou wilt be perfect, go *and* sell that thou hast, and give to the poor, and thou shalt have treasure in heaven : and come *and* follow me.

22 But when the young man heard that saying, he went away sorrowful : for he had great possessions.

23 Then said Jesus unto his disciples, Verily, I say unto you, That a rich man shall hardly enter into the kingdom of heaven.

24 And again I say unto you, It is easier for a camel to go through the eye of a needle, than for a rich man to enter into the kingdom of God.

25 When his disciples heard *it*, they were exceedingly amazed, saying, Who then can be saved ?

26 But Jesus beheld *them*, and said unto them, With men this is impossible, but with God all things are possible.

27 Then answered Peter, and said unto him, Behold, we have forsaken all, and followed thee ; what shall we have therefore ?

28 And Jesus said unto them, Verily, I say unto you, That ye which have followed me in the regeneration, when the Son of man shall sit in the throne of his glory, ye also shall sit upon twelve thrones, judging the twelve tribes of Israel.

29 And every one that hath forsaken houses, or brethren, or sisters, or father, or mother, or wife, or children, or lands, for my name's sake, shall receive a hundred-fold, and shall inherit everlasting life.

30 But many *that are* first shall be last, and the last *shall be* first.

CH. XX.

FOR the kingdom of heaven is like unto a man *that is* a householder,

MARK.
CH. X. 17–31.

21 Then Jesus beholding him, loved him, and said unto him, One thing thou lackest : go thy way, sell whatsoever thou hast, and give to the poor, and thou shalt have treasure in heaven ; and come, take up the cross, and follow me.

22 And he was sad at that saying, and went away grieved : for he had great possessions.

23 And Jesus looked round about, and saith unto his disciples, How hardly shall they that have riches enter into the kingdom of God !

24 And the disciples were astonished at his words. But Jesus answereth again, and saith unto them, Children, how hard is it for them that trust in riches to enter into the kingdom of God !

25 It is easier for a camel to go through the eye of a needle, than for a rich man to enter into the kingdom of God.

26 And they were astonished out of measure, saying among themselves, Who then can be saved ?

27 And Jesus, looking upon them, saith, With men *it is* impossible, but not with God : for with God all things are possible.

28 Then Peter began to say unto him, Lo, we have left all, and have followed thee.

29 And Jesus answered and said, Verily I say unto you, There is no man that hath left house, or brethren, or sisters, or father, or mother, or wife, or children, or lands, for my sake, and the gospel's,

30 But he shall receive a hundred-fold now in this time, houses, and brethren, and sisters, and mothers, and children, and lands, with persecutions ; and in the world to come, eternal life.

31 But many *that are* first shall be last ; and the last first.

LUKE.	JOHN.

LUKE.

CH. XVIII. 18—30.

22 Now, when Jesus heard these things, he said unto him, Yet lackest thou one thing : sell all that thou hast, and distribute unto the poor, and thou shalt have treasure in heaven : and come, follow me.

23 And when he heard this, he was very sorrowful : for he was very rich.

24 And when Jesus saw that he was very sorrowful, he said, How hardly shall they that have riches enter into the kingdom of God !

25 For it is easier for a camel to go through a needle's eye, than for a rich man to enter into the kingdom of God.

26 And they that heard *it*, said, Who then can be saved ?

27 And he said, The things which are impossible with men, are possible with God.

28 Then Peter said, Lo, we have left all, and followed thee.

29 And he said unto them, Verily, I say unto you, There is no man that hath left house, or parents, or brethren, or wife, or children, for the kingdom of God's sake,

30 Who shall not receive manifold more in this present time, and in the world to come life everlasting.

MATTHEW.	MARK.

MATTHEW.

CH. XIX. 16 – 30. CH. XX. 1 – 16.

which went out early in the morning to hire labourers into his vineyard.

2 And when he had agreed with the labourers for a penny a day, he sent them into his vineyard.

3 And he went out about the third hour, and saw others standing idle in the market-place,

4 And said unto them, Go ye also into the vineyard; and whatsoever is right, I will give you. And they went their way.

5 Again he went out about the sixth and ninth hour, and did likewise.

6 And about the eleventh hour he went out, and found others standing idle, and saith unto them, Why stand ye here all the day idle?

7 They say unto him, Because no man hath hired us. He saith unto them, Go ye also into the vineyard; and whatsoever is right, *that* shall ye receive.

8 So when evening was come, the lord of the vineyard saith unto his steward, Call the labourers, and give them *their* hire, beginning from the last unto the first.

9 And when they came that *were hired* about the eleventh hour, they received every man a penny.

10 But when the first came, they supposed that they should have received more; and they likewise received every man a penny.

11 And when they had received *it*, they murmured against the good man of the house,

12 Saying, These last have wrought *but* one hour, and thou hast made them equal unto us, which have borne the burden and heat of the day.

13 But he answered one of them, and said, Friend, I do thee no wrong: didst not thou agree with me for a penny?

14 Take *that* thine *is*, and go thy way: I will give unto this last, even as unto thee.

15 Is it not lawful for me to do what I will with mine own? is thine eye evil because I am good?

16 So the last shall be first, and the first last: for many be called, but few chosen.

MARK.

Laborers in the Vineyard. *Perea.*

LUKE.	JOHN.

§ 107. Jesus a third time foretells his Death

MATTHEW.	MARK.
CH. XX. 17–19.	CH. X. 32–34.
17 And Jesus, going up to Jerusalem, took the twelve disciples apart in the way, and said unto them,	32 And they were in the way, going up to Jerusalem; and Jesus went before them: and they were amazed; and as they followed, they were afraid. And he took again the twelve, and began to tell them what things should happen unto him,
18 Behold, we go up to Jerusalem; and the Son of man shall be betrayed unto the chief priests, and unto the scribes, and they shall condemn him to death,	33 *Saying*, Behold, we go up to Jerusalem; and the Son of man shall be delivered unto the chief priests, and unto the scribes; and they shall condemn him to death, and shall deliver him to the Gentiles;
19 And shall deliver him to the Gentiles to mock, and to scourge, and to crucify *him*: and the third day he shall rise again.	34 And they shall mock him, and shall scourge him, and shall spit upon him, and shall kill him: and the third day he shall rise again.

§ 108. James and John prefer their ambitious

CH. XX. 20–28.	CH. X. 35–45.
20 Then came to him the mother of Zebedee's children, with her sons, worshipping *him*, and desiring a certain thing of him.	35 And James and John, the sons of Zebedee, come unto him, saying, Master, we would that thou shouldest do for us whatsoever we shall desire.
21 And he said unto her, What wilt thou? She saith unto him, Grant that these my two sons may sit, the one on thy right hand, and the other on the left, in thy kingdom.	36 And he said unto them, What would ye that I should do for you? 37 They said unto him, Grant unto us that we may sit, one on thy right hand, and the other on thy left hand, in thy glory.
22 But Jesus answered and said, Ye know not what ye ask. Are ye able to drink of the cup that I shall drink of, and to be baptized with the baptism that I am baptized with? They say unto him, We are able.	38 But Jesus said unto them, Ye know not what ye ask: can ye drink of the cup that I drink of? and be baptized with the baptism that I am baptized with? 39 And they said unto him, We can. And Jesus said unto them, Ye shall indeed drink of the cup that I drink of; and with the baptism that I am baptized withal shall ye be baptized:
23 And he saith unto them, Ye shall drink indeed of my cup, and be baptized with the baptism that I am baptized with: but, to sit on my right hand, and on my left, is not mine to give, but *it shall be given to them* for whom it is prepared of my Father.	40 But to sit on my right hand and on my left hand, is not mine to give; but *it shall be given to them* for whom it is prepared.
24 And when the ten heard *it*, they were moved with indignation against the two brethren.	41 And when the ten heard *it*, they began to be much displeased with James and John.

Matth. xx. 21, *she saith*.] As all three came to Jesus, the *action* of the sons expressed, that they joined in the petition uttered by the mother. They are therefore represented as saying what was said with their consent, an[d] probably by their sug-

and Resurrection.　[See § 74, § 77.]　*Perea.*

LUKE.	JOHN.
cⁿ. xviii. 31 – 34.	

LUKE.

cⁿ. xviii. 31 – 34.

31 Then he took *unto him* the twelve, and said unto them, Behold, we go up to Jerusalem, and all things that are written by the prophets concerning the Son of man shall be accomplished.

32 For he shall be delivered unto the Gentiles, and shall be mocked, and spitefully entreated, and spitted on ;

33 And they shall scourge *him*, and put him to death : and the third day he shall rise again.

34 And they understood none of these things : and this saying was hid from them, neither knew they the things which were spoken.

request.　*Perea.*

gestion. Luke xix. 11, will show how suitable this request was to the time, according to the ideas of our Lord's disciples. NEWCOME.

§ 108. James and John prefer their ambitious

MATTHEW.	MARK.
CH. XX. 20 – 28.	CH. X. 35 – 45.
25 But Jesus called them *unto him*, and said, Ye know that the princes of the Gentiles exercise dominion over them, and they that are great exercise authority upon them.	42 But Jesus called them *to him*, and saith unto them, Ye know that they which are accounted to rule over the Gentiles, exercise lordship over them; and their great ones exercise authority upon them.
26 But it shall not be so among you : but whosoever will be great among you, let him be your minister ; 27 And whosoever will be chief among you, let him be your servant : 28 Even as the Son of man came not to be ministered unto, but to minister, and to give his life a ransom for many.	43 But so shall it not be among you : but whosoever will be great among you, shall be your minister : 44 And whosoever of you will be the chiefest, shall be servant of all. 45 For even the Son of man came not to be ministered unto, but to minister, and to give his life a ransom for many.

§ 109. The healing of two

CH. XX. 29 – 34.	CH. X. 46 – 52.
29 And as they departed from Jericho, a great multitude followed him. 30 And behold, two blind men sitting by the wayside, when they heard that Jesus passed by, cried out, saying, Have mercy on us, O Lord, *thou* son of David.	46 And they came to Jericho : and as he went out of Jericho with his disciples, and a great number of people, blind Bartimeus, the son of Timeus, sat by the highway side, begging. 47 And when he heard that it was Jesus of Nazareth, he began to cry out and say, Jesus, *thou* son of David, have mercy on me.
31 And the multitude rebuked them, because they should hold their peace : but they cried the more, saying, Have mercy on us, O Lord, *thou* son of David.	48 And many charged him that he should hold his peace : but he cried the more a great deal, *Thou* son of David, have mercy on me.
32 And Jesus stood still, and called them,	49 And Jesus stood still, and commanded him to be called : and they call the blind man, saying unto him, Be of good comfort, rise ; he calleth thee. 50 And he, casting away his garment, rose, and came to Jesus. 51 And Jesus answered and said unto him, What wilt thou that I
and said, What will ye that I shall do unto you?	should do unto thee ? The blind man

Luke xviii. 35, *come nigh.*] According to St. Mark, Jesus comes to Jericho ; by which may be meant that he is a temporary inhabitant of that city. See Mark vi. 1, and viii. 22. Jesus therefore may be represented, (Matth. xx. 29 ; Mark x. 46,) not as *finally leaving* Jericho for Jerusalem, but as *occasionally going out* of Jericho ; in which city he had made some abode, it matters not for how few days. See Mark xi. 19. Jericho was a very considerable city ; and we do not read that it was visited by our Lord at any other time. We may therefore suppose that Jesus, accompanied by his disciples and the multitude, and intent on his great work of propagating the gospel, went out of this city, knowing that a fit occasion of working a miracle would

request. *Perea.*

LUKE.	JOHN.

blind men near Jericho.

CH. XVIII. 35–43. CH. XIX. 1. 35 And it came to pass, that as he was come nigh unto Jericho, a certain blind man sat by the wayside begging; 36 And hearing the multitude pass by, he asked what it meant. 37 And they told him, that Jesus of Nazareth passeth by. 38 And he cried, saying, Jesus, *thou* son of David, have mercy on me. 39 And they which went before rebuked him, that he should hold his peace: but he cried so much the more, *Thou* son of David, have mercy on me. 40 And Jesus stood and commanded him to be brought unto him: and when he was come near, he asked him, 41 Saying, What wilt thou that I	

present itself; and that on his return, as he drew nigh unto Jericho, (Luke xviii. 35,) he restored the blind men to sight. It is likewise probable that Jesus, having given this proof of his divine mission, or foreseeing that so great a miracle would create too much attention in the people, prudently and humbly passed through Jericho on his return to it, (Luke xix. 1,) and continued his journey to Jerusalem.

As to the remaining difficulty, that Matthew mentions two blind men, and the other Evangelists only one, I must refer to Le Clerc's maxim, before quoted; (see § 57, note); adding that Bartimeus may have been the more remarkable of the two, and the more eminent for his faith in Jesus. NEWCOME.

§ 109. The healing of two

MATTHEW.	MARK.
CH. XX. 29 – 34.	CH. X. 46 – 52.
33 They say unto him, Lord, that our eyes may be opened.	said unto him, Lord, that I might receive my sight.
34 So Jesus had compassion *on them*, and touched their eyes : and immediately their eyes received sight, and they followed him.	52 And Jesus said unto him, Go thy way ; thy faith hath made thee whole. And immediately he received his sight, and followed Jesus in the way.

§ 110. The visit to Zaccheus. Parable of

blind men near Jericho.

LUKE.	JOHN.

CH. XVIII. 35–43. CH. XIX. 1.

shall do unto thee? And he said,
Lord, that I may receive my sight.

42 And Jesus said unto him, Receive thy sight: thy faith hath saved
thee.

43 And immediately he received his
sight, and followed him, glorifying
God: and all the people, when they
saw *it*, gave praise unto God.

CH. XIX.

AND *Jesus* entered and passed
through Jericho.

the ten Minae.   *Jericho.*

CH. XIX. 2–28.

2 And behold, *there was* a man
named Zaccheus, which was the
chief among the publicans, and he
was rich.

3 And he sought to see Jesus who
he was; and could not for the press,
because he was little of stature.

4 And he ran before, and climbed
up into a sycamore-tree to see him;
for he was to pass that *way*.

5 And when Jesus came to the
place, he looked up, and saw him, and
said unto him, Zaccheus, make haste,
and come down: for to-day I must
abide at thy house.

6 And he made haste, and came
down, and received him joyfully.

7 And when they saw *it*, they all
murmured, saying, That he was gone
to be guest with a man that is a sinner.

8 And Zaccheus stood, and said
unto the Lord; Behold, Lord, the
half of my goods I give to the poor;
and if I have taken any thing from
any man, by false accusation, I restore
him four-fold.

9 And Jesus said unto him, This
day is salvation come to this house,
forasmuch as he also is a son of Abraham.

10 For the Son of man is come to
seek and to save that which was lost.

11 And as they heard these things,
he added and spake a parable, because he was nigh to Jerusalem, and
because they thought that the kingdom of God should immediately appear.

§ 110. The visit of Zaccheus. Parable of

MATTHEW.	MARK.

Luke xix. 12.]   Here is a fine allusion to historical facts, first observed by Le Clerc. "Thus Herod the Great solicited the kingdom of Judea at Rome, (Jos. Antiq. Jud. XIV. xiv. 4, 5. XV. vi. 6, 7,) and was appointed king by the interest of Anthony with the senate; and afterwards he sailed to Rhodes, divested himself of his diadem, and received it again from Augustus. In like manner his sons Archelaus and Antipas

LUKE.
CH. XIX. 2–28.

12 He said therefore, A certain nobleman went into a far country to receive for himself a kingdom, and to return.

13 And he called his ten servants, and delivered them ten pounds, and said unto them, Occupy till I come.

14 But his citizens hated him, and sent a message after him, saying, We will not have this *man* to reign over us.

15 And it came to pass, that when he was returned, having received the kingdom, then he commanded these servants to be called unto him, to whom he had given the money, that he might know how much every man had gained by trading.

16 Then came the first, saying, Lord, thy pound hath gained ten pounds.

17 And he said unto him, Well, thou good servant: because thou hast been faithful in a very little, have thou authority over ten cities.

18 And the second came, saying, Lord, thy pound hath gained five pounds.

19 And he said likewise to him, Be thou also over five cities.

20 And another came, saying, Lord, behold *here is* thy pound, which I have kept laid up in a napkin:

21 For I feared thee, because thou art an austere man: thou takest up that thou layedst not down, and reapest that thou didst not sow.

22 And he saith unto him, Out of thine own mouth will I judge thee, *thou* wicked servant. Thou knewest that I was an austere man, taking up that I laid not down, and reaping that I did not sow:

23 Wherefore then gavest not thou my money into the bank, that at my coming I might have required mine own with usury?

JOHN.

repaired to the imperial city, that they might obtain the kingdom on their father's death; and we read, (Jos. Antiq. Jud. XIV. xi. 1, and xiii. 2,) that the Jews sent an embassy thither, with accusations against Archelaus. NEWCOME, Obs. on our Lord, p. 83.

25

§ 110.   The visit of Zaccheus.   The Parable of

MATTHEW.	MARK.

§ 111. Jesus arrives at Bethany six days

the ten Minae. *Jericho.*

LUKE.	JOHN.

LUKE.
CH. XIX.   2 – 28.

24 And he said unto them that stood by, Take from him the pound, and give *it* to him that hath ten pounds.

25 (And they said unto him, Lord, he hath ten pounds.)

26 For I say unto you, That unto every one which hath, shall be given ; and from him that hath not, even that he hath shall be taken away from him.

27 But those mine enemies, which would not that I should reign over them, bring hither, and slay *them* before me.

28 And when he had thus spoken, he went before, ascending up to Jerusalem.

before the Passover. *Bethany.*

JOHN.
CH. XI. 55 – 57.   CH. XII. 1, 9 – 11.

55 And the Jews' passover was nigh at hand : and many went out of the country up to Jerusalem before the passover, to purify themselves.

56 Then sought they for Jesus, and spake among themselves, as they stood in the temple, What think ye, that he will not come to the feast?

57 Now both the chief priests and the Pharisees had given a commandment, that, if any man knew where he were, he should shew *it*, that they might take him.

CH. XII.

THEN Jesus, six days before the passover, came to Bethany, where Lazarus was which had been dead, whom he raised from the dead.

9 Much people of the Jews therefore knew that he was there : and they came, not for Jesus' sake only, but that they might see Lazarus also, whom he had raised from the dead.

10 But the chief priests consulted that they might put Lazarus also to death ;

11 Because that by reason of him many of the Jews went away, and believed on Jesus.

PART VII.

OUR LORD'S PUBLIC ENTRY INTO JERUSALEM,

AND THE

SUBSEQUENT TRANSACTIONS

BEFORE

THE FOURTH PASSOVER.

TIME. Five days.

§ 112. Our Lord's public entry into Jerusalem.

MATTHEW.	MARK.
CH. XXI. 1–11, 14–17.	CH. XI. 1–11.
AND when they drew nigh unto Jerusalem, and were come to Bethphage, unto the mount of Olives, then sent Jesus two disciples,	AND when they came nigh to Jerusalem, unto Bethphage, and Bethany, at the mount of Olives, he sendeth forth two of his disciples,
2 Saying unto them, Go into the village over against you, and straightway ye shall find an ass tied, and a colt with her: loose *them*, and bring *them* unto me.	2 And saith unto them, Go your way into the village over against you : and as soon as ye be entered into it, ye shall find a colt tied, whereon never man sat ; loose him, and bring *him*.
3 And if any *man* say aught unto you, ye shall say, The Lord hath need of them ; and straightway he will send them.	3 And if any man say unto you, Why do ye this? say ye that the Lord hath need of him ; and straightway he will send him hither.
4 All this was done, that it might be fulfilled which was spoken by the prophet, saying,[a]	
5 Tell ye the daughter of Sion, Behold, thy King cometh unto thee, meek, and sitting upon an ass, and a colt the foal of an ass.	
6 And the disciples went, and did as Jesus commanded them,	4 And they went their way and found the colt tied by the door without, in a place where two ways met ; and they loose him.
	5 And certain of them that stood there said unto them, What do ye, loosing the colt ?
	6 And they said unto them even as Jesus had commanded : and they let them go.
7 And brought the ass and the colt, and put on them their clothes, and they set *him* thereon.	7 And they brought the colt to Jesus, and cast their garments on him ; and he sat upon him.
8 And a very great multitude spread their garments in the way : others cut down branches from the trees, and strewed *them* in the way.	8 And many spread their garments in the way : and others cut down branches off the trees, and strewed *them* in the way.

[a] Zech. ix. 9.

Matth. xxi. 7, *and put on them their clothes.*] Thus acknowledging him to be their *king ;* for this was a custom observed by the people when they found that God had appointed a man to the kingdom. When Jehu was anointed king by Elisha the prophet, at the command of God, and his captains knew what was done, *every man took his garment and spread it under him on the top of the steps, and blew the trumpets, saying Jehu is king.* 2 King ix. 13. A. CLARKE. See JENNINGS, Ant. vol. ii. p. 245. "*Thereon,*" that is, on the garments. The princes of Israel were forbidden to multiply *horses* to themselves. Deut. xvii. 16, and xx. 1. This law was imposed as a standing mark of distinction between them and other nations ; and a trial of prince and people, whether they had confidence in God their deliverer, who wanted neither horses nor footmen to fight his battles. It was observed for near four hundred

LUKE.	JOHN.
CH. XIX. 29 – 44.	CH. XII. 12 – 19.
29 And it came to pass, when he was come nigh to Bethphage and Bethany, at the mount called *the mount* of Olives, he sent two of his disciples,	12 On the next day, much people that were come to the feast, when they heard that Jesus was coming to Jerusalem,
30 Saying, Go ye into the village over against *you;* in the which at your entering ye shall find a colt tied, whereon yet never man sat: loose him, and bring *him hither*.	
31 And if any man ask you, Why do ye loose *him?* thus shall ye say unto him, Because the Lord hath need of him.	
32 And they that were sent went their way, and found even as he had said unto them.	
33 And as they were loosing the colt, the owners thereof said unto them, Why loose ye the colt!	
34 And they said, The Lord hath need of him.	
35 And they brought him to Jesus: and they cast their garments upon the colt and they set Jesus thereon.	
36 And as he went, they spread their clothes in the way.	

years, until some time in the reign of Solomon ; for David himself rode on a mule ; as did Solomon also on the day of his coronation. 1 Kings i. 33, 34. See Judges x. 4, and xii. 14 ; 1 Saml. xxv. 20. Subsequently the kings of Israel and Judah violated this command, by copying the example of the neighboring princes in the establishment of their cavalry. The displeasure of God for this offence is indicated by several of the prophets : Isaiah ii. 6, 7, and xxxi. 1 ; Hosea xiv. 3, and i. 7 ; Micah v. 10, 11. — In opposition to the character of these warlike and disobedient princes, it was predict- ed that Messiah would come as a just king, having salvation ; — a deliverer — riding upon an ass, after the manner of the ancient deliverers of Israel, who came only in the strength and power of the Lord. Zech. ix. 9. See Bishop SHERLOCK's Dissert. IV. MICHAELIS, vol. ii. pp. 439 – 449.

§ 112. Our Lord's public entry into Jerusalem.

MATTHEW.	MARK.
CH. XXI. 1–11, 14–17.	CH. XI. 1–11.
9 And the multitudes that went before, and that followed, cried, saying, Hosanna to the Son of David : Blessed *is* he that cometh in the name of the Lord : Hosanna in the highest.	9 And they that went before, and they that followed, cried, saying, Hosanna : Blessed *is* he that cometh in the name of the Lord.
	10 Blessed *be* the kingdom of our father David, that cometh in the name of the Lord : Hosanna in the highest.
10 And when he was come into Jerusalem, all the city was moved, saying, Who is this ?	
11 And the multitude said, This is Jesus the prophet of Nazareth of Galilee.	
14 And the blind and the lame came to him in the temple ; and he healed them.	
15 And when the chief priests and scribes saw the wonderful things that he did, and the children crying in the temple, and saying, Hosanna to the son of David ; they were sore displeased,	
16 And said unto him, Hearest thou what these say ? And Jesus saith unto them, Yea : have ye never read, Out of the mouth of babes and sucklings thou hast perfected praise ? [a]	
17 And he left them, and went out of the city into Bethany, and he lodged there.	11 And Jesus entered into Jerusalem, and into the temple : and when he had looked round about upon all things, and now the even-tide was come, he went out unto Bethany, with the twelve.

Ps. viii. 3.

LUKE.
CH. XIX. 29–44.

37 And when he was come nigh, even now at the descent of the mount of Olives, the whole multitude of the disciples began to rejoice and praise God with a loud voice, for all the mighty works that they had seen ;

38 Saying, Blessed *be* the King that cometh in the name of the Lord : Peace in heaven, and glory in the highest.

39 And some of the Pharisees from among the multitude said unto him, Master, rebuke thy disciples.

40 And he answered and said unto them, I tell you, that if these should hold their peace, the stones would immediately cry out.

41 And when he was come near, he beheld the city, and wept over it,

42 Saying, If thou hadst known, even thou, at least in this thy day, the things *which belong* unto thy peace ! but now they are hid from thine eyes.

43 For the days shall come upon thee, that thine enemies shall cast a trench about thee, and compass thee round, and keep thee in on every side,

44 And shall lay thee even with the ground, and thy children within thee : and they shall not leave in thee one stone upon another : because thou knewest not the time of thy visitation.

JOHN.
CH. XII. 12–19.

13 Took branches of palm-trees, and went forth to meet him, and cried, Hosanna ; Blessed *is* the King of Israel that cometh in the name of the Lord.[a]

14 And Jesus, when he had found a young ass, sat thereon ; as it is written,

15 Fear not, daughter of Sion : behold, thy King cometh, sitting on an ass's colt.

16 These things understood not his disciples at the first : but when Jesus was glorified, then remembered they that these things were written of him, and *that* they had done these things unto him.

17 The people therefore that was with him when he called Lazarus out of his grave, and raised him from the dead, bare record.

18 For this cause the people also met him, for that they heard that he had done this miracle.

19 The Pharisees therefore said among themselves, Perceive ye how ye prevail nothing ! behold, the world is gone after him.

[a] Ps. cxviii. 26.

§ 113. The barren Fig-tree. The cleansing of the

MATTHEW.	MARK.
CH. XXI. 12, 13, 18, 19.	CH. XI. 12–19.

18 Now in the morning, as he re-turned into the city, he hungered.

12 And on the morrow, when they were come from Bethany, he was hungry.

19 And when he saw a fig-tree in the way, he came to it, and found nothing thereon, but leaves only, and said unto it, Let no fruit grow on thee henceforward for ever. And presently the fig-tree withered away.

13 And seeing a fig-tree afar off, having leaves, he came, if haply he might find any thing thereon: and when he came to it, he found nothing but leaves: for the time of figs was not yet.

14 And Jesus answered and said unto it, No man eat fruit of thee hereafter for ever. And his disciples heard it.

12 And Jesus went into the temple of God, and cast out all them that sold and bought in the temple, and overthrew the tables of the money-changers, and the seats of them that sold doves,

15 And they come to Jerusalem: and Jesus went into the temple, and began to cast out them that sold and bought in the temple, and overthrew the tables of the money-changers, and the seats of them that sold doves;

16 And would not suffer that any man should carry any vessel through the temple.

13 And said unto them, It is writ-ten,[a] My house shall be called the house of prayer, but ye have made it a den of thieves.

17 And he taught, saying unto them, Is it not written, My house shall be called, of all nations, the house of prayer? but ye have made it a den of thieves.

18 And the scribes and chief priests heard it, and sought how they might destroy him: for they feared him, because all the people was astonished at his doctrine.

19 And when even was come, he went out of the city.

§ 114. The barren Fig-tree withers away.

CH. XXI. 20–22.	CH. XI. 20–26.

20 And in the morning, as they passed by, they saw the fig-tree dried up from the roots.

20 And when the disciples saw it, they marvelled, saying, How soon is the fig-tree withered away!

21 And Peter calling to remem-brance, saith unto him, Master, be-hold, the fig-tree which thou cursedst is withered away.

21 Jesus answered and said unto them, Verily, I say unto you, If ye have faith, and doubt not, ye shall not only do this which is done to the fig-tree, but also, if ye shall say unto

22 And Jesus answering, saith un-to them, Have faith in God.

23 For verily I say unto you, That whosoever shall say unto this moun-tain, Be thou removed, and be thou

a Isa. lvi. 7. Jer. vii. 11.

Matth. xxi. 20, the disciples. Mark xi. 21, Peter.] These may be thus reconciled. Peter addresses himself to Jesus: the disciples turn their attention to the object;

Temple. (SECOND DAY OF THE WEEK.) *Bethany.* *Jerusalem.*

LUKE.	JOHN.
CH. XIX. 45–48. CH. XXI. 37, 38.	

LUKE	JOHN
45 And he went into the temple, and began to cast out them that sold therein, and them that bought,	
46 Saying unto them, It is written, My house is the house of prayer, but ye have made it a den of thieves.	
47 And he taught daily in the temple. But the chief priests, and the scribes, and the chief of the people sought to destroy him,	
48 And could not find what they might do: for all the people were very attentive to hear him.	

CH. XXI.

37 And in the day-time he was teaching in the temple; and at night he went out, and abode in the mount that is called *the mount* of Olives.

38 And all the people came early in the morning to him in the temple, for to hear him.

(THIRD DAY OF THE WEEK.)   *Between Bethany and Jerusalem.*

Jesus addresses all. Or, Peter's remark may be attributed to all the disciples. See § 141. NEWCOME.

§ 114. The barren Fig-tree withers away.

MATTHEW.	MARK.
CH. XXI. 20 – 22.	CH. XI. 20 – 26.
this mountain, Be thou removed, and be thou cast into the sea ; it shall be done.	cast into the sea ; and shall not doubt in his heart, but shall believe that those things which he saith shall come to pass ; he shall have whatsoever he saith.
22 And all things whatsoever ye shall ask in prayer, believing, ye shall receive.	24 Therefore I say unto you, What things soever ye desire when ye pray, believe that ye receive *them*, and ye shall have *them*.
	25 And when ye stand praying, forgive, if ye have aught against any : that your Father also which is in heaven may forgive you your trespasses.
	26 But if ye do not forgive, neither will your Father which is in heaven forgive your trespasses.

§ 115. Christ's authority questioned. Parable of the

CH. XXI. 23 – 32.	CH. XI. 27 – 33.
23 And when he was come into the temple, the chief priests and the elders of the people came unto him as he was teaching, and said, By what authority doest thou these things ? and who gave thee this authority ?	27 And they come again to Jerusalem : and as he was walking in the temple, there come to him the chief priests, and the scribes, and the elders,
	28 And say unto him, By what authority doest thou these things ? and who gave thee this authority to do these things ?
24 And Jesus answered and said unto them, I also will ask you one thing, which if ye tell me, I in like wise will tell you by what authority I do these things.	29 And Jesus answered and said unto them, I will also ask of you one question, and answer me, and I will tell you by what authority I do these things.
25 The baptism of John, whence was it ? from heaven, or of men ? And they reasoned with themselves, saying, If we shall say, From heaven ; he will say unto us, Why did ye not then believe him ?	30 The baptism of John, was *it* from heaven, or of men ? answer me.
	31 And they reasoned with themselves, saying, If we shall say, From heaven ; he will say, Why then did ye not believe him ?
26 But if we shall say, Of men ; we fear the people : for all hold John as a prophet.	32 But if we shall say, Of men ; they feared the people : for all *men* counted John, that he was a prophet indeed.
27 And they answered Jesus, and said, We cannot tell. And he said unto them, Neither tell I you by what authority I do these things.	33 And they answered and said unto Jesus, We cannot tell. And Jesus answering saith unto them, Neither do I tell you by what authority I do these things.
28 But what think ye ? A *certain* man had two sons ; and he came to the first, and said, Son, go work to-day in my vineyard.	

LUKE.	JOHN.

two Sons.   (THIRD DAY OF THE WEEK.)   *Jerusalem.*

CH. XX.   1–8.

AND it came to pass, *that* on one of those days, as he taught the people in the temple, and preached the gospel, the chief priests and the scribes came upon *him*, with the elders,

2 And spake unto him, saying, Tell us, By what authority doest thou these things? or who is he that gave thee this authority?

3 And he answered and said unto them, I will also ask you one thing; and answer me:

4 The baptism of John, was it from heaven, or of men?

5 And they reasoned with themselves, saying, If we shall say, From heaven; he will say, Why then believed ye him not?

6 But and if we say, Of men; all the people will stone us: for they be persuaded that John was a prophet.

7 And they answered, That they could not tell whence *it was*.

8 And Jesus said unto them, Neither tell I you by what authority I do these things.

§ 115. Christ's authority questioned. Parable of the

MATTHEW.
CH. XXI. 23–32.

29 He answered and said, I will not ; but afterward he repented, and went.

30 And he came to the second, and said likewise. And he answered and said, I *go*, sir : and went not.

31 Whether of them twain did the will of *his* father? They say unto him, The first. Jesus saith unto them, Verily I say unto you, That the publicans and the harlots go into the kingdom of God before you.

32 For John came unto you in the way of righteousness, and ye believed him not : but the publicans and the harlots believed him : and ye, when ye had seen *it*, repented not afterward, that ye might believe him.

MARK.

---

§ 116. Parable of the wicked husbandmen.

CH. XXI. 33–46.

33 Hear another parable ; There was a certain householder, which planted a vineyard, and hedged it round about, and digged a wine-press in it, and built a tower, and let it out to husbandmen, and went into a far country :

34 And when the time of the fruit drew near, he sent his servants to the husbandmen, that they might receive the fruits of it.

35 And the husbandmen took his servants, and beat one, and killed another, and stoned another.

36 Again he sent other servants more than the first : and they did unto them likewise.

37 But last of all, he sent unto them his son, saying, They will reverence my son.

CH. XII. 1–12.

AND he began to speak unto them by parables. A *certain* man planted a vineyard, and set an hedge about *it*, and digged *a place for* the wine-fat, and built a tower, and let it out to husbandmen, and went into a far country.

2 And at the season he sent to the husbandmen a servant, that he might receive from the husbandmen of the fruit of the vineyard.

3 And they caught *him*, and beat him, and sent *him* away empty.

4 And again, he sent unto them another servant : and at him they cast stones, and wounded *him* in the head, and sent *him* away shamefully handled.

5 And again he sent another ; and him they killed, and many others ; beating some, and killing some.

6 Having yet therefore one son, his well-beloved, he sent him also last unto them, saying, They will reverence my son.

Matth. xxi. 34, 35, *servants*.] Many servants are sent ; some of whom are beaten, some slain, some stoned. Here St. Matthew is more circumstantial than the other two Evangelists, who mention only one servant as sent, and one of the three injurious modes of treatment. Some suppose that this servant was chief among the rest.

Matth. xxi. 36. Here Mark mentions one servant among the others, as stoned

two Sons. (THIRD DAY OF THE WEEK.) *Jerusalem.*

LUKE.	JOHN.

(THIRD DAY OF THE WEEK.) *Jerusalem.*

CH. XX. 9 – 19.

9 Then began he to speak to the people this parable : A certain man planted a vineyard, and let it forth to husbandmen, and went into a far country for a long time.

10 And at the season he sent a servant to the husbandmen, that they should give him of the fruit of the vineyard : but the husbandmen beat him, and sent *him* away empty.

11 And again he sent another servant : and they beat him also, and entreated *him* shamefully, and sent *him* away empty.

12 And again he sent a third : and they wounded him also, and cast *him* out.

13 Then said the lord of the vineyard, What shall I do? I will send my beloved son : it may be they will reverence *him* when they see him.

wounded in the head, and sent away dishonored ; and Luke selects the circumstance that that one was beaten. Then Mark and Luke mention a third message, about which Matthew is silent. But, "qui pauciora memorat, plura non negat." St. Luke may be understood as saying that a mortal wound was inflicted on the third messenger. NEWCOME.

§ 116. Parable of the wicked husbandmen.

MATTHEW.	MARK.
CH. XXI. 33 – 46.	CH. XII. 1 – 12.

38 But when the husbandmen saw the son, they said among themselves, This is the heir; come, let us kill him, and let us seize on his inheritance.

7 But those husbandmen said among themselves, This is the heir; come, let us kill him, and the inheritance shall be ours.

39 And they caught him, and cast *him* out of the vineyard, and slew *him.*

8 And they took him, and killed *him*, and cast *him* out of the vineyard.

40 When the lord therefore of the vineyard cometh, what will he do unto those husbandmen?

41 They say unto him, He will miserably destroy those wicked men, and will let out *his* vineyard unto other husbandmen, which shall render him the fruits in their seasons.

9 What shall therefore the lord of the vineyard do? He will come and destroy the husbandmen, and will give the vineyard unto others.

42 Jesus saith unto them, Did ye never read in the scriptures, The stone which the builders rejected, the same is become the head of the corner: this is the Lord's doing, and it is marvellous in our eyes? [a]

10 And have ye not read this scripture; The stone which the builders rejected is become the head of the corner:

11 This was the Lord's doing, and it is marvellous in our eyes?

43 Therefore say I unto you, The kingdom of God shall be taken from you, and given to a nation bringing forth the fruits thereof.

44 And whosoever shall fall on this stone, shall be broken: but on whomsoever it shall fall, it will grind him to powder. [b]

45 And when the chief priests and Pharisees had heard his parables, they perceived that he spake of them.

46 But when they sought to lay hands on him, they feared the multitude, because they took him for a prophet.

12 And they sought to lay hold on him, but feared the people; for they knew that he had spoken the parable against them: and they left him, and went their way.

§ 117. Parable of the Marriage of the King's Son.

CH. XXII. 1 – 14.

AND Jesus answered and spake unto them again by parables, and said,

2 The kingdom of heaven is like unto a certain king, which made a marriage for his son,

3 And sent forth his servants to call them that were bidden to the wedding: and they would not come.

4 Again, he sent forth other servants, saying, Tell them which are bidden, Behold, I have prepared my dinner: my oxen and *my* fatlings *are* killed, and all things *are* ready: come unto the marriage.

[a] Ps. cxviii. 22.　　[b] Isa. viii. 14, seq. Zech. xii. 3. Dan. ii. 34, seq., 44, seq.

LUKE.	JOHN.

LUKE.
CH. XX. 9 – 19.

14 But when the husbandmen saw him, they reasoned among themselves, saying, This is the heir: come, let us kill him, that the inheritance may be ours.

15 So they cast him out of the vineyard, and killed *him*. What therefore shall the lord of the vineyard do unto them?

16 He shall come and destroy these husbandmen, and shall give the vineyard to others. And when they heard *it*, they said, God forbid.

17 And he beheld them, and said, What is this then that is written, The stone which the builders rejected, the same is become the head of the corner?

18 Whosoever shall fall upon that stone, shall be broken: but on whomsoever it shall fall, it will grind him to powder.

19 And the chief priests and the scribes the same hour sought to lay hands on him; and they feared the people: for they perceived that he had spoken this parable against them.

§ 117. Parable of the marriage of the King's Son.

MATTHEW.	MARK.
CH. XXII. 1–14.	

5 But they made light of *it*, and went their ways, one to his farm, another to his merchandise.

6 And the remnant took his servants, and entreated *them* spitefully, and slew *them*.

7 But when the king heard *thereof*, he was wroth : and he sent forth his armies, and destroyed those murderers, and burned up their city.

8 Then saith he to his servants, The wedding is ready, but they which were bidden were not worthy.

9 Go ye therefore into the highways, and as many as ye shall find, bid to the marriage.

10 So those servants went out into the highways, and gathered together all as many as they found, both bad and good : and the wedding was furnished with guests.

11 And when the king came in to see the guests, he saw there a man which had not on a wedding-garment :

12 And he saith unto him, Friend, how camest thou in hither, not having a wedding-garment? And he was speechless.

13 Then said the king to the servants, Bind him hand and foot, and take him away, and cast *him* into outer darkness : there shall be weeping and gnashing of teeth.

14 For many are called, but few *are* chosen.

---

§ 118. Insidious question of the Pharisees.   Tribute

CH. XXII. 15–22.	CH. XII. 13–17.
15 Then went the Pharisees, and took counsel how they might entangle him in *his* talk.	13 And they send unto him certain of the Pharisees, and of the Herodians, to catch him in *his* words.

Matth. xxii. 11–13.] In the East, where the fashions of dress rarely if ever change, much of their riches consists in the number and splendor of their robes, or *caffetans.* Presents of garments are frequently alluded to in Scripture. Gen. xlv. 22. 2 Chron. ix. 24. Judges xiv. 12. 2 Kings v. 5. Ezra ii. 69. Neh. vii. 70, where "the Tirshatha gave five hundred and thirty priests' garments."

Presents were considered as tokens of honor ; — not meant as offers of payment or enrichment, (1 Sam. ix. 7) ; and especially presents of dresses. 1 Sam. xviii. 4. Luke xv. 22. *Tavernier*, p. 43, mentions a *nazar*, whose virtue so pleased a king of Persia, that he caused himself to be disappareled, and gave his own habit to the *nazar*, which is *the greatest honor a king of Persia can bestow on a subject.*

(THIRD DAY OF THE WEEK.)   *Jerusalem.*

LUKE.	JOHN.

to Cæsar.   (THIRD DAY OF THE WEEK.)   *Jerusalem.*

CH. XX. 20–26.

20 And they watched *him*, and sent forth spies, which should feign themselves just men, that they might take

---

Such presents are given by kings on great occasions, especially at the marriages of their children. The Sultan Achmet, at the marriage of his eldest daughter, " gave presents to above 20,000 persons." Knolles's Hist. of the Turks, p. 1311. So, Ahasuerus " gave gifts, *according to the state of the king.*" Esth. ii. 18.

The king gives his garment of honor *before* the wearer is admitted into his presence ; — De la Mottraye's Trav. p. 199 ; (Does this illustrate Zech. iii. 3, 4 ?) — and would resent it if any, having received robes of him, should appear in his presence without wearing these marks of his liberality. And to refuse such favors, when offered, is considered as one of the greatest indignities. Sir John Chardin relates an instance where such a refusal cost a vizier his life. See 4 CALM. DICT. p. 64, 126, 514.

§ 118. Insidious question of the Pharisees. Tribute

MATTHEW. CH. XXII. 15–22.	MARK. CH. XII. 13–17.
16 And they sent out unto him their disciples, with the Herodians, saying, Master, we know that thou art true, and teachest the way of God in truth, neither carest thou for any *man:* for thou regardest not the person of men.	14 And when they were come, they say unto him, Master, we know that thou art true, and carest for no man : for thou regardest not the person of men, but teachest the way of God in truth : Is it lawful to give tribute to Cesar, or not?
17 Tell us therefore, What thinkest thou? Is it lawful to give tribute unto Cesar, or not?	
18 But Jesus perceived their wickedness, and said, Why tempt ye me, *ye* hypocrites?	15 Shall we give, or shall we not give? But he, knowing their hypocrisy, said unto them, Why tempt ye me? bring me a penny, that I may see *it.*
19 Shew me the tribute-money. And they brought unto him a penny.	
20 And he saith unto them, Whose *is* this image, and superscription?	16 And they brought *it.* And he saith unto them, Whose *is* this image and superscription? And they said unto him, Cesar's.
21 They say unto him, Cesar's. Then saith he unto them, Render therefore unto Cesar, the things which are Cesar's ; and unto God, the things that are God's.	17 And Jesus answering, said unto them, Render to Cesar the things that are Cesar's, and to God the things that are God's. And they marvelled at him.
22 When they had heard *these words,* they marvelled, and left him, and went their way.	

§ 119. Insidious question of the Sadducees. The

CH. XXII. 23–33.	CH. XII. 18–27.
23 The same day came to him the Sadducees, which say that there is no resurrection, and asked him,	18 Then come unto him the Sadducees, which say there is no resurrection ; and they asked him, saying,
24 Saying, Master, Moses said, If a man die, having no children, his brother shall marry his wife, and raise up seed unto his brother.[a]	19 Master, Moses wrote unto us, If a man's brother die, and leave *his* wife *behind him,* and leave no children, that his brother should take his wife, and raise up seed unto his brother.
25 Now, there were with us seven brethren : and the first, when he had married a wife, deceased : and having no issue, left his wife unto his brother.	20 Now, there were seven brethren : and the first took a wife, and dying left no seed.
26 Likewise the second also, and the third, unto the seventh.	21 And the second took her, and died, neither left he any seed : and the third likewise.
27 And last of all the woman died also	22 And the seven had her, and left no seed : last of all the woman died also.

[a] Deut. xxv. 5

to Cæsar.   (THIRD DAY OF THE WEEK.)   *Jerusalem.*

LUKE.	JOHN.
CH. XX. 20 – 26.	
hold of his words, that so they might deliver him unto the power and authority of the governor.	
21 And they asked him, saying, Master, we know that thou sayest and teachest rightly, neither acceptest thou the person *of any,* but teachest the way of God truly :	
22 Is it lawful for us to give tribute unto Cesar, or no ?	
23 But he perceived their craftiness, and said unto them, Why tempt ye me ?	
24 Shew me a penny. Whose image and superscription hath it? They answered and said, Cesar's.	
25 And he said unto them, Render therefore unto Cesar the things which be Cesar's, and unto God the things which be God's.	
26 And they could not take hold of his words before the people : and they marvelled at his answer, and held their peace.	

Resurrection.   (THIRD DAY OF THE WEEK.)   *Jerusalem.*

CH. XX. 27 – 40.	
27 Then came to *him* certain of the Sadducees (which deny that there is any resurrection) and they asked him,	
28 Saying, Master, Moses wrote unto us, If any man's brother die, having a wife, and he die without children, that his brother should take his wife, and raise up seed unto his brother.	
29 There were therefore seven brethren : and the first took a wife, and died without children.	
30 And the second took her to wife, and he died childless.	
31 And the third took her ; and in like manner the seven also : and they left no children, and died.	
32 Last of all the woman died also.	

§ 119. Insidious question of the Sadducees.   The

MATTHEW.	MARK.
CH. XXII. 23–33.	CH. XII. 18–27.
28 Therefore, in the resurrection, whose wife shall she be of the seven? for they all had her.	23 In the resurrection therefore, when they shall rise, whose wife shall she be of them? for the seven had her to wife.
29 Jesus answered and said unto them, Ye do err, not knowing the scriptures, nor the power of God.	24 And Jesus answering, said unto them, Do ye not therefore err, because ye know not the scriptures, neither the power of God?
30 For in the resurrection they neither marry, nor are given in marriage, but are as the angels of God in heaven.	25 For when they shall rise from the dead, they neither marry, nor are given in marriage; but are as the angels which are in heaven.
31 But, as touching the resurrection of the dead, have ye not read that which was spoken unto you by God, saying,	26 And as touching the dead, that they rise; have ye not read in the book of Moses, how in the bush God spake unto him, saying, I am the God
32 I am the God of Abraham, and the God of Isaac, and the God of Jacob?[b] God is not the God of the dead, but of the living.	of Abraham, and the God of Isaac, and the God of Jacob? 27 He is not the God of the dead, but the God of the living: ye therefore do greatly err.
33 And when the multitude heard *this*, they were astonished at his doctrine.	

§ 120. A lawyer questions Jesus.   The two great

CH. XXII. 34–40.	CH. XII. 28–34.
34 But when the Pharisees had heard that he had put the Sadducees to silence, they were gathered together.	28 And one of the scribes came, and having heard them reasoning together, and perceiving that he had answered them well, asked him, Which is the first commandment of all?
35 Then one of them *which was a lawyer*, asked *him a question*, tempting him, and saying,	
36 Master, which *is* the great commandment in the law?	
	29 And Jesus answered him, The first of all the commandments *is*, Hear, O Israel; The Lord our God is one Lord:
37 Jesus said unto him, Thou shalt love the Lord thy God with all thy heart, and with all thy soul, and with all thy mind.[a]	30 And thou shalt love the Lord thy God with all thy heart, and with all thy soul, and with all thy mind,

[a] Ex. iii. 6.   [b] Deut. vi. 4, 5.

Luke xx. 36, *Neither can they die any more.*] Here is a minute indication of St. Luke's veracity, derived from his medical profession. No other Evangelist records

Resurrection.　(THIRD DAY OF THE WEEK.)　*Jerusalem.*

LUKE.	JOHN.

LUKE.
CH. xx. 27—40.

33 Therefore in the resurrection, whose wife of them is she? for seven had her to wife.

34 And Jesus answering, said unto them, The children of this world marry, and are given in marriage:
35 But they which shall be accounted worthy to obtain that world, and the resurrection from the dead, neither marry, nor are given in marriage:
36 Neither can they die any more: for they are equal unto the angels; and are the children of God, being the children of the resurrection.
37 Now that the dead are raised, even Moses shewed at the bush, when he calleth the Lord the God of Abraham, and the God of Isaac, and the God of Jacob.

38 For he is not a God of the dead, but of the living: for all live unto him.
39 Then certain of the scribes answering, said, Master, thou hast well said.
40 And after that, they durst not ask him any *question at all.*

Commandments.　(THIRD DAY OF THE WEEK.)　*Jerusalem.*

this remark; but it would not be likely to escape the notice of a physician. See on Luke xxii. 44.

§ 120. A lawyer questions Jesus. The two great

MATTHEW.	MARK.
CH. XXII. 34–40.	CH. XII. 28–34.
38 This is the first and great commandment.	and with all thy strength : this *is* the first commandment.
39 And the second *is* like unto it, Thou shalt love thy neighbour as thyself.[a]	31 And the second *is* like, *namely* this, Thou shalt love thy neighbour as thyself : there is none other commandment greater than these.
40 On these two commandments hang all the law and the prophets.	32 And the scribe said unto him, Well, Master, thou hast said the truth : for there is one God ; and there is none other but he :
	33 And to love him with all the heart, and with all the understanding, and with all the soul, and with all the strength, and to love *his* neighbour as himself, is more than all whole burnt-offerings and sacrifices.
	34 And when Jesus saw that he answered discreetly, he said unto him, Thou art not far from the kingdom of God. And no man after that durst ask him *any question.*

§ 121. How is Christ the Son of David ?

CH. XXII. 41–46.	CH. XII. 35–37.
41 While the Pharisees were gathered together, Jesus asked them,	
42 Saying, What think ye of Christ ? whose son is he ? They say unto him, *The son* of David.	35 And Jesus answered and said, while he taught in the temple, How say the scribes that Christ is the son of David ?
43 He saith unto them, How then doth David in spirit call him Lord, saying,	36 For David himself said by the Holy Ghost, The LORD said unto my Lord, Sit thou on my right hand, till I make thine enemies thy footstool.
44 The LORD said unto my Lord, Sit thou on my right hand, till I make thine enemies thy footstool ?[b]	37 David therefore himself calleth him Lord, and whence is he *then* his son ? And the common people heard him gladly.
45 If David then call him Lord, how is he his son ?	
46 And no man was able to answer him a word, neither durst any *man,* from that day forth, ask him any more *questions.*	

§ 122. Warnings against the evil example of the Scribes

CH. XXIII. 1–12.	CH. XII. 38, 39.
THEN spake Jesus to the multitude, and to his disciples,	38 And he said unto them in his doctrine, Beware of the scribes, which love to go in long clothing, and *love* salutations in the market-places,
2 Saying, The scribes and the Pharisees sit in Moses' seat :	39 And the chief seats in the synagogues, and the uppermost rooms at feasts :

[a] Lev. xix. 18.   [b] Ps. cx. 1.

Commandments.   (THIRD DAY OF THE WEEK.)   *Jerusalem.*

LUKE.	JOHN.

(THIRD DAY OF THE WEEK.)   *Jerusalem.*

CH. XX. 41–44.

41 And he said unto them, How say they that Christ is David's son?

42 And David himself saith in the book of Psalms, The LORD said unto my Lord, Sit thou on my right hand,

43 Till I make thine enemies thy footstool.

44 David therefore calleth him Lord, how is he then his son?

and Pharisees.   (THIRD DAY OF THE WEEK.)   *Jerusalem.*

CH. XX. 45, 46.

45 Then in the audience of all the people, he said unto his disciples,

46 Beware of the scribes, which desire to walk in long robes, and love greetings in the markets, and the highest seats in the synagogues, and the chief rooms at feasts;

§ 122. Warnings against the evil example of the Scribes

MATTHEW.	MARK.
CH. XXIII. 1–12.	

MATTHEW.
CH. XXIII. 1–12.

3 All therefore whatsoever they bid you observe, *that* observe and do : but do not ye after their works : for they say, and do not.

4 For they bind heavy burdens, and grievous to be borne, and lay *them* on men's shoulders; but they *themselves* will not move them with one of their fingers.

5 But all their works they do for to be seen of men : they make broad their phylacteries, and enlarge the borders of their garments,

6 And love the uppermost rooms at feasts, and the chief seats in the synagogues,

7 And greetings in the markets, and to be called of men, Rabbi, Rabbi.

8 But be not ye called Rabbi : for one is your Master, *even* Christ; and all ye are brethren.

9 And call no *man* your father upon the earth : for one is your Father which is in heaven.

10 Neither be ye called masters : for one is your Master, *even* Christ.

11 But he that is greatest among you, shall be your servant.

12 And whosoever shall exalt himself, shall be abased ; and he that shall humble himself, shall be exalted.

§ 123. Woes against the Scribes and Pharisees.   Lamentation

CH. XXIII. 13–39.   **CH. XII. 40.**

13 But wo unto you, scribes and Pharisees, hypocrites ! for ye shut up the kingdom of heaven against men : for ye neither go in *yourselves*, neither suffer ye them that are entering, to go in.

14 Wo unto you, scribes and Pharisees, hypocrites ! for ye devour widows' houses, and for a pretence make long prayer : therefore ye shall receive the greater damnation.

40 Which devour widows' houses, and for a pretence make long prayers : these shall receive greater damnation.

15 Wo unto you, scribes and Pharisees, hypocrites ! for ye compass sea and land to make one proselyte ; and when he is made, ye make him two-fold more the child of hell than yourselves.

16 Wo unto you, *ye* blind guides,

and Pharisees.　(THIRD DAY OF THE WEEK.)　*Jerusalem.*

LUKE.	JOHN.

over Jerusalem.　(THIRD DAY OF THE WEEK.)　*Jerusalem.*

CH. XX. 47.

47 Which devour widows' houses,
and for a shew make long prayers:
the same shall receive greater damnation.

§ 123. Woes against the Scribes and Pharisees. Lamentation

MATTHEW.
CH. XXIII. 13 – 39.

which say, Whosoever shall swear by the temple, it is nothing ; but whosoever shall swear by the gold of the temple, he is a debtor.

17 *Ye* fools, and blind ! for whether is greater, the gold, or the temple that sanctifieth the gold?

18 And whosoever shall swear by the altar, it is nothing ; but whosoever sweareth by the gift that is upon it, he is guilty.

19 *Ye* fools, and blind ! for whether *is* greater, the gift, or the altar that sanctifieth the gift ?

20 Whoso therefore shall swear by the altar, sweareth by it, and by all things thereon.

21 And whoso shall swear by the temple, sweareth by it, and by him that dwelleth therein.

22 And he that shall swear by heaven, sweareth by the throne of God, and by him that sitteth thereon.

23 Wo unto you, scribes and Pharisees, hypocrites! for ye pay tithe of mint, and anise, and cummin, and have omitted the weightier *matters* of the law, judgment, mercy, and faith : these ought ye to have done, and not to leave the other undone.

24 *Ye* blind guides, which strain at a gnat, and swallow a camel.

25 Wo unto you, scribes and Pharisees, hypocrites ! for ye make clean the outside of the cup and of the platter, but within they are full of extortion and excess.

26 *Thou* blind Pharisee, cleanse first that *which is* within the cup and platter, that the outside of them may be clean also.

27 Wo unto you, scribes and Pharisees, hypocrites! for ye are like unto whited sepulchres, which indeed appear beautiful outward, but are within full of dead *men's* bones, and of all uncleanness.

28 Even so ye also outwardly appear righteous unto men, but within ye are full of hypocrisy and iniquity.

29 Wo unto you, scribes and Pharisees, hypocrites ! because ye build the tombs of the prophets, and garnish the sepulchres of the righteous,

MARK.

over Jerusalem. (THIRD DAY OF THE WEEK.) *Jerusalem.*

LUKE.	JOHN.

§ 123. Woes against the Scribes and Pharisees. Lamentation

MATTHEW.
CH. XXIII. 13–39.

30 And say, If we had been in the days of our fathers, we would not have been partakers with them in the blood of the prophets.

31 Wherefore ye be witnesses unto yourselves, that ye are the children of them which killed the prophets.

32 Fill ye up then the measure of your fathers.

33 *Ye* serpents, *ye* generation of vipers, how can ye escape the damnation of hell?

34 Wherefore, behold, I send unto you prophets, and wise men, and scribes; and *some* of them ye shall kill and crucify, and *some* of them shall ye scourge in your synagogues, and persecute *them* from city to city:

35 That upon you may come all the righteous blood shed upon the earth, from the blood of righteous Abel, unto the blood of Zacharias, son of Barachias, whom ye slew between the temple and the altar.[a]

36 Verily, I say unto you, All these things shall come upon this generation.

37 O Jerusalem, Jerusalem, *thou* that killest the prophets, and stonest them which are sent unto thee, how often would I have gathered thy children together, even as a hen gathereth her chickens under *her* wings, and ye would not!

38 Behold, your house is left unto you desolate.[b]

39 For I say unto you, Ye shall not see me henceforth, till ye shall say, Blessed *is* he that cometh in the name of the Lord.[c]

MARK.

---

§ 124. The Widow's Mite. (THIRD DAY OF

CH. XII. 41–44.

41 And Jesus sat over against the treasury, and beheld how the people cast money into the treasury: and many that were rich cast in much.

42 And there came a certain poor widow, and she threw in two mites, which make a farthing.

---

[a] Gen. iv. 8.   2 Chron. xxiv. 20–22.
[b] Ps. lxix. 26.   Jer. xii. 7, and xxii. 5.   [c] Ps. cxviii. 26.

over Jerusalem. (THIRD DAY OF THE WEEK.) *Jerusalem.*

LUKE.	JOHN.

THE WEEK.) *Jerusalem.*

CH. XXI. 1 – 4. AND he looked up and saw the rich men casting their gifts into the treasury. 2 And he saw also a certain poor widow, casting in thither two mites.	

§ 124. The Widow's Mite. (THIRD DAY OF

MATTHEW.	MARK.
	CH. XII. 41–44.
	43 And he called *unto him* his disciples, and saith unto them, Verily, I say unto you, That this poor widow hath cast more in, than all they which have cast into the treasury.
	44 For all *they* did cast in of their abundance: but she of her want did cast in all that she had, *even* all her living.

§ 125. Certain Greeks desire to see Jesus.

THE WEEK.) *Jerusalem.*

LUKE.	JOHN.
CH. XXI. 1–4.	

3 And he said, Of a truth I say unto you, That this poor widow hath cast in more than they all.

4 For all these have of their abundance cast in unto the offerings of God : but she of her penury hath cast in all the living that she had.

(THIRD DAY OF THE WEEK.) *Jerusalem.*

CH. XII. 20–36.

20 And there were certain Greeks among them, that came up to worship at the feast.

21 The same came therefore to Philip, which was of Bethsaida of Galilee, and desired him, saying, Sir, we would see Jesus.

22 Philip cometh and telleth Andrew : and again, Andrew and Philip tell Jesus.

23 And Jesus answered them, saying, The hour is come, that the Son of man should be glorified.

24 Verily, verily, I say unto you, Except a corn of wheat fall into the ground and die, it abideth alone : but if it die, it bringeth forth much fruit.

25 He that loveth his life shall lose it ; and he that hateth his life in this world, shall keep it unto life eternal.

26 If any man serve me, let him follow me, and where I am, there shall also my servant be : if any man serve me, him will *my* Father honour.

27 Now is my soul troubled ; and what shall I say ? Father, save me from this hour : but for this cause came I unto this hour.

28 Father, glorify thy name. Then came there a voice from heaven, *saying*, I have both glorified *it*, and will glorify *it* again.

29 The people therefore that stood by, and heard *it*, said that it thundered. Others said, An angel spake to him.

30 Jesus answered and said, This voice came not because of me, but for your sakes.

31 Now is the judgment of this

§ 125. Certain Greeks desire to see Jesus.

MATTHEW.	MARK.

§ 126. Reflections upon the unbelief of the Jews.

LUKE.

JOHN.
CH. XII. 20 – 36.

world : now shall the prince of this world be cast out.

32 And I, if I be lifted up from the earth, will draw all *men* unto me.

33 (This he said, signifying what death he should die.)

34 The people answered him, We have heard out of the law that Christ abideth for ever : ᵃ and how sayest thou, The Son of man must be lifted up? Who is this Son of man?

35 Then Jesus said unto them, Yet a little while is the light with you. Walk while ye have the light, lest darkness come upon you : for he that walketh in darkness knoweth not whither he goeth.

36 While ye have light, believe in the light, that ye may be the children of light. These things spake Jesus, and departed, and did hide himself from them.

CH. XII. 37 – 50.

37 But though he had done so many miracles before them, yet they believed not on him.

38 That the saying of Esaias the prophet might be fulfilled, which he spake, Lord, who hath believed our report? and to whom hath the arm of the Lord been revealed? ᵇ

39 Therefore they could not believe, because that Esaias said again,

40 He hath blinded their eyes, and hardened their heart ; that they should not see with *their* eyes, nor understand with *their* heart, and be converted, and I should heal them. ᶜ

41 These things said Esaias, when he saw his glory, and spake of him. ᵈ

42 Nevertheless, among the chief rulers also many believed on him ; but because of the Pharisees they did not confess *him*, lest they should be put out of the synagogue :

43 For they loved the praise of men more than the praise of God.

44 Jesus cried, and said, He that

ᵃ 2 Sam. vii. 13. Ps. lxxxix. 30, 37 ; cx. 4.
ᵇ Is. liii. 1.   ᶜ Is. vi. 10.   ᵈ Is. vi. 1, seq.

126. Reflections upon the unbelief of the Jews.

MATTHEW.	MARK.

§ 127. Jesus, on taking leave of the Temple, foretells its destruction, etc.

CH. XXIV. 1–14.	CH. XIII. 1–13.
AND Jesus went out, and departed from the temple : and his disciples came to *him* for to shew him the buildings of the temple.	AND as he went out of the temple, one of his disciples saith unto him, Master, see what manner of stones, and what buildings *are here!*
2 And Jesus said unto them, See ye not all these things ? verily, I say unto you, There shall not be left here one stone upon another, that shall not be thrown down.	2 And Jesus answering, said unto him, Seest thou these great buildings ? there shall not be left one stone upon another, that shall not be thrown down.
3 And as he sat upon the mount of Olives, the disciples came unto him privately, saying, Tell us, when shall these things be ? and what *shall be* the sign of thy coming, and of the end of the world ?	3 And as he sat upon the mount of Olives, over against the temple, Peter, and James, and John, and Andrew, asked him privately,
	4 Tell us, when shall these things be ? and what *shall be* the sign when all these things shall be fulfilled ?
4 And Jesus answered and said unto them, Take heed that no man deceive you.	5 And Jesus answering them, began to say, Take heed lest any *man* deceive you :
5 For many shall come in my name, saying, I am Christ ; and shall deceive many.	6 For many shall come in my name, saying, I am *Christ ;* and shall deceive many.
6 And ye shall hear of wars, and rumours of wars : see that ye be not troubled : for all *these things* must come to pass, but the end is not yet.	7 And when ye shall hear of wars, and rumours of wars, be ye not troubled : for *such things* must needs be ; but the end *shall* not *be* yet.

LUKE.	JOHN.
	CH. XII. 37–50.
	believeth on me, believeth not on me, but on him that sent me.
	45 And he that seeth me, seeth him that sent me.
	46 I am come a light into the world, that whosoever believeth on me should not abide in darkness.
	47 And if any man hear my words, and believe not, I judge him not : for I came not to judge the world, but to save the world.
	48 He that rejecteth me, and receiveth not my words, hath one that judgeth him : the word that I have spoken, the same shall judge him in the last day.
	49 For I have not spoken of myself; but the Father which sent me, he gave me a commandment, what I should say, and what I should speak.
	50 And I know that his commandment is life everlasting : whatsoever I speak therefore, even as the Father said unto me, so I speak.

CH. XXI. 5–19.

5 And as some spake of the temple, how it was adorned with goodly stones, and gifts, he said,

6 *As for* these things which ye behold, the days will come, in the which there shall not be left one stone upon another, that shall not be thrown down.

7 And they asked him, saying, Master, but when shall these things be? and what sign *will there be* when these things shall come to pass?

8 And he said, Take heed that ye be not deceived : for many shall come in my name, saying, I am *Christ;* and the time draweth near : go ye not therefore after them.

9 But when ye shall hear of wars, and commotions, be not terrified : for these things must first come to pass; but the end *is* not by and by.

§ 127. Jesus, on taking leave of the Temple, foretells its destruction, etc.

MATTHEW.	MARK.
CH. XXIV. 1–14.	CH. XIII. 1–13.
7 For nation shall rise against nation, and kingdom against kingdom: and there shall be famines, and pestilences, and earthquakes in divers places.	8 For nation shall rise against nation, and kingdom against kingdom: and there shall be earthquakes in *divers* places, and there shall be famines, and troubles: these *are* the beginnings of sorrows.
8 All these *are* the beginning of sorrows.	
9 Then shall they deliver you up to be afflicted, and shall kill you: and ye shall be hated of all nations for my name's sake.	9 But take heed to yourselves: for they shall deliver you up to councils; and in the synagogues ye shall be beaten: and ye shall be brought before rulers and kings for my sake, for a testimony against them.
	10 And the gospel must first be published among all nations.
	11 But when they shall lead *you* and deliver you up, take no thought beforehand what ye shall speak, neither do ye premeditate: but whatsoever shall be given you in that hour, that speak ye: for it is not ye that speak, but the Holy Ghost.
10 And then shall many be offended, and shall betray one another, and shall hate one another.	12 Now, the brother shall betray the brother to death, and the father the son: and children shall rise up against *their* parents, and shall cause them to be put to death.
11 And many false prophets shall rise, and shall deceive many.	
12 And because iniquity shall abound, the love of many shall wax cold.	
13 But he that shall endure unto the end, the same shall be saved.	13 And ye shall be hated of all *men* for my name's sake: but he that shall endure unto the end, the same shall be saved.
14 And this gospel of the kingdom shall be preached in all the world, for a witness unto all nations; and then shall the end come.	

§ 128. The signs of Christ's coming to destroy Jerusalem, etc.

CH. XXIV. 15–42.	CH. XIII. 14–37.
15 When ye, therefore, shall see the abomination of desolation, spoken of by Daniel the prophet,[a] stand in the holy place, (whoso readeth, let him understand,)	14 But when ye shall see the abomination of desolation, spoken of by Daniel the prophet, standing where it ought not, (let him that readeth understand) then let them that be in Judea flee to the mountains:
16 Then let them which be in Judea flee into the mountains:	
17 Let him which is on the housetop not come down to take any thing out of his house:	15 And let him that is on the housetop not go down into the house, neither enter *therein*, to take any thing out of his house:

[a] Danl. ix. 27.

LUKE.	JOHN.
CH. XXI. 5–19.	

10 Then said he unto them, Nation shall rise against nation, and kingdom against kingdom :

11 And great earthquakes shall be in divers places, and famines, and pestilences : and fearful sights, and great signs shall there be from heaven.

12 But before all these they shall lay their hands on you, and persecute *you*, delivering *you* up to the synagogues, and into prisons, being brought before kings and rulers for my name's sake.

13 And it shall turn to you for a testimony.

14 Settle *it* therefore in your hearts, not to meditate before what ye shall answer.

15 For I will give you a mouth and wisdom, which all your adversaries shall not be able to gainsay nor resist.

16 And ye shall be betrayed both by parents, and brethren, and kinsfolks, and friends ; and *some* of you shall they cause to be put to death.

17 And ye shall be hated of all *men* for my name's sake.

18 But there shall not an hair of your head perish.

19 In your patience possess ye your souls.

CH. XXI. 20–36.

20 And when ye shall see Jerusalem compassed with armies, then know that the desolation thereof is nigh.

21 Then let them which are in Judea flee to the mountains ; and let them which are in the midst of it depart out ; and let not them that are in the countries enter thereinto.

22 For these be the days of vengeance, that all things which are written may be fulfilled.

§ 128. The signs of Christ's coming to destroy Jerusalem, etc.

MATTHEW.	MARK.
CH. XXIV. 15–42.	CH. XIII. 14–37.

MATTHEW.

18 Neither let him which is in the field return back to take his clothes.

19 And wo unto them that are with child, and to them that give suck in those days!

20 But pray ye that your flight be not in the winter, neither on the sabbath-day:

21 For then shall be great tribulation, such as was not since the beginning of the world to this time, no, nor ever shall be.

22 And except those days should be shortened, there should no flesh be saved: but for the elect's sake those days shall be shortened.

23 Then if any man shall say unto you, Lo, here *is* Christ, or there; believe *it* not.

24 For there shall arise false Christs, and false prophets, and shall shew great signs and wonders; insomuch that, if *it were* possible, they shall deceive the very elect.

25 Behold, I have told you before.

26 Wherefore, if they shall say unto you, Behold, he is in the desert; go not forth: behold, he *is* in the secret chambers; believe *it* not.

27 For as the lightning cometh out of the east, and shineth even unto the west; so shall also the coming of the Son of man be.

28 For wheresoever the carcass is, there will the eagles be gathered together.

29 Immediately after the tribulation of those days, shall the sun be darkened, and the moon shall not give her light, and the stars shall fall from heaven, and the powers of the heavens shall be shaken: [a]

30 And then shall appear the sign of the Son of man in heaven: and then shall all the tribes of the earth mourn, and they shall see the Son of man coming in the clouds of heaven with power and great glory.

31 And he shall send his angels with a great sound of a trumpet, and

MARK.

16 And let him that is in the field not turn back again for to take up his garment.

17 But wo to them that are with child, and to them that give suck in those days!

18 And pray ye that your flight be not in the winter.

19 For *in* those days shall be affliction, such as was not from the beginning of the creation which God created unto this time, neither shall be.

20 And except that the Lord had shortened those days, no flesh should be saved: but for the elect's sake, whom he hath chosen, he hath shortened the days.

21 And then, if any man shall say to you, Lo, here *is* Christ; or lo, *he is* there; believe *him* not.

22 For false Christs, and false prophets shall rise, and shall shew signs and wonders, to seduce, if *it were* possible, even the elect.

23 But take ye heed: behold, I have foretold you all things.

24 But in those days, after that tribulation, the sun shall be darkened, and the moon shall not give her light,

25 And the stars of heaven shall fall, and the powers that are in heaven shall be shaken.

26 And then shall they see the Son of man coming in the clouds with great power and glory.

27 And then shall he send his angels, and shall gather together his

[a] Is. xiii. 9, 10. Joel iii. 15.

LUKE.
CH. XXI. 20—36.

23 But wo unto them that are with child, and to them that give suck in those days! for there shall be great distress in the land, and wrath upon this people.

24 And they shall fall by the edge of the sword, and shall be led away captive into all nations : and Jerusalem shall be trodden down of the Gentiles, until the times of the Gentiles be fulfilled.

25 And there shall be signs in the sun, and in the moon, and in the stars ; and upon the earth distress of nations, with perplexity ; the sea and the waves roaring ;

26 Men's hearts failing them for fear, and for looking after those things which are coming on the earth : for the powers of heaven shall be shaken.

27 And then shall they see the Son of man coming in a cloud, with power and great glory.

28 And when these things begin to come to pass, then look up, and lift up your heads : for your redemption draweth nigh.

JOHN.

§ 128. The signs of Christ's coming to destroy Jerusalem, etc.

MATTHEW.	MARK.
CH. XXIV. 15—42.	CH. XIII. 14—37.
they shall gather together his elect from the four winds, from one end of heaven to the other.	elect from the four winds, from the uttermost part of the earth to the uttermost part of heaven.
32 Now learn a parable of the fig-tree ; When his branch is yet tender, and putteth forth leaves, ye know that summer *is* nigh :	28 Now learn a parable of the fig-tree : When her branch is yet tender, and putteth forth leaves, ye know that summer is near :
33 So likewise ye, when ye shall see all these things, know that it is near, *even* at the doors.	29 So ye in like manner, when ye shall see these things come to pass, know that it is nigh, *even* at the doors.
34 Verily, I say unto you, This generation shall not pass, till all these things be fulfilled.	30 Verily, I say unto you, That this generation shall not pass, till all these things be done.
35 Heaven and earth shall pass away, but my words shall not pass away.	31 Heaven and earth shall pass away : but my words shall not pass away.
36 But of that day and hour knoweth no *man*, no, not the angels of heaven, but my Father only.	32 But of that day and *that* hour knoweth no man, no, not the angels which are in heaven, neither the Son, but the Father.
37 But as the days of Noe *were*, so shall also the coming of the Son of man be.	33 Take ye heed, watch and pray : for ye know not when the time is.
38 For as in the days that were before the flood, they were eating and drinking, marrying and giving in marriage, until the day that Noe entered into the ark,[a]	34 *For the Son of man is* as a man taking a far journey, who left his house, and gave authority to his servants, and to every man his work ; and commanded the porter to watch.
39 And knew not until the flood came, and took them all away : so shall also the coming of the Son of man be.	
40 Then shall two be in the field ; the one shall be taken, and the other left.	
41 Two *women shall be* grinding at the mill ; the one shall be taken, and the other left.	
42 Watch therefore ; for ye know not what hour your Lord doth come.	35 Watch ye therefore : for ye know not when the master of the house cometh, at even, or at midnight, or at the cock-crowing, or in the morning :
	36 Lest coming suddenly, he find you sleeping.
	37 And what I say unto you, I say unto all, Watch.

[a] Gen. vii. 4, seq.

LUKE.	JOHN.
ᴄʜ. xxɪ. 20–36.	

29 And he spake to them a parable; Behold the fig-tree, and all the trees;

30 When they now shoot forth, ye see and know of your ownselves that summer is now nigh at hand.

31 So likewise ye, when ye see these things come to pass, know ye that the kingdom of God is nigh at hand.

32 Verily, I say unto you, This generation shall not pass away, till all be fulfilled.

33 Heaven and earth shall pass away: but my words shall not pass away.

34 And take heed to yourselves, lest at any time your hearts be overcharged with surfeiting and drunkenness, and cares of this life, and *so* that day come upon you unawares.

35 For as a snare shall it come on all them that dwell on the face of the whole earth.

36 Watch ye therefore, and pray always, that ye may be accounted worthy to escape all these things that shall come to pass, and to stand before the Son of man.

§ 129. Transition to Christ's final coming. Exhortation.

MATTHEW.
CH. XXIV. 43–51. CH. XXV. 1–30.

43 But know this, that if the good man of the house had known in what watch the thief would come, he would have watched, and would not have suffered his house to be broken up.

44 Therefore be ye also ready : for in such an hour as ye think not, the Son of man cometh.

45 Who then is a faithful and wise servant, whom his lord hath made ruler over his household, to give them meat in due season?

46 Blessed *is* that servant, whom his lord, when he cometh, shall find so doing.

47 Verily I say unto you, That he shall make him ruler over all his goods.

48 But and if that evil servant shall say in his heart, My lord delayeth his coming ;

49 And shall begin to smite *his* fellow-servants, and to eat and drink with the drunken ;

50 The lord of that servant shall come in a day when he looketh not for *him*, and in an hour that he is not aware of,

51 And shall cut him asunder, and appoint *him* his portion with the hypocrites : there shall be weeping and gnashing of teeth.

CH. XXV.

THEN shall the kingdom of heaven be likened unto ten virgins, which took their lamps, and went forth to meet the bridegroom.

2 And five of them were wise, and five *were* foolish.

3 They that *were* foolish took their lamps, and took no oil with them :

4 But the wise took oil in their vessels with their lamps.

5 While the bridegroom tarried, they all slumbered and slept.

6 And at midnight there was a cry made, Behold, the bridegroom cometh : go ye out to meet him.

7 Then all those virgins arose, and trimmed their lamps.

8 And the foolish said unto the wise, Give us of your oil : for our lamps are gone out.

MARK.

Parables. (THIRD DAY OF THE WEEK.) *Mount of Olives.*

LUKE.	JOHN.

§ 129. Transition to Christ's final coming. Exhortation.

MATTHEW.
CH. XXIV. 43–51. CH. XXV. 1–30.

9 But the wise answered, saying, *Not so;* lest there be not enough for us and you : but go ye rather to them that sell, and buy for yourselves.

10 And while they went to buy, the bridegroom came ; and they that were ready, went in with him to the marriage : and the door was shut.

11 Afterward came also the other virgins, saying, Lord, Lord, open to us.

12 But he answered and said, Verily, I say unto you, I know you not.

13 Watch therefore, for ye know neither the day nor the hour wherein the Son of man cometh.

14 For *the kingdom of heaven is* as a man travelling into a far country, *who* called his own servants, and delivered unto them his goods.

15 And unto one he gave five talents, to another two, and to another one ; to every man according to his several ability ; and straightway took his journey.

16 Then he that had received the five talents, went and traded with the same, and made *them* other five talents.

17 And likewise he that *had received* two, he also gained other two.

18 But he that had received one, went and digged in the earth, and hid his lord's money.

19 After a long time the lord of those servants cometh, and reckoneth with them.

20 And so he that had received five talents, came and brought other five talents, saying, Lord, thou deliveredst unto me five talents : behold, I have gained besides them five talents more.

21 His lord said unto him, Well done, *thou* good and faithful servant ; thou hast been faithful over a few things, I will make thee ruler over many things : enter thou into the joy of thy lord.

22 He also that had received two talents came, and said, Lord, thou deliveredst unto me two talents : be-

MARK.

Parables. (THIRD DAY OF THE WEEK.) *Mount of Olives.*

LUKE.	JOHN.

§ 129. Transition to Christ's final coming. Exhortation.

MATTHEW.	MARK.
CH. XXIV. 43–51. CH. XXV. 1–30.	

hold, I have gained two other talents besides them.

23 His lord said unto him, Well done, good and faithful servant ; thou hast been faithful over a few things, I will make thee ruler over many things : enter thou into the joy of thy lord.

24 Then he which had received the one talent came, and said, Lord, I knew thee that thou art an hard man, reaping where thou hast not sown, and gathering where thou hast not strewed :

25 And I was afraid, and went and hid thy talent in the earth: lo, *there* thou hast *that is* thine.

26 His lord answered and said unto him, *Thou* wicked and slothful servant, thou knewest that I reap where I sowed not, and gather where I have not strewed :

27 Thou oughtest therefore to have put my money to the exchangers, and *then* at my coming I should have received mine own with usury.

28 Take therefore the talent from him, and give *it* unto him which hath ten talents.

29 For unto every one that hath shall be given, and he shall have abundance : but from him that hath not, shall be taken away even that which he hath.

30 And cast ye the unprofitable servant into outer darkness : there shall be weeping and gnashing of teeth.

§ 130. Scenes of the Judgment Day.

CH. XXV. 31–46.

31 When the Son of man shall come in his glory, and all the holy angels with him, then shall he sit upon the throne of his glory :

32 And before him shall be gathered all nations : and he shall separate them one from another, as a shepherd divideth *his* sheep from the goats :

Matth. xxv. 26, *thou knewest*.] Interrogatively and sarcastically. That is, Was

Parables.　(THIRD DAY OF THE WEEK.)　*Mount of Olives.*

<table>
<tr><td align="center">LUKE.</td><td align="center">JOHN.</td></tr>
</table>

(THIRD DAY OF THE WEEK.)　*Mount of Olives.*

such thy wicked opinion?　Then "out of thine own mouth will I judge thee;" thou oughtest to have acted according to that opinion.　BP. SUMNER, in loc.

28

§ 130. Scenes of the Judgment Day.

MATTHEW.   MARK.
CH. XXV.   31–46.

33 And he shall set the sheep on his right hand, but the goats on the left.

34 Then shall the King say unto them on his right hand, Come, ye blessed of my Father, inherit the kingdom prepared for you from the foundation of the world :

35 For I was an hungered, and ye gave me meat : I was thirsty, and ye gave me drink : I was a stranger, and ye took me in :

36 Naked, and ye clothed me : I was sick, and ye visited me : I was in prison, and ye came unto me.

37 Then shall the righteous answer him, saying, Lord, when saw we thee an hungered, and fed *thee?* or thirsty, and gave *thee* drink?

38 When saw we thee a stranger, and took *thee* in? or naked, and clothed *thee?*

39 Or when saw we thee sick, or in prison, and came unto thee?

40 And the King shall answer and say unto them, Verily I say unto you, Inasmuch as ye have done *it* unto one of the least of these my brethren, ye have done *it* unto me.

41 Then shall he say also unto them on the left hand, Depart from me, ye cursed, into everlasting fire, prepared for the devil and his angels :

42 For I was an hungered, and ye gave me no meat : I was thirsty, and ye gave me no drink :

43 I was a stranger, and ye took me not in : naked, and ye clothed me not : sick, and in prison, and ye visited me not.

44 Then shall they also answer him, saying, Lord, when saw we thee an hungered, or athirst, or a stranger, or naked, or sick, or in prison, and did not minister unto thee?

45 Then shall he answer them, saying, Verily, I say unto you, Inasmuch as ye did *it* not to one of the least of these, ye did *it* not to me.

46 And these shall go away into everlasting punishment : but the righteous into life eternal.

(THIRD DAY OF THE WEEK.) *Mount of Olives.*

LUKE.	JOHN.

§ 131. The Rulers conspire. The Supper at Bethany. Treachery

MATTHEW. CH. XXVI. 1–16.	MARK. CH. XIV. 1–11.
AND it came to pass, when Jesus had finished all these sayings, he said unto his disciples,	
2 Ye know that after two days is *the feast of* the passover, and the Son of man is betrayed to be crucified.	AFTER two days was *the feast of* the passover, and of unleavened bread : and the chief priests, and the scribes, sought how they might take him by craft, and put *him* to death.
3 Then assembled together the chief priests, and the scribes, and the elders of the people, unto the palace of the high priest, who was called Caiaphas,	
4 And consulted that they might take Jesus by subtilty, and kill *him*.	
5 But they said, Not on the feast-*day*, lest there be an uproar among the people.	2 But they said, Not on the feast-*day*, lest there be an uproar of the people.
6 Now when Jesus was in Bethany, in the house of Simon the leper,	3 And being in Bethany, in the house of Simon the leper, as he sat at meat, there came a woman having
7 There came unto him a woman having an alabaster-box of very precious ointment, and poured *it* on his head as he sat *at meat*.	an alabaster-box of ointment of spikenard, very precious ; and she brake the box, and poured *it* on his head.
8 But when his disciples saw *it*, they had indignation, saying, To what purpose *is* this waste?	4 And there were some that had indignation within themselves, and said, Why was this waste of the ointment made?
9 For this ointment might have been sold for much, and given to the poor.	5 For it might have been sold for more than three hundred pence, and have been given to the poor. And they murmured against her.
10 When Jesus understood *it*, he said unto them, Why trouble ye the woman? for she hath wrought a good work upon me.	6 And Jesus said, Let her alone : why trouble ye her? she hath wrought a good work on me.

Matth. xxvi. 8, *his disciples*.] In St. John, Judas alone murmurs ; in St. Matthew, the disciples have indignation ; or, as St. Mark expresses it, some have indignation among themselves. Dr. Lardner says, Serm. v. 2, p. 316, "It is well known to be very common with all writers, to use the plural number when one person only is intended. Nor is it impossible that others might have some uneasiness about it, though they were far from being so disgusted at it as Judas was. And their concern for the poor was sincere ; his was self-interested, and mere pretence." See also Grotius in loc. NEWCOME.

John xii. 3, *the feet*.] It is nowhere asserted that the unction was of Jesus's head *only*, or of his feet *only*. Both actions are consistent ; and St. John, in his supplemental history, may very well have added the respectful conduct of Mary, that, after

of Judas. (FOURTH DAY OF THE WEEK.) *Jerusalem.* *Bethany.*

LUKE. CH. XXII. 1–6.	JOHN. CH. XII. 2–8.
Now the feast of unleavened bread drew nigh, which is called the Passover. 2 And the chief priests and scribes sought how they might kill him : for they feared the people.	
	2 There they made him a supper ; and Martha served : but Lazarus was one of them that sat at the table with him. 3 Then took Mary a pound of ointment of spikenard, very costly, and anointed the feet of Jesus, and wiped his feet with her hair : and the house was filled with the odour of the ointment. 4 Then saith one of his disciples, Judas Iscariot, Simon's *son*, which should betray him, 5 Why was not this ointment sold for three hundred pence, and given to the poor ? 6 This he said, not that he cared for the poor ; but because he was a thief, and had the bag, and bare what was put therein. 7 Then said Jesus, Let her alone : against the day of my burying hath she kept this.

having anointed Jesus's head, she proceeded to anoint his feet, and even to wipe them with her hair. NEWCOME.

John xii. 4, *Judas Iscariot.*] The other Evangelists mention that indignation was caused by the supposed waste of the ointment ; John fixes it upon Judas. That Judas went to the High Priest's on the evening or night of our Wednesday, may be collected from Matth. xxvi. 14, 17, and the parallel places ; and he seems to have acted partly from disgust at what had passed. The story has a remarkably apt connection with the preceding and subsequent history. The Jewish rulers consult how they may take Jesus by craft, and without raising a tumult among the people. An incident happens, which offends one of Jesus's familiar attendants, who immediately repairs to the enemies of Jesus, and receives from them a bribe to betray him in the absence of the multitude. NEWCOME.

§ 131. The Rulers conspire. The Supper at Bethany. Treachery

MATTHEW.	MARK.
CH. XXVI. 1–16.	CH. XIV. 1–11.
11 For ye have the poor always with you; but me ye have not always.	7 For ye have the poor with you always, and whensoever ye will ye may do them good: but me ye have not always.
12 For in that she hath poured this ointment on my body, she did *it* for my burial.	8 She hath done what she could: she is come aforehand to anoint my body to the burying.
13 Verily, I say unto you, Wheresoever this gospel shall be preached in the whole world, *there* shall also this, that this woman hath done, be told for a memorial of her.	9 Verily, I say unto you, Wheresoever this gospel shall be preached throughout the whole world, *this* also that she hath done shall be spoken of, for a memorial of her.
14 Then one of the twelve, called Judas Iscariot, went unto the chief priests,	10 And Judas Iscariot, one of the twelve, went unto the chief priests, to betray him unto them.
15 And said *unto them*, What will ye give me, and I will deliver him unto you? And they covenanted with him for thirty pieces of silver.	
16 And from that time he sought opportunity to betray him.	11 And when they heard *it*, they were glad, and promised to give him money. And he sought how he might conveniently betray him.

§ 132. Preparation for the Passover.

CH. XXVI. 17–19.	CH. XIV. 12–16.
17 Now the first *day* of the *feast of* unleavened bread, the disciples came to Jesus, saying unto him, Where wilt thou that we prepare for thee to eat the passover?	12 And the first day of unleavened bread, when they killed the passover, his disciples said unto him, Where wilt thou that we go and prepare, that thou mayest eat the passover?
18 And he said, Go into the city to such a man, and say unto him, The Master saith, My time is at hand; I will keep the passover at thy house with my disciples.	13 And he sendeth forth two of his disciples, and saith unto them, Go ye into the city, and there shall meet you a man bearing a pitcher of water: follow him.
	14 And wheresoever he shall go in, say ye to the good man of the house, The Master saith, Where is the guest-chamber, where I shall eat the passover with my disciples!
	15 And he will shew you a large upper room furnished *and* prepared: there make ready for us.
19 And the disciples did as Jesus had appointed them; and they made ready the passover.	16 And his disciples went forth, and came into the city, and found as he had said unto them: and they made ready the passover.

of Judas.   (FOURTH DAY OF THE WEEK.)   *Jerusalem.   Bethany.*

LUKE.	JOHN.
CH. XXII. 1–6.	CH. XII. 2–8.
	8 For the poor always ye have with you ; but me ye have not always.

3 Then entered Satan into Judas surnamed Iscariot, being of the number of the twelve.

4 And he went his way, and communed with the chief priests and captains, how he might betray him unto them.

5 And they were glad, and covenanted to give him money.

6 And he promised, and sought opportunity to betray him unto them in the absence of the multitude.

(FIFTH DAY OF THE WEEK.)   *Jerusalem.   Bethany.*

CH. XXII. 7–13.

7 Then came the day of unleavened bread, when the passover must be killed.

8 And he sent Peter and John, saying, Go and prepare us the passover, that we may eat.

9 And they said unto him, Where wilt thou that we prepare ?

10 And he said unto them, Behold, when ye are entered into the city, there shall a man meet you, bearing a pitcher of water ; follow him into the house where he entereth in.

11 And ye shall say unto the good man of the house, The Master saith unto thee, Where is the guest-chamber, where I shall eat the passover with my disciples?

12 And he shall shew you a large upper room furnished : there make ready.

13 And they went and found as he had said unto them : and they made ready the passover.

PART VIII.

THE FOURTH PASSOVER; OUR LORD'S PASSION;

AND THE

ACCOMPANYING EVENTS

UNTIL THE

END OF THE JEWISH SABBATH

TIME. Two days

§ 133.   The Passover Meal.   Contention among the Twelve.

MATTHEW.	MARK.
CH. XXVI. 20.	CH. XIV. 17.
20 Now when the even was come, he sat down with the twelve.	17 And in the evening he cometh with the twelve.

§ 134. Jesus washes the feet of his disciples.   (EVENING

LUKE.

CH. XXII. 14–18, 24–30.

14 And when the hour was come, he sat down, and the twelve apostles with him.

.15 And he said unto them, With desire I have desired to eat this passover with you before I suffer.

16 For I say unto you, I will not any more eat thereof, until it be fulfilled in the kingdom of God.

17 And he took the cup, and gave thanks, and said, Take this, and divide *it* among yourselves.

18 For I say unto you, I will not drink of the fruit of the vine, until the kingdom of God shall come.

24 And there was also a strife among them, which of them should be accounted the greatest.

25 And he said unto them, The kings of the Gentiles exercise lordship over them ; and they that exercise authority upon them are called benefactors.

26 But ye *shall* not *be* so : but he that is greatest among you, let him be as the younger; and he that is chief, as he that doth serve.

27 For whether *is* greater, he that sitteth at meat, or he that serveth? *is* not he that sitteth at meat? but I am among you as he that serveth.

28 Ye are they which have continued with me in my temptations.

29 And I appoint unto you a kingdom, as my Father hath appointed unto me ;

30 That ye may eat and drink at my table in my kingdom, and sit on thrones, judging the twelve tribes of Israel.

JOHN.

CH. XIII. 1–20.

Now before the feast of the passover, when Jesus knew that his hour was come that he should depart out of this world unto the Father, having loved his own which were in the world, he loved them unto the end.

2 And supper being ended, (the devil having now put into the heart of Judas Iscariot, Simon's *son*, to betray him,)

§134. Jesus washes the feet of his disciples. (EVENING

MATTHEW.	MARK.

LUKE.

JOHN.
CH. XIII. 1-20.

3 Jesus knowing that the Father had given all things into his hands, and that he was come from God, and went to God ;

4 He riseth from supper, and laid aside his garments; and took a towel, and girded himself.

5 After that, he poureth water into a basin, and began to wash the disciples' feet, and to wipe *them* with the towel wherewith he was girded.

6 Then cometh he to Simon Peter : and Peter saith unto him, Lord, dost thou wash my feet?

7 Jesus answered and said unto him, What I do thou knowest not now; but thou shalt know hereafter.

8 Peter saith unto him, Thou shalt never wash my feet. Jesus answered him, If I wash thee not, thou hast no part with me.

9 Simon Peter saith unto him, Lord, not my feet only, but also *my* hands and *my* head.

10 Jesus saith to him, He that is washed needeth not save to wash *his* feet, but is clean every whit : and ye are clean, but not all.

11 For he knew who should betray him : therefore said he, Ye are not all clean.

12 So after he had washed their feet, and had taken his garments, and was set down again, he said unto them, Know ye what I have done to you?

13 Ye call me Master, and Lord : and ye say well ; for *so* I am.

14 If I then, *your* Lord and Master, have washed your feet ; ye also ought to wash one another's feet.

15 For I have given you an example, that ye should do as I have done to you.

16 Verily, verily, I say unto you, The servant is not greater than his lord ; neither he that is sent greater than he that sent him.

17 If ye know these things, happy are ye if ye do them.

18 I speak not of you all ; I know whom I have chosen ; but that the

§ 134. Jesus washes the feet of his disciples. (EVENING

MATTHEW.	MARK.

§ 135. Jesus points out the traitor. Judas withdraws.

CH. XXVI. 21–25.	CH. XIV. 18–21.
21 And as they did eat, he said, Verily I say unto you, That one of you shall betray me.	18 And as they sat, and did eat, Jesus said, Verily I say unto you, One of you which eateth with me, shall betray me.
22 And they were exceeding sorrowful, and began every one of them to say unto him, Lord, is it I?	19 And they began to be sorrowful, and to say unto him one by one, *Is* it I? and another *said, Is* it I?
23 And he answered and said, He that dippeth *his* hand with me in the dish, the same shall betray me.	20 And he answered and said unto them, *It is* one of the twelve that dippeth with me in the dish.
24 The Son of man goeth, as it is written of him : but wo unto that man by whom the Son of man is betrayed! it had been good for that man if he had not been born.	21 The Son of man indeed goeth, as it is written of him : but wo to that man by whom the Son of man is betrayed! good were it for that man if he had never been born.
25 Then Judas, which betrayed him, answered and said, Master, is it I! He said unto him, Thou hast said.	

LUKE.	JOHN.
	CH. XIII. 1–20.

scripture may be fulfilled, He that eateth bread with me, hath lifted up his heel against me.[a]

19 Now I tell you before it come, that when it is come to pass, ye may believe that I am *he.*

20 Verily, verily, I say unto you, He that receiveth whomsoever I send, receiveth me ; and he that receiveth me, receiveth him that sent me.

CH. XXII. 21–23.	**CH. XIII. 21–35.**

21 But behold, the hand of him that betrayeth me *is* with me on the table.

22 And truly the Son of man goeth as it was determined : but wo unto that man by whom he is betrayed !

21 When Jesus had thus said, he was troubled in spirit, and testified, and said, Verily, verily, I say unto you, that one of you shall betray me.

22 Then the disciples looked one on another, doubting of whom he spake.

23 Now there was leaning on Jesus' bosom, one of his disciples, whom Jesus loved.

23 And they began to inquire among themselves, which of them it was that should do this thing.

24 Simon Peter therefore beckoned to him, that he should ask who it should be of whom he spake.

25 He then, lying on Jesus' breast, saith unto him, Lord, who is it ?

26 Jesus answered, He it is to whom I shall give a sop, when I have dipped *it.* And when he had dipped the sop, he gave *it* to Judas Iscariot *the son* of Simon.

27 And after the sop Satan entered into him. Then said Jesus unto him, That thou doest, do quickly.

28 Now no man at the table knew for what intent he spake this unto him.

29 For some *of them* thought, because Judas had the bag, that Jesus had said unto him, Buy *those things* that we have need of against the feast ; or, that he should give something to the poor.

30 He then, having received the sop, went immediately out : and it was night.

31 Therefore, when he was gone out, Jesus said, Now is the Son of

[a] Ps. xli. 10.

§ 135. Jesus points out the traitor. Judas withdraws.

MATTHEW.	MARK.

§ 136. Jesus foretells the fall of Peter, and the dispersion of the Twelve.

CH. XXVI. 31–35.	CH. XIV. 27–31.
31 Then saith Jesus unto them, All ye shall be offended because of me this night : for it is written, I will smite the Shepherd, and the sheep of the flock shall be scattered abroad.[a]	27 And Jesus saith unto them, All ye shall be offended because of me this night : for it is written, I will smite the Shepherd, and the sheep shall be scattered.
32 But after I am risen again, I will go before you into Galilee.	28 But after that I am risen, I will go before you into Galilee.
33 Peter answered and said unto him, Though all *men* shall be offended because of thee, *yet* will I never be offended.	29 But Peter said unto him, Although all shall be offended, yet *will* not I.
34 Jesus said unto him, Verily, I say unto thee, That this night, before the cock crow, thou shalt deny me thrice.	30 And Jesus saith unto him, Verily, I say unto thee, That this day, *even* in this night, before the cock crow twice, thou shalt deny me thrice.
35 Peter said unto him, Though I should die with thee, yet will not I deny thee. Likewise also said all the disciples.	31 But he spake the more vehemently, If I should die with thee, I will not deny thee in any wise. Likewise also said they all.

[a] Zech. xiii. 7.

Mark xiv. 30, *Before the cock crow twice.*] The other Evangelists simply say, Before the cock *crow.* — It is observed, that the cock crows about midnight : and about the fourth watch, or about three in the morning, when that watch began. When *gallicinium* (*cock-crowing*) stands alone, it means this latter time, which is referred to, Aristoph. Eccles. 390. Juv. Sat. ix. 107. The four Evangelists therefore denote the same time, — sc. galliciniis secundis, as Ammianus expresses it, l. 22 ; and any part of the period thus marked out, may be understood. See BOCHART de anim. pars, 2d. 119, and GROTIUS on Matth. xxvi. 34. NEWCOME.

Luke xxii. 36, *and he that hath no sword, let him sell his garment and buy one.*] In the animated language of the prophets, their predictions are often announced under the form of commands. The prophet Isaiah, in the sublime prediction he has given

LUKE.	JOHN.
	CH. XIII. 21–35.
	man glorified, and God is glorified in him.
	32 If God be glorified in him, God shall also glorify him in himself, and shall straightway glorify him.
	33 Little children, yet a little while I am with you. Ye shall seek me; and, as I said unto the Jews, Whither I go, ye cannot come, so now I say to you.
	34 A new commandment I give unto you, That ye love one another; as I have loved you, that ye also love one another.
	35 By this shall all *men* know that ye are my disciples, if ye have love one to another.

CH. XXII. 31–38.	CH. XIII. 36–38.
31 And the Lord said, Simon, Simon, behold, Satan hath desired *to have* you, that he may sift *you* as wheat:	36 Simon Peter said unto him, Lord, whither goest thou? Jesus answered him, Whither I go, thou canst not follow me now; but thou shalt follow me afterward.
32 But I have prayed for thee, that thy faith fail not: and when thou art converted, strengthen thy brethren.	
33 And he said unto him, Lord, I am ready to go with thee, both into prison, and to death.	37 Peter said unto him, Lord, why cannot I follow thee now? I will lay down my life for thy sake.
34 And he said, I tell thee, Peter, the cock shall not crow this day, before that thou shalt thrice deny that thou knowest me.	38 Jesus answered him, Wilt thou lay down thy life for my sake? Verily, verily, I say unto thee, The cock shall not crow, till thou hast denied me thrice.
35 And he said unto them, When I sent you without purse, and scrip, and shoes, lacked ye any thing? And they said, Nothing.	
36 Then said he unto them, But now, he that hath a purse, let him take *it,* and likewise *his* scrip: and he that hath no sword, let him sell his garment, and buy one.	

us of the fate of the king of Babylon, thus foretells the destruction of his family:— *Prepare slaughter for his children,* &c. Isa. xiv. 21. The prophet Jeremiah in like manner foretells the approaching destruction of the children of Zion:— *Call for the mourning women, that they may come: and send for cunning women; and let them make haste, and take up a wailing,* &c. Jer. ix. 17, 18. There, matter of sorrow is predicted, by commanding the common attendants on mourning and lamentation to be gotten in readiness; here, warning is given of the most imminent dangers, by orders to make the customary preparation against violence, and to account a weapon more necessary than a garment. CAMPBELL, *in loc.*

§ 136. Jesus foretells the fall of Peter, and the dispersion of the Twelve.

MATTHEW.	MARK.

§ 137. The Lord's Supper. (EVENING INTRODUCING

CH. XXVI. 26–29.	CH. XIV. 22–25.
26 And as they were eating, Jesus took bread, and blessed *it*, and brake *it*, and gave *it* to the disciples, and said, Take, eat; this is my body.	22 And as they did eat, Jesus took bread, and blessed, and brake *it*, and gave to them, and said, Take, eat: this is my body.
27 And he took the cup, and gave thanks, and gave *it* to them, saying, Drink ye all of it;	23 And he took the cup, and when he had given thanks, he gave *it* to them : and they all drank of it.
28 For this is my blood of the new testament, which is shed for many for the remission of sins.	24 And he said unto them, This is my blood of the new testament, which is shed for many.
29 But I say unto you, I will not drink henceforth of this fruit of the vine, until that day when I drink it new with you in my Father's kingdom.	25 Verily, I say unto you, I will drink no more of the fruit of the vine, until that day that I drink it new in the kingdom of God.

§ 138. Jesus comforts his disciples. The Holy Spirit promised.

Matth. xxvi. 26–29, &c.] This account of the institution of the Lord's Supper is corroborated by that of Paul, in 1 Cor. xi. 23–25, which is usually inserted by Harmonists in this place, as parallel testimony; but as the plan of this work leads me to deal with the four Gospels alone, the insertion of other parts of Scripture in the text, here and elsewhere, is omitted.

Matth. xxvi. 28, *my blood of the new testament.*] See Appendix, No. III.

Matth. xxvi. 26, *as they were eating.*] The Evangelists have determined, by some general expressions, the order of the following events between the sitting down to the paschal supper, and the going to Gethsemane. Before the eating of the paschal lamb, Jesus rises from supper to wash the disciples' feet. John xiii. 1, 4. While they are eating, a declaration is made of Judas's treachery, and the bread is instituted, Matth. xxvi. 21, 26. See also Mark. After, the cup is instituted, Luke xxii. 20; 1 Cor. xi.

LUKE.	JOHN.
CH. XXII. 31–38.	

37 For I say unto you, that this that is written must yet be accomplished in me, And he was reckoned among the transgressors: [a] for the things concerning me have an end.

38 And they said, Lord, behold, here *are* two swords. And he said unto them, It is enough.

THE SIXTH DAY OF THE WEEK.)   *Jerusalem.*

CH. XXII. 19–20.

19 And he took bread, and gave thanks, and brake *it*, and gave unto them, saying, This is my body which is given for you: this do in remembrance of me.

20 Likewise also the cup after supper, saying, This cup *is* the new testament in my blood, which is shed for you.

(EVENING INTRODUCING THE SIXTH DAY OF THE WEEK.)   *Jerusalem.*

CH. XIV. 1–31.

LET not your heart be troubled: ye believe in God, believe also in me.

2 In my Father's house are many mansions : if *it were* not *so*, I would have told you. I go to prepare a place for you.

3 And if I go and prepare a place for you, I will come again and receive you unto myself; that where I am, *there* ye may be also.

[a] Isa. liii. 12.

---

25. But as to the particular and precise order of the facts and discourses during this period, Pilkington's words relating to one of them are applicable to all. "It is observable that St. Luke mentions the institution of the communion before the declaration of Judas's treachery ; whereas the other Evangelists place these in a different order. But it is a liberty I think very allowable in any historian, to neglect taking notice of the exact order of all the facts, when he is only giving a general account of what was done at a certain time. And if so, whichsoever was the true successive order, there can be no just imputation upon any of the Evangelists for neglecting to observe it in the narration." Harm. p. 52. NEWCOME.

§ 138. Jesus comforts his disciples. The Holy Spirit promised.

MATTHEW.	MARK.

LUKE.

JOHN.

CH. XIV. 1 – 31.

4 And whither I go ye know, and the way ye know.

5 Thomas saith unto him, Lord, we know not whither thou goest; and how can we know the way?

6 Jesus saith unto him, I am the way, and the truth, and the life : no man cometh unto the Father, but by me.

7 If ye had known me, ye should have known my Father also : and from henceforth ye know him, and have seen him.

8 Philip saith unto him, Lord, shew us the Father, and it sufficeth us.

9 Jesus saith unto him, Have I been so long time with you, and yet hast thou not known me, Philip? he that hath seen me, hath seen the Father; and how sayest thou *then*, Shew us the Father?

10 Believest thou not that I am in the Father, and the Father in me? the words that I speak unto you, I speak not of myself : but the Father, that dwelleth in me, he doeth the works.

11 Believe me that I *am* in the Father, and the Father in me : or else believe me for the very works' sake.

12 Verily, verily, I say unto you, He that believeth on me, the works that I do shall he do also; and greater *works* than these shall he do; because I go unto my Father.

13 And whatsoever ye shall ask in my name, that will I do, that the Father may be glorified in the Son.

14 If ye shall ask any thing in my name, I will do *it*.

15 If ye love me, keep my commandments :

16 And I will pray the Father, and he shall give you another Comforter, that he may abide with you for ever;

17 *Even* the Spirit of truth; whom the world cannot receive, because it seeth him not, neither knoweth him : but ye know him; for he dwelleth with you, and shall be in you.

18 I will not leave you comfortless : I will come to you.

§ 138. Jesus comforts his disciples. The Holy Spirit promised.

MATTHEW.	MARK.

LUKE.	JOHN.
	CH. XIV. 1–31.

JOHN.

CH. XIV. 1–31.

19 Yet a little while, and the world seeth me no more; but ye see me: because I live, ye shall live also.

20 At that day ye shall know that I *am* in my Father, and ye in me, and I in you.

21 He that hath my commandments, and keepeth them, he it is that loveth me: and he that loveth me, shall be loved of my Father, and I will love him, and will manifest myself to him.

22 Judas saith unto him, (not Iscariot) Lord, how is it that thou wilt manifest thyself unto us, and not unto the world?

23 Jesus answered and said unto him, If a man love me, he will keep my words: and my Father will love him, and we will come unto him, and make our abode with him.

24 He that loveth me not, keepeth not my sayings: and the word which ye hear is not mine, but the Father's which sent me.

25 These things have I spoken unto you, being *yet* present with you.

26 But the Comforter, *which is* the Holy Ghost, whom the Father will send in my name, he shall teach you all things, and bring all things to your remembrance, whatsoever I have said unto you.

27 Peace I leave with you, my peace I give unto you: not as the world giveth, give I unto you. Let not your heart be troubled, neither let it be afraid.

28 Ye have heard how I said unto you, I go away, and come *again* unto you. If ye loved me, ye would rejoice, because I said, I go unto the Father: for my Father is greater than I.

29 And now I have told you before it come to pass, that when it is come to pass, ye might believe.

30 Hereafter I will not talk much with you: for the prince of this world cometh, and hath nothing in me.

31 But that the world may know that I love the Father; and as the Father gave me commandment, even so I do. Arise, let us go hence.

§ 139. Christ the true Vine. His disciples hated by the world.

MATTHEW.	MARK.

LUKE.

JOHN.

CH. XV. 1—27.

I AM the true vine, and my Father is the husbandman.

2 Every branch in me that beareth not fruit, he taketh away : and every *branch* that beareth fruit, he purgeth it, that it may bring forth more fruit.

3 Now ye are clean through the word which I have spoken unto you.

4 Abide in me, and I in you. As the branch cannot bear fruit of itself, except it abide in the vine : no more can ye, except ye abide in me.

5 I am the vine, ye *are* the branches : He that abideth in me, and I in him, the same bringeth forth much fruit : for without me ye can do nothing.

6 If a man abide not in me, he is cast forth as a branch, and is withered ; and men gather them, and cast *them* into the fire, and they are burned.

7 If ye abide in me, and my words abide in you, ye shall ask what ye will, and it shall be done unto you.

8 Herein is my Father glorified, that ye bear much fruit ; so shall ye be my disciples.

9 As the Father hath loved me, so have I loved you : continue ye in my love.

10 If ye keep my commandments, ye shall abide in my love ; even as I have kept my Father's commandments, and abide in his love.

11 These things have I spoken unto you, that my joy might remain in you, and *that* your joy might be full.

12 This is my commandment, That ye love one another, as I have loved you.

13 Greater love hath no man than this, that a man lay down his life for his friends.

14 Ye are my friends, if ye do whatsoever I command you.

15 Henceforth I call you not servants ; for the servant knoweth not what his lord doeth : but I have called you friends ; for all things that I have heard of my Father, I have made known unto you.

16 Ye have not chosen me, but I have chosen you, and ordained you, that ye should go and bring forth

§ 139. Christ the true Vine. His disciples hated by the world.

MATTHEW.	MARK.

§ 140. Persecution foretold. Further promise of the Holy Spirit.

LUKE.

JOHN.

CH. XV. 1–27.

fruit, and *that* your fruit should remain: that whatsoever ye shall ask of the Father in my name, he may give it you.

17 These things I command you, that ye love one another.

18 If the world hate you, ye know that it hated me before *it hated* you.

19 If ye were of the world, the world would love his own; but because ye are not of the world, but I have chosen you out of the world, therefore the world hateth you.

20 Remember the word that I said unto you, The servant is not greater than his lord. If they have persecuted me, they will also persecute you: if they have kept my saying, they will keep yours also.

21 But all these things will they do unto you for my name's sake, because they know not him that sent me.

22 If I had not come and spoken unto them, they had not had sin: but now they have no cloak for their sin.

23 He that hateth me, hateth my Father also.

24 If I had not done among them the works which none other man did, they had not had sin: but now have they both seen, and hated both me and my Father.

25 But *this cometh to pass,* that the word might be fulfilled that is written in their law, They hated me without a cause.[a]

26 But when the Comforter is come, whom I will send unto you from the Father, *even* the Spirit of truth, which proceedeth from the Father, he shall testify of me.

27 And ye also shall bear witness, because ye have been with me from the beginning.

CH. XVI. 1–33.

THESE things have I spoken unto you, that ye should not be offended.

2 They shall put you out of the synagogues: yea, the time cometh,

a Ps. lxix. 5.

§ 140. Persecution foretold.   Further promise of the Holy Spirit.

MATTHEW.	MARK.

LUKE.

JOHN.
CH. XVI. 1 – 33.

that whosoever killeth you, will think that he doeth God service.

3 And these things will they do unto you, because they have not known the Father, nor me.

4 But these things have I told you, that when the time shall come, ye may remember that I told you of them. And these things I said not unto you at the beginning because I was with you.

5 But now I go my way to him that sent me, and none of you asketh me, Whither goest thou?

6 But because I have said these things unto you, sorrow hath filled your heart.

7 Nevertheless, I tell you the truth: It is expedient for you that I go away: for if I go not away, the Comforter will not come unto you; but if I depart, I will send him unto you.

8 And when he is come, he will reprove the world of sin, and of righteousness, and of judgment:

9 Of sin, because they believe not on me;

10 Of righteousness, because I go to my Father, and ye see me no more;

11 Of judgment, because the prince of this world is judged.

12 I have yet many things to say unto you, but ye cannot bear them now.

13 Howbeit, when he, the Spirit of truth is come, he will guide you into all truth: for he shall not speak of himself; but whatsoever he shall hear, *that* shall he speak: and he will shew you things to come.

14 He shall glorify me: for he shall receive of mine, and shall shew *it* unto you.

15 All things that the Father hath are mine: therefore said I, that he shall take of mine, and shall shew *it* unto you.

16 A little while, and ye shall not see me: and again, a little while, and ye shall see me, because I go to the Father.

§ 140. Persecution foretold. Further promise of the Holy Spirit.

MATTHEW.	MARK.

LUKE.

JOHN.
CH. XVI. 1–33.

17 Then said *some* of his disciples among themselves, What is this that he saith unto us, A little while, and ye shall not see me: and again, a little while, and ye shall see me; and, Because I go to the Father?

18 They said therefore, What is this that he saith, A little while? we cannot tell what he saith.

19 Now Jesus knew that they were desirous to ask him, and said unto them, Do ye inquire among yourselves of that I said, A little while, and ye shall not see me: and again, a little while, and ye shall see me?

20 Verily, verily, I say unto you, that ye shall weep and lament, but the world shall rejoice: and ye shall be sorrowful, but your sorrow shall be turned into joy.

21 A woman when she is in travail hath sorrow, because her hour is come: but as soon as she is delivered of the child, she remembereth no more the anguish, for joy that a man is born into the world.

22 And ye now therefore have sorrow: but I will see you again, and your heart shall rejoice, and your joy no man taketh from you.

23 And in that day ye shall ask me nothing. Verily, verily, I say unto you, Whatsoever ye shall ask the Father in my name, he will give *it* you.

24 Hitherto have ye asked nothing in my name: ask, and ye shall receive, that your joy may be full.

25 These things have I spoken unto you in proverbs: but the time cometh when I shall no more speak unto you in proverbs, but I shall shew you plainly of the Father.

26 At that day ye shall ask in my name: and I say not unto you, that I will pray the Father for you:

27 For the Father himself loveth you, because ye have loved me, and have believed that I came out from God.

28 I came forth from the Father, and am come into the world: again, I leave the world, and go to the Father.

§ 140. Persecution foretold. Further promise of the Holy Spirit.

MATTHEW.	MARK.

§ 141. Christ's last prayer with his disciples. (EVENING

Christal.   (EVENING INTRODUCING THE SIXTH DAY OF THE WEEK.)   *Jerusalem.*

LUKE.	JOHN.

JOHN.
CH. XVI. 1 – 33.

29 His disciples said unto him, Lo, now speakest thou plainly, and speakest no proverb.

30 Now are we sure that thou knowest all things, and needest not that any man should ask thee : by this we believe that thou camest forth from God.

31 Jesus answered them, Do ye now believe ?

32 Behold, the hour cometh, yea, is now come, that ye shall be scattered every man to his own, and shall leave me alone : and yet I am not alone, because the Father is with me.

33 These things I have spoken unto you, that in me ye might have peace. In the world ye shall have tribulation, but be of good cheer : I have overcome the world.

INTRODUCING THE SIXTH DAY OF THE WEEK.)   *Jerusalem.*

CH. XVII. 1 – 26.

THESE words spake Jesus, and lifted up his eyes to heaven, and said, Father, the hour is come ; glorify thy Son, that thy Son also may glorify thee :

2 As thou hast given him power over all flesh, that he should give eternal life to as many as thou hast given him.

3 And this is life eternal, that they might know thee the only true God, and Jesus Christ whom thou hast sent.

4 I have glorified thee on the earth : I have finished the work which thou gavest me to do.

5 And now, O Father, glorify thou me with thine own self, with the glory which I had with thee before the world was.

6 I have manifested thy name unto the men which thou gavest me out of the world : thine they were, and thou gavest them me ; and they have kept thy word.

7 Now they have known that all things whatsoever thou hast given me are of thee :

8 For I have given unto them the words which thou gavest me ; and

§ 141. Christ's last prayer with his disciples. (EVENING

MATTHEW.	MARK.

LUKE.	JOHN.

JOHN.
CH. XVII. 1–26.

they have received *them*, and have known surely that I came out from thee, and they have believed that thou didst send me.

9 I pray for them : I pray not for the world, but for them which thou hast given me ; for they are thine.

10 And all mine are thine, and thine are mine ; and I am glorified in them.

11 And now I am no more in the world, but these are in the world, and I come to thee. Holy Father, keep through thine own name those whom thou hast given me, that they may be one, as we *are.*

12 While I was with them in the world, I kept them in thy name : those that thou gavest me I have kept, and none of them is lost, but the son of perdition ; that the scripture might be fulfilled.[a]

13 And now come I to thee, and these things I speak in the world, that they might have my joy fulfilled in themselves.

14 I have given them thy word ; and the world hath hated them, because they are not of the world, even as I am not of the world.

15 I pray not that thou shouldest take them out of the world, but that thou shouldest keep them from the evil.

16 They are not of the world, even as I am not of the world.

17 Sanctify them through thy truth : thy word is truth.

18 As thou hast sent me into the world, even so have I also sent them into the world.

19 And for their sakes I sanctify myself, that they also might be sanctified through the truth.

20 Neither pray I for these alone ; but for them also which shall believe on me through their word :

21 That they all may be one ; as thou, Father, *art* in me, and I in thee, that they also may be one in us : that the world may believe that thou hast sent me.

[a] Ps. xli. 9, and cix. 8, 17.

§ 141. Christ's last prayer with his disciples. (EVENING

MATTHEW.	MARK.

§ 142. The agony in Gethsemane. (EVENING

CH. XXVI. 30, 36–46.	CH. XIV. 26, 32–42.
30 And when they had sung a hymn, they went out into the mount of Olives.	26 And when they had sung an hymn, they went out into the mount of Olives.
36 Then cometh Jesus with them unto a place called Gethsemane, and saith unto the disciples, Sit ye here, while I go and pray yonder.	32 And they came to a place which was named Gethsemane : and he saith to his disciples, Sit ye here, while I shall pray.
37 And he took with him Peter, and the two sons of Zebedee, and began to be sorrowful and very heavy.	33 And he taketh with him Peter, and James, and John, and began to be sore amazed, and to be very heavy ;
38 Then saith he unto them, My soul is exceeding sorrowful, even unto death : tarry ye here, and watch with me.	34 And saith unto them, My soul is exceeding sorrowful unto death : tarry ye here, and watch.
39 And he went a little further, and fell on his face, and prayed, saying, O my Father, if it be possible, let this cup pass from me : nevertheless, not as I will, but as thou *wilt*.	35 And he went forward a little, and fell on the ground, and prayed that, if it were possible, the hour might pass from him.
	36 And he said, Abba, Father, all things *are* possible unto thee ; take away this cup from me : nevertheless, not what I will, but what thou wilt.

LUKE.

JOHN.

CH. XVII. 1–26.

22 And the glory which thou gavest me, I have given them ; that they may be one, even as we are one ;

23 I in them, and thou in me, that they may be made perfect in one ; and that the world may know that thou hast sent me, and hast loved them as thou hast loved me.

24 Father, I will that they also whom thou hast given me be with me where I am ; that they may behold my glory which thou hast given me : for thou lovedst me before the foundation of the world.

25 O righteous Father, the world hath not known thee : but I have known thee, and these have known that thou hast sent me.

26 And I have declared unto them thy name, and will declare *it :* that the love wherewith thou hast loved me, may be in them, and I in them.

INTRODUCING THE SIXTH DAY OF THE WEEK.) *Mount of Olives.*

CH. XXII. 39–46.

39 And he came out, and went, as he was wont, to the mount of Olives ; and his disciples also followed him.

40 And when he was at the place, he said unto them, Pray that ye enter not into temptation.

41 And he was withdrawn from them about a stone's cast, and kneeled down, and prayed,

42 Saying, Father, if thou be willing, remove this cup from me : nevertheless, not my will, but thine, be done.

43 And there appeared an angel unto him from heaven, strengthening him.

44 And being in an agony, he prayed more earnestly : and his sweat

CH. XVIII. 1.

WHEN Jesus had spoken these words, he went forth with his disciples over the brook Cedron, where was a garden, into the which he entered, and his disciples.

§ 142. The agony in Gethsemane. (EVENING

MATTHEW.	MARK.
CH. XXVI. 30, 36 – 46.	CH. XIV. 26, 32 – 42.

40 And he cometh unto the disciples, and findeth them asleep, and saith unto Peter, What! could ye not watch with me one hour?

41 Watch and pray, that ye enter not into temptation : the spirit indeed *is* willing, but the flesh *is* weak.

42 He went away again the second time, and prayed, saying, O my Father, if this cup may not pass away from me, except I drink it, thy will be done.

43 And he came and found them asleep again : for their eyes were heavy.

44 And he left them, and went away again, and prayed the third time, saying the same words.

45 Then cometh he to his disciples, and saith unto them, Sleep on now, and take *your* rest : behold, the hour is at hand, and the Son of man is betrayed into the hands of sinners.

46 Rise, let us be going : behold, he is at hand that doth betray me.

37 And he cometh, and findeth them sleeping, and saith unto Peter, Simon, sleepest thou? couldest not thou watch one hour?

38 Watch ye and pray, lest ye enter into temptation. The spirit truly *is* ready, but the flesh *is* weak.

39 And again he went away, and prayed, and spake the same words.

40 And when he returned, he found them asleep again, (for their eyes were heavy ;) neither wist they what to answer him.

41 And he cometh the third time, and saith unto them, Sleep on now, and take *your* rest : it is enough, the hour is come ; behold, the Son of man is betrayed into the hands of sinners.

42 Rise up, let us go ; lo, he that betrayeth me is at hand.

§ 143. Jesus betrayed and made prisoner. (EVENING

CH. XXVI. 47 – 56.	CH. XIV. 43 – 52.

47 And while he yet spake, lo, Judas, one of the twelve, came, and with him a great multitude with swords and staves, from the chief priests and elders of the people.

48 Now, he that betrayed him, gave them a sign, saying, Whomsoever I shall kiss, that same is he ; hold him fast.

43 And immediately while he yet spake, cometh Judas, one of the twelve, and with him a great multitude with swords and staves, from the chief priests, and the scribes, and the elders.

44 And he that betrayed him, had given them a token, saying, Whomsoever I shall kiss, that same is he ; take him, and lead *him* away safely.

Luke xxii. 44, *as it were great drops of blood.*] The strangeness of such a profusion of blood has been urged, first, against the probability, and then against the truth, of the narrative. But learned men have related instances of mental agony so great as to force the blood through the pores ; and if this has ever occurred, it may well be believed to have occurred in the present case. See *Bloomfield* and *A. Clarke,* in loc. It should be observed, however, that Luke does not directly affirm that it was blood. He only *compares* the sweat to that of blood, using a term of similitude, (*quasi grumi sanguinis — Beza : tanquam* demissiones sanguinis — *Tremellius ; sicut* guttæ sanguinis — *Vulg.* and *Molinæus ;*) which may signify no more than that the drops of sweat were as large as drops of blood, which, from its viscidity, are very large.

LUKE.	JOHN.
CH. XXII. 39–46.	
was as it were great drops of blood falling down to the ground.	
45 And when he rose up from prayer, and was come to his disciples, he found them sleeping for sorrow,	
46 And said unto them, Why sleep ye? rise and pray, lest ye enter into temptation.	

CH. XXII. 47–53.	CH. XVIII. 2–12.
47 And while he yet spake, behold a multitude, and he that was called Judas, one of the twelve, went before them, and drew near unto Jesus to kiss him.	2 And Judas also, which betrayed him, knew the place: for Jesus ofttimes resorted thither with his disciples.
	3 Judas then, having received a band *of men* and officers from the chief priests and Pharisees, cometh thither with lanterns, and torches, and weapons.

Luke xxii. 45, *sleeping for sorrow*] No other Evangelist mentions the cause of their slumber, except Luke, who ascribes it to their sorrow. It is observable, that Luke was a physician, (Col. iv. 14,) and therefore well knew that deep mental distress frequently induced sleep. To this cause may perhaps be referred the fact, that persons condemned to die are often waked from sound sleep by the executioner. The internal evidence here afforded of the truth of Luke's narrative, is corroborated by his notice of the bloody sweat, ver. 44, and of the miraculous healing of the ear of Malchus, ver. 51; facts which are not related by any other Evangelist, but which would naturally attract the attention of a physician.

§ 143. Jesus betrayed and made prisoner. (EVENING

MATTHEW.	MARK.
CH. XXVI. 47–56.	CH. XIV. 43–52.
49 And forthwith he came to Jesus, and said, Hail, Master; and kissed him.	45 And as soon as he was come, he goeth straightway to him, and saith, Master, Master; and kissed him.
50 And Jesus said unto him, Friend, wherefore art thou come? Then came they, and laid hands on Jesus, and took him.	46 And they laid their hands on him, and took him.
51 And behold, one of them which were with Jesus, stretched out *his* hand, and drew his sword, and struck a servant of the high priest, and smote off his ear.	47 And one of them that stood by, drew a sword, and smote a servant of the high priest, and cut off his ear.
52 Then said Jesus unto him, Put up again thy sword into his place: for all they that take the sword, shall perish with the sword.[a]	
53 Thinkest thou that I cannot now pray to my Father, and he shall presently give me more than twelve legions of angels?	
54 But how then shall the scriptures be fulfilled, that thus it must be?	
55 In that same hour said Jesus to the multitudes, Are ye come out as against a thief with swords and staves for to take me? I sat daily with you teaching in the temple, and ye laid no hold on me.	48 And Jesus answered and said unto them, Are ye come out as against a thief, with swords and *with* staves to take me?
	49 I was daily with you in the temple, teaching, and ye took me not: but the scriptures must be fulfilled.
56 But all this was done, that the scriptures of the prophets might be fulfilled. Then all the disciples forsook him, and fled.	50 And they all forsook him and fled.
	51 And there followed him a certain young man, having a linen cloth cast about *his* naked *body;* and the young men laid hold on him.
	52 And he left the linen cloth, and fled from them naked.

a Gen. ix. 6.

LUKE.	JOHN.
CH. XXII. 47–53.	CH. XVIII. 2–12.

LUKE. CH. XXII. 47–53.

48 But Jesus said unto him, Judas, betrayest thou the Son of man with a kiss?

49 When they which were about him, saw what would follow, they said unto him, Lord, shall we smite with the sword?

50 And one of them smote the servant of the high priest, and cut off his right ear.

51 And Jesus answered and said, Suffer ye thus far. And he touched his ear, and healed him,

52 Then Jesus said unto the chief priests, and captains of the temple, and the elders which were come to him, Be ye come out as against a thief, with swords and staves?

53 When I was daily with you in the temple, ye stretched forth no hands against me: but this is your hour, and the power of darkness.

JOHN. CH. XVIII. 2–12.

4 Jesus therefore, knowing all things that should come upon him, went forth, and said unto them, Whom seek ye?

5 They answered him, Jesus of Nazareth. Jesus saith unto them, I am *he*. And Judas also, which betrayed him, stood with them.

6 As soon then as he had said unto them, I am *he*, they went backward, and fell to the ground.

7 Then asked he them again, Whom seek ye? And they said, Jesus of Nazareth.

8 Jesus answered, I have told you that I am *he*. If therefore ye seek me, let these go their way:

9 That the saying might be fulfilled which he spake, Of them which thou gavest me, have I lost none.

10 Then Simon Peter, having a sword, drew it, and smote the high priest's servant, and cut off his right ear. The servant's name was Malchus.

11 Then said Jesus unto Peter, Put up thy sword into the sheath: the cup which my Father hath given me, shall I not drink it?

12 Then the band, and the captain, and officers of the Jews took Jesus, and bound him.

John xviii. 5, *I am he.*] In the order of events, Jesus first voluntarily discriminates himself; after which Judas gives the agreed sign to his enemies. NEWCOME.

John xviii. 10, *Simon Peter.*] Lenfant and Bp. Pearce think that Peter was named by John, because he was then dead; and that he was not named by the other Evangelists because when they wrote he was living, and the action might have subjected him to public justice, or at least to reproach. NEWCOME.

§ 144. Jesus before Caiaphas.   Peter thrice denies him.   (NIGHT

MATTHEW.	MARK.
CH. XXVI. 57, 58, 69 – 75.	CH. XIV. 53, 54, 66 – 72.
57 And they that had laid hold on Jesus, led *him* away to Caiaphas the high priest, where the scribes and the elders were assembled.	53 And they led Jesus away to the high priest: and with him were assembled all the chief priests, and the elders and the scribes.
58 But Peter followed him afar off, unto the high priest's palace, and went in, and sat with the servants to see the end.	54 And Peter followed him afar off, even into the palace of the high priest: and he sat with the servants, and warmed himself at the fire.
69 Now Peter sat without in the palace : and a damsel came unto him, saying, Thou also wast with Jesus of Galilee.	66 And as Peter was beneath in the palace, there cometh one of the maids of the high priest :
	67 And when she saw Peter warming himself, she looked upon him, and said, And thou also wast with Jesus of Nazareth.
70 But he denied before *them* all, saying, I know not what thou sayest.	68 But he denied, saying, I know not, neither understand I what thou sayest. And he went out into the porch ; and the cock crew.
71 And when he was gone out into the porch, another *maid* saw him, and said unto them that were there, This *fellow* was also with Jesus of Nazareth.	69 And a maid saw him again, and began to say to them that stood by, This is *one* of them.
72 And again he denied with an oath, I do not know the man.	70 And he denied it again. And a little after, they that stood by said again to Peter, Surely thou art *one* of them : for thou art a Galilean, and thy speech agreeth *thereto*.
73 And after a while came unto *him* they that stood by, and said to Peter, Surely thou also art *one* of them ; for thy speech bewrayeth thee.	

Matth. xxvi. 71, *into the porch*.] Here is a minute indication of veracity, which would have been lost upon us but for the narrative of John. Matthew only states the fact that the maid in the porch recognized Peter as one of the disciples of Jesus ; but John (xviii. 16,) informs us how she knew him to be so ; namely, because he was brought in by John, who was a frequent guest at the house of her master the high priest. BLUNT, Veracity, &c., sect. i. 12, 18.

LUKE.
CH. XXII. 54–62.

54 Then took they him, and led *him*, and brought him into the high priest's house. And Peter followed afar off.

55 And when they had kindled a fire in the midst of the hall, and were set down together, Peter sat down among them.

56 But a certain maid beheld him as he sat by the fire, and earnestly looked upon him, and said, This man was also with him.

57 And he denied him, saying, Woman, I know him not.

58 And after a little while another saw him, and said, Thou art also of them. And Peter said, Man, I am not.

59 And about the space of one hour after, another confidently affirmed, saying, Of a truth this *fellow* also was with him; for he is a Galilean.

JOHN.
CH. XVIII. 13–18, 25–27.

13 And led him away to Annas first, (for he was father-in-law to Caiaphas, which was the high priest that same year.)

14 Now Caiaphas was he which gave counsel to the Jews, that it was expedient that one man should die for the people.

15 And Simon Peter followed Jesus, and *so did* another disciple. That disciple was known unto the high priest, and went in with Jesus, into the palace of the high priest.

16 But Peter stood at the door without. Then went out that other disciple which was known unto the high priest, and spake unto her that kept the door, and brought in Peter.

18 And the servants and officers stood there, who had made a fire of coals; (for it was cold) and they warmed themselves : and Peter stood with them, and warmed himself.

17 Then saith the damsel that kept the door unto Peter, Art not thou also *one* of this man's disciples? He saith, I am not.

25 And Simon Peter stood and warmed himself. They said therefore unto him, Art not thou also *one* of his disciples? He denied *it*, and said, I am not.

26 One of the servants of the high priest (being *his* kinsman whose ear Peter cut off) saith, Did not I see thee in the garden with him ?

John xviii. 13, *to Annas first.*] Probably by way of compliment to the past high priest, who was also the father-in-law of Caiaphas. If this circumstance never happened, it is difficult to discover how the introduction of it could serve the purposes of fiction. See Roberts, Light shining, &c. pp. 171, 172.

§ 144. Jesus before Caiaphas. Peter thrice denies him. (NIGHT

MATTHEW.	MARK.
CH. XXVI. 57, 58, 69 – 75.	CH. XIV. 53, 54, 66 – 72.
74 Then began he to curse and to swear, *saying*, I know not the man. And immediately the cock crew.	71 But he began to curse and to swear, *saying*, I know not this man of whom ye speak.
	72 And the second time the cock crew. And Peter called to mind the word that Jesus said unto him, Before the cock crow twice, thou shalt deny me thrice. And when he thought thereon, he wept.
75 And Peter remembered the word of Jesus, which said unto him, Before the cock crow, thou shalt deny me thrice. And he went out, and wept bitterly.	

§ 145. Jesus before Caiaphas. He declares himself to be the

CH. XXVI. 59 – 68.	CH. XIV. 55 – 65.
59 Now the chief priests and elders, and all the council, sought false witness against Jesus, to put him to death ;	55 And the chief priests, and all the council sought for witness against Jesus to put him to death ; and found none :
60 But found none : yea, though many false witnesses came, *yet* found they none. At the last came two false witnesses,	56 For many bare false witness against him, but their witness agreed not together.
	57 And there arose certain, and bare false witness against him, saying,
61 And said, This *fellow* said, I am able to destroy the temple of God, and to build it in three days.	58 We heard him say, I will destroy this temple that is made with hands, and within three days I will build another made without hands.
	59 But neither so did their witness agree together.

§ 144.] Matthew and Mark relate Peter's denials of Christ after his condemnation, and the insults consequent upon it. It is plain that they happened while the High Priest and council were sitting in judgment. But instances of recurring in this manner to what had been omitted in its proper place are common in the Gospels ; and in this place the thread of the narration is preserved unbroken.

It having been expressly mentioned by each Evangelist, that Peter would *thrice* deny Jesus, we may conclude that each has related the *three* denials which Jesus foretold.

Peter's first denial. Peter was *without*, or *beneath*, in the hall of Caiaphas's house. Dr. Scott, on Matth. xxvi. 3, observes that *aule* signifies an house, (Luke xi. 21,) and that emphatically it signifies the king's house, or palace. But in Luke xxii. 55, it seems to signify a spacious apartment, probably the High Priest's judgment-hall. It was the place in which Jesus stood before the High Priest, (Luke xxii. 61,) and had an *atrium* or *vestibulum* at its entrance. This was an unfit place for the tribunal of the High Priest at such an hour, (John xviii. 18.) Sir John Chardin says, " In the lower Asia the day is always hot ; and in the height of summer the nights are as cold as at Paris in the month of March." It remains therefore that we understand it of a spacious chamber, such as Shaw mentions, Travels, 4to. p. 207, 8.

Peter was not in the *higher* part, where Jesus stood before the High Priest ; but *without* that division of the hall, and in the *lower* part, with the servants and officers. The damsel, who kept the door, had entered into the hall when she charged Peter.

Peter's second denial. Peter, having once denied Jesus, naturally retired from the

INTRODUCING THE SIXTH DAY OF THE WEEK.) *Jerusalem.*

LUKE.	JOHN.
CH. XXII. 54-62.	CH. XVIII. 13-18, 25-27.
60 And Peter said, Man, I know not what thou sayest. And immediately, while he yet spake, the cock crew.	27 Peter then denied again : and immediately the cock crew.
61 And the Lord turned, and looked upon Peter. And Peter remembered the word of the Lord, how he had said unto him, Before the cock crow, thou shalt deny me thrice.	
62 And Peter went out and wept bitterly.	

Christ, etc.   (MORNING OF THE SIXTH DAY OF THE WEEK.)   *Jerusalem.*

CH. XXII. 63-71.	CH. XVIII. 19-24.
66 And as soon as it was day, the elders of the people, and the chief priests, and the scribes, came together, and led him into their council, saying,	

place where his accuser was, to the vestibule of the hall, (Matth. xxvi. 71) ; and it was the time of the first cock-crowing, or soon after midnight. After remaining here a short time, perhaps near an hour, another damsel sees him, and says to those who were standing by in the vestibule, that he was one of them. Peter, to avoid this charge, withdraws into the hall, and stands and warms himself, (John xviii. 25.) The damsel, and those to whom she had spoken, follow him ; the communication between the places being immediate. Here *a man* enforces the charge of the damsel, according to Luke ; and *others* urge it, according to John, (though by him the plural may be used for the singular,) and Peter denies Jesus vehemently.

Peter's third denial. Peter was now in the hall. Observe Matth. xxvi. 75, and Luke xxii. 62. He was also within sight of Jesus, though at such a distance from him that Jesus could know what passed only in a supernatural way. About an hour after his second denial, those who stood by him on his being a Galilean, which, Luke says, one in particular strongly affirmed, (though here Matthew and Mark may use the plural for the singular,) and which, according to John, was supported by one of Malchus's relations. This occasioned a more vehement denial than before ; and immediately the cock crew the second time. The first denial may have been between our twelve and one ; and the second between our two and three. We must further observe, that Matth. xxvi. 57, lays the scene of Peter's denials in the house of Caiaphas ; whereas the transactions of John xviii. 15-23 seem to have passed in the house of Annas. But John xviii. 24 is here transposed to its regular place, with Le Clerc. NEWCOME.

Luke xxii. 60, *Man, I know not.*] The seeming contradiction between Luke, who relates that it was a *man* who charged Peter with being a follower of Jesus, and Matthew and Mark who state that he was accused by a *maid*, is reconciled by attending to the narrative of John, (xviii. 25,) who writes, "*They* said." Whence it appears that there were several who spake on this occasion, and that each Evangelist refers to the accusation which made the deepest impression on his own mind. See MICHAELIS and Bp. MIDDLETON, cited in 4 HORNE'S *Introd.* p. 258, note 1.

§ 145. Jesus before Caiaphas. He declares himself to be the

MATTHEW.	MARK.
CH. XXVI. 59–68.	CH. XIV. 55–65.
62 And the high priest arose, and said unto him, Answerest thou nothing? what *is it which* these witness against thee?	60 And the high priest stood up in the midst, and asked Jesus, saying, Answerest thou nothing? what *is it which* these witness against thee?
63 But Jesus held his peace. And the high priest answered and said unto him, I adjure thee by the living God, that thou tell us whether thou be the Christ, the Son of God.	61 But he held his peace, and answered nothing. Again the high priest asked him, and said unto him, Art thou the Christ, the Son of the Blessed?
64 Jesus saith unto him, Thou hast said: nevertheless, I say unto you, Hereafter shall ye see the Son of man sitting on the right hand of power, and coming in the clouds of heaven.	62 And Jesus said, I am : and ye shall see the Son of man sitting on the right hand of power, and coming in the clouds of heaven.
65 Then the high priest rent his clothes, saying, He hath spoken blasphemy ; what further need have we of witnesses? behold, now ye have heard his blasphemy.	63 Then the high priest rent his clothes, and saith, What need we any further witnesses?
66 What think ye? They answered and said, He is guilty of death.	64 Ye have heard the blasphemy : what think ye? And they all condemned him to be guilty of death.
67 Then did they spit in his face, and buffeted him ; and others smote *him* with the palms of their hands,	65 And some began to spit on him, and to cover his face, and to buffet him, and to say unto him, Prophesy : and the servants did strike him with the palms of their hands.
68 Saying, Prophesy unto us, thou Christ, Who is he that smote thee?	

§ 146. The Sanhedrim lead Jesus away to Pilate.

CH. XXVII. 1, 2, 11–14.	CH. XV. 1–5.
WHEN the morning was come, all the chief priests and elders of the people took counsel against Jesus to put him to death.	AND straightway in the morning the chief priests held a consultation with the elders and scribes, and the whole council, and bound Jesus, and carried *him* away, and delivered *him* to Pilate.
2 And when they had bound him, they led *him* away, and delivered him to Pontius Pilate the governor.	

Matth. xxvi. 68, *Prophesy unto us.*]   Matthew alone states this fact ; and he states nothing in explanation of it. The other Evangelists add another fact, which shows that the Jews were quite consistent in asking him to designate who struck him, namely, that they had previously " blindfolded him." Now these omissions of partic-

Christ.   (MORNING OF THE SIXTH DAY OF THE WEEK.)   *Jerusalem.*

LUKE.
CH. XXII. 63–71.

67 Art thou the Christ? tell us. And he said unto them, If I tell you, ye will not believe.

68 And if I also ask *you*, ye will not answer me, nor let *me* go.

69 Hereafter shall the Son of man sit on the right hand of the power of God.

70 Then said they all, Art thou then the Son of God? And he said unto them, Ye say that I am.

71 And they said, What need we any further witness? for we ourselves have heard of his own mouth.

63 And the men that held Jesus, mocked him, and smote *him.*

64 And when they had blindfolded him, they struck him on the face, and asked him, saying, Prophesy, who is it that smote thee?

65 And many other things blasphemously spake they against him.

JOHN.
CH. XVIII. 19–24.

19 The high priest then asked Jesus of his disciples, and of his doctrine.

20 Jesus answered him, I spake openly to the world; I ever taught in the synagogue, and in the temple, whither the Jews always resort; and in secret have I said nothing.

21 Why askest thou me? ask them which heard me, what I have said unto them: behold, they know what I said.

22 And when he had thus spoken, one of the officers which stood by, struck Jesus with the palm of his hand, saying, Answerest thou the high priest so?

23 Jesus answered him, If I have spoken evil, bear witness of the evil: but if well, why smitest thou me?

24 (Now Annas had sent him bound unto Caiaphas the high priest.)

(SIXTH DAY OF THE WEEK.)   *Jerusalem.*

CH. XXIII. 1–5.

AND the whole multitude of them arose, and led him unto Pilate.

2 And they began to accuse him, saying, We found this *fellow* perverting the nation, and forbidding to give tribute to Cesar, saying, That he himself is Christ, a King.

CH. XVIII. 28–38.

28 Then led they Jesus from Caiaphas unto the hall of judgment: and it was early; and they themselves went not into the judgment-hall, lest they should be defiled; but that they might eat the passover.

29 Pilate then went out unto them, and said, What accusation bring ye against this man?

30 They answered and said unto him, If he were not a malefactor, we would not have delivered him up unto thee.

31 Then said Pilate unto them, Take ye him, and judge him according to your law. The Jews therefore said unto him, It is not lawful for us to put any man to death:

---

ulars are characteristic of one to whom it never occurs that they are wanted to make his statement credible, but who, conscious of his own integrity, states his facts and leaves them to their fate; and they cannot fairly be accounted for, upon any other supposition than the truth of the narrative. BLUNT, Veracity, &c., sect. i. 10.

§ 146. The Sanhedrim lead Jesus away to Pilate.

MATTHEW.	MARK.
CH. XXVII. 1, 2, 11–14.	CH. XV. 1–5.
11 And Jesus stood before the governor: and the governor asked him, saying, Art thou the King of the Jews? And Jesus said unto him, Thou sayest.	2 And Pilate asked him, Art thou the King of the Jews? And he answering, said unto him, Thou sayest *it.*
12 And when he was accused of the chief priests and elders, he answered nothing.	3 And the chief priests accused him of many things : but he answered nothing.
13 Then saith Pilate unto him, Hearest thou not how many things they witness against thee ?	4 And Pilate asked him again saying, Answerest thou nothing? behold how many things they witness against thee.
14 And he answered him to never a word ; insomuch that the governor marvelled greatly.	5 But Jesus yet answered nothing : so that Pilate marvelled.

§ 147. Jesus before Herod.

John xviii. 36, *then would my servants fight.*] Jesus seems here almost to have challenged inquiry into the assault so lately committed by Peter upon the servant of the high priest. . St. Luke, however, states a fact which accounts for their not making such inquiry, ch. xxii. 51. *He touched his ear and healed him.* An inquiry into the

(SIXTH DAY OF THE WEEK.) *Jerusalem.*

LUKE.
CH. XXIII. 1–5.

3 And Pilate asked him, saying, Art thou the King of the Jews? And he answered him and said, Thou sayest *it*.

JOHN.
CH. XVIII. 28–38.

32 That the saying of Jesus might be fulfilled, which he spake, signifying what death he should die.

33 Then Pilate entered into the judgment-hall again, and called Jesus, and said unto him, Art thou the King of the Jews?

34 Jesus answered him, Sayest thou this thing of thyself, or did others tell it thee of me?

35 Pilate answered, Am I a Jew? Thine own nation, and the chief priests, have delivered thee unto me. What hast thou done?

36 Jesus answered, My kingdom is not of this world : if my kingdom were of this world, then would my servants fight, that I should not be delivered to the Jews : but now is my kingdom not from hence.

37 Pilate therefore said unto him, Art thou a king then? Jesus answered, Thou sayest that I am a king. To this end was I born, and for this cause came I into the world, that I should bear witness unto the truth. Every one that is of the truth, heareth my voice.

4 Then said Pilate to the chief priests, and *to* the people, I find no fault in this man.

5 And they were the more fierce, saying, He stirreth up the people, teaching throughout all Jewry, beginning from Galilee to this place.

38 Pilate saith unto him, What is truth? And when he had said this, he went out again unto the Jews, and saith unto them, I find in him no fault *at all*.

(SIXTH DAY OF THE WEEK.) *Jerusalem.*

CH. XXIII. 6–12.

6 When Pilate heard of Galilee, he asked whether the man were a Galilean.

7 And as soon as he knew that he belonged unto Herod's jurisdiction, he sent him to Herod, who himself was also at Jerusalem at that time.

8 And when Herod saw Jesus, he was exceeding glad: for he was desirous to see him of a long *season*,

---

truth would have frustrated the malicious purpose of the enemies of Jesus, by proving his own compassionate nature, his submission to the laws, and his miraculous powers. BLUNT, Veracity, &c., sect. i. 19.

§ 147. Jesus before Herod.

MATTHEW.	MARK.

§ 148. Pilate seeks to release Jesus.   The Jews demand

MATTHEW.	MARK.
CH. XXVII. 15 – 26.	CH. XV. 6 – 15.
15 Now at *that* feast, the governor was wont to release unto the people a prisoner, whom they would.	6 Now at *that* feast he released unto them one prisoner, whomsoever they desired.
16 And they had then a notable prisoner, called Barabbas.	7 And there was *one* named Barabbas, *which lay* bound with them that had made insurrection with him, who had committed murder in the insurrection.
	8 And the multitude crying aloud, began to desire *him to do* as he had ever done unto them.
17 Therefore, when they were gathered together, Pilate said unto them, Whom will ye that I release unto you? Barabbas, or Jesus, which is called Christ?	9 But Pilate answered them, saying, Will ye that I release unto you the King of the Jews?
18 (For he knew that for envy they had delivered him.)	10 (For he knew that the chief priests had delivered him for envy.)
19 When he was set down on the judgment-seat, his wife sent unto him, saying, Have thou nothing to do with that just man : for I have suffered many things this day in a dream, because of him.	
20 But the chief priests and elders persuaded the multitude that they should ask Barabbas, and destroy Jesus.	11 But the chief priests moved the people that he should rather release Barabbas unto them.
21 The governor answered and said unto them, Whether of the twain will ye that I release unto you? They said, Barabbas.	12 And Pilate answered, and said again unto them, What will ye then that I shall do *unto him* whom ye call the King of the Jews?
22 Pilate saith unto them, What shall I do then with Jesus, which is called Christ? *They* all say unto him, Let him be crucified.	13 And they cried out again, Crucify him.

LUKE.	JOHN.
CH. XXIII. 6 – 12.	

because he had heard many things of him; and he hoped to have seen some miracle done by him.

9 Then he questioned with him in many words; but he answered him nothing.

10 And the chief priests and scribes stood and vehemently accused him.

11 And Herod with his men of war set him at nought, and mocked *him*, and arrayed him in a gorgeous robe, and sent him again to Pilate.

12 And the same day Pilate and Herod were made friends together; for before they were at enmity between themselves.

Barabbas.   (SIXTH DAY OF THE WEEK.)   *Jerusalem.*

CH. XXIII. 13 – 25.	CH. XVIII. 39, 40.

13 And Pilate, when he had called together the chief priests, and the rulers, and the people,

14 Said unto them, Ye have brought this man unto me, as one that perverteth the people: and behold, I, having examined *him* before you, have found no fault in this man, touching those things whereof ye accuse him;

15 No, nor yet Herod: for I sent you to him; and lo, nothing worthy of death is done unto him:

16 I will therefore chastise him, and release *him*.

17 (For of necessity he must release one unto them at the feast.)

39 But ye have a custom that I should release unto you one at the passover: will ye therefore, that I release unto you the King of the Jews?

18 And they cried out all at once, saying, Away with this *man*, and release unto us Barabbas:

19 (Who, for a certain sedition made in the city, and for murder, was cast into prison.)

20 Pilate therefore, willing to release Jesus, spake again to them.

40 Then cried they all again, saying, Not this man, but Barabbas. Now Barabbas was a robber.

21 But they cried, saying, Crucify *him*, crucify him.

§ 148. Pilate seeks to release Jesus.   The Jews demand

MATTHEW.	MARK.
CH. XXVII. 15–26.	CH. XV. 6–15.
23 And the governor said, Why! what evil hath he done? But they cried out the more, saying, Let him be crucified.	14 Then Pilate said unto them, Why, what evil hath he done? And they cried out the more exceedingly, Crucify him.
24 When Pilate saw that he could prevail nothing, but *that* rather a tumult was made, he took water, and washed *his* hands before the multitude, saying, I am innocent of the blood of this just person : see ye *to it*.	
25 Then answered all the people, and said, His blood *be* on us, and on our children.	
26 Then released he Barabbas unto them :	15 And *so* Pilate, willing to content the people, released Barabbas unto them,

§ 149. Pilate delivers up Jesus to death.   He is scourged

CH. XXVII. 26–30.	CH. XV. 15–19.
26 And when he had scourged Jesus, he delivered *him* to be crucified.	15 And delivered Jesus, when he had scourged *him*, to be crucified.
27 Then the soldiers of the governor took Jesus into the common hall, and gathered unto him the whole band *of soldiers*.	16 And the soldiers led him away into the hall, called Pretorium ; and they call together the whole band ;
28 And they stripped him, and put on him a scarlet robe.	17 And they clothed him with purple, and platted a crown of thorns, and put it about his *head*,
29 And when they had platted a crown of thorns, they put *it* upon his head, and a reed in his right hand : and they bowed the knee before him, and mocked him, saying, Hail, King of the Jews!	18 And began to salute him, Hail, King of the Jews!
30 And they spit upon him, and took the reed, and smote him on the head.	19 And they smote him on the head with a reed, and did spit upon him, and bowing *their* knees, worshipped him.

§ 150. Pilate again seeks to release Jesus.

Luke xxiii. 24, *gave sentence*.] The accuracy of Luke, as a man of education, is observable in this statement of the formal judgment pronounced by Pilate, which is

Barabbas. (SIXTH DAY OF THE WEEK.) *Jerusalem.*

LUKE.	JOHN.
CH. XXIII. 13–25.	
22 And he said unto them the third time, Why, what evil hath he done? I have found no cause of death in him; I will therefore chastise him, and let *him* go.	
23 And they were instant with loud voices, requiring that he might be crucified: and the voices of them, and of the chief priests prevailed.	
24 And Pilate gave sentence that it should be as they required.	
25 And he released unto them him that for sedition and murder was cast into prison, whom they had desired; but he delivered Jesus to their will.	

and mocked. *Jerusalem.*

	CH. XIX. 1–3.
	THEN Pilate therefore took Jesus, and scourged *him.*
	2 And the soldiers platted a crown of thorns, and put *it* on his head, and they put on him a purple robe,
	3 And said, Hail, King of the Jews! and they smote him with their hands.

(SIXTH DAY OF THE WEEK.) *Jerusalem.*

	CH. XIX. 4–16.
	4 Pilate therefore went forth again, and saith unto them, Behold, I bring him forth to you, that ye may know that I find no fault in him.
	5 Then came Jesus forth, wearing the crown of thorns, and the purple robe. And *Pilate* saith unto them, Behold the man!
	6 When the chief priests therefore

only implied in the narratives of the other Evangelists. For an account of the two trials of Jesus, see Appendix, No. IV.

§ 150. Pilate again seeks to release Jesus.

MATTHEW.	MARK.

John xix. 14, *sixth hour.*] The apparent contradiction between John and Mark, (ch. xv. 25,) who mentions the third hour, is reconciled by Dr. Campbell, in a critical

(SIXTH DAY OF THE WEEK.) *Jerusalem.*

LUKE.

JOHN.
CH. XIX. 4—16.

and officers saw him, they cried out, saying, Crucify *him*, crucify *him*. Pilate saith unto them, Take ye him, and crucify *him:* for I find no fault in him.

7 The Jews answered him, We have a law, and by our law he ought to die, because he made himself the Son of God.

8 When Pilate therefore heard that saying, he was the more afraid ;

9 And went again into the judgment-hall, and saith unto Jesus, Whence art thou? But Jesus gave him no answer.

10 Then saith Pilate unto him, Speakest thou not unto me? knowest thou not, that I have power to crucify thee, and have power to release thee?

11 Jesus answered, Thou couldest have no power *at all* against me, except it were given thee from above : therefore he that delivered me unto thee hath the greater sin.

12 And from thenceforth Pilate sought to release him : but the Jews cried out, saying, If thou let this man go, thou art not Cesar's friend. Whosoever maketh himself a king, speaketh against Cesar.

13 When Pilate therefore heard that saying, he brought Jesus forth, and sat down in the judgment-seat, in a place that is called the Pavement, but in the Hebrew, Gabbatha.

14 And it was the preparation of the passover, and about the sixth hour : and he saith unto the Jews, Behold your King !

15 But they cried out, Away with *him*, away with *him*, crucify him. Pilate saith unto them, Shall I crucify your King? The chief priests answered, We have no king but Cesar.

16 Then delivered he him therefore unto them to be crucified.

---

note upon the force of the expressions in the original, which he interprets as equivalent to saying, in the one case, that it was *past three*, and in the other, that it was *towards six.* See CAMPBELL, *in loc.*

§ 151. Judas repents, and hangs himself.

MATTHEW.	MARK.
CH. XXVII. 3 – 10.	

3 Then Judas, which had betrayed him, when he saw that he was condemned, repented himself, and brought again the thirty pieces of silver to the chief priests and elders,

4 Saying, I have sinned in that I have betrayed the innocent blood. And they said, What *is that* to us? see thou *to that*.

5 And he cast down the pieces of silver in the temple, and departed, and went and hanged himself.

6 And the chief priests took the silver pieces, and said, It is not lawful for to put them into the treasury, because it is the price of blood.

7 And they took counsel, and bought with them the potter's field, to bury strangers in.

8 Wherefore that field was called, The field of blood, unto this day.

9 Then was fulfilled that which was spoken by Jeremy the prophet, saying, And they took the thirty pieces of silver, the price of him that was valued, whom they of the children of Israel did value;

10 And gave them for the potter's field, as the Lord appointed me.[a]

§ 152. Jesus is led away to be crucified.

CH. XXVII. 31 – 34.	CH. XV. 20 – 23.
31 And after that they had mocked him, they took the robe off from him, and put his own raiment on him, and led him away to crucify *him*.	**20** And when they had mocked him, they took off the purple from him, and put his own clothes on him, and led him out to crucify him.
32 And as they came out, they found a man of Cyrene, Simon by name: him they compelled to bear his cross.	**21** And they compel one Simon a Cyrenian, who passed by, coming out of the country, the father of Alexander and Rufus, to bear his cross.

a Zech. xi. 12, seq.   Jer. xxxii. 6, seq.

Matth. xxvii. 9, *Jeremy.*] The passage here quoted is found in the prophecy of Zechariah, and not in Jeremiah. Dr. Lightfoot says, that anciently among the Jews the Old Testament was divided into three parts. The first, beginning with the law, was called *The Law.* The second, beginning with Psalms, was called *The Psalms.* The third, beginning with the prophecy of Jeremiah, which anciently stood first, was called *Jeremiah*, under which name all quotations from the prophets were made. See A. CLARKE, in loc. JENNINGS, Jewish Antiq. pp. 594, 595. Others account for the apparent error in Matthew's quotation, by supposing that he omitted the name of the prophet, as he frequently did in his citations of scripture, and that the name of Jeremiah was inserted by a subsequent copyist. 1 HORNE's *Introd.* p. 582.

(SIXTH DAY OF THE WEEK.)   *Jerusalem.*

LUKE.	JOHN.

(SIXTH DAY OF THE WEEK.)   *Jerusalem.*

CH. XXIII. 26—33.	CH. XIX. 16—17.
26 And as they led him away, they laid hold upon one Simon a Cyrenian, coming out of the country, and on him they laid the cross, that he might bear *it* after Jesus.	16 And they took Jesus, and led *him* away.
27 And there followed him a great company of people, and of women,	17 And he bearing his cross

Mark xv. 21, *and Rufus.*]   Clement of Alexandria and Jerome both relate that Mark wrote this Gospel at *Rome,* and we find in Romans xiv. 13, that a disciple named Rufus, of considerable note, resided in that city. Admitting that both Mark and Paul speak of the same person, which is highly probable, as they refer to the same period of time and to a disciple of distinction, there is an evident consciousness of ve- racity in the Evangelist, in making this reference to Rufus, then living among them, since he could not but have known the particulars of the crucifixion, in which his own father was so intimately concerned. BLUNT'S Veracity, &c., sect. i. 14. See also EUSEBIUS, lib. 2, ch. 15.

§ 152. Jesus is led away to be crucified.

MATTHEW.	MARK.
CH. XXVII. 31 – 34.	CH. XV. 20 – 23.
33 And when they were come unto a place called Golgotha, that is to say, A place of a skull,	22 And they bring him unto the place Golgotha, which is, being interpreted, The place of a skull.
34 They gave him vinegar to drink, mingled with gall : and when he had tasted *thereof*, he would not drink.	23 And they gave him to drink, wine mingled with myrrh : but he received *it* not.

§ 153. The Crucifixion.

CH. XXVII. 35 – 38.	CH. XV. 24 – 28.
35 And they crucified him, and parted his garments, casting lots: that it might be fulfilled which was spoken by the prophet ; They parted my garments among them, and upon my vesture did they cast lots.ᵃ	24 And when they had crucified him, they parted his garments, casting lots upon them, what every man should take.
36 And sitting down, they watched him there :	25 And it was the third hour, and they crucified him.
37 And set up over his head his accusation written, THIS IS JESUS THE KING OF THE JEWS.	26 And the superscription of his accusation was written over, THE KING OF THE JEWS.

ᵃ Ps. xxii. 19.

Matth. xxvii. 37, *his accusation.*] As to the title itself, the precise wording may have differed in the different languages ; and MSS. represent it differently.

But the same verbal exactness is not necessary in historians, whose aim is religious instruction, as in recorders of public inscriptions. It is enough that the Evangelists agree as to the main article, "*the King of the Jews*," referred to, John xix. 21. That their manner is to regard the sense, rather than the words, appears from many places. Compare Matth. iii. 17, and ix. 11, and xv. 27, and xvi. 6, 9, and xix. 18, and xx. 33, and xxi. 9, and xxvi. 39, 64, 70, and xxviii. 5, 6, with the parallel verses in this Harmony. Compare also John xi. 40, with ver. 23, 25. One of the most solemn and aw-

LUKE.
CH. XXIII. 26–33.

which also bewailed and lamented him.

28 But Jesus turning unto them, said, Daughters of Jerusalem, weep not for me, but weep for yourselves, and for your children.

29 For behold, the days are coming, in the which they shall say, Blessed *are* the barren, and the wombs that never bare, and the paps which never gave suck.[a]

30 Then shall they begin to say to the mountains, Fall on us; and to the hills, Cover us.[b]

31 For if they do these things in a green tree, what shall be done in the dry?

32 And there were also two others, malefactors, led with him to be put to death.

33 And when they were come to the place which is called Calvary,

JOHN.
CH. XIX. 16–17.

went forth into a place called *the place* of a skull, which is called in the Hebrew, Golgotha.

CH. XXIII. 33, 34, 38.

33 There they crucified him, and the malefactors; one on the right hand, and the other on the left.

34 Then said Jesus, Father, forgive them: for they know not what they do. And they parted his raiment, and cast lots.

38 And a superscription also was written over him, in letters of Greek, and Latin, and Hebrew, THIS IS THE KING OF THE JEWS.

CH. XIX. 18–24.

18 Where they crucified him, and two other with him, on either side one, and Jesus in the midst.

19 And Pilate wrote a title, and put *it* on the cross. And the writing was, JESUS OF NAZARETH, THE KING OF THE JEWS.

[a] Isa. liv. 1.   [b] Hos. x. 8.

ful of our Lord's discourses is, in some parts, variously expressed. See Matth. xxvi. 28, Mark xiv. 24, Luke xxii. 20, 1 Cor. xi. 25. Now as each of these writers has, beyond all doubt, faithfully represented the meaning of Christ, we see that it might be truly done in different words, or in a different form of the same words. His sentences also, sometimes admitted a difference of arrangement; for the order in which two sentences, or the several members of the same sentence, are disposed by St. Matthew, is, in several places, inverted by St. Mark. And with regard to his actions, though the most material parts of whatever they were going to relate must command their attention, yet there was no such superior attraction in one specific number and order of

§ 153. The Crucifixion.

MATTHEW. CH. XXVII. 35-38.	MARK. CH. XV. 24-28.
38 Then were there two thieves crucified with him: one on the right hand, and another on the left.	27 And with him they crucify two thieves, the one on his right hand, and the other on his left. 28 And the scripture was fulfilled, which saith, And he was numbered with the transgressors.[b]

§ 154. The Jews mock at Jesus on the cross. He commends

CH. XXVII. 39-44.	CH. XV. 29-32.
39 And they that passed by, reviled him, wagging their heads, 40 And saying, Thou that destroyest the temple, and buildest *it* in three days, save thyself. If thou be the Son of God, come down from the cross. 41 Likewise also the chief priests mocking *him*, with the scribes and elders, said,	29 And they that passed by, railed on him, wagging their heads, and saying, Ah, thou that destroyest the temple, and buildest *it* in three days, 30 Save thyself, and come down from the cross. 31 Likewise also the chief priests mocking, said among themselves with the scribes, He saved others; himself he cannot save.

b Isa. liii. 12.

secondary circumstances, as could turn their thoughts absolutely and exclusively to them. This is plain from instances to the contrary. One Evangelist is sometimes distinct, while another is concise; and describes what the other passes over. Townson, pp. 60-1.

We may reasonably suppose St. Matthew to have cited the Hebrew,— St. John the Greek,— and St. Mark the Latin, which was the shortest, and without mixture of foreign words. St. Mark is followed by St. Luke; only that he has brought down " THIS IS " from above, as having a common reference to what stood under it. NEW-COME.

(SIXTH DAY OF THE WEEK.) *Jerusalem.*

LUKE.	JOHN.
	CH. XIX. 18–24.

20 This title then read many of the Jews : for the place where Jesus was crucified was nigh to the city : and it was written in Hebrew, *and* Greek, *and* Latin.

21 Then said the chief priests of the Jews to Pilate, Write not, The King of the Jews ; but that he said, I am King of the Jews.

22 Pilate answered, What I have written, I have written.

23 Then the soldiers, when they had crucified Jesus, took his garments, and made four parts, to every soldier a part ; and also *his* coat : now the coat was without seam, woven from the top throughout.

24 They said therefore among themselves, Let us not rend it, but cast lots for it whose it shall be : that the scripture might be fulfilled, which saith, They parted my raiment among them, and for my vesture they did cast lots. These things therefore the soldiers did.

---

his mother to John.   (SIXTH DAY OF THE WEEK.)   *Jerusalem.*

CH. XXIII. 35–37, 39–43.

35 And the people stood beholding. And the rulers also with them derided *him*, saying, He saved others ; let him save himself, if he be Christ, the chosen of God.

36 And the soldiers also mocked him, coming to him, and offering him vinegar,

37 And saying, If thou be the King of the Jews, save thyself.

John xix. 23, *four parts.*] We have here an incidental allusion to a practice well known at that time. The malefactor about to be crucified, having borne his own cross to the place of execution, was stripped, and made to drink a stupefying potion ; the cross was then laid on the ground, the sufferer distended upon it, and *four* soldiers, two on each side, were employed in driving four large nails through his hands and feet. For this service they had a right to his clothes, as a perquisite. See Dr. Harwood's Introd., cited in HORNE's *Introd.*, vol. i. pp. 94, 95.

Luke xxiii. 36, *vinegar.*] Here the common drink of the Roman soldiers is offered by them to Jesus on the cross, while they are deriding him ; which is a different act from that in Matth. xxvii. 34, 48, as appears by the place assigned to it. NEWCOME.

§ 154. The Jews mock at Jesus on the cross. He commends

MATTHEW.	MARK.
CH. XXVII. 39 – 44.	CH. XV. 29 – 32.
42 He saved others; himself he cannot save. If he be the King of Israel, let him now come down from the cross, and we will believe him.	32 Let Christ the King of Israel descend now from the cross, that we may see and believe. And they that were crucified with him, reviled him.
43 He trusted in God; let him deliver him now if he will have him : for he said, I am the Son of God.[a]	
44 The thieves also which were crucified with him, cast the same in his teeth.	

§ 155. Darkness prevails. Christ expires on the cross.

CH. XXVII. 45 – 50.	CH. XV. 33 – 37.
45 Now, from the sixth hour there was darkness over all the land unto the ninth hour.	33 And when the sixth hour was come, there was darkness over the whole land, until the ninth hour.

[a] Ps. xxii. 7, 8.

Luke xxiii. 39, *one of the malefactors.*] What was true of only one of the malefactors, is attributed to both in the concise relations of Matthew and Mark ; the plural being often used in the Gospels for the singular. This the Evangelists themselves show in some instances. Compare Mark vii. 17, and Matth. xv. 15 ; Mark v. 31, and Luke viii. 45 ; Matth. xiv. 17, and Mark vi. 38, Luke ix. 13, John vi. 8, 9 ; Matth. xxvi. 8, and Mark xiv. 4, John xii. 4 ; Matth. xxiv. 1, and Mark xiii. 1 ; Matth. xxvii. 37, and John xix. 19 ; Matth. xxvii. 48, and Mark xv. 36, John xix. 29. See also Luke xxii. 67. In the following places, the plural is used, while the sense shows that one is spoken of. John xi. 8, Luke xx. 21, 39, and xxiv. 5, Matth. xv. 1, 12. — The Evangelists, therefore, when from attention to brevity they avoid particularizing,

his mother to John. (SIXTH DAY OF THE WEEK.) *Jerusalem.*

LUKE.	JOHN.
CH. XXIII. 35 – 37, 39 – 43.	CH. XIX. 25 – 27.
39 And one of the malefactors, which were hanged, railed on him, saying, If thou be Christ, save thyself and us.	
40 But the other answering, rebuked him, saying, Dost not thou fear God, seeing thou art in the same condemnation? 41 And we indeed justly; for we receive the due reward of our deeds: but this man hath done nothing amiss. 42 And he said unto Jesus, Lord, remember me when thou comest into thy kingdom. 43 And Jesus said unto him, Verily, I say unto thee, To-day shalt thou be with me in paradise.	
	25 Now there stood by the cross of Jesus, his mother, and his mother's sister, Mary the *wife* of Cleophas, and Mary Magdalene. 26 When Jesus therefore saw his mother, and the disciple standing by whom he loved, he saith unto his mother, Woman, behold thy son! 27 Then saith he to the disciple, Behold thy mother! And from that hour that disciple took her unto his own *home*.

(SIXTH DAY OF THE WEEK.) *Jerusalem.*

CH. XXIII. 44 – 46.
44 And it was about the sixth hour, and there was a darkness over all the earth until the ninth hour.

often attribute to many what is said or done by single persons; nor does any striking peculiarity in the case omitted, lead them to deviate from their manner; for instance, the case of Judas, Matth. xxvi. 8, and the parallel places. NEWCOME.

Luke xxiii. 44, *over all the earth.*] The objection urged by infidels, upon this passage, against the veracity of the Evangelists, from the silence of profane writers concerning so remarkable an event, is met and answered by Bp. Watson in his Reply to Gibbon, Let. 5. The word translated *earth*, in Luke, is the same which is rendered *land*, in the others, and applies equally to both. Taken in the latter sense, it may limit the darkness to Judea. But the Evangelists do not mention the degree of darkness; if therefore it was slight, though it extended over the whole globe, the objection of its not being recorded by Pliny or Seneca vanishes at once.

§ 155. Darkness prevails. Christ expires on the cross.

MATTHEW.	MARK.
CH. XXVII. 45–50.	CH. XV. 33–37.
46 And about the ninth hour Jesus cried with a loud voice, saying, Eli, Eli, lama sabachthani? that is to say, My God, my God, why hast thou forsaken me? [a]	34 And at the ninth hour Jesus cried with a loud voice, saying, Eloi, Eloi, lama sabachthani? which is, being interpreted, My God, my God, why hast thou forsaken me?
47 Some of them that stood there, when they heard *that*, said, This *man* calleth for Elias.	35 And some of them that stood by, when they heard *it*, said, Behold, he calleth Elias.
48 And straightway one of them ran, and took a spunge, and filled *it* with vinegar, and put *it* on a reed, and gave him to drink.	36 And one ran and filled a spunge full of vinegar, and put *it* on a reed, and gave him to drink, saying, Let alone; let us see whether Elias will come to take him down.
49 The rest said, Let be, let us see whether Elias will come to save him.	
50 Jesus, when he had cried again with a loud voice, yielded up the ghost.	37 And Jesus cried with a loud voice, and gave up the ghost.

§ 156. The vail of the Temple rent. The graves opened.

CH. XXVII. 51–56.	CH. XV. 38–41.
51 And behold, the vail of the temple was rent in twain from the top to the bottom: and the earth did quake, and the rocks rent;	38 And the vail of the temple was rent in twain, from the top to the bottom.
52 And the graves were opened, and many bodies of the saints which slept, arose,	
53 And came out of the graves after his resurrection, and went into the holy city, and appeared unto many.	
54 Now, when the centurion, and they that were with him, watching Jesus, saw the earthquake, and those things that were done, they feared greatly, saying, Truly this was the Son of God.	39 And when the centurion which stood over against him, saw that he so cried out, and gave up the ghost, he said, Truly this man was the Son of God.
55 And many women were there (beholding afar off) which followed	40 There were also women looking on afar off, among whom was Mary

[a] Ps. xxii. 1.

Matth. xxvii. 48, *vinegar*.] *Hil* or *Hila* was the old Syriac for *vinegar*. Hence one of the bystanders, hearing our Saviour's exclamation on the cross, thought he wanted vinegar to alleviate his thirst, and straightway filled a spunge. See BUCHANAN'S *Researches*, p. 153.

Matth. xxvii. 49, *Elias*.] The Jews gave a literal interpretation to Mal. iv. 5, expecting Elijah to appear in person, as the forerunner of the Messiah; and hence they, on this occasion, sneeringly adverted to the want of this testimony to the mission of Christ. JONES, *Lect.* 147. This incidental allusion to the popular opinion, by Matthew and Mark, may be noticed as additional evidence of their veracity.

(SIXTH DAY OF THE WEEK.) *Jerusalem.*

LUKE. CH. XXIII. 44–46.	JOHN. CH. XIX. 28–30.
45 And the sun was darkened,	
	28 After this, Jesus knowing that all things were now accomplished, that the scripture might be fulfilled, saith, I thirst.[a]
	29 Now there was set a vessel full of vinegar: and they filled a sponge with vinegar, and put *it* upon hyssop, and put *it* to his mouth.
46 And when Jesus had cried with a loud voice, he said, Father, into thy hands I commend my spirit : and having said thus, he gave up the ghost.	30 When Jesus therefore had received the vinegar, he said, It is finished : and he bowed his head, and gave up the ghost.

The women at the cross.   (SIXTH DAY OF THE WEEK.)   *Jerusalem.*

CH. XXIII. 45, 47–49.
45   And the vail of the temple was rent in the midst.

47 Now, when the centurion saw what was done, he glorified God, saying, Certainly this was a righteous man.

48 And all the people that came together to that sight, beholding the

[a] Ps. lxix. 22.

Matth. xxvii. 55, *afar off.*] This and the parallel verses are reconciled with John xix. 25, by the following observation in Wall's critical notes, p. 116. "Mary stood as yet, (John xix. 25,) so nigh the cross as to hear what Christ said. But at the time of his departure, Matthew, Mark and Luke say, the women stood afar off." See also Watson's Reply to Gibbon, Let. 5, (Evangelical Family Library, Vol. xiv. pp. 276, 277.) It is natural to suppose that our Lord's relations and friends, mentioned in John xix. 25, were too much struck with commiseration and grief to remain long near the cross ; and that they would retire from the horror of the concluding scene. NEWCOME.

§ 156. The vail of the Temple rent. The graves opened.

MATTHEW.	MARK.
CH. XXVII. 51–56.	CH. XV. 38–41.
Jesus from Galilee, ministering unto him :	Magdalene, and Mary the mother of James the less, and of Joses, and Salome ;
56 Among which was Mary Magdalene, and Mary the mother of James and Joses, and the mother of Zebedee's children.	41 Who also, when he was in Galilee, followed him, and ministered unto him ; and many other women which came up with him unto Jerusalem.

§ 157. The taking down from the cross.

CH. XXVII. 57–61.	CH. XV. 42–47.
57 When the even was come, there came a rich man of Arimathea, named Joseph, who also himself was Jesus' disciple :	42 And now, when the even was come, (because it was the preparation, that is, the day before the sabbath,)
58 He went to Pilate, and begged the body of Jesus. Then Pilate commanded the body to be delivered.	43 Joseph of Arimathea, an honourable counsellor, which also waited for the kingdom of God, came, and went in boldly unto Pilate, and craved the body of Jesus.
	44 And Pilate marvelled if he were already dead : and calling *unto him*

Matth. xxvii. 58, *begged the body.*] Here is another of those incidental allusions to existing customs, which show the naturalness and veracity of the narrative. Those who were crucified by the Romans are said to have been usually exposed to the birds of prey ; and a guard was set to prevent their friends from burying the bodies. The

The women at the cross.   (SIXTH DAY OF THE WEEK.)   *Jerusalem.*

LUKE.	JOHN.
CH. XXIII. 45, 47–49.	
things which were done, smote their breasts and returned.	
49 And all his acquaintance, and the women that followed him from Galilee, stood afar off, beholding these things.	

The burial.   *Jerusalem.*

CH. XXIII. 50–56.	CH. XIX. 31–42.
	31 The Jews therefore, because it was the preparation, that the bodies should not remain upon the cross on the sabbath-day, (for that sabbath-day was an high day) besought Pilate that their legs might be broken, and *that* they might be taken away.
	32 Then came the soldiers, and brake the legs of the first, and of the other which was crucified with him.
	33 But when they came to Jesus, and saw that he was dead already, they brake not his legs :
	34 But one of the soldiers with a spear pierced his side, and forthwith came thereout blood and water.
	35 And he that saw *it*, bare record, and his record is true : and he knoweth that he saith true, that ye might believe.
	36 For these things were done, that the scripture should be fulfilled, A bone of him shall not be broken.[a]
	37 And again another scripture saith, They shall look on him whom they pierced.[b]
50 And behold, *there was* a man named Joseph, a counsellor : *and he was* a good man, and a just :	38 And after this, Joseph of Arimathea (being a disciple of Jesus, but secretly for fear of the Jews) besought Pilate that he might take away the body of Jesus : and Pilate gave *him* leave. He came therefore and took the body of Jesus.
51 (The same had not consented to the counsel and deed of them :) he was of Arimathea, a city of the Jews; who also himself waited for the kingdom of God.	
52 This *man* went unto Pilate, and begged the body of Jesus.	39 And there came also Nicodemus (which at the first came to Jesus by night) and brought a mixture of myrrh and aloes, about an hundred pounds *weight*.

[a] Ex. xii. 46.   Ps. xxxiv. 20.   [b] Zech. xii. 10.

body of Jesus therefore could not be obtained for burial, without leave from Pilate ; which the Evangelists relate was applied for, but without explaining the cause.

§ 157. The taking down from the cross.

MATTHEW.	MARK.
CH. XXVII. 57–61.	CH. XV. 42–47.
	the centurion, he asked him whether he had been any while dead.
	45 And when he knew *it* of the centurion, he gave the body to Joseph.
59 And when Joseph had taken the body, he wrapped it in a clean linen cloth,	46 And he bought fine linen, and took him down, and wrapped him in the linen, and laid him in a sepulchre
60 And laid it in his own new tomb, which he had hewn out in the rock; and he rolled a great stone to the door of the sepulchre, and departed.	which was hewn out of a rock, and rolled a stone unto the door of the sepulchre.
	47 And Mary Magdalene and Mary *the mother* of Joses beheld where he was laid.
61 And there was Mary Magdalene, and the other Mary, sitting over against the sepulchre.	

§ 158. The watch at the Sepulchre. (SEVENTH

CH. XXVII. 62–66.

62 Now, the next day that followed the day of the preparation, the chief priests and Pharisees came together unto Pilate,

63 Saying, Sir, we remember that that deceiver said, while he was yet alive, After three days I will rise again.

64 Command therefore that the sepulchre be made sure until the third day, lest his disciples come by night, and steal him away, and say unto the people, He is risen from the dead: so the last error shall be worse than the first.

65 Pilate said unto them, Ye have a watch: go your way, make *it* as sure as ye can.

66 So they went and made the sepulchre sure, sealing the stone, and setting a watch.

Matth. xxvii. 66, *setting a watch.*] The mention of this circumstance by Matthew, and not by the other Evangelists, is in perfect keeping with his previous occupation; which led him to watch for fraud, in all places where it might be perpetrated. See Preliminary Observations, *ante,* § 24.

The burial. *Jerusalem.*

LUKE.	JOHN.
CH. XXIII. 50–56.	CH. XIX. 31–42.

53 And he took it down, and wrapped it in linen, and laid it in a sepulchre that was hewn in stone, wherein never man before was laid.

54 And that day was the preparation, and the sabbath drew on.

55 And the women also, which came with him from Galilee, followed after, and beheld the sepulchre, and how his body was laid.
56 And they returned, and prepared spices and ointments; and rested the sabbath-day, according to the commandment.

40 Then took they the body of Jesus, and wound it in linen clothes with the spices, as the manner of the Jews is to bury.
41 Now in the place where he was crucified, there was a garden; and in the garden a new sepulchre, wherein was never man yet laid.
42 There laid they Jesus therefore, because of the Jews' preparation-*day;* for the sepulchre was nigh at hand.

DAY OF THE WEEK, OR SABBATH.) *Jerusalem.*

Luke xxiii. 54, *drew on.*] We must not understand this word of the morning light. The Jewish sabbath began at six in the evening, before which time our Lord's body was deposited in the tomb. NEWCOME.

PART IX.

OUR LORD'S RESURRECTION,

HIS SUBSEQUENT APPEARANCES,

AND

HIS ASCENSION.

TIME. Forty days

§ 159. The morning of the Resurrection.

MATTHEW.	MARK.
CH. XXVIII. 2–4.	CH. XVI. 1.

CH. XVI. 1.
AND when the sabbath was past, Mary Magdalene, and Mary the *mother* of James, and Salome, had bought sweet spices, that they might come and anoint him.

2 And behold, there was a great earthquake: for the angel of the Lord descended from heaven, and came and rolled back the stone from the door, and sat upon it.
3 His countenance was like lightning, and his raiment white as snow.
4 And for fear of him the keepers did shake, and became as dead *men*.

§ 160. Visit of the women to the Sepulchre.   Mary

CH. XXVIII. 1.
IN the end of the sabbath, as it began to dawn toward the first *day* of the week, came Mary Magdalene, and the other Mary to see the sepulchre.

CH. XVI. 2–4.
2 And very early in the morning, the first *day* of the week, they came unto the sepulchre at the rising of the sun:
3 And they said among themselves, Who shall roll us away the stone from the door of the sepulchre?
4 (And when they looked, they saw that the stone was rolled away,) for it was very great.

§ 161. Vision of angels in the Sepulchre.

CH. XXVIII. 5–7.

CH. XVI. 5–7.
5 And entering into the sepulchre, they saw a young man sitting on the right side, clothed in a long white garment; and they were affrighted.
6 And he saith unto them, Be not affrighted: ye seek Jesus of Nazareth, which was crucified: he is risen; he is not here: behold the place where they laid him.

5 And the angel answered and said unto the women, Fear not ye: for I know that ye seek Jesus, which was crucified.
6 He is not here: for he is risen, as he said. Come, see the place where the Lord lay.
7 And go quickly, and tell his disciples, that he is risen from the dead, and behold, he goeth before you into Galilee; there shall ye see him: lo, I have told you.

7 But go your way, tell his disciples and Peter, that he goeth before you into Galilee: there shall ye see him, as he said unto you.

(FIRST DAY OF THE WEEK.) *Jerusalem.*

LUKE.	JOHN.

Magdalene returns. (FIRST DAY OF THE WEEK.) *Jerusalem.*

CH. XXIV. 1–3.	CH. XX. 1–2.
Now upon the first *day* of the week, very early in the morning, they came unto the sepulchre, bringing the spices which they had prepared, and certain *others* with them.	THE first *day* of the week cometh Mary Magdalene early, when it was yet dark, unto the sepulchre, and seeth the stone taken away from the sepulchre.
2 And they found the stone rolled away from the sepulchre.	
3 And they entered in, and found not the body of the Lord Jesus.	
	2 Then she runneth, and cometh to Simon Peter, and to the other disciple whom Jesus loved, and saith unto them, They have taken away the Lord out of the sepulchre, and we know not where they have laid him.

(FIRST DAY OF THE WEEK.) *Jerusalem.*

XXIV. 4–8.

4 And it came to pass, as they were much perplexed thereabout, behold, two men stood by them in shining garments.

5 And as they were afraid, and bowed down *their* faces to the earth, they said unto them, Why seek ye the living among the dead?

6 He is not here, but is risen. Remember how he spake unto you when he was yet in Galilee,

7 Saying, The Son of man must be delivered into the hands of sinful men, and be crucified, and the third day rise again.

8 And they remembered his words,

§ 162. The women return to the city. Jesus meets them.

MATTHEW.	MARK.
CH. XXVIII. 8–10.	CH. XVI. 8.
8 And they departed quickly from the sepulchre, with fear and great joy; and did run to bring his disciples word.	6 And they went out quickly, and fled from the sepulchre; for they trembled, and were amazed: neither said they any thing to any *man*; for they were afraid.
9 And as they went to tell his disciples, behold, Jesus met them, saying, All hail. And they came, and held him by the feet, and worshipped him.	
10 Then said Jesus unto them, Be not afraid: go tell my brethren, that they go into Galilee, and there shall they see me.	

§ 163. Peter and John run to the Sepulchre.

§ 164. Our Lord is seen by Mary Magdalene at the

(first day of the week.)　*Jerusalem.*

LUKE.
ch. xxiv. 9–11.

9 And returned from the sepulchre, and told all these things unto the eleven, and to all the rest.

10 It was Mary Magdalene, and Joanna, and Mary *the mother* of James, and other *women that were* with them, which told these things unto the apostles.

11 And their words seemed to them as idle tales, and they believed them not.

JOHN.

(first day of the week.)　*Jerusalem.*

ch. xxiv. 12.

12 Then arose Peter, and ran unto the sepulchre, and, stooping down, he beheld the linen clothes laid by themselves, and departed, wondering in himself at that which was come to pass.

ch. xx. 3–10.

3 Peter therefore went forth, and that other disciple, and came to the sepulchre.

4 So they ran both together : and the other disciple did outrun Peter, and came first to the sepulchre.

5 And he stooping down, *and looking in*, saw the linen clothes lying ; yet went he not in.

6 Then cometh Simon Peter following him, and went into the sepulchre, and seeth the linen clothes lie ;

7 And the napkin that was about his head, not lying with the linen clothes, but wrapped together in a place by itself.

8 Then went in also that other disciple which came first to the sepulchre, and he saw, and believed.

9 For as yet they knew not the scripture, that he must rise again from the dead.

10 Then the disciples went away again unto their own home.

Sepulchre.　(first day of the week.)　*Jerusalem.*

ch. xx. 11–18.

11 But Mary stood without at the sepulchre weeping : and as she wept she stooped down *and looked* into the sepulchre,

12 And seeth two angels in white, sitting, the one at the head, and the other at the feet, where the body of Jesus had lain.

13 And they say unto her, Woman, why weepest thou ? She saith unto

§ 164. Our Lord is seen by Mary Magdalene at the

MATTHEW.	MARK. CH. XVI. 9-11.
	9 Now, when *Jesus* was risen early, the first *day* of the week, he appeared first to Mary Magdalene, out of whom he had cast seven devils.
	10 *And* she went and told them that had been with him, as they mourned and wept.
	11 And they, when they had heard that he was alive, and had been seen of her, believed not.

§ 165. Report of the watch.

CH. XXVIII. 11-15.

11 Now, when they were going, behold, some of the watch came into the city, and shewed unto the chief priests all the things that were done.

12 And when they were assembled with the elders, and had taken counsel, they gave large money unto the soldiers,

13 Saying, Say ye, His disciples came by night, and stole him *away* while we slept.

14 And if this come to the governor's ears, we will persuade him, and secure you.

15 So they took the money, and did as they were taught: and this saying is commonly reported among the Jews until this day.

Sepulchre.   (FIRST DAY OF THE WEEK.)   *Jerusalem.*

LUKE.	JOHN.
	CH. XX. 11–18.

them, Because they have taken away my Lord, and I know not where they have laid him.

14 And when she had thus said, she turned herself back, and saw Jesus standing, and knew not that it was Jesus.

15 Jesus saith unto her, Woman, why weepest thou? whom seekest thou? She, supposing him to be the gardener, saith unto him, Sir, if thou have borne him hence, tell me where thou hast laid him, and I will take him away.

16 Jesus saith unto her, Mary. She turned herself, and saith unto him, Rabboni, which is to say, Master.

17 Jesus saith unto her, Touch me not: for I am not yet ascended to my Father: but go to my brethren, and say unto them, I ascend unto my Father and your Father, and *to* my God and your God.

18 Mary Magdalene came and told the disciples that she had seen the Lord, and *that* he had spoken these things unto her.

(FIRST DAY OF THE WEEK.)   *Jerusalem.*

§ 166. Our Lord is seen of Peter; then by two disciples on the

MATTHEW.	MARK.
	CH. XVI. 12 – 13.
	12 After that, he appeared in another form unto two of them, as they walked, and went into the country.

sec. 166.]　　　THE GOSPELS.　　　499

way to Emmaus. (FIRST DAY OF THE WEEK.) *Emmaus.*

LUKE.
CH. XXIV. 13–35.

13 And behold, two of them went that same day to a village called Emmaus, which was from Jerusalem *about* threescore furlongs.

14 And they talked together of all these things which had happened.

15 And it came to pass, that, while they communed *together*, and reasoned, Jesus himself drew near, and went with them.

16 But their eyes were holden, that they should not know him.

17 And he said unto them, What manner of communications *are* these that ye have one to another, as ye walk, and are sad?

18 And the one of them, whose name was Cleopas, answering, said unto him, Art thou only a stranger in Jerusalem, and hast not known the things which are come to pass there in these days?

19 And he said unto them, What things? And they said unto him, Concerning Jesus of Nazareth, which was a prophet mighty in deed and word before God, and all the people:

20 And how the chief priests and our rulers delivered him to be condemned to death, and have crucified him.

21 But we trusted that it had been he which should have redeemed Israel: and besides all this, to-day is the third day since these things were done.

22 Yea, and certain women also of our company made us astonished, which were early at the sepulchre.

23 And when they found not his body, they came, saying, that they had also seen a vision of angels, which said that he was alive.

24 And certain of them which were with us, went to the sepulchre, and found *it* even so as the women had said: but him they saw not.

25 Then he said unto them, O fools, and slow of heart to believe all that the prophets have spoken!

26 Ought not Christ to have suffered these things, and to enter into his glory?

JOHN.

§ 166. Our Lord is seen of Peter; then by two Disciples on the

MATTHEW.	MARK.
	13 And they went and told *it* unto the residue : neither believed they them.

§ 167. Jesus appears in the midst of the Apostles, Thomas being absent.

	CH. XVI. 14–18. 14 Afterward he appeared unto the eleven, as they sat at meat, and upbraided them with their unbelief, and hardness of heart, because they believed not them which had seen him after he was risen.

Luke xxiv. 34, *appeared unto Simon.*] This appearance of Jesus is not alluded to be any other Evangelist; but it was a fact well known among the disciples, and is

LUKE.	JOHN.
CH. XXIV. 13-35.	

27 And beginning at Moses, and all the prophets, he expounded unto them in all the scriptures the things concerning himself.

28 And they drew nigh unto the village whither they went: and he made as though he would have gone further.

29 But they constrained him, saying, Abide with us : for it is toward evening, and the day is far spent. And he went in to tarry with them.

30 And it came to pass, as he sat at meat with them, he took bread, and blessed *it*, and brake, and gave to them.

31 And their eyes were opened, and they knew him : and he vanished out of their sight.

32 And they said one to another, Did not our heart burn within us while he talked with us by the way, and while he opened to us the scriptures?

33 And they rose up the same hour, and returned to Jerusalem, and found the eleven gathered together, and them that were with them,

34 Saying, The Lord is risen indeed, and hath appeared to Simon.

35 And they told what things *were done* in the way, and how he was known of them in breaking of bread.

(EVENING FOLLOWING THE FIRST DAY OF THE WEEK.) *Jerusalem.*

CH. XIV. 36-49.	CH. XX. 19-23.
36 And as they thus spake, Jesus himself stood in the midst of them, and saith unto them, Peace *be* unto you.	19 Then the same day at evening, being the first *day* of the week, when the doors were shut where the disciples were assembled for fear of the Jews, came Jesus and stood in the midst, and saith unto them, Peace *be* unto you.
37 But they were terrified and affrighted, and supposed that they had seen a spirit.	
38 And he said unto them, Why are ye troubled? and why do thoughts arise in your hearts?	

expressly stated by Paul, in 1 Cor. xv. 5,—"and that he was seen of Cephas, then of the twelve."

Mark xvi. 14, *unto the eleven.*] This appearance of Jesus is also affirmed by Paul, in 1 Cor. xv. 5.

§ 167. Jesus appears in the midst of the Apostles, Thomas being absent.

MATTHEW.	MARK. CH. XVI. 14–18.
	15 And he said unto them, Go ye into all the world, and preach the gospel to every creature. 16 He that believeth and is baptized, shall be saved; but he that believeth not, shall be damned. 17 And these signs shall follow them that believe: In my name shall they cast out devils; they shall speak with new tongues: 18 They shall take up serpents; and if they drink any deadly thing, it shall not hurt them; they shall lay hands on the sick, and they shall recover.

§ 168. Jesus appears in the midst of the Apostles, Thomas being present.

LUKE.
CH. XIV. 36–49.

39 Behold my hands and my feet, that it is I myself: handle me, and see; for a spirit hath not flesh and bones, as ye see me have.

40 And when he had thus spoken, he shewed them *his* hands and *his* feet.

41 And while they yet believed not for joy, and wondered, he said unto them, Have ye here any meat?

42 And they gave him a piece of a broiled fish, and of an honey-comb.

43 And he took *it*, and did eat before them.

44 And he said unto them, These *are* the words which I spake unto you, while I was yet with you, that all things must be fulfilled which were written in the law of Moses, and *in* the prophets, and *in* the psalms, concerning me.

45 Then opened he their understanding, that they might understand the scriptures.

46 And said unto them, Thus it is written, and thus it behoved Christ to suffer, and to rise from the dead the third day:

47 And that repentance and remission of sins should be preached in his name among all nations, beginning at Jerusalem.

48 And ye are witnesses of these things.

49 And behold, I send the promise of my Father upon you: but tarry ye in the city of Jerusalem, until ye be endued with power from on high.

JOHN.
CH. XX. 19–23.

20 And when he had so said, he shewed unto them *his* hands and his side. Then were the disciples glad when they saw the Lord.

21 Then said Jesus to them again, Peace *be* unto you: as *my* Father hath sent me, even so send I you.

22 And when he had said this, he breathed on *them*, and saith unto them, Receive ye the Holy Ghost.

23 Whose soever sins ye remit, they are remitted unto them; *and* whose soever *sins* ye retain, they are retained.

CH. XX. 24–29.

24 But Thomas, one of the twelve, called Didymus, was not with them when Jesus came.

25 The other disciples therefore said unto him, We have seen the Lord. But he said unto them, Except I shall see in his hands the print of the nails, and put my finger into the print of the nails, and thrust my hand into his side, I will not believe.

26 And after eight days again his disciples were within, and Thomas

§ 168. Jesus appears in the midst of the Apostles, Thomas being present.

MATTHEW.	MARK.

§ 169. The Apostles go away into Galilee. Jesus shows

CH. XXVIII. 16.
16 Then the eleven disciples went away into Galilee,

LUKE.	JOHN.
	CH. XX. 24–29.

with them : *then* came Jesus, the doors being shut, and stood in the midst, and said, Peace *be* unto you.

27 Then saith he to Thomas, Reach hither thy finger, and behold my hands; and reach hither thy hand, and thrust *it* into my side ; and be not faithless, but believing.

28 And Thomas answered and said unto him, My Lord and my God.

29 Jesus saith unto him, Thomas, because thou hast seen me, thou hast believed : blessed *are* they that have not seen, and *yet* have believed.

himself to seven of them at the Sea of Tiberias.　*Galilee.*

CH. XXI. 1–24.

AFTER these things Jesus shewed himself again to the disciples at the sea of Tiberias ; and on this wise shewed he *himself*.

2 There were together Simon Peter, and Thomas called Didymus, and Na-thanael of Cana in Galilee, and the *sons* of Zebedee, and two other of his disciples.

3 Simon Peter saith unto them, I go a fishing. They say unto him, We also go with thee. They went forth, and entered into a ship imme-diately ; and that night they caught nothing.

4 But when the morning was now come, Jesus stood on the shore ; but the disciples knew not that it was Jesus.

5 Then Jesus saith unto them, Children, have ye any meat ? They answered him, No.

6 And he said unto them, Cast the net on the right side of the ship, and ye shall find. They cast therefore, and now they were not able to draw it for the multitude of fishes.

7 Therefore that disciple whom Jesus loved saith unto Peter, It is the Lord. Now when Simon Peter heard that it was the Lord, he girt *his* fisher's coat *unto him*, (for he was naked) and did cast himself into the sea.

8 And the other disciples came in a little ship (for they were not far

§ 169. The Apostles go away into Galilee.   Jesus shows

MATTHEW.	MARK.

himself to seven of them at the Sea of Tiberias. *Galilee.*

LUKE.	JOHN.

JOHN.

CH. XXI. 1–24.

from land, but as it were two hundred cubits) dragging the net with fishes.

9 As soon then as they were come to land, they saw a fire of coals there, and fish laid thereon, and bread.

10 Jesus saith unto them, bring of the fish which ye have now caught.

11 Simon Peter went up, and drew the net to land full of great fishes, an hundred and fifty and three : and for all there were so many, yet was not the net broken.

12 Jesus saith unto them, Come *and* dine. And none of the disciples durst ask him, Who art thou? knowing that it was the Lord.

13 Jesus then cometh, and taketh bread, and giveth them, and fish likewise.

14 This is now the third time that Jesus shewed himself to his disciples, after that he was risen from the dead.

15 So when they had dined, Jesus saith to Simon Peter, Simon, *son* of Jonas, lovest thou me more than these? He saith unto him, Yea, Lord : thou knowest that I love thee. He saith unto him, Feed my lambs.

16 He saith to him again the second time, Simon, *son* of Jonas, lovest thou me? He saith unto him, Yea, Lord : thou knowest that I love thee. He saith unto him, Feed my sheep.

17 He saith unto him the third time, Simon, *son* of Jonas, lovest thou me? Peter was grieved because he said unto him the third time, Lovest thou me? And he said unto him, Lord, thou knowest all things ; thou knowest that I love thee. Jesus saith unto him, Feed my sheep.

18 Verily, verily, I say unto thee, When thou wast young, thou girdest thyself, and walkedst whither thou wouldest : but when thou shalt be old, thou shalt stretch forth thy hands, and another shall gird thee, and carry *thee* whither thou wouldest not.

19 This spake he, signifying by what death he should glorify God. And when he had spoken this, he saith unto him, Follow me.

§ 169. The Apostles go away into Galilee.　Jesus shows

MATTHEW.	MARK.

§ 170. Jesus meets the Apostles and above five hundred

CH. XXVIII.　16 – 20.

16　　　　　　　　　　　　into a mountain where Jesus had appointed them.

17 And when they saw him, they worshipped him : but some doubted.

18 And Jesus came, and spake unto them, saying, All power is given unto me in heaven and in earth.

19 Go ye therefore and teach all nations, baptizing them in the name of the Father, and of the Son, and of the Holy Ghost;

20 Teaching them to observe all things whatsoever I have commanded you : and lo, I am with you alway, *even* unto the end of the world. Amen.

Matth. xvi. 17, *they saw him.*]　Many and perhaps most Harmonists and Commentators refer 1 Cor. xv. 6, to this place, where it is related that Jesus was seen of above five hundred brethren at once.　Such is the opinion of Dr. Robinson and Bishop J. B. Sumner, and such seems to have been the opinion of Abp. Newcome, Dr. Macknight,

himself to seven of them at the Sea of Tiberias.   *Galilee.*

LUKE.	JOHN.
	CH. XXI. 1–24.
	20 Then Peter, turning about, seeth the disciple whom Jesus loved, following ; (which also leaned on his breast at supper, and said, Lord, which is he that betrayeth thee ?)
	21 Peter seeing him, saith to Jesus, Lord, and what *shall* this man *do ?*
	22 Jesus saith unto him, If I will that he tarry till I come, what *is that* to thee ? Follow thou me.
	23 Then went this saying abroad among the brethren, that that disciple should not die : yet Jesus said not unto him, He shall not die ; but, if I will that he tarry till I come, what *is that* to thee ?
	24 This is the disciple which testifieth of these things, and wrote these things : and we know that his testimony is true.

brethren on a mountain in Galilee.   *Galilee.*

and Dr. Pilkington. See Newcomе, in loc. The fact is deemed by some to have an important bearing upon the extent of the commission then given or repeated by our Lord ; but the plan of this work does not require any further notice of the question.

§ 171. Our Lord is seen of James;

MATTHEW.	MARK.

§ 171. The title of this section is inserted, for the sake of preserving the series of Dr. Robinson, whose arrangement has been followed in this Harmony; but as the appearances of Jesus which are here referred to, are related only by Luke in the Acts, i. 3 - 8, and by Paul in 1 Cor. xv. 7, the particular insertion of those passages

---

§ 172. The Ascension.

CH. XVI. 19–20.

19 So then, after the Lord had spoken unto them, he was received up into heaven, and sat on the right hand of God.

20 And they went forth, and preached every where, the Lord working with *them*, and confirming the word with signs following. Amen.

---

§ 173. Conclusion of

Luke xxiv. 50, *Bethany*.] This is perfectly consistent with the statement of Luke in Acts i. 12, as Bethany was not only the name of a town, but of a district of Mount

then of all the Apostles. *Jerusalem.*

LUKE.	JOHN.

is omitted, for the reasons already given. See § 137, note. The subject of this and the eleven preceding sections, respecting the resurrection of Jesus, is discussed in the Appendix, No. VI.

Bethany.

CH. XXIV. 50 – 53.

50 And he led them out as far as to Bethany : and he lifted up his hands, and blessed them.

51 And it came to pass, while he blessed them, he was parted from them, and carried up into heaven.

52 And they worshipped him, and returned to Jerusalem with great joy :

53 And were continually in the temple, praising and blessing God. Amen.

John's Gospel.

CH. XX. 30, 31.

30 And many other signs truly did Jesus in the presence of his disciples, which are not written in this book.

31 But these are written that ye might believe that Jesus is the Christ, the Son of God ; and that believing ye might have life through his name.

CH. XXI. 25.

25 And there are also many other things which Jesus did, the which, if they should be written every one, I suppose that even the world itself could not contain the books that should be written. Amen.

Olivet, adjoining the town. See WATSON's Reply to Gibbon, Letter vi. in Evangelical Family Library, Vol. xiv. p. [277].

APPENDIX.

The Genealogies. See § 13.

The Genealogy of Jesus, as given by Luke, in § 13, is there inverted for the sake of more convenient comparison with that given by Matthew.

The apparent discrepancies in these accounts are reconciled by Dr. Robinson, in the following manner:

"I. In the genealogy given by Matthew, considered by itself, some difficulties present themselves.

"1. There is some diversity among commentators in making out the three divisions, each of fourteen generations, v. 17. It is, however, obvious, that the first division begins with Abraham and ends with David. But does the second begin with David, or with Solomon? Assuredly with the former; because, just as the first begins *apo Abraham*, so the second also is said to begin *apo David*. The first extends *heos David*, and includes him; the second extends to an epoch and not to a person, and therefore the persons who are mentioned as coeval with this epoch are not reckoned before it. After the epoch the enumeration begins again with Jechoniah, and ends with Jesus. In this way the three divisions are made out thus:

1. Abraham.	1. David.	1. Jechoniah.
2. Isaac.	2. Solomon.	2. Salathiel.
3. Jacob.	3. Roboam.	3. Zorobabel.
4. Judah.	4. Abiah.	4. Abiud.
5. Phares.	5. Asa.	5. Eliakim.
6. Esrom.	6. Josaphat.	6. Azor.
7. Aram.	7. Joram.	7. Sadoc.
8. Aminadab.	8. Uzziah (Ozias).	8. Achim.
9. Naasson.	9. Jotham.	9. Eliud.
10. Salmon.	10. Ahaz.	10. Eleazar.
11. Boaz.	11. Hezekiah.	11. Matthan.
12. Obed.	12. Manasseh.	12. Jacob.
13. Jesse.	13. Amon.	13. Joseph.
14. David.	14. Josiah.	14. Jesus.

"2. Another difficulty arises from the fact, that between Joram and Ozias, in v. 8, three names of Jewish kings are omitted, viz. Ahaziah, Joash, and Amaziah; see 2 K. 8, 25 and Chr. 22, 1. 2 K. 11, 2. 21 and 2 Chr. 22, 11. 2 K. 12, 21. 14, 1 and 2 Chr. 24, 27. Further, between Josiah and Jechoniah in v. 11, the name of Jehoiakim is also omitted; 2 K. 23, 34. 2 Chr. 36, 4. comp. 1 Chr. 3, 15. 16. If these four names are to be reckoned, then the second division, instead of fourteen generations, will contain eighteen, in contradiction to v. 17. To avoid this difficulty, Newcome and some others have regarded v. 17 as a mere gloss, 'a marginal note taken into the text.' This indeed is in itself possible; yet all the external testimony of manuscripts and versions is in favor of the genuineness of that verse. It is better therefore to regard these names as having been customarily omitted in the current genealogical tables, from which Matthew copied. Such omissions of particular generations did sometimes actually occur, 'propterea quod malæ essent et impiæ,' according to R. Sal. Jarchi; Lightfoot. Hor. Heb. in Matth. 1, 8. A striking example of an omission of this kind, apparently without any such reason, is found in Ezra 7, 1-5, compared with 1 Chr. 6, 3-15. This latter passage contains the lineal descent of the high-priests from Aaron to the captivity; while Ezra, in the place cited, in tracing back his own genealogy through the very same line of descent, omits at least six generations. A similar omission is necessarily implied in the genealogy of David, as given Ruth 4, 20-22. 1 Chr. 2, 10-12. Matth. 1, 5, 6. Salmon was contemporary with the capture of Jericho by Joshua, and married Rahab. But from that time until David, an interval of at least four hundred and fifty years (Acts 13, 20,) there intervened, according to the list, only four generations, averaging of course more than one hundred years to each. But the highest average in point of fact is *three* generations to a century; and if reckoned by the eldest sons they are usually shorter, or three generations for every seventy-five or eighty years. See Sir I. Newton's Chronol. p. 53. Lond. 1728.

" We may therefore rest in the necessary conclusion, that as our Lord's regular descent from David was always asserted, and was never denied even by the Jews; so Matthew, in tracing this admitted descent, appealed to genealogical tables, which were public and acknowledged in the family and tribe from which Christ sprang. He could not indeed do otherwise. How much stress was laid by the Jews upon lineage in general, and how much care and attention were bestowed upon such tables, is well known. See Lightfoot Hor. Heb. in Matth. 1, 1. Comp. Phil. 3, 4, 5.

" II. Other questions of some difficulty present themselves, when we compare together the two genealogies.

" 1. Both tables at first view purport to give the lineage of our Lord through Joseph. But Joseph cannot have been the son by natural descent of both Joseph and Heli (Eli), Matth. 1, 16. Luke 3, 23. Only one of the tables therefore can give his true lineage by generation. This is done apparently in that of Matthew; because, beginning at Abraham, it proceeds by natural descent, as we know from history, until after the exile; and then continues on in the same mode of expression until Joseph. Here the phrase is changed; and it is no longer Joseph who 'begat' Jesus, but Joseph 'the husband of Mary, of whom was born Jesus who is called the Christ.' See Augustine de Consensu Evangel. II. 5.

" 2. To whom then does the genealogy in Luke chiefly relate? If in any way to Joseph, as the language purports, then it must be because he in some way bore the legal relation of son to Heli, either by adoption or by marriage. If the former simply, it is difficult to comprehend, why, along with his true personal lineage as traced by Matthew up through the royal line of Jewish kings to David, there should be given also another subordinate genealogy, not personally his own, and running back through a different and inferior line to the same great ancestor. If, on the other hand, as is most probable, this relation to Heli came by marriage with his daughter, so that Joseph was truly his *son-in-law* (comp. Ruth 1, 8. 11. 12); then it follows, that the genealogy in Luke is in fact that of Mary the mother of Jesus. This being so, we can perceive a sufficient reason, why this genealogy should be thus given, viz. in order to show definitely, that Jesus was in the most full and perfect sense a descendant of David not only by law in the royal line of kings through his reputed father, but also in fact by direct personal descent through his mother.

"That Mary, like Joseph, was a descendant of David, is not indeed elsewhere expressly said in the New-Testament Yet a very strong presumption to that effect is to be drawn from the address of the angel in Luke 1, 32 ; as also from the language of Luke 2, 5, where Joseph, as one of the posterity of David, is said to have gone up to Bethlehem, to *enroll himself with Mary his espoused wife.* The ground and circumstances of Mary's enrollment must obviously have been the same as in the case of Joseph himself. Whether all this arose from her having been an only child and heiress, as some suppose, so that she was espoused to Joseph in accordance with Num. 36, 8, 9, it is not necessary here to inquire. See Michaelis 'Commentaries on the Laws of Moses,' Part II. § 78.

"It is indeed objected, that it was not customary among the Jews to trace back descent through the female line, that is, on the mother's side. There are, however, examples to show that this was sometimes done ; and in the case of Jesus, as we have seen, there was a sufficient reason for it. Thus in 1 Chr 2, 22, Jair is enumerated among the posterity of Judah by regular descent. But the grandfather of Jair had married the daughter of Machir, one of the heads of Manasseh, 1 Chr. 2, 21. 7, 14 ; and therefore in Num. 32, 40 41, Jair is called the son (descendant) of Manasseh. In like manner, in Ezra 2, 61, and Neh 7, 63, a certain family is spoken of as 'the children of Barzillai ,' because their ancestor 'took a wife of the daughters of Barzillai the Gileadite, and was called after their name.'.

"3 A question is raised as to the identity, in the two genealogies, of the Salathiel and Zorobabel named as father and son, Matth 1, 12. Luke 3, 27. The Zorobabel of Matthew is no doubt the chief, who led back the first band of captives from Babylon, and rebuilt the temple, Ezra c. 2 – 6. He is also called the son of Salathiel in Ezra 3, 2. Neh. 12, 1. Hagg 1, 1. 2, 2. 23. Were then the Salathiel and Zorobabel of Luke the same persons ? Those who assume this, must rest solely on the identity of the names , for there is no other possible evidence to prove, either that they were contemporary, or that they were not different persons. On the other hand, there are one or two considerations, of some force, which go to show that they were probably not the same persons.

"First, if Salathiel and Zorobabel are indeed the same in both genealogies, then Salathiel, who according to Matthew, was the son of Jechoniah by natural descent, must have been called the son of Neri in Luke either from adoption or marriage. In that case, his connection with David through Nathan, as given by Luke, was not his own personal genealogy. It is difficult, therefore, to see, why Luke, after tracing back the descent of Jesus to Salathiel, should abandon the true personal lineage in the royal line of kings, and turn aside again to a merely collateral and humbler line. If the mother of Jesus was in fact descended from the Zorobabel and Salathiel of Matthew, she, like them, was descended also from David through the royal line. Why rob her of this dignity, and ascribe to her only a descent through an inferior lineage ? See Spanheim Dubia Evangel. I. p 108 sq.

"Again, the mere identity of names under these circumstances, affords no proof , for nothing is more common even among cotemporaries. Thus we have two Ezras , one in Neh. 12, 1. 13, 33 , from whom Ezra the scribe is expressly distinguished in v. 36. We have likewise two Nehemiahs , one who went up with Zorobabel, Ezra 2, 2 ; and the other the governor who went later to Jerusalem, Neh 2, 9 sq. So too, as cotemporaries, Joram son of Ahab, king of Israel, and Joram (Jehoram,) son of Jehoshaphat, king of Judah ; 2 K. 8, 16, coll. v. 23. 24. Also, Joash king of Judah, and Joash king of Israel ; 2 K. 13, 9, 10. Further, we find in succession among the descendants of Cain the following names . Enoch, Irad, Mehujael, Methusael, Lamech, Gen. 4, 17, 18 ; and later among the descendants of Seth these similar ones : Enoch, Methuselah, Lamech, Gen. 5, 21 - 25. See Dr. Robinson's Greek Harmony of the Gospels, p. 183 - 187.

NO. II. See § 67.

The Traditions of the Elders were unwritten ordinances of indefinite antiquity, the principal of 'which, as the Pharisees alleged, were delivered to Moses in the mount, and all of which were transmitted through the High Priests and Prophets, down to the members of the great Sanhedrim in their own times ; and from these, as the Jews say, they were handed down to Gamaliel, and ultimately to Rabbi Jehudah, by whom they were digested and committed to writing, toward the close of the second century. This collection is termed the Mishna ; and in many cases it is esteemed among the Jews as of higher authority than the law itself. In like manner, there are said to be many Christians, at the present day, who receive ancient traditionary usages and opinions as authoritative exponents of Christian doctrine. They say that the preached gospel was before the written gospel , and that the testimony of those who heard it is entitled to equal credit with the written evidence of the Evangelists ; especially as the latter is but a brief record, while the oral preaching was a more full and copious announcement of the glad tidings.

These traditions, both of the Jewish and the Christian Church, seem to stand *in pari ratione*, the arguments in favor of the admissibility and effect of the one, applying with the same force, in favor of the other. All these arguments may be resolved into two grounds, namely, contemporaneous practice subsequently and uniformly continued ; and contemporaneous declarations, as part of the *res gestæ*, faithfully transmitted to succeeding times. It is alleged that those to whom the law of God was first announced. best knew its precise import and meaning, and that therefore their interpretation and practice, coming down concurrently with the law itself, is equally obligatory.

But this argument assumes what cannot be admitted ; for it still remains to be shown that those who first heard the law, when orally announced, had any better means of understanding it than those to whom the same words were afterwards read. The Ten Commandments were spoken in the hearing of Aaron and all the congregation of Israel , immediately after which they made and worshipped a golden calf. Surely this will not be adduced as a valid contemporaneous exposition of the second commandment. The error of the argument lies in the nature of the subject. The human doctrine of contemporaneous exposition is applicable only to human laws and the transactions of men, as equals, and not to the laws of God. Among men, when *their own* language is doubtful and ambiguous, *their own* practice is admissible, to expound it , because both the language and the practice are but the outward and visible signs of the meaning and intention of one and the same mind and will, which inward meaning and intention is the thing sought after. It is on the same ground, that where a statute, capable of divers interpretations, has uniformly been acted upon in a certain way, this is held a sufficient exposition of its true intent. In both cases it is the conduct of *the parties* themselves which is admitted to interpret their own language ; expressed, in cases of contract, by themselves in person, and in statutes, through the medium of the legislators, who were their agents and representatives ; and in both cases, it is merely the interpretation of what a man says, by what he does. But this rule has never been applied, in the law, to the language of any other person than the party himself; never, to the command or direction of his superior or employer. And even the language of the *parties*, when it is contained in a sealed instrument, is at this day held incapable of being expounded by their actions, on account of the greater solemnity of the instrument. See Baynham *v* Guy's Hospital, 3 Vesey's Rep. 295. Eaton *v.* Lyon, Ibid. 690, 694. The practice of men, therefore, can be no just exponent of the law of God. If they have mistaken the meaning of his command from the beginning, the act of contravention remains a sin in the last transgressor, as well as the first; for the word of God cannot be changed or affected by the gloss of human interpretation.

The other ground, namely, that the testimony of those who heard Jesus and his apostles preach, is of equal authority with the Scriptures, being contemporaneous declarations, and parts of the *res gestæ*, and therefore admissible in aid of the exposition of the written word, is equally inconsistent with the sound and settled rules of law respecting writings. When a party has deliberately committed his intention and meaning to writing, the law regards the writing as the sole repository of his mind and intention, and does not admit any oral testimony to alter, add to, or otherwise affect it. The reasons for this rule are two; first, because the writing is the more solemn act, by the party himself, designed to prevent mistake, and to remain as the perpetual memorial of his intention; and, secondly, because of the great uncertainty and weakness of any secondary evidence. For no one can tell whether the by-standers heard precisely what was said, nor whether they heard it all, nor whether they continued to remember it with accuracy until the time when they wrote it down or communicated it to those who wrote it; to say nothing of the danger of their mixing up the language of the speaker with what was said by others, or with their own favorite theories. And where the witnesses were not the original auditors of what was said, no one knows how much the truth may have suffered from the many channels through which it has passed, in coming from the first speaker to the last writer or witness. On all these accounts, the law rejects oral testimony of what the parties said, in regard to anything that has already been solemnly committed to writing by the parties themselves, and rejects the secondary evidence of hearsay, when evidence of an higher degree, as, for example, a written declaration of the party, can be obtained

Now, inasmuch as the writings of the Evangelists and Apostles were penned under the inspiration of the Holy Spirit, why should not the documentary evidence of the Gospel, thus drawn up by them, be treated with at least as much respect, as other written documents? If they were inspired to write down those great truths for a perpetual memorial to after ages, then this record is the primary evidence of those truths. It is the word of God, penned by his own dictation, and sealed, as it were, with his own seal. If it were a man's word and will, thus solemnly written, no verbal or secondary evidence could be admitted, by the common law, to explain, add to, or vary it, nothing could be engrafted upon it; nor could any person be admitted to testify what he heard the party say, in regard to what was written The courts would at once reject all such attempts, and confine themselves strictly to the writing before them, the only inquiry being as to the meaning of the language contained in that document, and not as to what the party may elsewhere have spoken. The law presumes that the writing alone is the source to which he intended that resort should be had, in order to ascertain his meaning 'But by calling in the fathers, with their traditions, to prove what Christ and his Apostles taught, beyond what is solemnly recorded in the Scriptures, the principle of this plain and sound rule of law is violated, resort is had to secondary evidence of the truths of our religion, when the primary evidence is already at hand; and the pure fountain is deserted for the muddy stream.

34

NO. III. See § 137.

The use of the word *testament*, (*diatheke*,) in a sense involving also the idea of a *covenant*, and in connexion with the circumstances of a compact, has greatly perplexed many English readers of the Bible. The difficulty occurs in Matth. 26. 28, and the parallel places, where our Lord employs the word *testament*, or last will, in connexion with the sacrificial shedding of his own blood ; a ceremony which, by means of a suitable animal, usually was adopted among the ancients, upon the making of the most solemn engagements ; and instead of which, the mutual partaking of the sacrament of the Lord's Supper, by the contracting parties, was substituted among Christians in later times. The same embarrassment occurs, perhaps in a greater degree, in the exposition of several passages in the eighth and ninth chapters of the Epistle to the Hebrews, (manifestly written by a profound lawyer, be he Paul or Apollos,) where he uses language applicable indifferently both to a covenant *inter vivos* and a last will. For with us, a testament is simply a declaration of the last will of the testator, in regard to the disposition of his property after his decease, irrespective of any consent or even knowledge, at the time, on the part of him to whom the estate is given ; while a covenant requires the mutual consent of both parties, as essential to its existence. The one is simply the *ultima voluntas* of an individual, the other is the *aggregatio mentium* of both or all.

The solution of this difficulty belongs rather to theologians, whose province it is by no means intended here to invade ; but perhaps a reference to the laws and usages in force in Judea in the times of our Saviour and his Apostles may furnish some aid, which a lawyer might contribute without transgressing the limit of his profession.

It is first to be observed that the municipal laws of Greece and Rome were strikingly similar ; those of Greece having been freely imported into the Roman jurisprudence. In like manner, the similarity of the Grecian laws and usages with those extant in Asia Minor, indicated a common origin ; and thus, what Greece derived from Egypt and the states of Asia Minor, these states, after many ages, received again as the laws of their Roman masters. It should also be remembered that Palestine had been reduced to a Roman province some years before the time of our Saviour ; long enough, indeed, to have become familiar with Roman laws and usages, even had they been previously unknown ; and that Paul, to whom the Epistle to the Hebrews is generally attributed, was himself a thorough-bred lawyer, well versed in the customs of his country, whether ancient or modern. Among those nations, the civil magistrate often exercised the functions of the priesthood, these dignities being in some respects identical ; and thus, whatever was transacted before the magistrate, might naturally seem to partake of the character of an act of religion. Covenants were always made with particular formalities, and to those of graver nature, religious solemnities were often superadded. They were frequently confirmed by an oath, the most solemn form of which was taken standing before the altar ; and whosoever swore by the altar, swore by the sacrifice thereon, and was held as firmly bound as though he had passed between the dismembered parts of the victim. Of the latter kind was the oath, by which God confirmed his covenant with Abraham, (Gen. xv.) when the visible light of his presence passed between the pieces which the patriarch had divided and laid " each piece one against another."

With these things in view, we may now look at some of the modes of transferring property, practised by the nations alluded to.

Among the methods of alienation or sale of property by the owner, in his lifetime, was that which in the Roman law was termed *mancipatio ;* a mode by which the vendor conveyed property to the purchaser, each party being present, either in person, or by his agent, representative, or factor. Five witnesses were requisite, one of whom was called *libripens*, or the balance-holder. This form had its origin in the sale of goods by weight, but was gradually extended to all sales; and the practice was for the buyer to strike the balance with a piece of money called a *sestertius*, which was immediately paid over to the vendor as part of the price, and hence the expression *per æs et libram vendere.*

Wills or testaments were made with great solemnity. One method among the Romans, probably common, in its principal traits, to the other nations before mentioned, was termed the testament *per æs et libram*, it being effected in the form of a sale. This mode seems to have been resorted to whenever the estate was given to a stranger, (*hæres extraneus*,) to the exclusion of the *hæres suus*, or *necessarius*, or, as we should say, the heir at law; and it was founded on a purchase of the estate by the adopted heir, who succeeded to the privileges of the child. The forms of a sale by *mancipatio* were therefore scrupulously observed, the presence and agreement of the purchaser, either in person or by his representative or negotiator, being necessary to its validity. The reason for requiring this form was because it *involved a covenant* on the part of the adopted heir or legatee, by which he became bound to pay all the debts of the testator. Having entered into this covenant, he had the best possible title in law to the inheritance, namely, that of a purchaser for a valuable consideration. Among the Greeks, and probably among the Romans also, this was transacted in the presence of a magistrate, who sanctioned it by his sentence of approval. This was the most ancient form of a will; and it does not seem to have been abrogated until the time of Constantine.

Now, when our Saviour speaks of the *new testament in his blood*, or of his *blood of the new testament*, and when Paul uses similar forms of expression may not the figure have reference to the custom above stated? And if so, may not this custom guide us to the true meaning of the words? Does it intimate to us that the promised inheritance was first given to man, as it were by a testament in this ancient form, upon a covenant of *his own* perfect *obedience* to every part of the law of God; that having broken this covenant, his title became forfeited, that the inheritance was afterwards promised, in the same manner, to every one, Jew or Gentile, upon a new covenant and condition, namely, of a true *faith* in Christ; a faith evinced in the fruits of a holy life, that this inheritance by a new testament and covenant was negotiated, as it were, and obtained for man by the mediation of Jesus Christ, ("the mediator of the new testament," Heb. 9. 15,) as the representative of all who should accept it by such faith, and their surety for the performance of its conditions; that it was purchased by *his* obedience and solemnized by the sacrifice of himself as the victim?

This solution is suggested with much diffidence. That it carries these passages clear of all difficulty is not pretended. The very nature of the subject renders it difficult of illustration by any reference to human affairs; and the embarrassment is proportionally increased, whenever the simile is pressed beyond its principal point of resemblance.

See Ayliffe's Pandect, pp. 349, 393, *367-*369. Book iii tit. xii. xv. Leges Atticæ, De Testamentis, &c. tit. vi. S. Petit. Comm. in Leges Attic. p. 479-481 Justin. Inst. lib. 2. tit 10, § 1 Ibid. tit. 19, § 5, 6 Cooper's Justinian, p. 487. Cod lib. 6. tit. 23, l 15. Fuss's Roman Antiq ch 1, § 87, 97, 103, 107, 183. Michaelis, LL. Moses, vol. 4, art 302. Bp Patrick, quoted in Bush's Illustrations, p. 254.

NO. IV.

The Trial of Jesus.

The death of Jesus is universally regarded among Christians as a cruel murder, perpetrated under the pretence of a legal sentence, after a trial, in which the forms of law were essentially and grossly violated. The Jews to this day maintain, that, whatever were the merits of the case, the trial was at least regular, and the sentence legally just; that he was accused of blasphemy, and convicted of that offence by legal evidence. The question between them involves two distinct points of inquiry, namely, first, whether he was guilty of blasphemy; and, secondly, whether the arraignment and trial were conducted in the ordinary forms of law. But there will still remain a third question, namely, whether, admitting that, as a mere man, he had violated the law against blasphemy, he could legally be put to death for that cause; and if not, then whether he was justly condemned upon the new and supplemental accusation of treason or of sedition, which was vehemently urged against him. The first and last of these inquiries it is proposed briefly to pursue; but it will be necessary previously to understand the light in which he was regarded by the Jewish rulers and people, the state of their criminal jurisprudence and course of proceeding, and especially the nature and extent of the law concerning blasphemy, upon which he was indicted.

In the early period of the ministry of Jesus, he does not appear to have excited among the Pharisees any emotion but wonder and astonishment, and an intense interest respecting the nature of his mission. But the people heard him with increasing avidity, and followed him in countless throngs. He taught a purer religion than the Scribes and Pharisees, whose pride and corruption he boldly denounced. He preached charity and humility, and perfect holiness of heart and life, as essential to the favor of God, whose laws he expounded in all the depth of their spirituality, in opposition to the traditions of the elders, and the false glosses of the Scribes and Pharisees. These sects he boldly charged with making void and rejecting the law of God, and enslaving men by their traditions; he accused them of hypocrisy, covetousness, oppression, and lust of power and popularity; and denounced them as hinderers of the salvation of others, as a generation of serpents and vipers, doomed to final perdition. It was natural that these terrific denunciations, from such a personage, supported by his growing power and the increasing acclamations of the people, should alarm the partisans of the ancient theocracy, and lead them to desire his destruction. This alarm evidently increased with the progress of his ministry; and was greatly heightened by the raising of Lazarus from the dead, on which occasion the death of Jesus was definitively resolved on;[1] but no active measures against him seem to have been attempted, until the time when, under the parable of the wicked husbandmen who cast the heir out of the vineyard and slew him, he declared that the kingdom of God should be taken from them, and given to others more worthy. Perceiving that he spake this parable against them, from that hour they sought to lay hands on him, and were restrained only by fear of the popular indignation.[2]

Having thus determined to destroy Jesus at all events, as a person whose very existence was fatal to their own power, and perhaps, in their view, to the safety of their nation, the first step was to render him odious to the people; without which the design would undoubtedly recoil on the heads of its contrivers, his popularity being unbounded. Countless numbers had received the benefit of his miraculous gifts; and it was therefore deemed a vain at-

[1] See John xi. 47–54.
[2] Matth. xxi. 33–46. Mark xxii. 1–12. Luke xx. 9–19.

tempt to found an accusation, at that time, on any past transaction of his life. A new occasion was accordingly sought, by endeavoring to "entangle him in his talk," a measure, planned and conducted with consummate cunning and skill The Jews were divided into two political parties. One of these consisted of the Pharisees, who held it unlawful to acknowledge or pay tribute to the Roman emperor, because they were forbidden, by the law of Moses,[1] to set a king over them who was a stranger, and not one of their own countrymen The other party was composed of the partisans of Herod, who understood this law to forbid only the voluntary election of a stranger, and therefore esteemed it not unlawful to submit and pay tribute to a conqueror. These two parties, though bitterly opposed to each other, united in the attempt to entrap Jesus, by the question, — "Is it lawful to give tribute to Cæsar, or not?"[2] If he answered in the negative, the Herodians were to accuse him to Pilate, for treason, if in the affirmative, the Pharisees would denounce him to the people, as an enemy to their liberties.[3] This insidious design was signally frustrated by the wisdom of his reply, when, referring to Cæsar's image and legend, on the coins which they all received as legally current, he showed the inconsistency of withholding the honor due to one thus implicitly acknowledged by both parties to be their lawful sovereign.

Defeated in this attempt to commit him politically, their next endeavor was to render him obnoxious to one or the other of the two great religious sects, which were divided upon the doctrine of the resurrection, the Pharisees affirming, and the Sadducees denying, that the dead would rise again. The latter he easily silenced, by a striking exposition of their own law. They asked him which, of several husbands, would be entitled in the next world to the wife whom they successively had married in this, and in reply, he showed them that in heaven the relation of husband and wife was unknown [4]

Their last trial was made by a lawyer, who sought to entrap him into an assertion that one commandment in the law was greater than another, a design rendered abortive by his reply that they were all of equal obligation [5]

It being apparent, from these successive defeats, that any farther attempt to find new matter of accusation would result only in disgrace to themselves, the enemies of Jesus seem to have come to the determination to secure his person secretly, and afterwards to put him to death, in any manner that would not render them odious to the people. In execution of this design, they first bribed Judas to betray him by night into their hands. This object being attained, the next step was to destroy his reputation, and if possible to render him so vile in the public estimation, as that his destruction would be regarded with complacency. Now no charge could so surely produce this effect, and none could so plausibly be preferred against him, as that of blasphemy; a crime which the Jews regarded with peculiar horror. Even their veneration of Jesus, and the awe which his presence inspired, had not been sufficient to restrain their rising indignation on several occasions, when they regarded his language as the blasphemous arrogation of a divine character and power to himself; and could they now be brought to believe him a blasphemer, and see him legally convicted of this atrocious crime, his destruction might easily be brought about, without any very scrupulous regard to the form, and even with honor to those by whom it might be accomplished.

It will now be necessary to consider more particularly the nature of the crime of blasphemy, in its larger signification, as it may be deduced from the law of God. That the spirit of this law requires from all men, everywhere, and at all times, the profoundest veneration of the Supreme Being, and the

---

[1] Deut xvii 15.
[2] Matth. xxii 15-22. Mark xii. 13-17. Luke xx 20-26.
[3] Tappan's Jewish Ant. p. 239
[4] Matth. xxii. 23-33. Mark xii. 18-27. Luke xx. 27-39.
[5] Matth. xxii. 25-40, 46. Mark xii 28-34.

most submissive acknowledgment of Him as their rightful Sovereign, is too plain to require argument. If proof were wanted, it is abundantly furnished in the Decalogue,[1] which is admitted among Christians to be of universal obligation. At the time when the Jewish Theocracy was established, idolatry had become generally prevalent, and men had nearly lost all just notions of the nature and attributes of their Creator. It is therefore supposed that the design of Jehovah, in forming the Jewish constitution and code of laws, was to preserve the knowledge of himself as the true God, and to retain that people in the strictest possible allegiance to him alone ; totally excluding every acknowledgment of any other being, either as an object of worship or a source of power. Hence the severity with which he required that sorceries, divinations, witchcrafts and false prophecies, as well as open idolatries, should be punished, they being alike acts of treason, or, as we might say, of *præmunire*, amounting to the open acknowledgment of a power independent of Jehovah. Hence, too, the great veneration in which he commanded that his name and attributes should be held, even in ordinary conversation. It is the breach of this last law, to which the term *blasphemy*, in its more restricted sense, has usually been applied ;[2] but originally the command evidently extended to every word or act, directly in derogation of the sovereignty of Jehovah, such as speaking in the name of another god,[3] or omitting, on any occasion that required it, to give to Jehovah the honor due to his own name.[4] Thus, when Moses and Aaron, at the command of God,

[1] Exodus xx. 1 - 7. And God spake all these words, saying, I *am* the Lord thy God, which have brought thee out of the land of Egypt, out of the house of bondage. Thou shalt have no other gods before me. Thou shalt not make unto thee any graven image, or any likeness *of any thing* that *is* in heaven above, or that *is* in the earth beneath, or that *is* in the water under the earth : Thou shalt not bown down thyself to them, nor serve them : for I the Lord thy God *am* a jealous God, visiting the iniquity of the fathers upon the children unto the third and fourth *generation* of them that hate me ; And shewing mercy unto thousands of them that love me, and keep my commandments. Thou shalt not take the name of the Lord thy God in vain : for the Lord will not hold him guiltless that taketh his name in vain.

[2] Lev. xxiv. 11 - 16. And the Israelitish woman's son blasphemed the name *of the Lord*, and cursed ; and they brought him unto Moses : (and his mother's name *was* Shelomith, the daughter of Dibri, of the tribe of Dan :) And they put him in ward, that the mind of the Lord might be shewed them. And the Lord spake unto Moses, saying, Bring forth him that hath cursed without the camp, and let all that heard *him* lay their hands upon his head, and let all the congregation stone him. And thou shalt speak unto the children of Israel, saying, Whosoever curseth his God shall bear his sin. And he that blasphemeth the name of the Lord, he shall surely be put to death, *and* all the congregation shall certainly stone him : as well the stranger, as he that is born in the land, when he blasphemeth the name *of the Lord*, shall be put to death. See A. Clarke on Matth. ix. 3.

[3] Deut. xiii. 6 - 10. If thy brother, the son of thy mother, or thy son, or thy daughter, or the wife of thy bosom, or thy friend, which *is* as thine own soul, entice thee secretly, saying, Let us go and serve other gods, which thou hast not known, thou, nor thy fathers ; *Namely*, of the gods of the people which *are* round about you, nigh unto thee, or far off from thee, from the *one* end of the earth even unto the *other* end of the earth ; Thou shalt not consent unto him, nor hearken unto him : neither shall thine eye pity him, neither shalt thou spare, neither shalt thou conceal him : But thou shalt surely kill him ; thine hand shall be first upon him to put him to death, and afterwards the hand of all the people. And thou shalt stone him with stones that he die ; because he hath sought to thrust thee away from the Lord thy God, which brought thee out of the land of Egypt from the house of bondage. Deut. xviii. 20. But the prophet, which shall presume to speak a word in my name, which I have not commanded him to speak, or that shall speak in the name of other gods, even that prophet shall die.

[4] It is true that in the Mishna it is written — "Blasphemus non tenetur, nisi expressit Nomen." Mishna, Pars iv. p. 242. Tractatus de Synedriis, cap. 7, § 5. But these traditions were not written until 150 years after the time of our Saviour ; and the passage, moreover, seems properly to refer to that form of blasphemy which consists in evil speaking of the Supreme Being, in a direct manner, rather than to the other forms in which this offence, in its larger acceptation, might be committed. See Michælis, Comm. Art. 251. Vol. 4, p. 67 - 70.

smote the rock in Kadesh, that from it waters might flow to refresh the fam-
ishing multitude, but neglected to honor him as the source of the miraculous
energy, and arrogated it to themselves, saying, "Hear now, ye rebels, must
we bring you water out of this rock?"[1] this omission drew on them his severe displeasure. "And the Lord spake unto Moses and Aaron, Because
ye believed me not, to sanctify *me* in the eyes of the children of Israel, therefore *ye* shall not bring this congregation into the land which I have given
them." Accordingly, both Moses and Aaron died before the Israelites entered into the promised land[2] No other deity was permitted to be invoked ;
no miracle must be wrought, but in the name of God alone. "I am Jehovah ; that is my name ; and my glory will I not give to another, neither my
praise to graven images "[3] This was ever a cardinal principle of his law,
neither newly announced by Isaiah, nor by Moses Its promulgation on
Mount Sinai was merely declaratory of what had been well understood at
the beginning, namely, that God alone was the Lord of all power and might,
and would be expressly acknowledged as such, in every exertion of superhuman energy or wisdom. Thus Joseph, when required to interpret the
dream of Pharaoh, replied, "It is not in me . God shall give Pharaoh an answer of peace."[4] And Moses, in all the miracles previously wrought by
him in Egypt, expressly denounced them as the judgments of God, by whose
hand alone they were inflicted.[5] After the solemn re-enactment of this law
on Mount Sinai, its signal violation by Moses and Aaron deserved to be made
as signal an example of warning ; and this judgment of Jehovah may be said
to constitute the leading case under this article of the law , forming a rule of
action and of judgment for all cases of miracles which might be wrought in
all coming time. The same principle was afterwards expressly extended to
prophesying. "The prophet — that shall speak in the name of other gods,
even that prophet shall die."[6] His character of prophet, and even his inspiration, shall not authorize him to prophesy but in the name of the Lord.
He shall not exercise his office in his own name, nor in any name but that of
Jehovah, from whom his power was derived

That such was understood to be the true meaning of this law of God, is
further evident from the practice of the prophets, in later times, to whom
was given the power of working miracles. These they always wrought in
his name, expressly acknowledged at the time. Thus, the miracle of thun-
der and rain in the season of the wheat-harvest, called for by Samuel, he
expressly attributed to the Lord[7] So did Elijah, when he called fire from
heaven to consume his sacrifice, in refutation of the claims of Baal[8] So did
Elisha, when he divided the waters of Jordan, by smiting them with the
mantle of Elijah ;[9] and again, when he miraculously multiplied the loaves of
bread, for the people that were with him ;[10] and again, when he caused the
young man's eyes to be opened, that he might behold the hosts of the Lord
around him, and smote his enemies with blindness[11] And even the angel

[1] Numb xx. 10, 12
[2] Numb. xx 24 Deut i. 37, and xxxiv. 4, 5
[3] Is xlii. 8, and xlviii. 2   [4] Gen. xli 16, 25, 28
[5] Exod viii ix. x per tot.   [6] Deut xviii 20.
[7] "Now, therefore, stand and see this great thing, which the Lord will do before
your eyes " 1 Sam xii 16–18.
[8] "And it came to pass, at the time of the offering of the evening sacrifice, that Elijah the prophet came near and said, Lord God of Abraham, Isaac, and of Israel, let it
be known this day that *thou art God in Israel*," &c 1 Kings xviii. 36–38
[9] "And he took the mantle of Elijah that fell from him, and smote the waters, and
said, *Where is the Lord God of Elijah?* " &c. 2 Kings ii 14.
[10] "For *thus saith the Lord*, they shall eat and shall leave thereof," &c. 2 Kings
iv. 43
[11] See 2 Kings vi. 16, 17, 18, 20 In some other places, where there is no express
reference to the power of God, the omission may be attributed to the brevity of the
narrative ; but even in those cases, such reference is plainly implied.

Gabriel, when sent to interpret to Daniel the things which should befall his people in the latter days, explicitly announced himself as speaking in Jehovah's name.[1]

The same view of the sinfulness of exercising superhuman power without an express acknowledgment of God as its author, and of any usurpation of his authority, continued to prevail, down to the time of our Saviour. Thus, when he said to the sick of the palsy, " Son, be of good cheer, thy sins be forgiven thee," certain of the Scribes said within themselves, " This man blasphemeth. Who can forgive sins, but God alone ? "[2] And again, when the Jews, on another occasion, took up stones to stone him, and Jesus, appealing to his good works done among them, asked for which of them he was to be stoned ; they replied, " For a good work we stone thee not, but for blasphemy, and because that thou, being a man, makest thyself God."[3] Yet Jesus had on no occasion mentioned the *name* of Jehovah, but with profound reverence.

Thus it appears that the law of blasphemy, as it was understood among the Jews, extended not only to the offence of impiously using the name of the Supreme Being, but to every usurpation of his authority, or arrogation, by a created being, of the honor and power belonging to him alone.[4] Like the crime of treason among men, its essence consisted in acknowledging or setting up the authority of another sovereign than one's own, or invading the powers pertaining exclusively to him ; an offence, of which the case of Moses, before cited, is a prominent instance, both in its circumstances and in its punishment. Whether a false god was acknowledged or the true one denied, and whether the denial was in express terms, or by implication, in assuming to do, by underived power, and in one's own name, that which God only could perform, the offence was essentially the same. And in such horror was it held by the Israelites, that in token of it every one was obliged, by an early and universal custom, to rend his garments, whenever it was committed or related in his presence.[5] This sentiment was deeply felt by the whole people, as a part of their religion.

Such being the general scope and spirit of the law, it would seem to have

---

[1] Dan. ix. 21, 23, and x. 11, 12. See further, 2 Kings xviii. 30 – 35, and xix. 1 – 3.
[2] Matt. ix. 2, 3. Luke v. 20, 21.
[3] John x. 31 – 33.
[4] This view of the Jewish law may seem opposed to that of Dr. Campbell, in his Preliminary Dissertations on the Gospels ; (Vol. 2, Diss. ix. Part 2,) but it is evident, on examination, that he is discussing the *word blasphemy*, and the propriety of its application, taken in its more restricted sense of intentional and direct malediction of Jehovah ; and not whether the assumption of his attributes and authority was or was not a violation of his law. That this assumption was a heinous transgression, seems universally agreed. The question, therefore, is reduced to this — whether the offence was properly *termed* blasphemy. For the *act*, by whatever name it were called, was a capital crime. The Jewish judges of that day held it to amount to blasphemy ; and in so doing, they do not appear to have given to their law a construction more expanded and comprehensive than has been given by judges in our own times, to the law of treason, or of sedition.
[5] This was judicially and solemnly done by the members of the Sanhedrim, rising from their seats, when the crime was testified to. Only one witness was permitted to repeat the words ; the others simply stating that they heard the same which he had related. The practice is thus described in the Mishna : " Exactis omnibus, interrogant vetustissimum testium, dicendo, — *Edissere, quodcumque audiisti expresse.* Tum ille hoc refert. Judices autem stant erecti, vestesque discerpunt, non resarciendas. Dein secundus tertiusque ait, — *Ego idem, quod ille, audivi.*" Mishna, Pars 4. Tractat. de Synedriis, cap. 7, § 5. Upon which, Coccejus remarks : — "Assurgunt reverentiæ causâ. Mos discendarum vestium probatur ex 2do Regum, xviii. 37. Hinc nata est regula, — *Qui blasphemiam audit, vel ab ipso auctore vel ex alio, tenetur vestem discerpere.* Ratio est, ut semper ob oculos et animum versetur mæroris aut indignationis mnemosynon." Coccej. in loc. § 11, 12. The custom is fully explained, with particular reference to the high priest at the trial of Jesus, by Hedenus, *De Scissione Vestium,* 38, 42. (In Ugolini Thesauro, Tom. xxix. fol. 1025, &c.)

been easy to prove that Jesus had repeatedly incurred its penalties. He had performed many miracles, but never in any other name than his own In his own name, and without the recognition of any higher power, he had miraculously healed the sick, restored sight to the blind and strength to the lame, cast out devils, rebuked the winds, calmed the sea, and raised the dead. In his own name, also, and with no allusion to the Omniscient, no " Thus saith the Lord," he had prophesied of things to come. He had by his own authority forgiven sins, and promised, by his own power, not only to raise the dead, but to resume his own life, after he should, as he predicted, be put to death. Finally, he had expressly claimed for himself a divine origin and character, and the power to judge both the quick and dead [1] Considered as a man, he had usurped the attributes of God. That he was not arrested at an earlier period, is to be attributed to his great popularity, and the astounding effect of his miracles. His whole career had been resplendent with beneficence to the thousands who surrounded him. His eloquence surpassed all that had been uttered by man. The people were amazed, bewildered and fascinated, by the resistless power of his life. It was not until his last triumphal visit to Jerusalem, after he had openly raised Lazarus from the dead, when the chief priests and elders perceived that " the world was gone after him," that they were stricken with dismay and apprehension for their safety, and under this panic resolved upon the perilous measure of his destruction.

The only safe method in which this could be accomplished, was under the sanction of a legal trial and sentence. Jesus, therefore, upon his apprehension, was first brought before the great tribunal of the Sanhedrim, and charged with the crime of blasphemy. What were the specifications under this general charge, or whether any were necessary, we are not informed. But that this was the offence charged, is manifest both from the evidence adduced and from the judgment of conviction.[2] Such was the estimation in which he was held, that it was with great difficulty that witnesses could be found to testify against him, and the two who at last were procured, testified falsely, in applying his words to the temple of Solomon, which he spake of the temple of his body. When, upon the occasion of his scourging the money-changers out of the temple, the Jews demanded by what authority he did this, Jesus replied, alluding to his own person, " Destroy *this* temple, and in three days I will raise it up."[3] But though the witnesses swore falsely in testifying that he spake of the Jewish temple, yet his words, in either sense, amounted to a claim of the power of working miracles, and so brought him within the law. The high priest, however, still desirous of new evidence, which might justify his condemnation in the eyes of the people, proceeded to interrogate Jesus concerning his character and mission. " I adjure thee, by the living God, that thou tell us whether thou be the Christ, the Son of God. Jesus saith to him, Thou hast said nevertheless, I say unto you, hereafter ye shall see the Son of Man sitting on the right hand of power, and coming in the clouds of heaven Then the high priest *rent his*

[1] That the Jews understood Jesus to make himself equal with God, is maintained by Mr Salvador, himself a Jew, in his Histoire des Institutions de Moire, et du peuple Hebreu, Liv iv ch 3, p 81, of which chapter a translation is given at the end of this article Mr Noah, also a Jew, seems to be of opinion, that Jesus was brought to trial under the law in Deut xiii. 1-11 See his Discourse on the Restoration of the Jews, p 19. But whether he was charged with a blasphemous usurpation of the attributes of Deity, or with sedition, in inciting the people to serve another god, meaning himself, the difference is of no importance ; the essence of the offence in both cases being the same
[2] Matth xxvi. 60-65 This view of the nature of the offence with which Jesus was charged, is confirmed by the learned jurist, Chr Thomasius, in his Dissertatio de injusto Pilati judicio, § 11, 12, and by the authors whom he there cites. Dissert. Thomasii vol 1, p 5.
[3] John ii. 13-22

clothes, saying He hath *spoken blasphemy;* what *further* need have we of witnesses? Behold, now *ye have heard* his *blasphemy.* What think ye? They answered and said, *He is guilty of death.*" [1] We may suppose the multitude standing without the hall of judgment, able, through its avenues and windows, to see, but not to hear, all that was transacting within. It became important, therefore, to obtain some reason upon which the high priest might rend his clothes in their sight, thus giving to the people, by this expressive and awful sign, the highest evidence of blasphemy, uttered by Jesus in the presence of that august assembly. This act turned the tide of popular indignation against him, whose name, but a short time before, had been the theme of their loudest hosannas. There was now no need to go into the past transactions of his ministry, for matter of accusation. His friends might claim for him on that score all that the warmest gratitude and love could inspire; and all this could be safely conceded. But here, his accusers might say, was a new and shocking crime, just perpetrated in the presence of the most sacred tribunal; a crime so shocking, and so boldly committed, that the high priest rent his clothes with horror, in the very judgment seat, in the presence of all the members of the Sanhedrim, who, with one accord, upon that evidence alone, immediately convicted the offender and sentenced him to death.

If we regard Jesus simply as a Jewish citizen, and with no higher character, this conviction seems substantially right in point of law, though the trial were not legal in all its forms. For, whether the accusation were founded on the first or second commands in the decalogue, or on the law, laid down in the thirteenth chapter of Deuteronomy, or on that in the eighteenth chapter and twentieth verse, he had violated them all, by assuming to himself powers belonging alone to Jehovah. And even if he were recognized as a prophet of the Lord, he was still obnoxious to punishment, under the decision in the case of Moses and Aaron, before cited. It is not easy to perceive on what ground his conduct could have been defended before any tribunal, unless upon that of his superhuman character. No lawyer, it is conceived, would think of placing his defence upon any other basis.

The great object of exciting the people against Jesus being thus successfully accomplished, the next step was to obtain legal authority to put him to death. For though the Sanhedrim had condemned him, they had not the power to pass a capital sentence; this being a right which had passed from the Jews by the conquest of their country, and now belonged to the Romans alone. They were merely citizens of a Roman province; they were left in the enjoyment of their civil laws, the public exercise of their religion, and many other things relating to their police and municipal regulations; but they had not the power of life and death. This was a principal attribute of sovereignty, which the Romans always took care to reserve to themselves in order to be able to reach those individuals who might become impatient of the yoke, whatever else might be neglected *Apud quos (Romanos), vis imperii valet; inania transmittuntur.* [2] The jurisdiction of capital cases belonged or-

---

[1] Matth. xxvi. 63–66.

[2] Tacit. Annal. xv. 31. See M. Dupin's Trial of Jesus, p. 57–59, (Amer. Ed.) Chr. Thomasius, Dissertatio de injusto Pilati judicio, § 12, 60. The want of this power was admitted by the Jews, in their reply to Pilate, when he required them to judge Jesus according to their own law, and they replied, "It is not lawful for us to put any man to death." John xviii. 31.

This point has been held in different ways by learned men. Some are of opinion that the Sanhedrim had power to inflict death for offences touching religion, though not for political offences; and that it was with reference to the charge of treason that they said to Pilate what has just been cited from St. John. They say that, though the Sanhedrim had convicted Jesus of blasphemy, yet they dared not execute that sentence, for fear of a sedition of the people: — that they therefore craftily determined to throw on Pilate the odium of his destruction, by accusing him of treason; and hence, after con-

dinarily to the governor general or *Præses* of a province, the *Procurator* having for his principal duty only the charge of the revenue and the cognizance of revenue causes. But the right of taking cognizance of capital crimes was, in some cases, given to certain *Procurators*, who were sent into small provinces, to fill the places of governors, (*Vice Præsides*,) as clearly appears from the Roman laws. The government of all Syria was at this time under a governor general, or *Præses*, of which Judea was one of the lesser dependencies, under the charge of Pilate as *Vice Præses*, with capital jurisdiction.[1]

It could not be expected that Pilate would trouble himself with the cognizance of any matter, not pertaining to the Roman law; much less with an alleged offence against the God of the Jews, who was neither acknowledged nor even respected by their conquerors. Of this the chief priests and elders were fully aware, and therefore they prepared a second accusation against Jesus, founded on the Roman law, as likely to succeed with Pilate, as the former had done with the people. They charged him with attempting to restore the kingdom of Israel, under his own dominion as king of the Jews. " We found this fellow, said they, perverting the nation, and forbidding to give tribute to Cesar, saying, That he himself is Christ, a king."[2]

It was a charge of high treason against the Roman state and emperor; a charge which was clearly within Pilate's cognizance, and which, as they well knew, no officer of Tiberius would venture lightly to regard. Pilate accordingly forthwith arraigned Jesus, and called upon him to answer this accusation. It is worthy of note, that from the moment when he was accused of treason before Pilate, no further allusion was made to the previous charge of blasphemy, the Roman governor being engaged solely with the charge newly preferred before himself. The answer of Jesus to this charge satisfied Pilate that it was groundless, the kingdom which he set up appearing plainly to be not a kingdom of this world, but his spiritual reign in righteousness and holiness and peace, in the hearts of men. Pilate therefore acquitted him of the offence. "He went out again unto the Jews, and saith unto them, *I find in him no fault at all.*"[3] Here was a sentence of acquittal, judicially pronounced, and irreversible, except by a higher power, upon appeal; and it was the duty of Pilate thereupon to have discharged him. But the multitude, headed now by the priests and elders, grew clamorous for his execution; adding, "He stirreth up the people, teaching throughout all Jewry,

---

demning him, they consulted further, as stated in Matth. xxvii. 1, 2. Mark xv 1, how to effect this design — that when Pilate found no fault in him, and directed them to take and crucify him, some replied, " we have a law, and by our law he ought to die," (John xix. 7,) to intimate to Pilate that Jesus was guilty of death by the Jewish law also, as well as the Roman, and that therefore he would not lose any popularity by condemning him. See Zornius, Hist. Fisci Judaici, ch. 2, § 2, (in Ugolini Thesaur. Tom. 26. col. 1001 - 1003) The same view is taken by Deylingius, De Judæorum Jure Gladii, § 10, 11, 12, (in Ugolin. Thesaur, Tom. 29, col. 1189 - 1192) But he concludes that in all capital cases, there was an appeal from the Sanhedrim to the Prætor; and that without the approval of the latter, the sentence of the Sanhedrim could not be executed. Ibid. § 15, col 1196 Molinæus understood the Jewish law in the same manner. See his Harmony of the Gospels, note on John 18 31. C. Molinæi Opera, Tom 5, pp 603, 604. But this opinion is refuted by what is said by M Dupin, Trial, &c § 8, and by Thomasius, above cited

[1] See M. Dupin's Trial of Jesus, pp 55 - 62 His authorities are Loiseau, Godefroy, and Cujas, the two latter of whom he cites as follows , — " Procurator Cæsaris *fungens vice præsidis* potest cognoscere *de causis criminalibus* Godefroy, in his note (letter S) upon the 3d law of the Code, *Ubi causæ fiscales*, &c And he cites several others, which I have verified, and which are most precise to the same effect. See particularly the 4th law of the Code, *Ad leg fab. de plag* , and the 2d law of the Code, *De pœnis* — Procuratoribus Cæsaris data est jurisdictio in causis fiscalibus pecuniariis, non in criminalibus, nisi quum fungebantur *vice præsidum; ut* Pontius Pilatus fuit procurator Cæsaris *vice præsidis* in Syria. Cujas, Observ xix. 13."

[2] Luke xxiii. 2.   [3] John xviii. 38.

beginning from Galilee to this place." [1] Hearing this reference to Galilee,
Pilate seized the opportunity, thus offered, of escaping from the responsibility
of a judgment, either of acquittal or of condemnation, by treating the case as
out of his jurisdiction, and within that of Herod tetrarch of Galilee, who was
then in Jerusalem on a visit. He therefore sent Jesus and his accusers to
Herod; before whom the charge was vehemently renewed and urged. But
Herod, too, perceived that it was utterly groundless, and accordingly treated
it with derision, arraying Jesus in mock habiliments of royalty, and remand-
ing him to Pilate.[2] The cause was then solemnly reëxamined by the Roman
governor, and a second judgment of acquittal pronounced. For "Pilate,
when he had called together the chief priests and the rulers, and the people,
said unto them, Ye have brought this man unto me, as one that perverteth
the people; and behold, I having examined him before you, have found no
fault in this man, touching those things whereof ye accuse him : No, nor yet
Herod : for I sent you to him ; and lo, nothing worthy of death is done unto
him. I will therefore chastise him and release him." [3]

It may seem strange to us that after a judgment of acquittal thus solemnly
pronounced, any judge, in a civilized country, should venture to reverse it,
upon the same evidence, and without the pretence of mistake or error in the
proceedings. Probably, in the settled jurisprudence of the city of Rome, it
could not have been done. But this was in a remote province of the empire,
under the administration not of a jurist, but a soldier ; and he, too, irresolute
and vascillating ; fearful for his office, and even for his life, for he served
the "dark and unrelenting Tiberius." As soon as he proposed to release
Jesus, "the Jews cried out, saying, If thou let this man go, *thou art not
Cæsar's friend. Whosoever maketh himself a king, speaketh against Cæsar.*" [4]
Whereupon "Pilate gave sentence that it should be as they required." [5]
That Jesus was executed under the pretence of treason, and that alone, is
manifest from the tenor of the writing placed over his head, stating that he
was king of the Jews ; such being the invariable custom among the Romans,
in order that the public might know for what crime the party had been condemned.[6] The remaining act in this tragedy is sufficiently known.

In the preceding remarks, the case has been considered only upon its general merits, and with no reference to the manner in which the proceedings
were conducted. But M. Dupin, in his tract on the Trial of Jesus before the
Sanhedrim, in reply to Mr. Salvador's account of it, has satisfactorily shown
that throughout the whole course of that trial the rules of the Jewish law of
procedure were grossly violated, and that the accused was deprived of rights,
belonging even to the meanest citizen. He was arrested in the night, bound
as a malefactor, beaten before his arraignment, and struck in open court
during the trial ; he was tried on a feast day, and before sunrise ; he was
compelled to criminate himself, and this, under an oath or solemn judicial
adjuration ; and he was sentenced on the same day of the conviction. In all
these particulars the law was wholly disregarded.[7]

---

[1] Luke xxiii. 5.   [2] Luke xxiii. 10, 11.

[3] Luke xxiii. 13, 14, 15. I regard this judgment as conclusive evidence of the innocence of the accused. Pilate's strenuous endeavors to release him instead of Barabbas,
and his solemn washing his own hands of the guilt of his blood, though they show the
strength of his own convictions, yet add no legal force to the judgment itself.

[4] John xix. 12.   [5] Luke xxiii. 24.

[6] See M. Dupin's Trial of Jesus, pp. 82-84.

[7] See M. Dupin's Trial of Jesus, pp. 7-15. Jahn's Bibl. Ant. § 246.

NO. V.

M. Joseph Salvador, a physician and a learned Jew, a few years ago published at Paris, a work, entitled, "Histoire des Institutions de Moise et du Peuple Hebreu," in which, among other things, he gives an account of their course of criminal procedure, in a chapter on "The Administration of Justice;" which he illustrates, in a succeeding chapter, by an account of the trial of Jesus. As this is the recent work of a man of learning, himself a Jew, it may be regarded as an authentic statement of what is understood and held by the most intelligent and best informed Jews, respecting the claims of our Lord, the tenor of his doctrines, the nature of the charge laid against him before the Sanhedrim, and the grounds on which they condemned him. The following translation of the last-mentioned chapter will therefore not be unacceptable to the reader. It will be found in Book IV. chapter iii., entitled, "The Trial and Condemnation of Jesus." The reader will bear in his mind, that it is the language of an enemy of our Saviour, and in justification of his murderers.

"According to this exposition of judicial proceedings," says the Jew, "I shall follow out the application of them in the most memorable trial in history, that of Jesus Christ. I have already explained the motives which have directed me, and the point of view in which I have considered the subject; I have already shown, that among the Jews no title was a shelter against a prosecution and sentence. Whether the law or its forms were good or bad, is not the object of my present investigation; neither is it to ascertain whether we ought to pity the blindness of the Hebrews in not discovering a Deity in Jesus, or to be astonished that a God personified could not make himself comprehended when he desired it. But since they regarded him only as a citizen, did they not try him according to their law and its existing forms? This is my question, which can admit of no equivocation. I shall draw all my facts from the Evangelists themselves, without inquiring whether all this history was developed after the event, to serve as a form to a new doctrine, or to an old one which had received a fresh impulse.

Jesus was born of a family of small fortune; Joseph, his supposed father, perceived that his wife was big before they had come together. If he had brought her to trial, in the ordinary course of things, Mary, according to the 23d verse of the 22d chapter of Deuteronomy, would have been condemned, and Jesus, having been declared illegitimate, could never, according to the 2d verse of the 23d chapter, have been admitted to a seat in the Sanhedrim.[1] But Joseph who, to save his wife from disgrace, had taken the resolution of sending her away privately, soon had a dream which consoled him.[2]

After having been circumcised, Jesus grew like other men, attended the solemn feasts, and early displayed surprising wisdom and sagacity. In the assembly on the Sabbath, the Jews, eager for the disputes to which the interpretation of the law gave rise, loved to hear him. But he soon devoted himself to more important labors; he pronounced censures against whole towns, Capernaum, Chorazin and Bethsaida.[3] Recalling the times of Isaiah and Jeremiah, he thundered against the chiefs of the people with a vehemence which would in our day be terrific.[4] The people then regarded him as a prophet;[5] they heard him preach in towns and country without opposition; they saw him surrounded with disciples according to the custom of the learned men of the age; whatever may have been the resentment of the chief men, they were silent as long as he confined himself to the law.

[1] Deut. xxii. 22, and xxiii. 2. Selden, De Synedriis, lib. 3, cap. 4, 5.
[2] Matth. i. 19, 20.   [3] Matth. xi. 20–24. Luke iv. &c.
[4] Matth. xxiii. per tot.   [5] Matth. xxi. 11, 46. John vii. 40.

But Jesus, in presenting new theories, and in giving new forms to those already promulgated, speaks of himself as God; his disciples repeat it; and the subsequent events prove in the most satisfactory manner, that they thus understood him.[1] This was shocking blasphemy in the eyes of the citizens: the law commands them to follow Jehovah alone, the only true God; not to believe in gods of flesh and bone, resembling men or women; neither to spare nor listen to a prophet who, even doing miracles, should proclaim a new god, a god whom neither they nor their fathers had known.[2]

Jesus having said to them one day: "I have come down from heaven to do these things," the Jews, who till then had listened to him, murmured and cried: "Is not this Jesus, the son of Joseph and of Mary? we know his father, his mother, and his brethren; why then does he say that he has come down from heaven?"[3] On another day, the Jews, irritated from the same cause, took stones and threatened him. Jesus said unto them, "I have done good works in your eyes by the power of my Father, for which of these works would you stone me? It is for no good work," replied the Jews, who stated the whole process in few words, "but because of thy blasphemy; for being a man,[4] thou makest thyself God."[5]

His language was not always clear. Often his disciples themselves did not comprehend him. Among his maxims, some of which showed the greatest mildness, there were some which the Hebrews, who were touched only through their natural sense, thought criminal. "Think not that I am come to send peace on earth; I came not to send peace, but a sword. For I am come to set a man at variance against his father, and the daughter against her mother, and the daughter-in-law against her mother-in-law. And a man's foes shall be they of his own household. He that loveth father or mother more than me, is not worthy of me."[6] Finally, if he wrought miracles before certain of the people, his replies to the questions of the doctors were generally evasive.[7]

In regard to political relations, he caused dissensions.[8] A great number of disorderly persons whom he had the design of reclaiming, but who inspired dread in the national council, attached themselves to him;[9] his discourse flattered them inasmuch as he pronounced anathemas against riches. "Know," said he, "that it is easier for a camel to go through the eye of a needle, than for a rich man to enter the kingdom of heaven."[10] In this state of affairs, the council deliberates; some are of opinion that he should be regarded as a madman,[11] others say that he seeks to seduce the people.[12] Caiaphas, the high priest, whose dignity compels him to defend the letter of the law, observes that these dissensions would furnish an excuse to the Romans for overwhelming Judea, and that the interests of the whole nation must

---

[1] The expression *son of God* was in common use among the Jews, to designate a man of remarkable wisdom and piety. It was not in this sense that Jesus Christ used it; for in that case it would have occasioned no great sensation. Besides, if we should assume, in order to make it a subject of accusation against these Jews, that Jesus did not expressly declare himself to be God, we should be exposed to this rejoinder: why then do you believe in him?

[2] See Deut. iv. 15, and xiii. per tot.

[3] John vi. 39 – 42. Matth. xiii. 55.

[4] This fact is as clearly established as possible; and we must observe that till then there had been neither opposition nor enmity in the minds of this people, since they had listened to him with the greatest attention, and did not hesitate to acknowledge in him all that the public law permitted them to do, viz. a prophet, a highly inspired man.

[5] John x. 30 – 33.   [6] Matth. x. 34.   Mark x. 29.

[7] Matth. xvi. 1 – 4.   John viii. 13 – 18.

[8] John vii. 43.   Luke xxiii. 5.

[9] Matth. ix. 10.   Mark ii. 15.   Luke xv. 1.

[10] Matth. xix. 24.   [11] John x. 20.   [12] John vii. 12.

outweigh those of a single individual ; he constitutes himself the accuser of Jesus.[1]

The order is given to seize him. But let us pause here upon a fact of the highest importance. The senate did not begin by actually seizing Jesus, as is now the practice ; they begin by giving, after some debate, an order that he should be seized.[2] This decree is made public ; it is known to all, especially to Jesus. No opposition is offered to his passing the frontier : his liberty depends entirely upon himself. This is not all ; the order for his arrest was preceded by a decree of admonition. One day, Jesus having entered the temple, took upon himself authority contrary to the common law ; then he preached to the people, and said : "That those who should believe in him should be able to do all things, so that if they should say to a mountain, remove thyself and cast thyself into the sea, it would obey." Then the chief priest and senators went to find him, and said to him, "By what authority doest thou these things ? who gave thee this power?"[3]

Meanwhile a traitor discloses the place whither the accused had retired ; the guards, authorized by the high priest and by the elders,[4] hasten to seize him. One of his disciples, breaking into open rebellion, with a stroke of his sword cuts off the ear of one of them, and brings upon himself the reproof of his master.[5] As soon as Jesus is arrested, the zeal of the apostles is extinguished ; all forsake him.[6] He is brought before the grand council, where the priests sustain the accusation. The witnesses testify, and they are numerous ; for the deeds of which he is accused were done in the presence of all the people. The two witnesses whom St. Matthew and St. Mark accuse of perjury, relate a discourse which St. John declares to be true, with regard to the power which Jesus arrogates to himself.[7] Finally, the high priest addresses the accused, and says : "Is it true that thou art Christ, that thou art the Son of God?" "I am he," replies Jesus ; "you shall see me hereafter at the right hand of the majesty of God, who shall come upon the clouds of heaven." At these words, Caiaphas rent his garments in token of horror.[8] "You have heard him." They deliberate. The question already raised among the people was this : has Jesus become God ? But the senate having adjudged that Jesus, son of Joseph, born at Bethlehem, had profaned the name of God by usurping it to himself, a mere citizen, applied to him the law of blasphemy, and the law in the 13th chapter of Deuteronomy, and the 20th verse in chapter 18, according to which every prophet, even he who works miracles, must be punished, when he speaks of a god unknown to the Jews and their fathers :[9] the capital sentence was pronounced. As to

[1] John xi. 47 – 50.
[2] Matth. xxvi. 4. John xi. 53, 54.
[3] Matth. xxi. 23.
[4] It will be recollected, that the senate held its sessions in one of the porticos of the temple. At this time the high priest presided over the senate, so that the guards of the high priest, of the elders and the temple, were no other than the legal militia.
[5] John xviii. 10, 11.   [6] Mark xiv. 50. Matth. xxvi. 56.
[7] Matth. xxvi. 60, 61. And the last came two false witnesses, and said, this fellow said, I am able to destroy the temple of God, and to build it in three days. Mark xiv. 57, 58. And there arose certain and bare false witness against him, saying, We heard him say, I will destroy this temple that is made with hands, and within three days I will build another made without hands. John ii. 19, 21, 22. Jesus answered and said unto them, Destroy this temple, and in three days I will raise it up. But he spake of the temple of his body. When, therefore, he was risen from the dead, his disciples remembered that he had said this unto them ; and they believed the scripture, and the word which Jesus had said.
[8] I repeat that the expression *son of God*, includes here the idea of God himself ; the fact is already established, and all the subsequent events confirm it. Observe, also, that I quote the narrative of only one of the parties to this great proceeding.
[9] Deut. xxviii. 20. But the prophet, which shall presume to speak a word in my name, which I have not commanded him to speak, or that shall speak in the name of other gods, even that prophet shall die.

the ill-treatment which followed the sentence, it was contrary to the spirit of
the Jewish law; and it is not in the course of nature, that a Senate composed of the most respectable men of a nation, who, however they might
have been deceived, yet intended to act legally, should have permitted such
outrages against him whose life was at their disposal. The writers who
have transmitted to us these details, not having taken a part in the prosecution, have been disposed to exaggerate the picture, either on account of their
prejudices, or to throw greater obloquy on the judges.

One thing is certain, that the council met again on the morning of the next
day or of the day following that,[1] as the law requires, to confirm or to annul
the sentence: it was confirmed. Jesus was brought before Pilate, the procurator that the Romans had placed over the Jews. They had retained the
power of trying according to their own laws, but the executive power was in
the hands of the procurator alone: no criminal could be executed without his
consent: this was in order that the Senate should not have the means of
reaching men who were sold to foreigners.[2] Pilate, the Roman, signed the
decree. His soldiers, an impure mixture of diverse nations, were charged
with the punishment. These are they who brought Jesus to the judgment
hall, who stripped him before the whole cohort, who placed upon his head a
crown of thorns, and a reed in his hand, who showed all the barbarity to
which the populace in all ages is disposed; who finally caused him to under-
go a punishment common at Rome, and which was not in use among the Jews.[3]
But before the execution, the governor had granted to the condemned an appeal to the people, who, respecting the judgment of their own council, would
not permit this favor, couching their refusal in these terms: "We have a
law; and by our law he ought to die, because he made himself the Son of
God."[4]   Then Pilate left them the choice of saving Jesus, or a man accused
of murder in a sedition; the people declared for the latter; saying that the
other would scatter the seeds of discord in the bosom of the nation, at a time
when union was most necessary.[5]

Jesus was put to death. The priests and elders went to the place of punishment; and as the sentence was founded upon this fact, that he had unlaw-
fully arrogated to himself the title of Son of God, God himself, they appealed
to him thus: "Thou wouldst save others; thyself thou canst not save. If
thou art indeed the king of Israel, come down into the midst of us, and we
will believe in thee; since thou hast said, I am the Son of God, let that God
who loves thee come now to thine aid."[6]   According to the Evangelist, these
words were a mockery; but the character of the persons who pronounced
them, their dignity, their age, the order which they had observed in the trial,
prove their good faith. Would not a miracle at this time have been decisive?"

[1] Matt. xxvii. 1. Mark xv. 1.
[2] The duties of Pilate were to inform himself whether the sentences given did or
did not affect the interests of Rome; there his part ended. Thus it is not astonishing
that this procurator, doubtless little acquainted with the Jewish laws, signed the decree for the arrest of Jesus, although he did not find him guilty. We shall see hereafter that there were then many parties among the Jews, among whom were the Herodians or serviles, partisans of the house of Herod, and devoted to the foreign interests. These are they who speak continually of Cæsar, of rendering to Cæsar the tribute due to Cæsar; they also insist that Jesus called himself *king of the Jews:* but
this charge was reckoned as nothing before the senate, and was not of a nature alone
to merit capital punishment.
[3] See Matth. xxvii. 27.   Mark xv. 16.   John xix. 2.   [4] John xix. 7.
[5] The sending back of Jesus to Herod, which, according to the Gospel of St. Luke,
Pilate would have done, is not stated by the other Evangelists, and does not at all
change the judicial question. Herod Antipas, tetrarch of Galilee, and of Perea, had no
authority in Jerusalem. Upon his visit to this city, Pilate, according to St. Luke,
would, out of respect, have caused Jesus to appear before this ally of the Romans, because Jesus was surnamed the Galilean, though originally from Judea. But to whatever tribe he belonged, the nature of the accusation would still have required, according to the Hebrew law, that he should be judged by the senate of Jerusalem.
[6] Matth. xvii. 42, 43

NO. VI.   See § 159 to § 171.

The accounts of the Resurrection and of the subsequent appearances of our Lord, have been harmonized in various methods ; of which the latest, and probably the best, is that of Professor Robinson, in an Article published in the Bibliotheca Sacra for February, 1845, vol. ii. pp. 162 – 189   As the best service the present writer could do to the English reader, he has therefore here abridged that Article, by omitting the introduction, and such parts as relate to the Greek text, and a few other passages, which it seemed might be spared without injury to the narrative itself.

§ 1.   *The Time of the Resurrection.*
Matt 26 : 1, 2.   Mark 16 · 1, 2, 9   Luke 24 · 1.   John 20 . 1.

That the resurrection of our Lord took place before full daylight, on the first day of the week, follows from the unanimous testimony of the Evangelists respecting the visit of the women to the sepulchre.   But the exact time at which he rose is nowhere specified.   According to the Jewish mode of reckoning, the Sabbath ended and the next day began at sunset ; so that had the resurrection occurred even before midnight, it would still have been upon the first day of the week, and the third day after our Lord's burial.   The earthquake had taken place and the stone had been rolled away before the arrival of the women ; and so far as the immediate narrative is concerned, there is nothing to show that all this might not have happened some hours earlier.   Yet the words of Mark in another place render it certain, that there could have been no great interval between these events and the arrival of the women ; since he affirms in v. 9, that Jesus " had risen *early*, the first day of the week ," while in v. 2, he states that the women went out " *very early.*" A like inference may be drawn from the fact, that the affrighted guards first went to inform the chief priests of these events, when the women returned to the city (Matt 28 11) ; for it is hardly to be supposed, that after having been thus terrified by the earthquake and the appearance of an angel, they would have waited any very long time before sending information to their employers. — The body of Jesus had therefore probably lain in the tomb not less than about thirty-six hours.

§ 2.   *The Visit of the Women to the Sepulchre.*
Matt. 28 : 1 – 8.   Mark 16 . 1 – 8.   Luke 24 : 1 – 11.   John 20 : 1, 2.

The first notices we have of our Lord's resurrection, are connected with the visit of the women to the sepulchre, on the morning of the first day of the week.   According to Luke, the women who had stood by the cross, went home and rested during the sabbath (23 · 56) ; and Mark adds that after the sabbath was ended, that is, after sunset, and during the evening, they prepared spices in order to go and embalm our Lord's body.   They were either not aware of the previous embalming by Joseph and Nicodemus ; or else they also wished to testify their respect and affection to their Lord, by completing, more perfectly, what before had been done in haste ; John 19 : 40 – 42.

It is in just this portion of the history, which relates to the visit of the women to the tomb and the appearance of Jesus to them, that most of the alleged difficulties and discrepancies in this part of the Gospel narratives are found.   We will therefore take up the chief of them in their order.

I. *The Time.*   All the Evangelists agree in saying that the women went out *very early* to the sepulchre.   Matthew's expression is, *as the day was*

35

dawning. Mark's words are, *very early;* which indeed are less definite, but are appropriate to denote the same point of time. Luke has the more poetic term: *deep morning,* i. e. early dawn. John's language is likewise definite: *early, while it was yet dark.* All these expressions go to fix the time at what we call *early dawn,* or *early twilight;* after the break of day, but while the light is yet struggling with darkness.

Thus far there is no difficulty; and none would ever arise, had not Mark added the phrase, *the sun being risen;* or, as the English version has it, *at the rising of the sun.* These words seem, at first, to be at direct variance both with the *very early* of Mark himself, and with the language of the other Evangelists. To harmonize this apparent discrepancy, we may premise, that since Mark himself first specifies the point of time by a phrase sufficiently definite in itself, and supported by all the other Evangelists, we must conclude that when he adds, *at the rising of the sun,* he did not mean to contradict himself, but used this latter phrase in a broader and less definite sense. As the sun is the source of light and of the day, and as his earliest rays produce the contrast between darkness and light, between night and dawn, so the term *sunrising* might easily come in popular language, by a metonymy of cause for effect, to be put for all that earlier interval, when his rays, still struggling with darkness, do nevertheless usher in the day.

Accordingly we find such a popular usage prevailing among the Hebrews; and several instances of it occur in the Old Testament. Thus in Judg. 9: 33 the message of Zebul to Abimelech, after directing him to lie in wait with his people in the field during the night, goes on as follows: " and it shall be, in the morning, as soon as the sun is up thou shalt rise early and set upon the city;" yet we cannot for a moment suppose that Abimelech with his ambuscade was to wait until the sun actually appeared above the horizon, before he made his onset. So the Psalmist (104: 22), speaking of the young lions that by night roar after their prey, goes on to say: " The sun ariseth, they gather themselves together, and lay them down in their dens." But wild animals do not wait for the actual appearance of the sun ere they shrink away to their lairs; the break of day, the dawning light, is the signal for their retreat. See also Sept. 2 K. 3: 22. 2 Sam. 23: 4. In all these passages the language is entirely parallel to that of Mark; and they serve fully to illustrate the principle, that the rising of the sun is here used in a popular sense as equivalent to the *rising of the day* or early dawn.

II. *The Number of the Women.* Matthew mentions Mary Magdalene and the other Mary; v. 1. Mark enumerates Mary Magdalene, Mary the mother of James, and Salome; v. 1. Luke has Mary Magdalene, Joanna, Mary the mother of James, and others with them; v. 10. John speaks of Mary Magdalene alone, and says nothing of any other. The first three Evangelists accord then in respect to the two Marys, but no further; while John differs from them all. Is there here a real discrepancy?

We may at once answer, No; because, according to the sound canon of Le Clerc:[1] " *Qui plura narrat, pauciora complectitur; qui pauciora memorat, plura non negat.*" Because John, in narrating circumstances with which he was personally connected, sees fit to mention only Mary Magdalene, it does not at all follow that others were not present. Because Matthew, perhaps for like reasons, speaks only of the two Marys, he by no means excludes the presence of others. Indeed, the very words which John puts into the mouth of Mary Magdalene, (v. 2), presuppose the fact, that others had gone with her to the sepulchre. That there was something in respect to Mary Magdalene, which gave her a peculiar prominence in these transactions, may be inferred from the fact, that not only John mentions her alone,

---

[1] Harm p. 525. Can. XII. fin.

but likewise all the other Evangelists name her first, as if holding the most conspicuous place.

The instance here under consideration is parallel to that of the demoniacs of Gadara, and the blind men at Jericho; where, in both cases, Matthew speaks of two persons, while Mark and Luke mention only one.[1] Something peculiar in the station or character of one of the persons, rendered him in each case more prominent, and led the two latter Evangelists to speak of him particularly. But there, as here, their language is not exclusive, nor is there in it anything that contradicts the statements of Matthew

III. *The Arrival at the Sepulchre* According to Mark, Luke, and John, the women on reaching the sepulchre find the great stone, with which it had been closed, already rolled away. Matthew, on the other hand, after narrating that the women went out to see the sepulchre, proceeds to mention the earthquake, the descent of the angel, his rolling away the stone and sitting upon it, and the terror of the watch, as if all these things took place in the presence of the women. The angel too (in v. 5) addresses the women, as if still sitting upon the stone he had rolled away

The apparent discrepancy, if any, here arises simply from Matthew's brevity in omitting to state in full what his own narrative presupposes. According to v. 6, Christ was already risen, and, therefore the earthquake and its accompaniments must have taken place at an earlier point of time, to which the sacred writer returns back in his narration And although Matthew does not represent the women as entering the sepulchre, yet in v. 8, he speaks of them as going out of it, so that of course their interview with the angel took place, not outside of the sepulchre, but in it, as narrated by the other Evangelists When therefore the angel says to them in v. 6, "Come, see the place where the Lord lay," this is not said without the tomb to induce them to enter, as Strauss avers, but within the sepulchre, just as in Mark v. 6.

IV. *The Vision of Angels in the Sepulchre.* Of this John says nothing. Matthew and Mark speak of one angel; Luke of two. Mark says he was sitting, Luke speaks of them as standing. This difference in respect to numbers is parallel to the case of the women, which we have just considered; and requires therefore no further illustration.

There is likewise some diversity in the language addressed to the women by the angels In Matthew and Mark, the prominent object is the charge to the disciples to depart into Galilee. In Luke this is not referred to; but the women are reminded of our Lord's own previous declaration, that he would rise again on the third day. Neither of the Evangelists here professes to report *all* that was said by the angels; and of course there is no room for contradiction.

§ 3. *The return of the Women to the city, and the first appearance of our Lord.*

Matt. 28 · 7 -10 Mark 16 : 8. Luke 24 : 9-11. John 20 : 1, 2

John, speaking of Mary Magdalene alone, says that having seen that the stone was taken away from the sepulchre, she went in haste (ran) to tell Peter and John He says nothing of her having seen the angels, nor of her having entered the sepulchre at all The other Evangelists, speaking of the women generally, relate that they entered the tomb, saw the angels, and then returned into the city On their way Jesus meets them. They recognize

[1] Matt 8. 23 Mark 5 2 Luke 8. 27. — Matt 20. 30. Mark 10. 46. Luke 18 35.

him; fall at and embrace his feet; and receive his charge to the disciples. — Was Mary Magdalene now with the other women? Or did she
enter the city by another way? Or had she left the sepulchre before the
rest?

It is evident that Mary Magdalene was not with the other women when
Jesus thus met them. Her language to Peter and John forbids the supposition, that she had already seen the Lord: "They have taken away the
Lord out of the sepulchre, and we know not where they have laid him."
She therefore must have entered the city by another path and gate; or else
have left the sepulchre before the rest; or possibly both these positions may
be true. She bore her tidings expressly to Peter and John, who would seem
to have lodged by themselves in a different quarter of the city; while the
other women went apparently to the rest of the disciples. But this supposition of a different route. is essential, only in connection with the view, that
she left the tomb with the other women. That, however, she actually
departed from the sepulchre before her companions, would seem most probable; inasmuch as she speaks to Peter and John only of the absence of the
Lord's body; says nothing in this connection of a vision of angels; and
when, after returning again to the tomb, she sees the angels, it is evidently
for the first time; and she repeats to them as the cause of her grief her
complaint as to the disappearance of the body; John 20: 12, 13. She may
have turned back from the tomb without entering it at all, so soon as she
saw that it was open; inferring from the removal of the stone, that the
sepulchre had been rifled. Or, she may first have entered with the rest,
when, according to Luke, "they found not the body of the Lord Jesus,"
and "were much perplexed thereabout," before the angels became visible
to them. The latter supposition seems best to meet the exigencies of the
case.

"As the other women went to tell his disciples, behold, Jesus met them,
saying, All hail. And they came, and held him by the feet, and worshipped
him. Then Jesus said unto them, Be not afraid; go, tell my brethren,
that they go into Galilee, and there shall they see me." The women had
left the sepulchre "with fear and great joy" after the declaration of the
angels that Christ was risen; or, as Mark has it, "they trembled and were
amazed." Jesus meets them with words of gentleness to quiet their terrors;
"Be not afraid." He permits them to approach, and embrace his feet, and
testify their joy and homage. He reiterates to them the message of the
angels to his "brethren," the eleven disciples; see v. 16.

This appearance and interview is narrated only by Matthew; none of the
other Evangelists give any hint of it. Matthew here stops short. Mark
simply relates that the women fled from the tomb; "neither said they anything to any one, for they were afraid." This of course can only mean,
that they spoke of what they had thus seen to no one while on their way to
the city; for the very charge of the angels, which they went to fulfil, was,
that they should "go their way and tell his disciples;" v. 7. Luke narrates more fully, that "they returned from the sepulchre, and told all these
things unto the eleven, and to all the rest. — And their words seemed to
them as idle tales, and they believed them not." We may perhaps see in
this language one reason why the other Evangelists have omitted to mention
this appearance of our Lord. The disciples *disbelieved the report of the
women*, that they had seen Jesus. In like manner they afterwards disbelieved the report of Mary Magdalene to the same effect; Mark 16: 11.
They were ready, it would seem, to admit the testimony of the women to
the absence of the body, and to the vision of angels; but not to the
resurrection of Jesus and his appearance to them; Luke 24: 21–24. And
afterwards, when the eleven had become convinced by the testimony of their

own senses, those first two appearances to the women became of less importance and were less regarded. Hence the silence of three Evangelists as to the one; of two as to the other, and of Paul as to both; 1 Cor. 15: 5, 6.

§ 4. *Peter and John visit the Sepulchre. Jesus appears to Mary Magdalene.*
John 20· 3–18. Luke 24· 12. Mark 16. 9–11.

The full account of these two events is given solely by John. Matthew has not a word of either; Luke merely mentions, in general, that Peter, on the report of the women, went to the sepulchre; while Mark speaks only of our Lord's appearance to Mary Magdalene, which he seems to represent as his *first* appearance.

According to John's account, Peter and the beloved disciple, excited by the tidings of Mary Magdalene that the Lord's body had been taken away, hasten to the sepulchre. They run; John outruns Peter, comes first to the tomb, and stooping down, sees the grave-clothes lying, but he does not enter. The other women are no longer at the tomb; nor have the disciples met them on the way. Peter now comes up; he enters the tomb, and sees the grave-clothes lying, and the napkin that was about his head not lying with the rest, but wrapped together in a place by itself. John too now enters the sepulchre; "and he saw, and believed."

What was it that John thus believed? The mere report of Mary Magdalene, that the body had been removed? So much he must have believed when he stooped down and looked into the sepulchre. For this, there was no need that he should enter the tomb. His belief must have been of something more and greater. The grave-clothes lying orderly in their place, and the napkin folded together by itself, made it evident that the sepulchre had not been rifled nor the body stolen by violent hands, for these garments and spices would have been of more value to thieves, than merely a naked corpse; at least, they would not have taken the trouble thus to fold them together. The same circumstances showed also that the body had not been removed by friends; for they would not thus have left the grave-clothes behind. All these considerations produce in the mind of John the germ of a belief that Jesus was risen from the dead. He believed *because* he saw; "*for* as yet they knew not the Scripture," (v. 9). He now began more fully to recall and understand our Lord's repeated declaration, that he was to rise again on the third day; [1] a declaration on which the Jews had already acted in setting a watch.[2] In this way, the difficulty which is sometimes urged of an apparent want of connection between verses 8 and 9, disappears.

The two disciples went their way, "wondering in themselves at what was come to pass." Mary Magdalene who had followed them back to the sepulchre, remained before it weeping. While she thus wept, she too, like John, stooped down and looked in, "and seeth two angels, in white, sitting, the one at the head and the other at the feet, where the body of Jesus had lain." To their inquiry why she wept, her reply was the same report which she had before borne to the two disciples· "Because they have taken away my Lord, and I know not where they have laid him," v. 13. Of the angels we learn nothing further. The whole character of this representation seems to show clearly, that Mary had not before seen the angels; and also that she had not before been told, that Jesus was risen. We must otherwise regard her as having been in a most unaccountably obtuse and unbelieving frame of mind; the very contrary of which seems to have been the fact. If also she had before informed the two disciples of a vision of angels and of

[1] Matt. 16. 21. 17: 23. Luke 9: 22. 24: 6, 7 al.   [2] Matt. 28: 63 sq.

Christ's resurrection, it is difficult to see, why John should omit to mention this circumstance, so important and so personal to himself.

After replying to the angels, Mary turns herself about, and sees a person standing near, whom, from his being present there, she takes to be the keeper of the garden. He too inquires, why she weeps. Her reply is the same as before ; except that she, not unnaturally, supposes him to have been engaged in removing the body, which she desires to recover. He simply utters in reply, in well-known tones, the name, Mary ! and the whole truth flashes upon her soul ; doubt is dispelled, and faith triumphs. She exclaims : " Rabboni ! " as much as to say, " My dearest Master ! " and apparently, like the other women,[1] falls at his feet in order to embrace and worship him. This Jesus forbids her to do, in these remarkable words : " Touch me not ; for I am not yet ascended to my Father. But go to my brethren, and say unto them, I ascend unto my Father and your Father, and to my God and your God ;" v. 17.

There remains to be considered the circumstance, that Mark, in v. 9, seems to represent this appearance of Jesus at the sepulchre to Mary Magdalene, as his first appearance : " Now, being risen early the first of the week, he appeared *first* to Mary Magdalene." In attempting to harmonize this with Matthew's account of our Lord's appearance to the other women on their return from the sepulchre, several methods have been adopted ; but the most to the purpose is the view which regards the word *first*, in Mark v. 9, as put not absolutely, but relatively. That is to say, Mark narrates three, and only three, appearances of our Lord ; *of these three*, that to Mary Magdalene takes places *first*, and that to the assembled disciples the same evening occurs *last*, v. 14. A similar example occurs in 1 Cor. 15 : 5 – 8, where Paul enumerates those to whom the Lord showed himself after his resurrection, viz. to Peter, to the twelve, to five hundred brethren, to James, to all the apostles, and *last of all* to Paul also. Now had Paul written here, as with strict propriety he might have done, " he was seen *first* of Cephas," assuredly no one would ever have understood him as intending to assert that the appearance to Peter was the first absolutely ; that is, as implying that Jesus was seen of Peter before he appeared to Mary Magdalene and the other women. In like manner when John declares (21 : 14) that Jesus showed himself to his disciples by the lake of Galilee for the *third* time after he was risen from the dead ; this is said relatively to the two previous appearances to the assembled apostles ; and does by no means exclude the four still earlier appearances, viz. to Peter, to the two at Emmaus, to Mary Magdalene, and to the other women, — one of which John himself relates in full.

In this way the whole difficulty in the case before us disappears ; and the complex and cumbrous machinery of earlier commentators becomes superfluous.

After her interview with Jesus, Mary Magdalene returns to the city, and tells the disciples that she had seen the Lord and that he had spoken these things unto her. According to Mark (vs. 10, 11), the disciples were " mourning and weeping ;" and when they heard that Jesus was alive and had been seen of her, they believed not.

§ 5.   *Jesus appears to two disciples on the way to Emmaus.   Also to Peter.*

Luke 24 : 13 – 35.   Mark 16 : 12, 13.   1 Cor. 15 : 5.

This appearance on the way to Emmaus is related in full only by Luke. Mark merely notes the fact ; while the other two Evangelists and Paul (1 Cor. 15 : 5) make no mention of it.

[1] Matt. 28 : 9.

On the afternoon of the same day on which our Lord arose, two of his disciples, one of them named Cleopas, were on their way on foot to a village called Emmaus, sixty stadia or seven and a half Roman miles distant from Jerusalem, — a walk of some two or two and a half hours. They had heard and credited the tidings brought by the women, and also by Peter and John, that the sepulchre was open and empty ; and that the women had also seen a vision of angels, who said that Jesus was alive. They had most probably likewise heard the reports of Mary Magdalene and the other women, that Jesus himself had appeared to them; but these they did not regard and do not mention them (v. 24); because they, like the other disciples, had looked upon them "as idle tales, and they believed them not ;" v. 11. As they went, they were sad, and talked together of all these things which had happened. After some time, Jesus himself drew near and went with them. But they knew him not. Mark says he was in another form; Luke affirms that "their eyes were holden, that they should not know him ;" v. 16. Was there in this anything miraculous ? The "another form" of Mark, Doddridge explains by "a different habit from what he ordinarily wore." His garments, of course, were not his former ones , and this was probably one reason why Mary Magdalene had before taken him for the keeper of the garden.[1] It may be, too, that these two disciples had not been intimately acquainted with the Lord. He had arrived at Jerusalem only six days before his crucifixion ; and these might possibly have been recent converts, who had not before seen him. To such, the change of garments, and the unexpectedness of the meeting, would render a recognition more difficult ; nor could it be regarded as surprising, that under such circumstances they should not know him. Still, all this is hypothesis ; and the averment of Luke, that "their eyes were holden," and the manner of our Lord's parting from them afterwards, seem more naturally to imply that the idea of a supernatural agency, affecting not Jesus himself, but the eyes or minds of the two disciples, was in the mind of the sacred writer.

Jesus inquires the cause of their sadness; chides them for their slowness of heart to believe what the prophets had spoken ; and then proceeds to expound unto them "in all the Scriptures the things concerning himself" They feel the power of his words ; and their hearts burn within them. By this time they drew nigh to the village whither they went , it was toward evening and the day was far spent. Their journey was ended ; and Jesus was about to depart from them. In accordance with oriental hospitality they constrained him to remain with them. He consents ; and as he sat at meat with them, he took bread, and blessed, and brake, and gave unto them. At this time, and in connection with this act, their eyes were opened ; they knew him ; and he vanished away from them. Here too the question is raised, whether the language necessarily implies anything miraculous ? Our English translators have rendered this passage in the margin, " he ceased to be seen of them ;" and have referred to Luke 4 . 30, and John 8 . 59, as illustrating this idea. They might also have referred to Acts 8 39. Still, the language is doubtless such as the sacred writers would most naturally have employed in order directly to express the idea of supernatural agency.

Full of wonder and joy, the two disciples set off the same hour and return to Jerusalem. They find the eleven and other disciples assembled ; and as they enter, they are met with the joyful exclamation · "The Lord is risen indeed, and hath appeared unto Simon ;" v. 34. They then rehearse what had happened to themselves ; but, according to Mark, the rest believed them not. As in the case of the women, so here, there would seem to have been something in the position or character of these two disciples, which led the

[1] See also John 21 ; 4.

others to give less credit to their testimony, than to that of Peter, one of the leading apostles.

This appearance to Peter is mentioned by no other Evangelist; and we know nothing of the particular time, nor of the attending circumstances. It would seem to have taken place either not long before, or else shortly after, that to the two disciples. It had not happened when they left Jerusalem for Emmaus; or at least they had not heard of it. It had occurred when they returned; and that long enough before to have been fully reported to all the disciples and believed by them. It may perhaps have happened about the time when the two disciples set off, or shortly afterwards.

Paul, in enumerating those by whom the Lord was seen after his resurrection (1 Cor. 15 : 5), mentions Peter first; passing over the appearances to the women, and also that to the two disciples; probably because they did not belong among the apostles.

§ 6. *Jesus appears to the Apostles in the absence of Thomas; and afterwards when Thomas is present.*

Mark 16 : 14 - 18.　Luke 24 : 36 - 48.　John 20 : 19 - 29.　1 Cor. 15 : 5.

The narrative of our Lord's first appearance to the apostles is most fully given by Luke; John adds a few circumstances; and Mark as well as Luke, has preserved the first charge thus privately given to the apostles, to preach the Gospel in all the world, — a charge afterwards repeated in a more public and solemn manner on the mountain in Galilee. When Paul says the Lord appeared to *the twelve*, he obviously employs this number as being the usual designation of the apostles; and very probably includes both the occasions narrated in this section. Mark and Luke speak in like manner of *the eleven;* and yet we know from John, that Thomas was not at first among them; so that of course only *ten* were actually present.

According to Mark, the disciples were at their evening meal; which implies a not very late hour. John says the doors were shut, for fear of the Jews. While the two who had returned from Emmaus were still recounting what had happened unto them, Jesus himself "came and stood in the midst of them, and saith unto them, Peace be unto you!" The question here again is raised, whether this entrance of our Lord was miraculous? That it might have been so, there is no reason to doubt. He who in the days of his flesh walked upon the waters, and before whose angel the iron gate of the prison opened of its own accord so that Peter might pass out; [1] he who was himself just risen from the dead; might well in some miraculous way present himself to his followers in spite of bolts and bars. But does the language here necessarily imply a miracle? The doors indeed were shut; but the word used does not of itself signify that they were bolted or fastened. The object no doubt was, to prevent access to spies from the Jews; or also to guard themselves from the danger of being arrested; and both these objects might perhaps have been as effectually accomplished by a watch at or before the door. Nor do the words used of our Lord strictly indicate anything miraculous. We do not find here a form of the word commonly employed to express the sudden appearance of angels; but, "he *came* and stood in the midst of them;" implying *per se* nothing more than the ordinary mode of approach. There is in fact nothing in the whole account to suggest a miracle, except the remark of John respecting the doors; and as this circumstance is not mentioned either by Mark or Luke, it may be doubtful, whether we are necessarily compelled by the language to regard the mode of our Lord's entrance as miraculous.

[1] Acts 12 : 10.

At this interview Thomas was not present. On his return the other disciples relate to him the circumstances. But Thomas now disbelieved the others; as they before had disbelieved the women. His reply was, "except I shall see in his hands the print of the nails, and put my finger into the print of the nails, and thrust my hand into his side, I will not believe." Our Lord had compassion upon his perverseness. Eight days afterwards, when the disciples were again assembled and Thomas with them, our Lord came as before, and stood in the midst, and said, Peace be unto you? He permits to Thomas the test he had demanded; and charges him to be not faithless, but believing. Thomas, convinced and abashed, exclaims in the fulness of faith and joy, My Lord and my God! recognizing and acknowledging thereby the divine nature thus manifested in the flesh. The reply of our Lord to Thomas is strikingly impressive and condemnatory of his want of faith. "Thomas, because thou hast seen me, thou hast believed, blessed are they that have not seen, and yet have believed!" He and the other disciples, who were to be the heralds of the Lord's resurrection to the world as the foundation of the hope of the Gospel, refused to believe except upon the evidence of their own senses, while all who after them have borne the Christian name, have believed this great fact of the Gospel solely upon their testimony. God has overruled their unbelief for good, in making it a powerful argument for the truth of their testimony in behalf of this great fact, which they themselves were so slow to believe. Blessed, indeed, are they who have received their testimony.

§ 7. *Our Lord's Appearance in Galilee.*

John 21. 1 - 24. Matt 28: 16–20 1 Cor. 15· 6.

It appears from the narrative of Matthew, that while the disciples were yet in Jerusalem, our Lord had appointed a time, when he would meet them in Galilee, upon a certain mountain.[1] They therefore left Jerusalem after the passover, probably soon after the interview at which Thomas was present, and returned to Galilee, their home. While waiting for the appointed time, they engaged in their usual occupation of fishermen. On a certain day, as John relates, towards evening, seven of them being together, including Peter, Thomas, and the sons of Zebedee, they put out upon the lake with their nets in a fishing-boat, but during the whole night they caught nothing. At early dawn Jesus stood upon the shore, from which they were not far off, and directed them to cast the net upon the right side of the boat. "They cast therefore, and now they were not able to draw it for the multitude of the fishes." Recognizing in this miracle their risen Lord, they pressed around him. Peter with his characteristic ardour, threw himself into the water in order to reach him the sooner. At their Lord's command they prepared a meal from the fish they had thus taken. "Jesus then cometh and taketh bread, and giveth them, and fish likewise" This was his third appearance to the eleven; or rather to a large number of them together. It was on this occasion, and after their meal, that our Lord put to Peter the touching and thrice repeated question, "Lovest thou me?·"

At length the set time arrived; and the eleven disciples went away into the mountain "where Jesus had appointed them" It would seem most probable, that this time and place had been appointed of our Lord for a solemn and more public interview, not only with the eleven, whom he had already met, but with all his disciples in Galilee; and that therefore it was on this same occasion, when, according to Paul, "he was seen of above five hundred brethren at once."[2] That the interview was not confined to the

---

[1] See Matt. 26· 32. [2] 1 Cor 15 6.

eleven alone, would seem evident from the fact that "some doubted;" for this could hardly be supposed true of any of the eleven, after what had already happened to them in Jerusalem and Galilee, and after having been appointed to meet their risen Lord at this very time and place. The appearance of the five hundred must at any rate be referred to Galilee; for even after our Lord's ascension, the number of the names in Jerusalem were together only about an hundred and twenty.[1] I do not hesitate, therefore, to hold with Flatt, Olshausen, Hengstenberg and others, that the appearances thus described by Matthew and Paul, were identical. It was a great and solemn occasion. Our Lord had directed that the eleven and all his disciples in Galilee should thus be convened upon the mountain. It was the closing scene of his ministry in Galilee. Here his life had been spent. Here most of his mighty works had been done and his discourses held. Here his followers were as yet most numerous. He therefore here takes leave on earth of those among whom he had lived and laboured longest; and repeats to all his disciples in public the solemn charge, which he had already given in private to the apostles: "Go ye therefore and teach all nations: — and lo, I am with you alway, even unto the end of the world." It was doubtless his last interview with his disciples in that region, — his last great act in Galilee.

§ 8.   *Our Lord's further Appearances at Jerusalem, and his Ascension.*

1 Cor. 15 : 7.   Acts 1 : 3 – 12.   Luke 24 : 49 – 53.   Mark 16 : 19, 20.

Luke relates, in Acts 1 : 3, that Jesus showed himself alive to the apostles, "after his passion, by many infallible proofs, being seen of them forty days, and speaking of the things pertaining to the kingdom of God." This would seem to imply interviews and communications, as to which we have little more than this very general notice. One of these may have been the appearance to James, mentioned by Paul alone (1 Cor. 15 : 7), as subsequent to that to the five hundred brethren. It may be referred with most probability to Jerusalem, after the return of the apostles from Galilee. That this return took place by the Lord's direction, there can be no doubt; although none of the Evangelists have given us the slightest hint as to any such direction. Indeed, it is this very brevity, — this omission to place on record the minor details which might serve to connect the great facts and events of our Lord's last forty days on earth, — that has occasioned all the doubt and difficulty with which this portion of the written history of these events has been encompassed. — The James here intended was probably our Lord's brother; who was of high consideration in the church, and is often, in the latter books, simply so named without any special designation.[2] At the time when Paul wrote, the other James, "the brother of John," as he is called, was already dead.[3]

After thus appearing to James, our Lord, according to Paul, was seen "of all the apostles." This, too, was apparently an appointed meeting; and was doubtless the same of which Luke speaks, as occurring in Jerusalem immediately preceding the ascension. It was, of course, the Lord's last interview with his apostles. He repeats to them the promise of the baptism with the Holy Spirit as soon to take place; and charges them not to depart from Jerusalem until this should be accomplished.[4] Strange as it may appear, the twelve, in this last solemn moment, put to him the question, "Lord, wilt thou at this time restore the kingdom to Israel?" How, indeed, were they to believe! Their gross and darkened minds, not yet enlightened by the baptism of the Spirit, clung still to the idea of a temporal

[1] Acts 1 : 15.   [2] See Acts 12 : 17.   15 : 13.   21 : 18.   Gal. 2 : 9, 12 al.
[3] Acts 12 : 1.   [4] To this interview belongs also Luke 24 : 44.

Prince and Saviour, who should deliver his people, not from their sins, but from the galling yoke of Roman dominion. Our Lord deals gently with their ignorance and want of faith · "It is not for you to know the times and seasons, — but ye shall receive the power of the Holy Ghost coming upon you, and ye shall be witnesses unto me — unto the uttermost part of the earth"

During this discourse, or in immediate connection with it, our Lord leads them out *as far as to* Bethany, and lifting up his hands he blessed them; Luke 24 . 50. This act of blessing must be understood, by all the laws of language, as having taken place at or near Bethany. "And it came to pass, *while* he blessed them, he was parted from them, and carried up into heaven." Our Lord's ascension, then, took place at or near Bethany. Indeed, the sacred writer could hardly have found words to express this fact more definitely and fully, and a doubt on this point could never have suggested itself to the mind of any reader, but for the language of the same writer, in Acts 1 · 12, where he relates that after the ascension the disciples "returned unto Jerusalem from the mount called Olivet." Luke obviously did not mean to contradict himself; and the most that this expression can be made to imply, is, that from Bethany, where their Lord had ascended, which lies on the eastern slope of the Mount of Olives, a mile or more below the summit of the ridge, the disciples returned to Jerusalem by a path across the mount.

As these disciples stood gazing and wondering, while a cloud received their Lord out of their sight, two angels stood by them in white apparel, announcing unto them, that this same Jesus, who was thus taken up from them into heaven, shall again so come, in like manner as they had seen him go into heaven. With this annunciation closes the written history of our Lord's resurrection and ascension.

CPSIA information can be obtained
at www.ICGtesting.com
Printed in the USA
LVHW080149290522
720005LV00003B/39